OUR GRANDMOTHERS' DRUMS

OUR GRANDMOTHERS' DRUMS

MARK HUDSON

An Owl Book

Henry Holt and Company · New York

Library of Congress Cataloging-in-Publication Data
Hudson, Mark.
Our grandmothers' drums / Mark Hudson. — 1st Owl book ed.
p. cm.
ISBN 0-8050-1620-1
1. Women, Mandingo (African people) 2. Mandingo (African people)—
Social life and customs. 3. Dulaba (Gambia)—Social life and
customs. I. Title.
[DT509.45.M34H87 1991]
305.48'896306651—dc20 90-49451
CIP

Henry Holt books are available at special discounts
for bulk purchases for sales promotions, premiums,
fund-raising, or educational use. Special editions
or book excerpts can also be created to specification.
For details contact:
Special Sales Director, Henry Holt and Company, Inc.,
115 West 18th Street, New York, New York 10011.

First published in hardcover in Great Britain by
Martin, Secker and Warburg Ltd.
First American publication in 1989 by Grove Weidenfeld.

First Owl Book Edition—1991

Printed in the United States of America
Recognizing the importance of preserving the written word,
Henry Holt and Company, Inc., by policy, prints all of its
first editions on acid-free paper. ∞

1   3   5   7   9   10   8   6   4   2

I would like to thank many people in the Gambia and in Britain. Any errors, indiscretions or offences are entirely my fault and not attributable to any of these people.

A NOTE ON PRONUNCIATION

The surname Sise is pronounced 'Ceessay', and is sometimes spelt like that. In the Mandinka language, the sound 'ng' is pronounced always as in 'ringing', rather than in 'bingo'. The 'af' in kafo and safo is pronounced as in 'café', rather than as in 'safe'. Tubab is pronounced 'toobab'. The 't' in marabout is not pronounced; the 't' in griot is.

CONTENTS

OUR GRANDMOTHERS' DRUMS

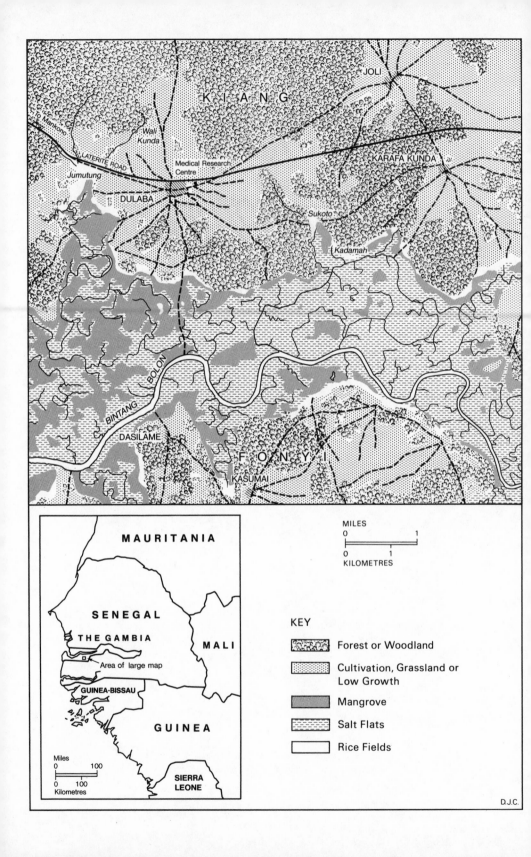

KIANG

JOLI

To Manfono

Wali
Kunda

LATERITE ROAD

Jumutung

Medical Research
Centre

KARAFA KUNDA

DULABA

Sukoto

GOLD AREA KUNDA ROAD

Kadamah

BOLON

BINTANG

DASILAME

F O N Y I

KASUMAI

MAURITANIA

SENEGAL

THE GAMBIA

MALI

Area of large map

GUINEA-BISSAU

GUINEA

SIERRA
LEONE

Miles
0   100

0   100
Kilometres

MILES
0   1

0   1
KILOMETRES

KEY

Forest or Woodland

Cultivation, Grassland or
Low Growth

Mangrove

Salt Flats

Rice Fields

D.J.C.

A WOMAN HAS NO PLACE TO STAY

I had no visa for Senegal.

The plane flew low over the Mauritanian desert. One could pick out the routes of ancient dried-up rivers cut into the eternity of mountainous, uninhabitable rock. But at this height it all looked reassuringly small, like a child's excavations on a beach.

Further south all detail dissolved into a haze of yellow-grey dust which seemed to rise into the sky to meet the plane. Banks of cloud lay on the horizon, like slabs of frosted icing, beneath a cold, pale moon. It rapidly became dark, and soon only a ribbon of pink separated the blackness of the sky from the blueness of the haze over the earth, into which we descended as though into an abyss.

It hadn't occurred to me that a visa would be necessary for a twelve-hour stop in transit, but as I walked across the tarmac towards the airport buildings I had a sudden feeling of trepidation. I waited in the dimly-lit customs hall till the other passengers had gone through, then headed for the desk where the most serious and responsible-looking policeman was sitting.

'*You have no visa for Senegal?*'

'Er . . . no.'

A younger policeman, a large, cheerful-looking man, leant into the booth and threw a rubber stamp onto the desk. The serious-looking policeman leapt to his feet and followed him out of the booth, where he began vehemently berating him. When it looked as though the younger man was about to burst into tears the serious-looking policeman returned to the booth shaking his head. He sat down at his desk and looked at me absently.

'What do you speak?'

'Sorry?'

'What do you speak?'

'Only English.'

'No, no. What is your problem?'

'I have no visa for Senegal.'

'Ah yes.' He read my passport from cover to cover, studying the various passport control stamps. 'You did not know you need a visa for Senegal?' he asked, genuinely surprised.

'Er, yes . . . No.'

'Do you have a hotel?'

'No.'

'Where will you sleep?'

'In the airport.'

He thought this over for some moments. He was aquiline, neatly bearded. He was in no sense a light person.

'You will leave at nine tomorrow morning: Nigeria Airways.'

'Yes.'

He scrawled some notes on my card of disembarkation, and I went through.

The other passengers from my flight were still waiting for their luggage. Soon it came bumping through on a rickety conveyor belt. Then there was a fight to get through the cursory baggage check, and the various residents of Dakar – French, Lebanese, Senegalese – who had come on that flight were free.

Through the glass front of the airport I could see a great crowd of people standing waiting in the darkness. I could make out nothing of their faces but their white teeth and their eager, hungry eyes. I walked towards the small exit door tightly clutching my baggage. As I passed through into the warm night the crowd closed in around me. Most of them seemed to be very tall. Hands grabbed at my arms and body.

'*Monsieur*. Taxi, taxi . . . Hotel, hotel . . . *Monsieur*. Change, change . . . Hotel . . . taxi . . . *Monsieur*.'

I pushed my way through, mechanically intoning the word '*non*'. A figure detached itself from the edge of the crowd to follow me, its eyes lighting up with pleasure, as though in recognition. It was wearing a striped jacket. I quickly looked away. '*Non*,' I shouted, before he had the chance to say anything.

'American? English?'

'*Non*,' I said.

'Can I help you?'

'*Non*.'

Within moments I was inside the main part of the airport building, heaving my luggage across the entrance hall. There were a lot of lights, but not enough to make much impact on the recesses of the immense, gloomy concourse. There were booths housing the offices of airline companies and car-hire firms. There was a self-service café, unpatronized, and a stall selling masks, drums and other tourist artefacts, like a lightship anchored in the middle of the great floor.

My travel agent in London had told me to go straight to the Nigeria Airways office to confirm my reservation on the flight leaving the following morning. It took only a few minutes to discover that there was no Nigeria Airways office. At the information desk I was told to go to the Air Afrique office. At the Air Afrique office they told me to come back at eight the following morning. I went and sat in one of the fibreglass bucket seats that ran along the middle of the concourse, and put my feet up on my luggage. There was little light except for that emanating from the tourist stall opposite. In the brilliantly-lit area at the far end of the concourse a group of French tourists sat chatting and laughing. They obviously felt safe enough. But then, they were leaving Africa. I was arriving.

Thin, hungry-looking boys carrying shoeshine apparatus moved soundlessly along the rows of fibreglass seats. They were so downtrodden in their manner it was easy to wave them away. But there were other bigger men, fashionably dressed, whose function was less clear. They walked this way and that across the concourse. They seemed purposeful enough. But who were they? And what was their purpose?

I became aware of a figure sitting two seats to my left. I didn't turn, but kept staring straight ahead at the production-line fetish figures in the stall opposite. At length, the figure greeted me in English. I returned the greeting without turning.

'Where are you going?'

I couldn't see what harm it could do to tell him.

'You're going to the Gambia. Will you be staying at Fajara?'

'No.'

'Banjul?'

'No.'

From the corner of my eye I could see that he was slumped well back in his seat. He was not looking at me, but at or towards something on the other side of the concourse. He spoke with no great urgency or insinuation, and that reassured me. I turned to look at him, and at the same moment he turned to me with a smile. He was wearing a striped jacket.

'So where will you stay in the Gambia?'

'In a small village in the interior.'

'What is the name of that village?'

'Dulaba.'

'I've never heard of it.'

'It's very small,' I said.

'You just want to go there. To travel.'

'In a way.'

'I also like to travel. I've been to the Gambia many times. I used to drive tourists there in a bus. Banjul, Fajara, Serekunda.' He smiled again. 'I know the Gambia very well.' I took a better look at him. His skin was quite violet; he was handsome, his features small and regular, his moustache neatly trimmed. His slanting eyes gave him an appearance of almost Buddhic composure. Except that he was obviously blind in one of them.

'What are you doing here?' I asked.

'I've just been visiting some friends who work here.' He paused. 'Now I'm tired.' And he stared into space once more.

'You will take the nine o'clock flight, tomorrow morning,' he said. 'Nigeria Airways.'

'Yes,' I said, rather surprised.

'Do you have a reservation?' he asked, his voice curiously dry.

'No.'

'That won't be a problem. Don't worry.' He got to his feet. 'I'm going home now,' he said with a smile. 'It was nice talking to you. Till tomorrow.' And he walked off into the half-light towards the exit.

Till tomorrow? I puzzled. What did he mean by that? Maybe it was just what people in this part of the world always said. I gave it no more thought.

I felt a tap on my shoulder. A figure in a bomber jacket was proffering a packet of Camel cigarettes. I declined.

'*Américain?*'

'*Non.*'

'English?'

'*Non.*'

He disappeared. A few seconds later he reappeared with a thin boy in a hooded gown whose eyes were very close together.

'*Monsieur,*' said the latter, slurring appallingly. 'You must take your things to the "Baggage". Here is . . . *not safe!*' He gestured wildly round the hall. He was out of his head, though what on it was difficult to say.

'*Monsieur,* I beg you. You must take these things to the "Baggage". Here is not safe. There are many bad people here. Some of these boys are very bad.' He hiccuped violently.

'*Monsieur,* why is it that you will not take your baggage to that place?'

'I have no money.'

'You can change money. Come with me. We will go together to the bank.'

'No, no.'

'Please, *monsieur.* Change some money.'

'No.'

He stood leaning over me, his bloodshot eyes very close to mine. '*Monsieur.*'

'What?'

'Do you wish to eat?'

'No.'

'I know a restaurant where you can eat fish and rice. It is very cheap. My sister is the owner.'

'What do you want?'

'Work! I want to work. I have no work, but I want to work . . . *for you!*' At this point he nearly fell over.

'I don't need anybody to work for me.'

He sat down on the floor beside me. '*Monsieur* . . . this place is not safe. *Monsieur,* please. Let me work.' He tried to take my hand. I shook him off.

'Go away.'

'Oh, *monsieur.* That is not good. Please, just give me something.' I took out a fifty-pence piece, which was the only coin I had.

'What's this?' he asked.

'It's worth 250 CFA,' I said.

'250 CFA,' he repeated disgustedly. '*Two hundred and fifty CFA?*'

A French woman sitting nearby watched this pantomime through narrowed eyes. I felt deeply embarrassed.

'I don't want 250 CFA,' said the boy, standing up. 'I want to work.' And slapping the fifty-pence down on the seat beside me, he lolloped off.

I exhaled deeply. Was it going to go on like this all night?

A few minutes later another figure appeared in front of me.

'Are you the guy who's going to the Gambia?'

'Yes,' I said, looking up past a pair of blue jeans and a thick leather belt into the hardest pair of eyes I'd ever seen. He was grizzled, tough-looking, in perhaps his late thirties. The vowel of the last word had been spoken with an American twang, though he clearly wasn't American.

'Come on,' he said. 'Let's go to the restaurant.'

'What for?'

'To be *cool!*'

'Cool? In what way?'

He raised his hands in exasperation. 'This is not a good place to stay. There are many bad people here . . . Criminals. In the restaurant nobody will disturb you.'

'But I haven't got any CFA.'

'Don't worry.'

The restaurant was situated at the far end of the concourse. Beside the entrance an ornamental rock-garden jutted out of the wall on a kind of platform. Behind the glass wall, lace curtains protected the diners from the stares of those who could not afford to enter. The place was full of the cigarette smoke and conversation of Frenchmen, all very big and pink in complexion. Through the picture window of the bar there was a fine view of the floodlit runway.

My companion ordered me the coffee I had asked for.

'Aren't you going to have something?' I asked.

'No, no,' he said with a dismissive wave of his hand.

'How did you know I was going to the Gambia?' I asked.

'A friend of mine, a policeman who works for the customs told me to keep an eye out for you. He said you might need some help.'

I laughed. 'Right.'

'Anyone who comes to speak to you, just tell them "*No*". Don't say anything else. But don't worry. You can spend the night here. I'll speak to someone and arrange your reservation. Tomorrow morning at eight o'clock you can collect your reservation, and then you can leave.' His voice was as hard and as angry as his eyes, but I felt completely safe with him.

'Who are you?' I asked

'My name is Gabriel. I work around this airport. Helping people. Doing whatever's necessary. I've seen a lot of travellers come through this airport. I know what they want.' He gestured around the bar. 'This place. It's all right?'

'It's fine.'

'Some of the travellers who come here are not good. They don't like blacks. But you are not like that. You are nice. What I'm doing for you, I'm not charging you for it. But later you can give me something if you wish. Wait here. I'm going to go and check your reservation.'

I sat back with a sense of relief that was only momentary. I took a book out of my bag and began to read. But I was unable to frame the words into sentences. What was this place I'd arrived in? I was sitting in a bar in an airport. It could have been anywhere. It could almost have been England. But I had the feeling that a different set of rules applied here. The other

Europeans, all drinking, smoking and laughing so noisily, seemed to know what they were. But I didn't. I felt like a child or an invalid who is unable to act for himself and is at the mercy of whatever guardians are available. I was out of my depth, and I hadn't even got further than the airport.

I noticed that the waiters were looking at me searchingly from behind the bar. One of them, a stocky man in a white jacket and black tie, strode over and handed me the bill. I explained weakly that I had no CFA and gave him a pound coin. He looked at it with disapproval then returned to the bar.

'Is this your book?' said the hard voice at my elbow. 'I love books. *Slowly Down the . . .* what?'

'*The Ganges.* It's a river in India.'

'Ah, *la fleuve Gange.* You are reading a book about *la fleuve Gange.* You are nice.' He sat down, clearly tired. 'I couldn't find anybody to speak to about your reservation. But if you go there at eight tomorrow morning they will arrange everything for you.' He looked at the book again. 'Have you finished with this?'

'I've just started it.'

'In that case I couldn't take it from you.'

The waiter came over with the pound coin, and began talking rapidly and vehemently in Wolof, the language of Dakar, prodding the air with the coin and pointing at me. I noted the extraordinarily forceful shape of his shaven head.

'Yes, yes,' said the hard man, wearily waving him to silence. He spoke for a few minutes in Wolof and the waiter went away, apparently highly disgruntled. Moments later he returned with a handful of change, which he slammed down on the table in front of me before returning to the bar.

'I'm going to go home now,' said Gabriel. 'I'm very tired. I've been working here since early morning. You can sit here in the restaurant all night. I've spoken to the waiters. No one will disturb you. If you want to give me something you can do it now.'

I explained that I didn't have any CFA.

'None at all?'

'None.'

'Come on, let's go to the bank. You can change some money there. Leave your bags. They'll be safe here.'

I found myself getting to my feet and following him out of the bar.

When we'd been to the bureau de change I gave him what I thought was a lot of money. He looked at it for a moment. 'I have a wife and six children to feed. It is late, I will have to get a taxi home. But I only stayed here so that I could help you.'

I gave him another note.

'I knew you were nice,' he said.

At about one, the flight for Paris left, and the bar and the restaurant were suddenly empty and silent. The waiters had long since stopped looking at me. Now I looked at them; their white jackets and black ties, the way their shaven heads gleamed in the soft electric light of the bar. They were constantly polishing the glasses, dusting the table-tops – everything was immaculate. I listened to their speech: the harsh consonants, the way the vowels seemed to bend. I wondered what they did when they weren't polishing glasses, what their lives were like outside the airport.

I had visited Dakar before. I had been there only three days before a fifteen-year-old had tried ineptly to mug me in one of the busiest streets of the city. It had been the capital of France's empire in West Africa; a show-place, perched on a temperate promontory at the westernmost point of the immense bulge of the continent. It had been of Dakar, of its coolness, of its sophistication, that the administrators of the colonial period, beleaguered in some of the hottest places on the earth, had dreamed. It retained an uneasy European glamour, but behind the façades of marble, steel and glass, Africa started immediately. Only a few feet along the backstreets stood the tenements of the people, the rooms dimly lit by paraffin lamps, or at this hour immersed in darkness. And beyond them, in the endless sprawling suburbs, many would still be up sitting in the darkness in the cramped yards of their compounds, listening to their radios, if they had the batteries to power them.

Since the Second World War, the population of Dakar had grown ten-fold. And of these one and a half million, only one in ten had regular employment. Since the beginning of the drought in the Sahel, fifteen years ago, the young men had come pouring into the city from the villages of the bush at the beginning of every dry season. As one walked along the boulevards, robed figures came darting from the shadows, trying to thrust a bangle, a bar of soap, a towel, a fistful of cassettes into one's hands. In some streets one had to fight one's way along great queues of such people. They pushed their way after one, desperately, and furtively – furtively, because such unlicensed street trade was illegal. Now, as the rainy season approached, they would be returning to their villages to prepare the land in anticipation of the rain they hoped would come.

But as I tried to imagine the city outside, memories of my previous visit came only in dream-like flashes, as though I had imagined it, or seen it only on film. I had no idea where the airport was in relation to the rest of the city – whether it began immediately outside the glass walls, or twenty miles away. I conceived of it now as a sort of dark hive – a city of cells, in which nothing would be fixed, nothing would be quite as substantial as it seemed. And the systems of interrelationship and interdependence that existed between these cells would remain to the outsider forever mysterious. The policeman in the customs hall, Gabriel, the waiters in this restaurant – what were they to each other? Now I was sitting in this bar, comfortably enough. But I felt rather as though I were sitting on a stage set – that at any moment the furniture might be taken away, the lace curtains rolled up; the waiters would take off their white jackets, and the whole place would be revealed as something utterly *other*. But what?

Four months before, I had travelled to the neighbouring country, the Gambia, to a village where the Medical Research Council of the United

Kingdom (the MRC) had maintained a research station since 1949. It lay in the middle of a land mass between the great river that gave the country its name and the Bintang Bolon, a saline creek that led off it. Thus cut off from the main overland routes into the interior it had been bypassed for centuries by slave traders, colonists and missionaries alike, so that although it was not physically very distant from the coast and the centres of contact with the outside world, it had remained one of the least developed areas of that country. The MRC had chosen this neglected hinterland because of the complete absence of medical facilities, and the village of Dulaba because, from a medical point of view, it was the 'worst' of all those visited.

Since then, research into every area of medicine, not to mention sociology, anthropology and even entomology had been carried out in Dulaba. It was, medically speaking, one of the most thoroughly documented communities in the world. I had spent four weeks there, visiting an old school-friend who was doing research into the nutritional needs of pregnant and lactating women. It was my first time in Africa.

In the 1950s, an anthropologist named Gamble made a census of the village, which took the form of a family tree of each of the different compounds. Subsequently redrafted and annotated, it now filled two enormous box files which were kept in the computer room of the MRC compound. It was in its time the most complete record ever to have been made of such a village, but the relevant information had long since been transferred to card index and other more convenient forms of record, and it was now seldom looked at.

There they were, however, the names of every person who had lived or died in the village since the early years of the century – recorded in the cramped but definite script of an HMSO manual typewriter, the more recent names hastily added in biro. And as one turned the pages, dog-eared and discoloured by the red dust of the region, one saw the same names repeated over and over again. More than half of them had the surname Sise. The first son was always called Lamin (al Amin) or Momodou (Mohammed), and the first daughter was always Fatoumata (Fatima) after the Prophet's daughter. After a time, this monotony began to suggest a similar sense of limitation in the attitudes of the people themselves. One was tempted to wonder what the point had been, not so much of this monolithic study which was now so seldom looked at, but of all the relentless and apparently obsessive procreation it recorded. For each of the men had had up to four wives, and many of these women had had as many as twelve children. Who could say how many Lamin Sises, how many Momodou Mintes there had been since the foundation of the village? And what in retrospect had there been to differentiate one of them from any of the others? They had all been Muslims, and they had all been farmers, scraping just enough from the grey earth to continue their survival as a community. Knowing nothing of the outside world, unaware even of Africa as a geographical entity, they called themselves simply the *mofingos* – the blacks – and they believed that God had made them to be the poorest people of the earth. They had left behind nothing but their progeny, whose lives would be exactly the same as theirs had been.

As one looked more carefully at this document, however, one began to notice how many of these people had died at a very young age – had been born dead, had died before they'd been named, or had died in infancy. About half of them had died before the age of five. There were women in the village who had given birth to ten children, none of whom had survived. Some had lived to the age of eighteen, and then he or she had gone in the blinking of an eye. A European might have said that this child had died before its time, but the people knew that no one could die before their time was due. A human being created by God can only be destroyed by God. The moment of that person's death is God's decision and when it comes, nothing can postpone it.

One afternoon, a few days before my departure, I was walking in the bush not far from the village. The sky was overcast, the air thick and hot. As I made my way slowly back along the rocky path through the low forest, I suddenly saw three women walking briskly and purposefully along the path towards me. I felt a slight sense of trepidation. I knew that in Africa it was always necessary to greet, but should I greet them or wait for them to greet me first? As they drew level with me they paused. They were, I suppose, about my own age. The first was a tall, powerful-looking woman, very dark in complexion. She had a large, blunt face, and small eyes. The second woman was only a little shorter, and stockier – fair in complexion, with slanting eyes and three tiny ritual scars in the middle of each broad cheek. Of the third woman I can remember little, except that she was smaller than the others – though none of them were the sort of person one would take lightly. They stood regarding me – unsmiling, almost accusing. The tall woman drew herself to her full height.

'*Tubab*,' she snapped. 'Where are the people of your compound?' On her lips, this inconsequential, almost meaningless question sounded like a challenge, a threat almost.

'They are there.' I blurted out the prescribed response.

'Are they in peace?'

'Peace only.'

'I hope there's no trouble.'

'No trouble.'

When the two other women had each 'greeted' me in exactly the same way, they continued on their way, sniggering and cackling to themselves.

When these women died, the dates of their death would be written in the annals of the MRC, as all the others had been for the last forty years. By studying the endless routines of work that had structured their existence, and the code of traditional laws that had circumscribed it, an anthropologist would be able to build up a picture of what their lives had been like. But of them themselves, what they had actually been like as individuals, the things that had made them different from each other, and from all other human beings, nothing would be known.

When I returned to England I was haunted by the image of those three

women disappearing into the bush, as I was by much else that I had
observed on my brief visit. What had they been going so eagerly to do, out
there in that thin, featureless forest, on that dismal afternoon? But of
course it was not featureless to them. It was part of their world. They lived
from it. And for them every rock, every stick, every lump of earth was
known – was of importance.

Even before I had arrived in Dulaba I had heard about the women. Of
how they spent their lives in a continual round of childbearing, domestic
labour and manual agriculture, much of it amounting to little more than
slavery. Of how they were unable to make even the most basic decisions
concerning their own lives and the upbringing of their children. Of how
they were circumcised to dull the edge of their sexuality. Of how they
were prevented even from fully participating in their own religion.

They said that 'a woman has no place to stay', because after five years of
marriage, when she had had one or two children, a woman would leave
her parents' compound, and go – 'transfer', as they called it – to live in her
husband's compound. And because she had gone to his compound, to be
his wife, she would believe herself to be under his authority. She would
not go anywhere, or do anything, without first asking his permission.
When she returned from the fields, or presented her husband with his
bowl of food, she would go down on one knee before him. For the women
believed that this was the only way that they could be blessed. When they
died they would be judged, not according to their own independent
actions, but on the way they had behaved towards their husbands. If they
had not obeyed him, if they had not pleased him, if they had not worked
hard for him, they would never, ever enter heaven.

And yet, as I had observed them, they were far from abject. I had seen
them each day, gathering at the Infant Supplement Centre, from which
the MRC distributed porridge to the children aged between three and
twelve months. There would be women there of every conceivable size,
shape and age, and of every colour, from a very light brown to black.
Most, however, were of a violet so deep that when they stood against a
dark background they seemed to disappear. It covered them in a dense,
matt evenness; many of them were very beautiful.

They spilled out of the building into the shade of the baobab opposite,
holding bawled conversations with their fellows inside as they stirred the
porridge to cool it before spooning it swiftly into their infants' mouths.
They didn't care whether they exposed their breasts or not, but they
never, ever showed their legs – covering them with a *faneau*, a piece of
cloth tied at the waist to form a skirt. And they had been taught by their
religion that it is immodest for a woman to go bare-headed, so they would
always cover their scalp with a kind of turban. They weighed slightly less
than their European counterparts, but the difference was in fat rather
than in active tissue, so they were relatively thin and muscular. They had
about them a vigour and a vitality that made their husbands seem mean,
insubstantial, even shadow-like in comparison. And it seemed to me that,
in spite of everything, their lives were as rich in their way as they could
have been under any other circumstances. In what this richness resided, I

had only the vaguest idea. But I felt that in the memory of those three women disappearing off along the path into the bush, I had a clue. It had something to do with their close physical involvement with that blank, unpromising landscape, and with each other.

Even after so brief an experience of Africa, life in England seemed extraordinarily lacklustre, and what was most difficult to bear was the thought that those women's lives were continuing in that other world, and that I would never know anything more about it. I had been in some way touched, both by my short, generalized experience of the continent, and by being among the people of Dulaba. I had been both humbled by my ignorance in the face of virtually everything I had seen, and stimulated by it in a way that I knew would be a rare occurrence in my life. I realized then that, unless I went back there as soon as possible, this adventure in consciousness that I had seen opening so briefly before me would pass by. The essential mystery of the lives of the women of Dulaba: of in what the richness of their lives resided, of how they were able to face the difficulties of their circumstances with such courage and good humour, of whether these factors even existed, or were merely products of my well-meaning imagination, would remain forever clouded by the vast physical and emotional distance between England and Africa. Soon my friend the Professor would return to England, I would move on to other things, and I would remain not knowing. From my room in North London I calculated that in two months' time the rainy season would begin in Dulaba, and life there would move into a new phase. I would have to take what money I had out of the bank, buy a ticket on the cheapest flight available, and get back there before the onset of the first storms. I would try to find out more about the lives of the women and I would try to write about them. Now I was on my way. But how I was going to set about this task when I got there, I had absolutely no idea.

I had waited so long for the sunrise, and in the end it happened so quickly that I scarcely noticed it. One moment it was night, and the next it was morning, and a row of grey hills were visible on the other side of the runway.

I emerged onto the stairs to see the waiter with the shaven head kneeling in prayer in the ornamental rock-garden. On the ground floor, the fibreglass bucket seats were full of fantastically dressed women. I felt excited. It was morning, and I was in Africa. Then I saw the man in the striped jacket. He took my bags. 'Come on,' he said, and led me off across the concourse.

What the hell's going on? I wondered. I hadn't slept all night, and I suddenly felt very tired and very confused.

'I don't need anyone to help me,' I said.

'That's OK,' he said. 'No problem.'

Along one side of the far end of the hall were the baggage check-in desks of the various airlines. Over one of them was the green and white insignia of Nigeria Airways. The man in the striped jacket put my luggage on the weighing machine.

'Thanks very much,' I said, 'I'm OK now.'

'You don't understand,' he said. 'The flight is full.'

'But I've got a seat on it,' I said, panic rising in my voice.

'Let me see your ticket.'

Where the flight number should have been, the word 'Unreserved' was written. In the corner of the page someone had written in ballpoint the number of the nine o'clock flight from Dakar to Banjul.

'What's this?' he asked, pointing to the number.

'It's the number of the flight,' I said.

'Who wrote it there?'

'The people in London who issued the ticket.'

'This isn't correct,' he said. 'The number of the flight should be written here.' He pointed to where the word 'Unreserved' was written.

'But I'm booked on this plane,' I said. 'It's just the reservation of the seat.'

'No, no,' he said. 'That will not work here. The plane is full. My friend works for Nigeria Airways. He told me.'

What was I going to do? Wait for the next one? I wanted to get out of that place as quickly as possible.

'Don't worry,' I heard him saying. 'My friend works for Nigeria Airways. He will arrange everything. It's not going to be a problem.'

'If I can just speak to the officials myself, I'm sure I'll be able to sort it out.'

'No, no. You do not know these people. I know them very well. I've been working with tourists for many years. In an organization.'

'What sort of organization?'

'An independent organization. Don't worry.'

I heard the bland voice of my travel agent in Muswell Hill, telling me to go straight to the Nigeria Airways office when I arrived in Dakar. Such people didn't know what was going on in the world. They should be struck off. They should be illegal.

I turned to the tall, well-dressed man on my right. He gave me a bland reassuring smile.

Another tall young man, well-built, a red pullover tight over his muscular chest, came strolling nonchantly towards us behind the check-in desks. The man in the striped jacket winked at me with his good eye. The young man in the red pullover stopped at the Nigeria Airways counter and shook hands with the man in the striped jacket. They greeted each other copiously in Wolof, then the young man turned to me. 'Ça va?' he grunted, proffering his hand. He seemed rather informal to be an airline official. But then this was Africa; anything might be possible.

The man in the striped jacket showed my ticket to the young man, pointing to the number written in ballpoint and the word 'Unreserved' and exclaiming vehemently in Wolof. The man from Nigeria Airways took the ticket disdainfully and peered at it for some moments. He turned and looked down at me through half-closed eyes. 'The flight is full,' he said effortfully in English.

I took hold of the ticket. 'Look, I was booked onto this flight in London. I just want to confirm my seat.'

'*Non, non.* Is not booked.' He pointed dismissively to the number written in ballpoint. 'This is nothing. The number of the flight must be 'ere.' He straightened and looked off across the concourse. 'The flight is full.'

'This is what I told you,' said the man in the striped jacket. He took the ticket and leant across the counter. He spoke long and deep to the man from Nigeria Airways in Wolof. Gradually the man seemed to melt slightly. '*Wow, wow,*' he said at length. '*Wow.*' (Yes, yes – yes.)

The man in the striped jacket turned to me and smiled. 'He will help us. You can travel on this plane. The plane is full, but he will do this for you because he is my friend.'

I could feel myself sinking. I didn't know what these people were planning to do to get me on the plane, but whatever it was I didn't want to be involved in it. I should have just told the man in the striped jacket to go away as soon as he appeared, but I had somehow been unable to do so. Now I felt as though I were drowning in my own inability to act.

'He is not the boss,' I heard him saying. 'He is the assistant. When the boss comes he will speak to him. Afterwards you can give him something. Whatever you have. Do you have CFA?'

'No.'

'We can go to the bank. You can change it there. This man will help us. He and I are from the same village.'

I tried to imagine the cramped compound in which this man must live with his extended family. He had no job. There was no social security in Senegal. One lived off the largesse of one's relatives or one went back to the land. This man was of an age when he should have been supporting his family, not being supported by it. The shame must have been very great.

And yet he was so cool and so assured. He spoke English so well. And he had turned up at the airport at six o'clock in the morning. For what? I looked into his face as I tried to imagine the social existence, the human life behind it. But I could see nothing in the regular features, perfect except for the skew-whiff blind eye – nothing but coldness and hardness in the slight smirk of bland well-being. This man would do absolutely anything, I thought. I looked at the heavy, satiated features of the man from Nigeria Airways, leaning forward against the counter in his tight red pullover. He was no more from Nigeria Airways than I was. I felt a queasy, sickening sensation in my stomach.

People were walking this way and that across the concourse, going about their business. But it was as though they were on a different plane of existence; as though if I called to them for assistance they would be unable to hear me – as though I would be invisible to them. These two men were going to rob me, and I wasn't going to be able to do anything to stop them.

A queue was beginning to form behind us: Africans in safari suits, Africans in robes. Immediately behind me was a man of some Caucasian origin with a pointed grey beard. I asked him if he had a seat reserved for this flight. He showed me his ticket. The number of the flight was written in the correct place.

'You see,' interceded the man in the striped jacket. 'This is where the number should be written. But it is not on yours. This is why you have a problem.'

A man in a khaki suit began ripping the labels off my luggage.

'Hey, what's he doing?' I shouted.

'He's going to put new labels on your bags.'

'It's already got labels. It's routed direct to Banjul.'

'No,' he laughed. 'Those labels are no good. He's going to put new labels on it. This man is my friend.' He smiled at the man in the khaki suit, and the man in the khaki suit smiled back.

It was well past eight o'clock, the time when the Nigeria Airways people were due to arrive. I'd long since lost track of time. I was a prisoner of these two men, but how long I'd been in this position was difficult to tell.

Suddenly the man in the red pullover jumped over the weighing machine and stood beside us. A man in a Nigeria Airways uniform walked breezily up and slammed his briefcase down on the counter. A spectacularly plaited woman sat down calmly at the desk. The man in the striped jacket began waving my ticket at her and talking rapidly in Wolof.

'Wow, wow,' said the woman dismissively. The man in the red pullover grabbed the ticket and continued the argument.

'These people have got my ticket,' I said to the woman.

'Take it from them then,' she said.

I took it from them.

She took out the sheet on which the reservations would be written. It was completely blank. The man in the striped jacket pointed at the paper, talking rapidly in Wolof all the time. She ignored him.

He flashed a smile at me. 'I'm helping you,' he said.

She took my ticket and wrote the details impassively on the sheet of paper. It was the first reservation. New labels were put on my luggage. The man in the khaki suit fed it onto the conveyor belt. I wondered if I would ever see it again.

Clutching my passport and ticket I began walking towards the passport control. The man in the striped jacket and the man in the red pullover blocked the way. They were big. They stood in front of me like a wall.

'Now you must pay us,' said the man in the red pullover.

'Give us what you have,' said the man in the striped jacket. The expression of geniality had suddenly disappeared. I looked around. Everywhere there were soldiers and policemen. But when I looked at their faces, I saw only the faces of these two men. They were the same people. They would be from the same village. They would be their brothers. They would laugh at me.

I opened my wallet and took out the meagre remains of CFA I had changed the previous night, two pound coins and a Gambian banknote. I thrust it at the man in the red pullover.

'What's this?' he said angrily.

'That's all you're getting,' I said.

'We have helped you very much,' said the man in the striped jacket.

'You've done nothing for me,' I said, by now as angry as they were. I pushed past them and ran towards the passport control. The policemen at the first booth was chatting to a friend. 'Wait a minute,' he said. I didn't. At the second barrier the policemen stood talking in a group. They paid no attention as I ran past.

The departures lounge was cool and white and empty. I breathed a sigh of relief.

A few minutes later I was sitting on the toilet. I was almost asleep where I sat when I heard the outside door opening. I froze. 'This is it,' I thought. 'Now they're going to kill me.' I pulled my trousers up, threw open the door and ran into the departures lounge, sending the aged cleaner sprawling against the sink.

'I couldn't believe it when I got your letter,' said the Professor as he drove me from the airport. 'I went over to the lab and told Helene. I said, "He wants to come back here. He must be mad." She agreed.'

It was midday. The flame-trees were in bloom. But apart from their brilliant vermilion blossoms the world was almost entirely devoid of colour. Thin skeins of smoke, where people were burning the remains of last year's crops, drifted up into the empty sky. Much of the land had already been cleared, and for miles the grey earth was bare except for the tall termite hills, and a few skeletal trees. Everything looked fragile in its parched brittleness, as though it could have been levelled with the sweeping movement of an arm. Yet already tiny leaves had started to appear on the baobabs, and small bushes with shiny green leaves had sprung up in even the most barren places. They were called manonkaso, and they were said to be a sure sign that the rain would come.

The Professor drove fast along the tar road, which shone as though drawn onto the land with lead, unrolling inexorably over the gently undulating landscape from the pencil of an unseen hand. In the hard light, the villages of mud and corrugated iron looked appallingly ramshackle and run down. Apart from the odd figure sitting hunched on a verandah, they appeared to be completely deserted. It was Ramadan – the month in which Muslims are enjoined to fast between sunrise and sunset – and the people had retreated from the heat of the day. Even the donkeys, sheep, and goats who normally rushed into the road lay sleeping in the shade.

There was no other traffic on the road, and the Professor explained that this was because there was almost no petrol in the country. 'The MRC can usually find just enough to keep us going, but we've had to turn the generators off at night. In fact,' he added, a note of grimness in his voice, 'we've been having a few problems with accommodation at the camp. So you may not find it as easy to carry out this project of yours as you may have thought. To be honest, I don't know if you'll be able to do it at all. I'm sorry about that, when you've come all this way.'

'That's all right,' I said.

When I first entered the village, it was as though I were entering a different dimension of life, and at the same time a place I had always known existed. It was the middle of the afternoon, and only an insane person would have walked out into the virulent sunlight without a hat, but in those days I didn't know anything about the sun. I felt ludicrously exposed and self-conscious as I trod the almost empty streets. The few old men seated on their log benches watched impassively as I passed. The women carrying huge containers on their heads glanced searchingly, their skins so dark the sunlight seemed to shatter against them. A crowd of children, almost naked and grey with dust, appeared as if from nowhere, and followed me through the streets, laughing and giggling and falling over each other. Where I had come from, I now realized, one was always distanced from one's environment by the hard edges of the constructed world – the pavements finished with kerbstones, the buildings fronted with concrete, steel and glass. Here there was nothing between one and the rough, dry surfaces of the people's lives – the pink sand of the streets, littered with ashes and animal droppings; the brittle grey thatch; the corrugated iron, orange with rust; the mud walls of the houses; the scrawny animals who wandered through the compounds and even into the houses – all illuminated with almost preternatural clarity by the hard white light. This sudden physical nearness of the people and their lives came as a shock.

It was all exactly as one would have expected having seen hundreds of photographs of African villages, even of this particular village. But a photograph is only an idea; this was real. And as I was confronted, moment by moment, by the physical actuality of it, my preconceptions fell away. It is at such moments that one feels truly alive. Even immediately afterwards I couldn't tell how long I had spent in the village on that first visit, or even on my subsequent visits. Everything seemed concentrated into short, dream-like flashes; fifteen minutes felt like fifteen seconds – or was it the other way around? And when I got back to the camp I scarcely glanced at the pile of books I'd brought with me; all that seemed irrelevant now.

On my return to the village four months later, I saw it without mystery or atmosphere, without the magic of otherness. I saw it as a collection of shed-like buildings, dilapidated, with corrugated-iron roofs. The sky was often dull and overcast, the fasting population blank and listless: their voices faint, their movements slow. I tried to remember what it was that had brought me to that place rather than anywhere else in the world. I didn't realize then, any more than I had that first time I entered the village, that what happened to me there would change me completely and forever.

2

A WOMAN OF SUBSTANCE

The walls of dark, unplastered mud were riven by long cracks, which appeared to be getting wider, suggesting that the sides of the house would soon be parting company. There were no windows; the light came from the doorways, and the gaps around the roof beams, through which mosquitoes would pour in the humidity of the rainy season. Nets hung over the three beds, translucent, almost ghostly in the dimness. The beds were made from branches, supported by forked posts buried in the rocky, uneven floor. Apart from a clay water jar and a wooden chest with a broken lid, there was no other furniture.

This was the *muso-bungo* – the house of the women – where they lived with their husband's mother and the children. This one was relatively small. There were houses in the village that accommodated dozens of people – wives, mothers, children, relatives. Their husband lived in his own house, which was often on the other side of the compound.

In a corner beside the doorway, one of the Professor's fieldworkers and I sat on tiny stools. He was keeping an 'activity diary' on one of the women of the house – one of the Professor's 'survey mothers'. On his knee rested a clipboard with an electronic alarm device attached to it. Every two and a half minutes the device would sound, and he would note down whatever the woman was doing at that moment.

It was hot and close. The woman's three-month-old son, who was sick with a fever, lay under one of the nets. Outside, clouds of dust swirled through the compounds. I could hear the sound of a pestle and mortar, each beat resonating deep into the hard, empty earth. Apart from a few scattered dribblings, it had not rained for eight months.

The woman, who had momentarily left the room, re-entered carrying an old tomato-paste tin full of water. She folded back the mosquito net and sat down on the edge of the bed. She sprinkled some water over the child's head, then she took off her head-tie and sprinkled some of the water over her own face; it glittered as it trickled over her violet skin. She was a tall, slender, gentle-looking woman. It was Ramadan. She could feel the water on her skin, but she could not drink it. She had risen before dawn and eaten porridge with the other people of the compound; she would not drink again until nightfall. It was only mid-morning, and clearly she was already exhausted. She took off one of her rubber flip-flop sandals and began to fan herself with it.

I was surrounded by details. By following the Professor's fieldworkers, I was able to walk in and out of the women's lives with remarkable freedom. But always, whether it was in the houses, or at the fields, or at the wells, I had the feeling that I was alienated, that I was being pushed back by these details. It was as though they formed a kind of shell, transparent but impenetrable, between me and the women, and whatever interpretation I placed upon these details, I could only guess at the significance they had for the women themselves.

I had hoped to involve myself in the women's lives through work – through participating in their agricultural labours – but every time I attempted to join in the hoeing of the rice fields, I was told to stop. I was a *tubab* – a European – and it was apparently inconceivable that a tubab should work. At night I would sit with the Professor and Helene in the almost antiseptic brightness of their living-room, reading or listening to music. Sometimes I would hear laughter coming from the warm darkness only yards away, and I would be almost painfully aware that the real life of the place – all the things I had come there to write about – was going on out there, just beyond the edge of the light. I felt that I shouldn't just be sitting there, a prisoner of nothing more sinister than my own shyness, waiting for the life of the village to reveal itself to me. But whenever I strayed from the paths open to me through the Professor's work, I felt that I was an intruder.

Once I had emerged from the house, only to virtually fall over a great group of people kneeling in prayer in the darkness outside the lab. I had turned round and gone straight back indoors.

The fact that I had arrived in the middle of Ramadan was a further distancing factor. The people's exhaustion hung over the village, as tangible as the haze of grey dust that filled the air. It was like having arrived in a place where the entire population was suffering from some minor but demoralizing illness.

The fieldworker took out a small pocket radio, and an English pop record – 'I Was Born To Take Care Of You' by Freddy Mercury – erupted tinnily into the room.

'Don't they mind you playing your radio?' I asked.

'No,' he said. 'They like music.'

He flicked the dial, and tuned into a broadcast from the Casamance, the southern region of Senegal, the border of which lay only a few miles away. It was in Jola, his own language. It urged people to plant trees before the rains started, for the benefit of 'the population that will come'.

His name was Yaya Bojang. He was a small, compact man in his early twenties, with a surprisingly deep, resonant voice. But he was not much given to talking to strangers, and as he was also fasting, he was not keen to talk at all. None the less, I asked him when he thought it would rain.

'Not yet. It will be very hot, both by day and by night. Then, suddenly, it will rain.'

'When will this be?'

'Around . . . let's say the twenty-first of June.'

'Why the twenty-first?'

'It is just my feeling.'

Every year the water-table sank a little lower, the wells had to be dug a little deeper, and at this time of year the women had to wait long into the morning for the thick, gluey water to drain through the earth. It was at the wells that the women heard the news and the gossip, and normally the air resounded with the sound of their laughter and the clattering of their basins, the sunlight glinting and flashing on their brilliantly coloured clothes as they pulled vigorously on the ropes. In the fasting month, however, there was no hurry. There was no lunch to be cooked. They sat in silence, their faces glazed and expressionless, their eyes as empty as the wells.

I went for a walk into the bush, following the path that led east across the football pitch, the old bush path to the neighbouring village of Karafa Kunda. It was early evening, and I walked for about a mile and a half without meeting anyone, except two skinny, bug-eyed boys with shiny tins a foot high perched on their heads. They paused just long enough to shake hands, before continuing earnestly on their way. The bush became denser, the trees taller, and the rocky path began to slope downhill. Then to the right the bush suddenly opened out into a huge glade, which grew wider as it stretched away towards the salt flats. The grey earth had been cleared, and in places it had already been tilled in expectation of the rain. This must be one of the rice fields, I thought. This must be Sukoto – 'the old home' – where the village of Dulaba had once been sited.

Narrow banks of earth showed where the fields would be divided. The trunks of trees, burnt away at the roots, lay still smouldering. Narrow trees clambered up the exhausted-looking palms, strangling them, and enormous bare branches lay across the fields like dinosaur bones. Monkeys scampered away into the thick bush. Despite the evidence of human occupation only hours before, the place had a desolate, strangely haunted atmosphere.

A fierce wind began to blow as the sky darkened. The rains were preceded by strong winds, but they came always from the east. This was from the west. In the MRC compound, the petals of flame-tree and bougainvillaea – vermilion and magenta – swirled over the dusty ground. Suddenly it was dark.

The village had been founded by four families. Three brothers named Sise had met a pagan named Cho Jammeh. They had converted him and started a village at Sukoto, beside the salt flats. The Minte family joined them from the north bank of the great river, and they had all married with people of the surrounding villages of Joli, Karafa Kunda and Kulli Kunda.

It was, however, very cramped and very hot at that place. There were many devils and spirits, and the people began to die. Their marabout told them to move the village to the higher, open ground to the west, which was known as 'Dula-ba' – a wide place. The Bajo family were already living there. But the king, who lived in Mankono, the next village to the west, would attack them and take them as slaves. So they had taken refuge with their relatives at Joli. When they heard that the people from Sukoto were clearing the land at the wide place, they went back to join them. Their group of houses became the first compound of the village. But, because they were considered by the other families to have 'arrived late', they were treated as strangers, and made the *falifos* of the village. They took the news to the people, distributed kola nuts at naming ceremonies and funerals, and divided the meat on prayer days.

That original compound was still there. It was known as Old Bajo Kunda, and it lay behind the much larger compound of Kafuli Kunda, in what was still the most densely populated part of the village. From there the village had spread slowly up the faint incline towards where the MRC compound now stood. When 'the camp' had been built, forty years before, the village had ended at Mbara Kunda. The camp was considered to be quite separate from the village, to be out in the bush. Now Mbara Kunda was in the middle of the village, and the compounds and gardens closely surrounded the camp on three sides.

A compound was simply the houses of an extended family grouped together. Each of them was named after the family who lived there, or the person who had founded it: Bajo Kunda, the place of the Bajo family; Minteba Kunda, the largest compound of the Minte family; Fili Kunda, named after the first Imam of Dulaba, Madifili Sise.

The larger compounds were like separate districts that could only be entered by two or three pathways. They had expanded first outwards, until they touched the boundaries of the other compounds, and then inwards, people building new houses inside the yards, till they became so overcrowded that the young men left to build their own compounds on the edge of the village.

Lanes ran to, and often through, the yards of the smaller compounds from the street, which ran like a thick vein from the MRC compound to the bottom of the village. Two further streets ran along the edges of the village, parallel with the main street, so that it was rather a long, sloping village; though it was only if you were standing at the very bottom of the village street that you were aware of it.

As it passed through the middle of the village the sides of the street became steeper, and during the rainy season the waters would rush along it in a great torrent, washing away the sand, and exposing the deeply-pitted banks of pink rock. Through the gaps between the houses one could see into the yards of the larger compounds, some broad and dusty, others narrow and rocky, the entrances to the courts beyond obscured by screens of millet stalks, which gave them a mysterious, almost secretive aspect. The mud brick parapets of the grander houses which gave onto them were worn by the rain into an appearance of almost organic ancientness. Yet the great quantities of corrugated iron, in various stages of rusting disintegration, prevented these places from seeming pretty or picturesque. Where the houses had been whitewashed, it had chipped or worn away, or been buried under a layer of graffiti, filth and children's handprints. The rough posts that supported the verandahs had become twisted from position, giving the impression that these battered awnings were on the verge of collapse. Sheep, goats and chickens wandered where they wished, defecating at their convenience.

The *bantabas*, the meeting places of the men, were low platforms of logs, sited to overlook the life that might be likely to pass in such a place. The largest was at the bottom of the village street, close to the corner of the avenue that led towards the mosque, in the shade of a huge mango tree. There the men sat through the long months of the dry season, old and young alike, sprawled out in sleep or simply sitting as they waited for the time of the next prayer. For them work was something that happened at specific times of the year, and when there was no rain, there was little for them to do. Some were very much older than their wives; though many seemed older than they actually were, hiding their powerful bodies under their often filthy and tattered gowns, while they sat somnolent and heavy-eyed, as though drugged by their own inertia.

During the long Ramadan afternoons, the village appeared deserted. The men retired into their houses, while the women sat in groups in the deep shade of the mango trees at the backs of the compounds or at the corners of the lanes near their houses. Dazed and speechless with the effort of fasting, their shirts discarded to let the air to their breasts, they sat or sprawled on their mats, some picking lice from each other's hair, or plaiting it; some working on their crochet, others just staring, at nothing. This was the most difficult time of the day, when the energy of the morning had been dissipated, and there was nothing left but a long wait for the relief of the evening.

Travellers, women undergoing their monthly period, and pregnant women were exempted from fasting, but when Ramadan was over they would have to atone for this by fasting two days for every one they had missed. Everyone knew that it was more difficult to fast when others were eating, to cook meals one would not be able to eat, so in Dulaba the women would fast till within a few days of their delivery. They could have given away the amount of food they had eaten during Ramadan as a charity to the poor. But that was not considered so effective in the sight of God – and anyway it was unusual in Dulaba to find people who had that amount of food to give away.

There will come a day, the Muslims believe, when the world will be rolled away, and the second world will come. The angel Serafil will blow his trumpet and everyone who is alive on this earth will die. It will rain for forty years, and all the world will be destroyed. Then the angel will blow his trumpet again, and everyone will wake up. Each person's soul will return to his or her body. They will be naked. But they will not see each other, because everyone will be looking up.

Everything that has been created, whether angel, devil or human being, will gather in the place where judgement will be done. There will be a bridge. Heaven will be in front. You have to cross this bridge. If your deeds in this earth have been good, if you have obeyed God's words, if you have prayed and fasted as He has asked, you will cross that bridge. But if you have been bad you will fall; and in hell there will be only fire. The people who fall into this fire will be burnt quickly and completely. Then God, the Creator, will cause them to be born again. And they will burn again. That is how they will remain. They will not die. But they will keep on burning, forever.

It wasn't until the arrival of the Cass Nutrition Unit in 1974 that the Europeans established a permanent, full-time presence in Dulaba. Until then their visits had been only periodic, but the Cass, an autonomous unit of the MRC based at Cambridge University, had been expelled from Uganda by Idi Amin, and in return for co-operation in their research, they offered to provide free medical treatment for the people of Dulaba and the neighbouring villages of Mankono and Karafa Kunda.

Their first area of investigation was the cause of poor growth in the village children, because that was the first step in the slide towards severe clinical malnutrition, which could overtake a child before the mother even realized it.

It was discovered that nine out of ten children in Dulaba had suffered weight-loss caused by diarrhoea before they were one year old. Their systems weakened in this way, they would succumb to the first minor infection. This diarrhoea was caused by faecio-oral contamination. It wasn't that their mothers were particularly dirty in their personal habits, but under the conditions in which they lived, it was impossible to achieve a high degree of sanitation.

The women breast-fed their children for at least eighteen months, and some up to three years after birth. Recognizing that their breast milk alone was inadequate to support the child after three months, they would begin to supplement it with the traditional weaning food, a watery gruel of pounded rice or millet. It contained little in the way of energy or nutriments, and the child had to consume vast quantities in order to grow at a normal rate. A large bowl of it would be prepared early in the morning and carried out to the fields or wherever the woman was working, so that she could feed it to the child during the course of the day. As the porridge lay there under the sun, bacteria would proliferate. For although the porridge was boiled during cooking, it was then poured into bowls which had been washed in infected water. Young children would defecate on the floors of the cramped yards at the back of the houses, where the women did the cooking. It was immediately swept away, but the sand from which it had been swept might then be used to scour the bowls into which the children's porridge would be poured. It was worse in the rainy season, when the humid conditions encouraged bacterial growth, and the rain washed faeces into the wells.

So it was that the Child Supplement Centre came to be built on the area of waste ground between the MRC laboratory and the village. The Cass had decided to introduce its own weaning food, an energy-dense blend of aid foods it had been asked to find a use for by the government of the country: wheat flour, oil, sugar, dried skimmed milk. The administering of this new porridge was supervised and annotated, and it was drunk immediately, from the Cass's own plastic mugs.

Despite good population compliance the Child Supplement did not have the dramatic results hoped for. In terms of 'achieved energy intake and improved growth', its impact was relatively small. None the less, along with the improved standard of health care provided in their clinic, the Cass had managed to reduce the infant mortality rate from 50% to 0.2% in less than fifteen years.

For the first few years of its residence in Dulaba, the Cass's director was met on each of his visits by a group of the village elders wanting to know if the Cass had any plans to leave the village. When they had been assured that it had not, they returned to their compounds, apparently greatly relieved. After a time, however, these deputations ceased. The people had accepted the Cass as part of their landscape and their world. And while they were strict in the practice of their own religion, they refrained from judgement of the Europeans. For if God had made the blacks to be Muslims, only God could say what He had made the tubabs to be.

The flame-trees were in bloom, and the MRC compound stood out, an island of vermilion in the grey exhaustion of the surrounding bush. The laboratory itself, a two-storey building of 1930s design, stood four-square opposite the main gate, its upper portions smothered in cerise bougainvillaea – as unlikely in that setting as a Greek temple in the Brecon Beacons. Through the sliding glass doors at the side, one could see into the gleaming interior of formica and stainless steel. Immediately outside, the rock-like red earth was riddled with termite holes. They covered the parched grasses, the bushes, the trees, and even, in places, the walls of the houses with a brittle layer of red dust so that they could eat without ever emerging from the earth. One would see a branch that the termites had covered, and when one touched it, it crumbled to powder. For they had already eaten it from within, leaving only the shell of dust behind.

The bungalows of the Europeans stood close by among the trees, their assiduously watered gardens providing them with a measure of privacy. There were six other tubabs: Sarah and Richard Innes, the doctors, and their two young daughters; Susan Lawrence, the second scientist, and her husband Rajiv, an agriculturist with the charity Action Aid, who was only periodically present; and Barbara Smith, the midwife, who had her own flat on top of the laboratory. The 'Staff' – the thirty or so technicians, fieldworkers and drivers, and their wives and children – lived mostly in the 'Quarters', a long blockhouse facing the perimeter fence.

In the lonely north-western corner of the compound was the tennis court. It was not much used now, and the net lay sadly trampled in the red dust. It had never been a very good place to play, for the dust quickly coloured the ball, and once lost it was impossible to find.

The days passed, alternating between blazing white light and a thick overcast greyness. The country's fuel supplies were diminishing daily, and at night the compound generators were turned off. I slept in the Professor's office, where the windows were kept closed against insects, and every night I would wake in the small hours hardly able to breathe.

I'd take the sheet, stagger out into the living room and curl up on the sofa. All around I could hear the sound of the earth – a grunting and a heaving – as though it were an animal, dozing but not sleeping.

Then, before dawn, the first cock would crow, immediately followed by the massed hooting, howling and honking of the other animals, and above it all the braying of a donkey, like the grinding of a rusting iron door. Finally, beneath this barrage of animal noises could be heard, faintly, distantly, the voice of the muezzin, calling the faithful to prayer. Whether this latter sound came from the mosque on the other side of the village or the gatekeeper's radio I never found out, for I'd fall back into a sleep as muggy as the grey dawn. The next thing I'd be aware of would be Natoma, the child's nursemaid, standing in the doorway in the half light. I'd wrap myself in my sheet and stagger back into the office.

At eight o'clock it became suddenly light. I'd get up and make my breakfast under the mildly disapproving gaze of Natoma. She was in her early thirties, svelte of physique, lissom of movement, and apparently mild in manner; though you could sense the severity in her, as if she'd been toughened inside with unbreakable wire. She and Ousmane Koujabi, the 'house-boy', seemed like ancient guardians of the house, who had watched over it and inhabited it years before the Professor arrived and would be there for ever after, regardless of who was ostensibly living there. In fact, Natoma had only been working there for about four months, since the Professor and Helene brought their infant daughter Gabby from England.

Her husband was old and in poor health, and though he still maintained a groundnut field, he got very little from it. It was left to Natoma to support him and their seven children. Last year the rain had been very poor, and Natoma had only got a quarter of what she had expected from her rice field. She had been hoping to send her eldest son to secondary school, so she went to the camp and asked Helene for a job.

Helene had laughed. Natoma was one of the 'survey mothers', and she had not been the easiest to deal with. It had been necessary for the purpose of the survey for Helene to measure the thickness of the layers of subcutaneous fat around the women's hips. There had been resistance from some of them, as they didn't like to expose their nether regions, even to each other. Natoma had been particularly difficult about this. Ultimately she had complied, but afterwards whenever she saw Helene her deep-set, rather sad eyes would take on a look of intense and determined disapproval, which made the white woman feel most uncomfortable. 'You think you can make my life miserable, and then ask me for a job?' Helene had said to herself. None the less the woman was evidently a competent mother – all of her seven children had lived, and they had all grown well. So when the time had come for Helene and the Professor to find a nursemaid for their child, they had given her the job.

Ousmane Koujabi was a Jola from the Casamance. He could speak five languages, including French, but he only ever seemed to communicate in any of them in a series of hoarse grunts. He had a broad face of extraordinary sculptural simplicity and definiteness – the look of someone who carries no information other than what is necessary for what he has to do. He padded around with his broom dressed only in a pair of ragged shorts, exposing his muscles, which curved magnificently around his back and thighs, like those of a wrestler on an ancient Greek vase. A fisherman, a hunter, a person of many practical skills, he was very fond of the Europeans' child, and would sit holding her and mooning at her for long periods of time. He was twenty-nine years old.

Two years before, he had returned from a weekend away with a young woman, his new wife. He had never met her before, and was not at all pleased about the situation. For a long time he had refused to speak to her.

Helene had asked him if he had known someone he would have preferred to marry. He said he had. She asked him why he hadn't told his father of this. He said it was because his wife was a twin. Her sister was going to be married, and if she did not marry at the same time, it would bring great evil on all of them.

On the corner of the street opposite the entrance to the compound of Li Kunda, there stood an enormous baobab tree. As with all the baobabs, the bark had been stripped from the trunk to make rope, but it had re-formed, leaving a curious rim around the base of the branches, like a roll of skin that had been pulled effortfully back to reveal the mass of sinuous muscle, now frozen into a grey, rock-like stillness. At its base, the tree had formed itself into a number of columnular masses, like a set of monstrous knuckles forever digging into the earth. From this immense girth grew three branches, each the width of an ordinary tree, from which more huge branches spread up into the sky.

Recently branches had started to fall from the tree, and in the winds that preceded the first storms, it would become a danger to human life. So the inhabitants of the compound decided to cut it down. For days, late every afternoon, they hacked away from all angles at the base of the tree. The wood was flaky and gave easily to their axes. Ibou Sanyang, one of the MRC fieldworkers, who was also the leader of the Dulaba Boy Scouts, went over to have a look. 'You should use ropes,' he told them. 'The Scouts always use ropes when they do these things.' But they paid no attention. The old men looked on impassively. The small boys watched with mounting excitement, and the young men took it in turns with the axes, as they cut deeper and deeper into the hollow centre of the tree.

At midday on the third day, when the wind was blowing strongly, the great tree began to rock. Panicking, the people quickly cleared the area. The tree fell, banging like a gun as it smashed a house to pieces. The owner of the house, who had rented it out from time to time, had to laugh with everyone else; a human life is worth more than a house.

'These people are very stupid,' said Ibou Sanyang bitterly. 'If they had used ropes like I said, the house would not have been destroyed.'

The next day the trunk filled the street like an immense torso. The boys clambered over it, stripping off the smaller branches, which they laid in neat piles around it. The base had been chopped into shards of more or less equal size. The hollow of the tree yawned like the inside of a giant ribcage.

'What is your name?' asked a boy of about twelve who was standing on the highest point of the trunk.

I told him.

The other boys echoed in an insistent chorus. 'Mark! Mark! What is your name?'

'Mark, what is your time?' asked the older boy.

I looked at my watch. 'Half-past twelve.'

'Mark, what is your past?' asked one small boy.

The others all howled in derision.

Children under the age of fourteen were not required to fast, and their society was one of the few aspects of village life that functioned normally during Ramadan. As soon as any European appeared in the village, they would come running from all directions, shrieking at the tops of their voices: 'Tubabo fele! Tubabo fele!' 'The white man is here! The white man is here!' They were as much a part of the texture, the physical substance of the village, as the rough wood of the bantabas or the mud of the houses. They were one with the dust they rolled in, and naked or clothed it covered them from their toes to their shaven scalps. They moved in great gangs, scarcely controllable. The girls were allowed to look after other children from the age of seven, though many started earlier, and it was often not clear who was supposed to be carrying who, as they stumbled through the compounds – fighting, tormenting animals, laying waste to the fragile fences with their constant comings and goings, leaving behind the shattered wreckage of their playthings: rags, sticks, old tins and any other bits of manufactured European refuse they could lay their hands on.

The upper lips of the younger children were perpetually covered in a layer of gleaming snot, frequently causing hideous sores. With their heads shaven against lice, it would have been difficult to tell which sex was which, except that the girls wore tiny rings of blue metal in their ears. They were all festooned with jujus – amulets to protect them from witches and devils: Koranic spells sewn into pieces of leather or cloth, cowries, pieces of root or horn, tiny bottles of holy water. They wore them bound to their arms or ankles, hanging from their necks, or on long strings slung around their bodies like bandoliers.

In the early evening, the village suddenly came alive. People began hurrying to their compounds in readiness for the breaking of the fast. Everywhere one could hear the pestles thudding in eager syncopation, the rhythms becoming faster and faster as the moment of relief came closer. The children, catching the mood of exhilaration, started to chatter and run about even more excitedly than usual. The yellow millet stalks of the fences began to glow as though incandescent in the last light of the setting sun. The pink colour of the sand deepened to a dusky lilac. The air thickened with the smoke of cooking fires, the darkness pouring from the shadows between the houses, and within moments the village was engulfed in night.

The end of Ramadan was fast approaching. On Sunday the moon would disappear. On Monday it would rest. On Tuesday night the people would go out and look for the new moon – the ming-karo – the moon of drinking. If they saw it, the next day would be Koriteh, the great feast that marked the end of Ramadan.

'That is a great day,' said Helene. 'They dress up. They eat a lot, and everyone is very happy. But it will not happen here on Wednesday, I am sure of that. Here they always have to fast longer than anywhere else. If they fast thirty days on the coast, they will fast thirty-one days here. They will not stop until they themselves have actually seen the moon. It is the same every year. They have always to be more pious than anyone else.'

In the afternoons the fieldworkers would lay bamboo mats out under the trees in front of the community centre, and lie down to sleep or rest. They were very pleased when they heard that I would fast on the last day of Ramadan. Fabakary Manneh, a young lad of eighteen and the most recent recruit, raised himself on his elbow.

'But you must not look at a woman's legs if you are fasting.'

'The women here cover their legs,' I said.

'But these white women, Sarah, Helene and others, they are exposing their legs. So on that day you can rest from looking at them.'

'I'll try,' I said. 'Will I have to spit?'

'It is not always necessary to spit. If you have these big salivas . . .' A woman hawked violently in a nearby house. '. . . like that woman, you can spit them out. But if you just have some small salivas, God will not mind if you swallow them.'

Jere Jarjou, a tall, thin young man, rolled onto his back. 'Mark, if you fast, I will invite you for dinner on Tuesday night. But you must fast.'

'I will,' I said.

Jarra Njai Sise wore her hair plaited along her scalp in tight ridges. She had small eyes, slanting above high cheek-bones, and a long jaw with prominent teeth. When she smiled she showed a great deal of her gums, which had been tattooed blue. Her body was lean and well-proportioned; her biceps rippled as she hugged them against her body. But her breasts hung flaccidly between them; two shrivelled, emaciated sacs, as though the life had been drained out of them by some terrible and overwhelming force. She had suckled four of her five children, the first having died at birth.

> 'Jarra Njai is a great woman,' sang the other women.
> 'She can forgive at any time.
> And she has taken the position of a man,
> Because of her greatness.'

She was twenty-eight – the same age as the Professor and myself.

'Fasting,' she said, 'is something that God has commanded us to do. He has put us in this world so that he can place any difficulties on us that he wishes. We are his slaves, and whatever he commands us to do, we must do it. Because whatever he says he means it.'

She was the tall, black woman I had met with her two friends on the path into the bush that afternoon, four months before. She was renowned for the strident quality and the sheer volume of her voice, but on that day she was fasting and sounded hoarse and drained, as she sat limply on the edge of her bed in the room she shared with her husband's mother, the second wife, and all the children. I had gone there to interview her, with the fieldworker Ibou Sanyang acting as translator. Despite her evident weariness, she had agreed to speak to us, and her small eyes betrayed a certain amount of curiosity – not so much with the questions themselves, but with the hidden purpose behind them. We had gone there to get something from her. She also might be able to get something from us.

She had been with her husband for six years, she said, before they started quarrelling. Whenever she spoke to him he would be angry. And whenever he spoke to her she would be angry. They would quarrel, and he would beat her. It was around this time that he had taken the second wife; though whether they had quarrelled because he was taking a second wife, or whether he had taken a second wife because they were quarrelling, was not made clear.

The second wife sat and listened to the conversation. She looked, in her way, remarkably similar to Jarra Njai; a smaller, younger, milder version. I recognized her as the third person I had seen going into the bush on that afternoon. The two women were now on good terms, though if two people lived together, they would always have occasional differences.

Since my last visit, the husband had moved them from his father's compound in the oldest and most crowded part of the village, to this new compound beside the laterite road. He slept at one end of the long blockhouse, and the women at the other. From the verandah that ran along the front of the building under the broad expanse of dully gleaming new corrugate, a bare yard stretched down to the fence of wooden stakes that separated the compound from the road. It was only the second compound to have been built on the north side of the road, and beyond it the bush stretched uninterrupted for seven miles, to the banks of the great river.

I asked Jarra Njai what she would ask for if she could have anything in the world.

'I would ask that that chest be filled with clothes, and new covers be put on the bed. But if I was asking God, I would ask for peace, wealth and happiness. Because, you know, God will never give you anything directly. He will never come out of the sky or the ground and say, "Here is the thing you were asking for." He will give it to you through somebody or something. So if you don't accept that person or that thing, you will lose what you are seeking. For example, you have come to talk to me today. After you leave this compound, if I go into the village and find a coin, it will be because of you.'

'What she is trying to say,' said Sanyang, 'is that she will be very happy if you can find her a job washing clothes at the camp.'

I was astonished. I said I was only a visitor at the camp. I had no power to employ anybody.

She sat very still, and I thought for a moment she was going to become angry. Then she said, 'We will always help you. No matter how many times you come to us, we will always answer your questions.'

Sanyang was the leader of the Dulaba Boy Scouts – in fact he had founded the troop when he was teaching at the Dulaba Primary School. He was twenty-six, well-built in a plumply muscular way. He had a naturally pedagogical temperament; he was articulate, fond of voicing his good intentions, of saying what he would and would not do under a wide variety of unlikely circumstances. Three years before, however, he had given up teaching to become a fieldworker at the MRC. For although the pay was much the same, and the work at the MRC was less demanding and less stimulating, the conditions of employment were infinitely better: the pay arrived on a regular basis, there was free transport to the coast on the MRC vehicles, and the status of working for a 'foreign company' was just a little higher.

He had been married for three years, but he had brought his wife from her home village in the Casamance only six months before, because it was their custom that the first child should be born in the mother's parents' compound. Previously she had lived in Dakar and Banjul, and she seemed quite different from the women of the village. She plaited her hair into extravagant whorls on the side of her head or twisted it into long, thin spikes that stuck out like the branches of a baobab tree. She was slender, and beautiful, and you could tell that he was deeply proud of her.

It was said that on Sunday night the moon would disappear, and as we walked through the streets of the village, I could see nothing whatsoever. Only the swish of cloth against cloth, and the faint slap of their rubber sandals, betrayed the presence of the people passing. A low moaning sound and a flurry of feet would tell us we had disturbed a flock of sheep or goats. The warm air was thick with their smell and the smoke of cooking firs. I kept close to Sanyang. I didn't want to fall over or get lost.

'Is it true,' asked Sanyang, 'that in Europe there are so many lights, 'that even if it is the middle of the night and you drop a pin in the street, you will be able to find it?'

'No.'

'All of the blacks can see very well in the dark,' he said. 'When I came to work for the MRC, they gave me a torch for when I work in the village at night. But if I didn't work for the MRC, I would never use a torch.'

It was Kitimo, the twenty-sixth night of Ramadan, when the Koran would be recited by the people, and interpreted by those educated in God's words. Sanyang stopped and I bumped into him. 'Let us go into this compound,' he said. I heard the rattling and creaking of a corrugated-iron door, and followed him through. There was a murmured exchange of greetings. I was led to a seat and sat down. All I could see were the tips of lighted cigarettes. I counted seven.

'Hello, Mr Hudson,' said a clear and rather clipped voice. 'And how are you enjoying the environment?'

'Very much,' I said.

'That is good.'

'Who are you?' I asked.

'My name is Momodou Jopp. I am a teacher at Dulaba Primary School. We are all teachers in this compound.' There were grunts and murmurs of affirmation. 'Mr Hudson, I would like to ask you a question.'

'Go ahead,' I said.

'What is your opinion of smoking?'

'It's bad,' I said.

A harsh voice broke in. 'These European doctors all say that smoking is bad, yet most of them are smoking. Can you answer that?'

Before I had a chance to respond, Mr Jopp had continued. 'The reason smoking is bad is not because of health, it is because of money.' He inhaled deeply. 'A farmer is buying cigarettes at ten batuts each, and he is smoking twenty a day. When he sells his groundnuts for 1,500 dalasis, he must support his family for a year on that money. But first he must settle his debt with the shopkeeper for the previous eight months. How much will it cost him?'

'I've no idea.'

'Exactly. This is why I'm saying smoking is an economic problem.'

Shortly afterwards, we left that compound and turned a corner to find ourselves facing an open space, in the middle of which a hurricane-lamp had been placed on a table. Around it there must, one would have thought from the volume and strength of the singing, have been a very great crowd of people. But it was difficult to tell as beyond the feeble glow of the lamp the darkness was as thick and impenetrable as ever. I was led to the verandah of a building which turned out to be a shop. Behind me I could see people buying cigarettes in the muggily lit interior. As I didn't smoke, a black mint was passed out for me to suck. We must have been beside one of the main thoroughfares of the village, but I had no idea which one for I had long since lost any sense of where we were.

Around the table sat the elder Koranic students – young men in their late teens – and behind them the younger boys. The light of the lamp shone into their joyful faces, and upwards into the dark foliage of the mango tree that hung over the place. They sang a long refrain, the rough voices of the men singing from the darkness, and the sharp, clean voices of the boys chiming together. A man in dark glasses and a white robe, standing among the figures close to the table, led the singing, his head thrown back, calling out into the darkness in the stylized, slightly nasal manner of the Muslim liturgy – a sound cold, almost stellar in its lonely longing. He had a strong, bullish voice, and the long, undulating refrains came rolling effortlessly forth, to be met immediately by the surging chorus.

'What are they singing?' I asked Sanyang.

'They are just saying that there is no God but God.'

'And what else?'

'I don't know. I'm not much educated in the Koran. I was sent there when I was very small, but I can't remember any of it. Even the small children in this village know more about the Koran than I do.'

A rangy figure in a long white gown came towards us, puffing on a cigarette. He shook hands with both of us. 'Yes, Mr Hudson,' he said in a clipped voice. 'I hope you're enjoying the environment.' And then he lolloped off.

'Hurh!' chuckled Sanyang. 'Momodou Jopp! He is dressing like a pure Muslim, while he is smoking ganja and drinking alcohol – rampantly!' He laughed again at the cheek of it.

'Are you a pure Muslim?' I asked.

'No!' he exclaimed emphatically. 'I am a Rasta.'

'A Rasta?' I said, astonished. 'But your hair?'

'I do not have the locks, because I do not need to show anyone that I am a Rasta.'

'So what do you do to be a Rasta?'

'To be a Rasta you must be of good heart. You must be good to all people. If you do something bad to me, I will not do anything to you. I will know that you have done it – but I will not do anything back. A Muslim prays five times a day, but I only pray when I need to speak to Jah.'

'Are there many Rastas in the Gambia?' I asked.

'Very many. One day I hope that the Rasta faith will take over the whole of our country.'

The singing had come to a temporary halt, and a youngish man in a light-coloured safari suit got to his feet. Sanyang told me he was a teacher at the Arabic school.

There were two schools in Dulaba: the government school, where the teaching was in English, and the Arabic school. English was for this world, Arabic for the next. If a man sent two children to the government school, he would send two to the Arabic school. Most of the girls went to the Arabic school.

'It was on a day like today,' said the young teacher, 'the twenty-sixth day of Ramadan, that the Koran was revealed to the Prophet Mohammed. God sent the angel Gabriel to tell him that he should learn. But Mohammed said that he was not someone who was meant to learn. The angel came to him again, and again told him that he should learn. But Mohammed told him that he was a poor man, that he was not a person who should learn. Then the angel came to him a third time, and Mohammed said, "What should I learn?" Then the angel revealed to him the words of the Holy Koran.

'The tubabs have offered us their knowledge, and we should learn from them. But what they teach us can only help us to make our living easier on the earth. It cannot lead us to heaven.

'It is the tubabs who invented this expression, "Mind your business, save your life". They are the ones who brought it to Africa. The Africans are the poorest people on earth, but now we are taking this attitude even more than the Europeans. Please, let us not forget our own religion, because it is only through our religion that we can get to heaven. Pray five times a day! And if you see a Muslim doing something wrong you should stop him. If you see a child misbehaving you should discipline it, even if it is not your own. This is how a Muslim should behave. We are very fond of saying that God will punish that person. But who knows what God will do tomorrow?'

On the last day of Ramadan, I fasted. I woke late and realized I'd missed the porridge I should have eaten at four-thirty in the morning. By mid-morning, I noticed that my thoughts lacked order – they floated slowly but aimlessly backwards and forwards across my mind. But slow as they were I could not catch them. By lunchtime – or what would have been lunchtime – I had a headache, as though someone had wrapped a wet cloth around my brain and was slowly tightening it. To have fasted properly, I should have gone about my normal duties. Instead I retreated into the Professor's office and lay down on my bed with the air-conditioning full on. Whenever I ventured out into the living-room, I felt as though I were drowning, as the heat came rushing from all directions, flooding my brain so that I could hardly stand.

By half-past seven it was almost dark. I was putting my shoes on, when Jere Jarjou appeared at the window. 'It is time,' he said, and I hurried after him to the staff quarters.

It is better to break your fast with something hot. If you began with the iced water you had been craving all day, you would probably be sick. So we started by drinking a mixture of tea, Ovaltine and evaporated milk, each mug sweetened with two dessertspoons of sugar. We knocked this concoction back, expressions of great gratitude and relief on our faces, then we fell on the platefuls of food spread out on the low table – chicken cut up and fried in sauce, the head and feet served on the plate, fish with a sauce of macaroni and prawns, fish fried with potatoes, and a *mélange* of vegetable. We tore hunks from loaves of bread and dipped them into the juices before cramming them into our mouths. As we ate, each of my companions seemed to light up from the inside, and I too could feel my body returning to normal with the warm food inside me. Across the table Demba Tamba, smallest and most punctilious of the fieldworkers, leant forward eagerly to eat, talking animatedly in Jola all the time. His short hair seemed wilder than usual, his eyes wider, the orange whites gleaming brilliantly.

However much you may feel that you lack material security in your own country, and that you can thus identify with the uprooted and the disinherited of the earth, you may find, when you arrive in a radically different cultural environment, that you are almost immediately distanced from this position – not through any failure of empathy, or even because of the social and physical distance, but because of these very people's perception of you as something completely and profoundly *other*.

None of the people with whom I was eating – Demba, Ibou Sanyang, Jere, Yaya Bojang or Bakary Sanneh – could have been said to have fallen into that category. They came across as typical young men of West Africa: smilingly amiable in the easy-going manner of the region; casually but always smartly dressed in clothes of European cut. They all had secure employment, and they had none of them gone a day without eating. They were, none the less, even by the standards of their own country, from extremely humble backgrounds. They would never be part of the élite, they would never receive scholarships to study abroad. They would never reach the higher echelons of the civil service. They were the sons of provincial farmers who had managed to scrape together just enough money to send them to secondary school, that they might be spared the drudgery and the uncertainty of life on the land. They were, in all cases, the first generation of their families to be educated in the European way.

But though they were friendly enough, and though they clearly recognized me as someone of their own age-group – in local terms a *kambano*: a boy – I could tell that I was for them first and foremost a tubab, and that it would take some time to get beyond that.

Demba was twenty-five. He had been with the Cass for five years, Before that he had worked as a barman and a waiter in one of the hotels on the coast. He said he admired the British very much, and he nurtured the hope that he might one day go to Britain to study. He had a friend, Lamin Bojang, an MRC fieldworker, who had been sent by the Cass to their head office in Cambridge to train as a laboratory technician. This was the example he dreamed of following.

Yaya Bojang was slightly younger than Demba, but they came from the same village, and they had known each other since childhood. He was an athlete, the head of the football team; he prided himself on his expertise in all forms of play, into which he threw himself with almost passionate absorption. He explained his diminutive stature by the fact that he had suffered very seriously from measles as a child, and despite his initial reserve, it was quickly obvious that in his soul he was a big person.

There was Sanyang, whom I already knew. Then there was Jere Jarjou, the one who had invited me to the meal. He was tall, slightly gangling and oddly bug-eyed. He was only twenty-one, one of the most recent recruits to the MRC, and one of the most qualified. But he remained something of an enigma: humorous and melancholic by turns, one never knew which aspect of himself he would show next.

They were all Jolas, and perceived of themselves as being quite different from the Mandingkos – the Mandinka people of Dulaba. They came from Fonyi, the ancient country of the Jolas, which began only a few miles away on the other side of the Bintang Bolon, and stretched south as far as Ziguinchor on the Casamance river. Now the border ran through the middle of this area, but it was well known that the Jolas paid little attention to such details. They had been there long before the Mandingkos came from the east, in their ancestors' time. In those days they called themselves Ajamat. When the first Mandingko arrived in that part of the world, he asked them what he must do to live beside them in peace. 'Whatever good thing you do to us,' they said, 'we will repay you with good. But whatever evil you do to us, we will repay you with evil.' So the Mandingko said, 'I will call you Jo-la', which in the Mandinka language means 'someone who pays back'. And today, except in the very remote areas, even the Ajamat referred to themselves as Jolas.

I listened to Demba speaking in the Jola language. It sounded unutterably strange to me at that moment; it seemed to consist only of consonants, which bumped and crashed into each other as they came spilling from his mouth, punctuated by throaty guffaws, high nasal exclamations of surprise, and the odd curse in Arabic.

The only person there who was not a Jola, and was thus excluded from the conversation as much as I, was Bakary Sanneh. He was a Mandingko from the neighbouring village of Joli, but he had been sent as a boy to Banjul, where relatives had taken care of his education. He had been working for the Cass in Dulaba for ten years. Recently he had taken five O levels in his spare time, and he had passed them all. He was fair in complexion, leanly good-looking, cool – like an attorney in a cop series. He sat back, bare-chested in the wooden armchair, nonchalantly blowing clouds of cigarette smoke into the air. If anyone was going to follow Lamin Bojang to Cambridge, it would be he.

'You say you do not have a car,' he said. 'But it is not because you cannot afford one. It is because you do not want one. If you wanted one you would have one.'

'He is not poor,' said Jere Jarjou. 'I believe he is poorer than these other tubabs here. But he is not poor. He cannot say he is poor.'

After dinner we sat outside in the cool breeze, and drank cold water. All over the country, in the open spaces of the bush, on the beaches and by the riversides, people would be out looking for the moon. If they saw it they would run and tell the Imam, and then everyone would know that Ramadan was at an end. Above us the sky was utterly black – an immense black nothing opening up beyond the feeble glow of the electric light on the verandah.

Someone turned on the radio to see if the moon had been seen in Senegal. The others went off to pray, while Jere stayed and sat with me. He had invited me, and he wouldn't hear of my leaving yet. A recording of a Jola initiation ceremony came over on the radio, broadcast for the pleasure of Jola listeners. The ecstatic voices rose and fell like waves on a choppy sea, while beneath, the brittle drums beat. Two small children who had been playing with a broom on the verandah began cavorting to the rhythm. Jere encouraged them by clapping his hands. They obliged with a display of knock-kneed stamping. 'You see,' he said. 'Even they can do it. This is our dance, everyone here can do it . . .' He gestured round the forecourt of the quarters, empty as people were at prayer. 'But me, I cannot do it. I was brought up in the town, so I did not learn it.'

At midnight a message had been sent from the Ministry of the Interior in Dakar to the Gambian government, informing them that the moon had been seen in Senegal. News of sightings had also come from Guinea and Mauritania. In the Gambia the moon was spotted in East Jarra, where the chief sent a message to the government.

The MRC staff and the schoolteachers had stopped fasting that Tuesday night, and nothing would have induced them to start again. But the rest of the population continued to fast, because they themselves had not yet seen the moon.

At ten o'clock on Wednesday night, as I sat drinking green tea in the teachers' compound, it was announced that the moon had still not appeared, and the villagers would continue to fast the following day. Now, in the whole country, it was only the people of Dulaba, and the neighbouring villages of Joli and Karafa Kunda, who were still fasting. The fieldworkers and the teachers who sat with me in the compound were furious. They said that if another Muslim tells you he has seen the moon, you should believe him. But these people here in this village were quite impossible! They would only believe the evidence of their own eyes.

The teachers and the MRC staff saw themselves as a group apart, quite separate from the rest of the village. They called themselves the 'Civil Servants', for though the MRC staff did not work for the government, they had all had the benefit of a Western education. They were none of them citizens of Dulaba, for it was only very recently that the elders had allowed a European school to be built in the village.

'These people are very wicked,' said Jere Jarjou. 'They think they are the most pious people on earth while they know nothing.'

The following day, however, they were not so sure. It was said that if the moon had been seen on Tuesday night in a cloudy sky, it should have appeared early on Wednesday evening. Maybe those people on the radio had been lying. What if the moon did not appear tonight either?

'No, no,' said Demba Tamba. 'It must appear tonight. It is not possible that it will not.'

At seven-thirty in the evening it was announced in the compound that the moon had appeared. Everyone went out into the forecourt to look at it. The sky was still very bright, and at first no one could see it. Then Helene spotted it, framed by the pods of a flame-tree – a tiny sliver of a moon hanging upside down in the pale lilac sky – like a fragment of feather lost in an enamel bathtub.

3

THE GOLDEN CHAIN

At ten o'clock the following morning the villagers prayed. They had been wrong. They admitted they had been wrong. Last night the moon had been high in the sky – it must also have appeared the previous night.

In the 'praying ground', the area of street in front of the mosque, facing the burial ground, the men prostrated themselves before God. Beside them in the enclosure of the mosque, the old women knelt to pray with them, their heads draped in long white shawls. Behind them the younger boys, shaven-headed, dressed in their best tunics and trousers, and behind them the girls and small children all rose and knelt in prayer. The women of child-bearing age watched from the wells, where, dressed in some of their best clothes, they continued with their tasks. They were not allowed to go into the praying ground or enter the mosque, for it was said that if a man became sexually aroused he would not be able to concentrate on his prayers.

As the prayer came to an end, a great drum sounded twice from the Imam's compound to signal that the feasting could begin, and with a tremendous thundering of feet the children ran howling and shrieking into the village.

Late in the afternoon crowds of children began to gather at the gates of the MRC compound. They had come for their *salibo*, their prayer-day present. They stood there, all looking very solemn and very clean. The brightly-patterned dresses of the girls, and the tunics, shirts and shorts of the boys were all immaculately ironed. The girls' head-ties – *tikos* – were arranged in rings on the tops of their heads like little haloes. Many of them were made up with lipstick and eyebrow pencil.

The Professor had told Momodou Jallo, the night-watchman, that the children could come into the compound at six o'clock. And come they did, rushing towards the house, pouring in through the rickety garden gate and along the verandah. Helene beat them back and shut the gate. Then she produced several packets of 'Camel Biscuits de Medina', which she had bought that afternoon at the village shop, and she and I began passing the hard round little biscuits over the fence. Immediately dozens of tiny arms thrust up into the air, furiously grasping for the biscuits, the tiny bodies crushing against each other. Little voices screamed from the sea of anguished, desperate faces: 'Mark, Mark! Try it! Try it!' Some would take their biscuits and dart out of the crowd. Others would immediately thrust their other empty hand forwards. Still others would quickly shove their prizes in their mouths and continue to shout, 'Me! Me! I haven't had anything,' through mouthfuls of half-chewed biscuit.

The bigger children had pushed their way to the front and were getting most of the action. We tried to pass the biscuits over their heads, but immediately their hands would go up: 'Mark! Mark! Yes, yes!' At the side of the crowd, tiny, bug-eyed infants were trying to climb up the fence to get to the biscuits. 'Here, Mark, here.' Little faces at the front were disappearing into the mass. Enough! Time to stop! We retreated into the house after only three minutes.

Once it was dark, the older girls and the young women began to arrive. Soon the doorway of the Professor's house was piled high with plastic and rubber sandals like the entrance to a mosque. On the sofa, on the Habitat armchairs and on the cane-backed dining chairs, the young women and girls sat clutching mugs of lemonade, expressions of intense seriousness on their faces. Their deep violet skin seemed to absorb the yellowish light, so that they radiated a glowing darkness.

They were all dressed in their finest clothes – tight-fitting blouses that zipped up the back, frilling out at the waist and the shoulders, the frills often stiffly ironed so that they stood out like butterfly wings. In places they were embellished with imitation satin, and all in the gaudiest of colours. It was a style that had been developed by the Wolof women on the coast from French fashion of the time of Marie-Antionette.

Occasionally someone would try to make conversation:
'Where are the people of your compound?'
'They are there.'
'Are they in peace?'
'Peace only.'
'I hope there's no trouble.'
'No trouble.'

I spent most of the evening in the kitchen with the Professor, endlessly refilling mugs with lemonade. The Professor shook his head. 'No matter how long I live here, I don't think I'd ever get over finding these situations embarrassing,' he said. 'I mean there's just nothing to say.'

Back in the living-room, the Professor's daughter Gabby was brought out, and the girls took it in turns to hold her. Some of them looked through Helene's magazines. They pored over the illustrations: photographs of women showing their legs and platefuls of strange food. A small boy who had managed to get in sat in a corner looking round himself as though at the interior of a cathedral. Helene gave out presents to the girls: sachets of perfume, nail varnish, headscarves, small necklaces and earrings.

As the evening wore on fewer of the girls came and more of the women. Last to arrive, as we were sitting down to dinner, was Fatounding Sise, with her co-wife Isatou, and a tall thin woman called Musakeba Sise, who lived in the same compound. Fatounding was the second woman I had seen going into the bush with Jarra Njai that afternoon – the broad fair one. She came rolling into the living-room, a slow and rather roguish smile on her face. Her body, beneath the black shawl she wore around her shoulders, looked as though it had been constructed from a series of slabs. The European men liked her because she was funny and handsome, and a bit of a character. The women were not so sure. She had the habit of just turning up and demanding things; and if she didn't get them she'd wander off muttering darkly to herself. Not that she was poor. Her husband was a rice merchant, and one of the wealthier people in the village.

The three women sat down at the table with us, and sipped at their glasses of Grenadine syrup.

'It's very nice,' said Fatounding slowly. 'But it's not much.'

By now all the biscuits, the small coins, the jewellery and the items of make-up had been given away. The only thing I could think of to give them was some CFA coins I had left over from Dakar airport.

'What's this?' asked Fatounding.

'Senegalese money,' I said.

'We don't want Senegalese money. We want Gambian money.'

'Yes,' echoed Musakeba. 'We want Gambian money.'

'If you go to Casamance,' I said, 'you can buy a very nice scarf with that.'

'I never go there,' said Fatounding. 'I'm always here.'

And they gave the money back – all except Isatou, who kept hers. Helene hunted around and found some proper salibos; a headscarf and a bottle of nail varnish. She told Fatounding she'd have to share the nail varnish with Isatou.

'Oh, no,' she said. 'I'm not doing that.'

That night there was a disco dance in the community centre, a long shed-like building which stood in the middle of the waste ground adjacent to the Child Supplement Centre. A cassette player belonging to Alioune Sware, the MRC driver, was set up on the verandah, while inside, from the tall speakers he had bought from Bill, the previous doctor, reggae and African pop were blaring out through a fog of distortion. One red light bulb illuminated the concrete floor, over which water appeared to have been poured with great liberality.

I was rather surprised to note that most of the dancers were of no more than waist height. The boys danced singly: leaping from side to side, kicking their legs in the air, wildly shaking their arms and torsos. There was no particular venue for their dancing. They danced inside, they danced outside. Some danced with their shadows in front of walls. The little girls, their head-ties still in place, danced in groups, twisting their little bodies in thoughtless abandon, like members of some miniature Tamla Motown ensemble. They were certainly more enterprising in their dancing than the adults, who favoured the kind of laboured twitching one would see in a youth club in the suburbs of London – expressions of pained solemnity on their faces. It was as though they were aiming for a certain style, a specifically 'pop' style, to which they felt bound to adhere. Occasionally there would be bursts of frenetic enthusiasm, but they were of brief duration.

The older men – those in their thirties – the 'elders' of the youth, sat in a group on the verandah near the cassette console, while the young men danced under the red bulb near the speakers. The adolescent girls were found mostly at the other, darker end of the long room, and along the brilliantly-lit verandahs. They talked constantly and conspiratorially among themselves, forming and reforming into groups, pausing briefly to dance, and then wandering from the verandah to the dancefloor, from the dancefloor to the verandah; always looking about themselves, and always looking away when looked at. The noise of their chatter was so great it threatened to drown out the already muffled music.

The numbers were usually quite long, each followed by a round of applause and a pause while Alioune cued up the next cassette. In any disco there is always one record which stirs people more than the others, which on the first flush of recognition has everyone rushing for the dancefloor with involuntary abandon. That night it was a song by Super Jamano, a band from Dakar. The rhythm throbbed through the distortion and the spluttering of the tam-tams like the pulsing of a great engine, the horns endlessly repeating the same melancholy phrase. There was an organ solo that sounded as though it was being played by someone who was already dead, and above it all a voice intoned coolly in Wolof, occasionally raising itself with that sense of possession, that lonely, almost desolate yearning that characterizes the call of the muezzin. High above the community centre the stars shone brilliantly, and in the distance lightning shot up into the sky. The dancers swayed in rapt, ecstatic absorption; I with five nine-year-old girls. The rhythm began to slow as though the engine was seizing up, while the beating of the tam-tams became more and more frenetic. Then everything became faster and faster, and the dancers shook their bodies almost violently as the song came to a crashing conclusion. There was a tumultuous round of applause, then everyone headed for the verandahs. The nine-year-old girls thanked me for dancing. 'What is your wife's name?' they asked politely.

'Mariyama,' I said, lying instinctively.

In the darkness at the end of the far verandah I found Ibou Sanyang sitting with Momodou Jopp and one of the other teachers, a tall, round-faced young man. He smiled and held out his hand. 'My name is Mr Sambali. I'm a Rasta supporter, as you can see from this badge.' He proffered his shirt to reveal in the dim light a badge bearing the image of Paul McCartney.

'What's that?' I asked.

'That,' said Mr Sambali, 'is the late, great Bob Marley.'

'It's Paul McCartney, isn't it?' I said.

They roared with laughter. 'I think it's Bob,' said Ibou.

I must have looked sceptical.

'Mark,' said Ibou. 'What colour was Bob Marley?'

'I suppose he must have been a light brown,' I said.

'Well . . .' said Ibou, gesturing at the badge. I looked again to see McCartney's visage transmogrified into a feverish orange. 'Mark, who do you think this man was?' said Ibou.

I gave a brief resume of McCartney's career to date, but ended, 'If you say it's Bob Marley, it must be Bob Marley.'

'Now Mark, why do you say that? Is it because it is Sambali's property?

If you don't think it is Bob Marley, you don't have to say that it is.'

We moved on to other subjects. Ibou told me that until recently the youth of Dulaba only liked 'Kenyan' music. 'Now we are educating them to like funk and reggae. They used to dance with *power* – like this . . .' He made an obscene thrusting movement with his pelvis, swinging his arms in an apelike fashion. 'Now we have shown them how to dance in a civilized way. So they don't dance with power any more.'

'What's wrong with dancing with power?' I asked.

'Well, if you dance with power for three minutes you'll be exhausted. But if you dance in a civilized way you can keep going for a long time.'

Along the verandahs and inside the hall, the girls continued to move, still talking with unabated enthusiasm. They were dressed in their finest clothes. They were made-up. They were wearing all the jewellery they possessed. But few of the men showed any interest in dancing with them. Nor did the girls seem to expect to be asked. Occasionally one of them would dance with one of the teachers, but it was a cursory, passionless business.

For they were all married. By the time she was twelve, virtually every woman in the village would be married. At fifteen or sixteen she would be given to her husband, but until she finally transferred to his compound when she was in her early twenties, she would remain under the authority of her mother. So on the nights she was not sleeping with her husband, she was free to come and go in the village more or less as she pleased. But she knew that once she had transferred to her husband's compound she would never be able to attend such a dance again.

For now, if any man could persuade her to dance she was free to do so, and even if her husband was present he couldn't do anything to stop them. Nor would she expect her husband to want to dance with her. If she had a lover she would never speak to him here. She would meet him somewhere far away; somewhere secret.

Momodou Balde was one of the schoolteachers. He was a tall, soft-spoken, rather serious young man. 'Before this community centre was built they used to hold their dances under the big mango tree at the bottom of the high street. In the old days they did not have these cassette systems. They had a little gramophone, which they called an "echo". Initially the boys and the girls used to stay in completely separate groups, but when we teachers came here we did not like that, so we used to invade the girls' groups – we used to walk into their groups and talk to them. When the village boys saw what we were doing, they started to follow us. But still it doesn't happen much. Because it is not something they are familiar with. For a woman to dance with a man is not part of their culture. They don't even know it.'

Bana and Nene Sise were employed as nursemaids, to look after the survey mothers' children while they were taking part in the Professor's experiments in the laboratory. They walked self-importantly around the compound with the children tied on their backs, trying to see their reflections in the glass windows of the laboratory. Bana was the daughter of Mabinta, the Professor's laundress, and was round-faced, doll-like, with wide eyes. Nene was in comparison almost Moorish looking, with a narrow, flat nose and slanting eyes – though they were both extremely black.

Although few of the villagers knew how old they were in terms of numbers of years, they all knew exactly how old they were in relation to the people around them; for they remained in a *kafo*, a group, with the other people of their age throughout their lives. Bana was thus highly aware that she was a member of a kafo slightly older than Nene's. She was, I suppose, sixteen. I decided to interview them to find out what they thought about their lives.

Sanyang sighed with exasperation. 'He doesn't want you to say that you don't know,' he shouted. 'He wants you to say what you think!'

'I don't think,' said Bana, rather put out.

'You are wasting your time with this girl,' he said. 'She is extremely foolish. The other girl is also foolish. But not as foolish as this one.'

The interview was taking place at the Professor's dining table. I had begun to feel almost immediately that it was a fatuous exercise, but we carried on.

She was married. She had been married for three years, but she had not yet been given to her husband. One night her father had called her to his room and said, 'You will be married.' Then he told her the name of the man. She waited in the room for some seconds, then she left. But she had already known she would be married, because a few days before she had heard them dancing and beating a basin in a nearby compound. People told her they were dancing because a boy from that compound would be married to her.

Did she feel special or important because those people were dancing on account of her?

No.

The husband was twenty-six, and he lived in Serekunda, where he worked as a driver. When he came to Dulaba she would go to his compound with two of her age-mates and spend time with him. They would chat and make jokes, and she would help with the cooking.

So she knew the husband well?

Yes.

Did she love him?

Yes.

Why?

Because he is her husband. A woman should love her husband.

Would she love him if he was old and ugly?

'Even if her parents give her to a marabout with one buttock, she will be happy about it,' said Sanyang.

'Is that what she said?'

'No, but this is what they think. I know these people very well.'

Did she know when she would be given to the husband?

She had no idea. The other girls didn't know when they would be given either, whether it would be tomorrow or next year, though sometimes they joked about it.

We moved on to the subject of religion, of how a Muslim should behave.

A Muslim, she said, should behave like a Muslim.

How does a Muslim behave?

In a Muslim way.

'I told you it's a waste of time asking her anything,' said Sanyang.

In contrast to Bana's robust complacency, Nene was shy and soft-spoken almost to the point of inaudibility. She responded to most of the questions with a high-pitched nasal droning, and would then say softly, 'Sanyang!'

'She does not believe you are asking these questions,' he said. 'She thinks I am making them up to make a fool of her.'

I asked if anything had ever happened to her which, when she thought of it, made her feel happy.

Her mother had given her a goat, she said. The goat had died, but she still had the kids. When she thought of that goat she felt happy.

Her husband was a citizen of the village, but lived in Brikama, near the coast. He was about forty. She had met him twice, briefly, before they told her she would marry him, but she hadn't spoken to him since. As for the co-wife, she had seen her, but she hadn't met her, so she didn't know whether she would be on good terms with her or not.

Did she know when she would be given to the husband?

No.

Was she looking forward to it?

No.

Why not?

Because she was a child.

When she went there would it be nice?

No.

Why not?

Because she is a child.

But when she went there, she would be old enough, so would it be a nice thing then?

Yes.

Why?

Because she would be old enough.

Should a woman get married?

If she is old enough she should be married.

Why?

Because she is a Muslim.

She didn't look like a child, but in West Africa women begin menstruating later than in Europe, and they reach the menopause earlier. It was believed by the Europeans that the relative shortness of this reproductive period was due to inferior nutrition.

As soon as she began to bleed, she would, usually within a matter of days, be taken to the husband. She would go there at night with her mother, and even if she did not like him, even if he disgusted her, she had to let him enter her, or she would bring a terrible disgrace upon her family.

From then on she would take her turn with the other wives, each sleeping with the husband for two nights in a row. But each morning she would return to her mother's compound, and she would remain under her mother's authority. She was no longer a child, but she was still a girl. She would be called *sunkuto ba* – big girl.

Binta Sise was as big and as broad as a Greek statue. She wasn't fat, she was just tall and massive, with fine, strong features and deep, thoughtful eyes, like one of those powerful Italian actresses of the 1940s, like Anna Magnani; though she was black in colour – a rich, shining black. When she was young and she went to the fields with the other girls of her age group, they would mock her and run away from her because she was such a joker. And she would run after them and fight them, because she didn't care. She was ashamed in front of the almighty God, but apart from that she was afraid of no one.

If her husband beat her, she would fight back. She would run out into the compound and taunt him, then everyone would know that they were fighting. She didn't care; she wanted people to know what was going on. She was twenty-four years of age.

She lived in Fili Kunda in a house that was like a little island around which the paths passed into a labyrinth of alleys and yards, where the blackened, smoke-filled doorways of the cooking huts gaped like mouths, to tiny, secretive gardens, or to courtyards where the elders sat reading the Koran under a tree. In front of the house was an open area where children played football, and the carpenter who lived over the way – Sajonding Minte's husband – did his work. Beyond that the yard broadened out into the street, so there was a constant traffic of people moving in and out of the compound around Binta Sise's house.

The two rooms of the house were small and dark, the walls of bare mud brick unadorned. The bedroom was barely six feet square and had one short single bed made of branches wedged between the walls. Her husband did not have his own house, but slept on another bed in the minuscule entrance area. Through the bedroom was a tiny yard with a small square hut for cooking. There were no cattle, sheep, or goats. There was a clay water jar in each of the rooms, a dusty Koran on a shelf, and that, apart from Binta's basins and cooking pots, was all they had.

Her husband was a lean, untidy man with narrow eyes and an array of long, uneven teeth. He seemed slighter than he actually was, because he managed to appear both furtive and half-asleep at the same time. He was a fisherman, but the proportion of his time he spent at the Bintang Bolon was not great. He was said by many to be the laziest man in the village. This reputation stemmed from the fact that he did not grow groundnuts –which, in a village where groundnuts were the only cash crop, was unheard of.

Binta had never made any secret of her contempt for him. She had threatened to divorce him if he did not plant a groundnut field. But her mother had told her that if she did that she would never enter their compound again, and as she had nowhere else to go, she had had to forget the idea.

She had no co-wife, and no daughter old enough to help her. She had had three sons by Junkung, and Bill, the previous doctor, had noted that because she despised the husband she had taken very little interest in his children. Once she had brought the youngest son to the clinic suffering from diarrhoea. He was defecating all over the seat, but she paid no attention. She just let him lie in it. Bill had noticed, however, that when at last she had a daughter, she had shown her more affection because she had felt able to identify with her.

Binta herself said that she preferred boys. If you had a daughter you would feed her and clothe her for many years, and then she would go and get married somewhere else, whereas boys could be educated, go to Europe and make a lot of money for you. Who knew which was the real answer? Maybe there wasn't one.

That afternoon she sat shelling groundnuts with the other women of her compound, sprawled in the shade, her legs spread out in front of her, casually cracking the nuts against a stone. She had just had her hair plaited into a series of thick ridges that curled like black snakes around her head, rearing at the top of her scalp into a crown of small spikes. She had discarded her head-tie to reveal the dramatic effect. As they worked, the women discussed times past, quarrels which had been serious at the time but seemed funny when viewed across the years.

Tomaring Sise, a small woman, whose hooked nose gave an impression of severity, recalled that when they were young Binta Sise had made fun of her and her elder sister. Binta laughed a deep, husky laugh. 'So now you should treat us with extra respect,' said Tomaring. 'To show that you are ashamed.' Binta laughed again. 'Don't laugh,' said Tomaring, her voice rising. She grabbed Binta's hand in a fierce clench and shook it from side to side. 'Yes, you should!' Binta giggled and tried to pull her hand away. Tomaring took off her rubber flip-flop sandal and hit Binta Sise's hand – hard.

The other women paused in their shelling to see if it would become serious. But Tomaring let go of Binta's hand, giving her a glare.

Binta looked ruefully at her thumb. 'You've broken it,' she said. Then they went on with their work.

Around the women sat a group of children, the older ones helping spasmodically with the shelling, the younger ones just talking and occasionally fighting among themselves. Suddenly a bigger boy hit one of the smaller children. Seeing this, Binta got to her feet, walked over to the boy and hurled him to the ground. Then she sat on him. The boy screamed as though he were about to die. But Binta just sat there impassively, her arms folded. When it seemed that the child's rib-cage must inevitably cave in under her great weight, she got to her feet, and the child hobbled away whimpering.

In the early evening, as the husband sat on the wooden seat outside their house, the baby on his knee, Binta Sise stood behind him, staring into space as the sky darkened. Living crammed together in their tiny house in the middle of one of the biggest compounds in Dulaba, they resembled for a moment a European nuclear family. 'Why should I be afraid of my husband?' said Binta Sise. 'I am stronger than him, more intelligent than him, and more beautiful than him.' But sometimes she looked utterly lost.

In the afternoon the bush was a dangerous place. Once off the main path one could easily become lost. The light of the sun glaring through the sparse foliage threw a mesh of thin shadows over the brittle, colourless vegetation, to create a bewildering uniformity of tone in which shadow and substance became interchangable. Everything looked exactly the same whichever way one looked, and one's sense of distance and direction quickly became confused. Here and there one of the stiff, hard leaves would glint uncannily where it caught the direct light of the sun. It was only the termite hills that seemed to have any fixedness of position by which one could guide oneself. They erupted suddenly from the grey soil, towers of bullet-hard pink earth, often twice the height of a man.

This was the *wulokono ba* – the real bush – just beyond the limits of cultivation. The villagers, particularly the women, were reluctant to go there, as it was said to be the territory of devils. Human beings are surrounded by devils, and they may have a malevolent influence on our lives at any time. Normally they remain invisible, but in the bush they are more numerous, and the loneliness of those remote places makes them dangerous. There were people in the village who had gone insane or died long, lingering deaths because of what they had seen in the bush. Most people had only the sketchiest idea of what these devils looked like. Some said they were as tall as trees, others that their hair was long and hideously matted. For they had never seen one, and they were not, as they said, praying to see one; they preferred not even to think about them.

Late in the afternoon the leaves began to rattle in the mango trees. The dust started to rise from the ground in sudden gusts. The wind became faster. It was coming from the east. The women at the wells picked up their almost empty basins and, averting their faces, hurried for home. Quickly it grew dark. People went into their houses and shut the doors. The wind roared. There was a clattering as the wind threw dead leaves and groundnut shells and other bits of rubbish onto the iron roofs. There were a few drops of rain, and then it stopped. People opened the doors of their houses to see the light fading in the west. Then it was night.

It had rained in Jarra to the east. It had rained in Fonyi to the south. It had rained on the coast. But it hadn't rained in Dulaba. They had fasted for more than thirty days. Maybe God was punishing them for that.

The first scorpion appeared skulking among the shoes in the Professor's doorway. Ousmane Koujabi swept it into a dustpan and dropped it on the concrete outside. It immediately assumed the combat posture, its tail, in which the terrible sting was located, raised above its head. It was about two inches long and of a translucent amber hue. Ousmane lowered the dustpan and neatly beheaded it.

Later Daouda Jarjou, the mechanic, found another in the generator building. It was about six inches long, fat and black, like a baby lobster. He gave it to Richard, the doctor, who kept it preserved in a jar in his living-room, to the awed revulsion of visitors – though its sting was apparently less painful than that of the smaller variety.

Heavy rain had fallen during the night. It lay about the camp in pools stained the colour of blood by the earth. The grass was already starting to grow, as though someone had sprinkled a grey-green powder over the red earth. Inside the house, everything was damp: the carpet, the covers on the seats, even people's hair. Above the world, the sky was bursting with puffy white clouds.

The men went immediately to the *kankangos* – the large garden areas behind the compounds. After months of inactivity they attacked the land with an almost inhuman speed and energy. By lunchtime, the bare, dusty wastes of the village had been converted into rich, deep, black earth. The men walked barefoot, pushing the seeds of maize and sorghum into the earth with their toes. In the streets the little girls plaited leaves into their hair so that they fell over their faces in long green streaks.

By afternoon, the sky was getting darker, and a warm wind blew over the plain as I walked towards the rice field of Jumutung. Eagles soared above the trees; cattle crashed through the undergrowth. Although it had rained, the ground was already hard underfoot. Half-way across I met an old woman, quite tall and upright, with one tooth. I greeted her.

'My name is Njai,' she said. 'Say to me, "You are working, Njai".'

'You are working, Njai.'

'All right,' she said, and passed on her way.

The rice field of Jumutung opened up in a great glade around the tip of the salt flats. At first it seemed to be deserted. Then I picked out the figures of the women, working singly or in groups, dwarfed by the tall palms and the immense trees. In the lowest places the grey-green mud was still wet and sprouting a profusion of tiny weeds. The narrow embankments of earth stemming from the roots of the trees, and twisting their way across the network of tiny fields, seemed to have helped to trap the rainwater. Some of the women had long-handled hoes which they manipulated with both hands, but most had the shorter hoes, and they had to bend double as they pulled the soft soil into ridges. They would pause frequently to wipe the sweat from their faces or shout across to a friend at another field.

I came across an old woman working alone in her field. She gave me her short-handled hoe, and pointed at the ground. I took it, and began to pull at the soil where she had left off. I expected that at any moment she would tell me to stop, but she didn't. Instead she began to clap in time. It was a brisk time she clapped, and she soon began to speed up, singing along in rhythm:

> 'The tubab is working – Yo!
> Mark is working – Yo!
> The tubab is working – Yo!
> Mark is working – Yo!'

'Marky-o! Nimbara! Nimbara!' she would shout at intervals.

Soon I was having trouble keeping up. The dark clouds seemed to have given way to intense sunlight. I could feel the blood rushing to my head. I kept going at the frenetic pace set by the old woman, who kept on clapping and chanting with great glee: 'Marky-o-Marky! Nimbara!'

By now I was struggling to keep up. My arms felt weak. 'I've got to stop,' I thought. 'I'm going to faint.' I stopped and handed her the hoe.

'Nimbara!' she beamed. 'You are working.'

I'm going to be sick, I thought.

A tall, elegant young woman stood waiting at the gate to Jarra Njai's compound. She had a rather large upper lip which curled naturally with disdain, and she looked at me over it, without appetite, clearly wondering what I was doing there. Her name was Manlafi, which in the Mandinka language means 'I don't want'. If a woman had lost many children, she might call her child Manlafi, because if the spirits thought she did not want the child they might not bother to take it from her.

She was married to Seikouba Drammeh, one of the MRC fieldworkers, and she had transferred from her home village of Joli only the year before. When she arrived she had asked Jarra Njai if she could help her at her field. Jarra Njai had agreed, and now she had to pay back that day's work. So a bond had been established between then – what they called *badiya*.

It was ten in the morning, and though the ground was still damp after the night's rain, the sun was already hard and bright. The laterite road glowed a deep orange as it ran away, disappearing and reappearing over the low, undulating landscape. Above, the sky was the colour of iron.

Jarra Njai suddenly appeared, trotting along the road towards us from the other direction, her body swaying under the weight of two enormous basins full of washing piled on her head, one on top of the other. She went quickly into the compound, deposited the clothes, and re-emerged carrying a hoe and a small enamel basin which contained her lunch.

We walked quickly towards the field, which lay not far away in the bush at the back of the compound. Jarra Njai carried the two basins of lunch on her head, Manlafi a green plastic bucket of water.

The bush to the north was unrecognizable as what it had been even a week before – a thick profusion of grass and weeds was bursting from the earth, and the leaves of the bushes, many of which had appeared to be dead, now shone an almost synthetic green. A great many figures, some ploughing with donkeys, but most bending to the earth, were scattered apparently at random over the plain.

We arrived at a large rectangle of tilled earth just off the main path, with no indication as to why it should have been there rather than anywhere else in the great expanse. We began hoeing immediately, the three of us in a line, moving forward quickly from one of the short sides of the rectangle. The two women were close on either side of me. I was acutely aware of their muscular proximity, and of my paleness in comparison.

The blades of the hoes sighed as they sliced into the hot, damp earth. We advanced quickly, hacking the grey crust into a mauvish rubble. I looked up for some sort of natural barrier to our labours, but looked only into an endless nothingness of pure brilliance. The two women talked ceaselessly, with Jarra Njai, the elder of the two, taking the lead in the conversation and the work. Occasionally there'd be a short burst of song, which seemed mostly to relate to the fact that I was there working with them.

Soon we turned an abrupt corner, and then another, and were working our way back along the other side of the rectangle. My thighs were starting to ache, and the hoe seemed to become heavier. Jarra Njai swapped my hoe for her own, which was lighter and sharper. Then when some women came past, she swapped it again for an even smaller one. The work was now much easier, but large blisters were starting to appear on the palms of my hands. It was midday, the sun was at its fiercest, and I was desperate to drink. After an hour and a quarter, two of the blisters on my right hand had burst.

I retired to the shade of the tree where we'd left our things. I took great draughts of MRC water. It was still icy and cut agonizingly into my insides. I squatted on a root but could hardly manage to support myself, and fell back against the trunk. I remained slumped there in a state of semi-consciousness for some time. I began to wonder if I should go back to the camp, or try to continue with the work. I picked up the small hoe, and returned to the women.

They were just hacking up the last few feet of the rectangle. 'Lunch,' said Jarra Njai with a grin of enthusiasm.

Her lunch consisted of rice with *kutcha*, a tart, glutinous sauce of green leaves. Manlafi's consisted of rice with a sauce of fish, potatoes and pasta, flavoured with tomato and chilli. Mine consisted of a lump of dry bread that had spent the greater part of its life in the MRC freezer. They dug eagerly into each other's bowls, and heartily encouraged me to do the same. I declined, partly because they'd only brought the amount they would normally have eaten anyway, and partly because my hands were covered in sweat, grit, snot and liquidescent sun lotion. In fact, my water container, the plastic bag that had contained my repast, and my entire person were covered in filth.

The two women, who both looked quite spruce and personable after the refreshment of their lunch, watched me discreetly as I wrestled with my lump of bread. Manlafi, particularly, evinced a sense of incredulous revulsion: how could someone so rich be so incompetent in matters of simple hygiene?

As soon as we'd finished eating we returned to the place of our labours, and began another rectangle the same size as the one we'd completed before lunch. The light of the sun was now less fierce, though the actual heat was greater. It was as though it were rising in waves to meet us as we bent over the earth. The bread I'd eaten had formed a solid, rock-like lump in my stomach. I could feel its dryness as a constant presence in my mouth. I hacked away listlessly and mindlessly. Dislocated thoughts of no value or significance wandered in and out of my mind at random – occasionally repeating themselves to the rhythm of the hoes – fragments of songs I had forgotten existed, things people had once said. It was a state like that on the verge of nausea. The conversation of the women grew less, but they continued to work with unflagging energy. After a further hour and a half, the area of untilled earth in the middle of the rectangle had become very small. I picked up speed in a final burst of energy, fired with enthusiasm at the prospect of stopping. As we walked back to the tree I tried to spit, but my saliva had become so thick and elastic it refused to leave my mouth. Jarra Njai took the last of my water and poured it carefully over my forearms, my plastic bag, and my watch. Then she began to rub the dirt from them with her hands.

Early in the evening the following day, a great column of violet-grey cloud was seen advancing on the village from the west. It stretched massively into the distance and seemed to be bearing down on the village with ominous force. As it passed overhead its colour and mass were so uniform that it was difficult to tell if it was fifteen or fifteen hundred feet above us. The wind, unaccountably, was blowing from the west. It became stronger. The trunks of the baobabs glowed strangely, as though emitting an unearthly golden light. The leaves began to rattle violently in the trees. The ground seemed to ripple and shudder as the wind passed through the short grass. Large drops of rain appeared, flicking against one, as if from nowhere. And then there were more, splashing from side to side in all directions at once. Everyone began running for cover.

As soon as the Professor and I reached the house there was a massive thunderclap directly overhead. And then it began to rain, in great spasms, each more powerful than the last. The force of the rain pounding on the corrugated-iron roof was so great I wondered if it would hold. It sounded as though the sheer force from above would drive the house into the ground. The water poured from the edge of the roof in solid sheets. The football pitch disappeared in a haze of bouncing water. Then, almost immediately, it was dark.

After half an hour the rain stopped, but the thunder continued in the distance, and to the east the sky was lit to its very apex by flashes so bright and so sudden they were painful to watch. The sodden, pitted earth seemed to come leaping towards one in these split seconds of white lucidity, and for moments after its every detail could be seen, photographed onto the darkness. Above, every scrap of cloud thown out across the heavens would, for a fraction of a moment, be clearly visible, and on the horizon the shattered branches of the trees reached into the sky like the mirror image of one's own nerve endings.

At the Staff Quarters, the wives moved to and fro as they continued clearing away the empty dinner basins by the warm comforting glow of the electric light, unconcerned with the great silver firmament which at split-second intervals was opening up above their heads.

Before it rained, the wind would whistle through the house, blowing the papers from the tables, making the pictures flap and rattle as it tried to drag them from the walls. When the thunder came during the night, it sounded like the world was coming to an end – as though the very earth was being split open.

But the following morning it would all still be there. Once I was awoken just after dawn by a tremendous clattering, and looked out to see the garden completely blackened by flame-tree pods – the long, brittle sheaths shaken from the trees by the wind, covering the ground like thousands of discarded scabbards.

The grass grew thickly in the grove of mango trees on the south side of the village, giving it the temporary appearance of a Kentish orchard. But by nine o'clock, the sun shone into the humid air with such ferocity that one could see the swirling currents of moisture as it came steaming and seething out of the earth; it was as though the very air was boiling. And against the gleaming, rain-drenched flora, the colours of the clothes of the women rushing into the bush stood out with an exhilarating clarity and freshness – each pink, each blue, each yellow, each red having its own unique brilliance.

Now I went almost daily to the fields to work, and as they hurried along the paths out of the village, hoes hooked over their shoulders, their heads laden with basins of lunch and buckets of water, the rice seed tied into the cloths around their waists, the women would be in a buoyant mood. The rain had come, and there was not a moment to be lost. Some just hurled the seeds onto the tilled earth and cursorily scraped the soil over them. Others had cut their fields into furrows and now sprinkled them with seed, pulling the soil up onto the ridges and burying the seed beneath it. Most women tried both methods in their different fields. If one system failed, God might cause another to succeed.

The women were extremely courteous to me – they were always anxious that I should eat some of their lunch and rest as often as possible. But otherwise they paid me little attention. They accepted me as one might accept the presence of a lump of rock; I was neither a good thing nor a bad thing – I was just there. Occasionally I would look up to see one of them regarding me with a glacial curiosity, but they would quickly look away. Sometimes they would have to re-do areas I'd hoed. Far from helping, I seemed to be merely adding to their difficulties. But they didn't seem to mind..They showed no sign of annoyance or even amusement at my incompetence.

I would stay out there in the bush as long as I could, usually returning when they did. But sometimes I felt so weak from the effects of the sun that I would have to leave early. By now the colour would have drained from the world, and often the sun had withdrawn behind the white clouds, leaving a layer of shuddering heat over the earth. As I stumbled back along the rocky paths through the bush my mind would start to tremble at the thought of the cool liquid standing in its tall bottles in the Professor's fridge. I would have drooled at the idea of the silvery gurgling of it, but I could summon no saliva. There was only an aching dryness, as though my mouth and throat were being pulled back into my body.

Later, as I lay numbed and exhausted on the sofa in the Professor's living-room, I would wonder what possible purpose these exertions could be serving. I didn't seem to be learning very much from them, nor could they be said to be bringing me much closer to the women. I was completely excluded from their protracted and often lively conversations by my ignorance of the language. Sarah, the doctor, and I were taking lessons in Mandinka from Demba Tamba, but so far we'd got no further than 'This is a pen.'

Towards the end of Ramadan I had come across a large group of women sitting in one of the smaller yards of the village, shelling groundnuts. They were all talking, or rather shouting, at once, nobody paying any attention to anybody else – it sounded as though dozens of pieces of slate were being slapped together at high speed. I was struck by the fact that they all seemed to be of roughly the same age – around their mid-thirties. Sanyang told me that these women were all indeed of one kafo – one age-group; this was their society, their club, and these were the groundnuts they would plant at their kafo farm.

There was a different society for each age-group. They formed these groups when they were children, and they remained in them until they were too old to be socially active. Each kafo had its own farm, and on the first Saturday after the first 'big rain' they would head out into the bush to till the earth. It was a day that was traditionally associated with singing and celebration. Jarra Njai and Fatounding were the leaders of their respective kafos. I decided that when the time came, I would follow both of these groups to their fields.

After an afternoon storm the water came rushing in a great torrent through the middle of the village, and as it came swelling, strong and deep around the slight bend at the bottom of the high street, it was suddenly nothing but children – falling, diving, leaping; hundreds of almost naked children, their sinuous, wriggling brown flesh one with the water stained by the red earth, celebrating this moment of effusion with shrieking and laughter as they jumped splashing from the rippling torrent.

And in the MRC compound the singing of the birds swarming in the flame-trees was so loud that human conversation was impossible.

The earth was seething with new insects – tiny scarlet beetles, their wings thick and furry like velvet; copper-coloured beetles the size of a new penny piece working over the heaps of cattle dung, rolling it into balls and pushing it away over the earth with their back legs. Groups collaborated over the larger pieces, occasionally stopping to argue over who was pushing and who was pulling.

The termites had emerged from the earth. Every night they made a muffled rattling sound as they fluttered in their thousands against the windows. Through a small gap under the mosquito mesh they seeped into the kitchen and crowded harmlessly but uncomfortably around the bodies of the inhabitants.

The Professor was making a curry. The termites swarmed around the rank meat as he tried to cut it up. They drowned themselves in the stock.

They got lost in his beard. They were slow moving and easy to swat, but there were so many it would have taken all night to have got rid of them all. The only assistance he had was from the lizards who lay in the darkness on the wall outside the windows. Darting their heads forward, they nonchalantly snapped up the termites by their ones and twos, calmly munching them in their long thin jaws.

By the time I arrived in the kitchen there were so many termites in the room that it was almost dark. 'That meat smells disgusting,' I said.

'It is disgusting,' he said.

I was already sweating as I hurried back towards the village. It was still early in the morning, but I was carrying my tape-recorder, which hung like a rock around my neck, and I could feel the heat hardening as the light, which had arrived soft and hazy, became clearer and brighter and stronger.

Jarra Njai and Fatounding had come early to the camp to tell me that this was the day their respective kafos would be going to their farms. It appeared they were both going to the same place. 'If you go along the road towards Mankono,' said Fatounding, 'the farm will be on your left.'

I had walked along the road for about two miles before I realized I was walking through the Mankono groundnut fields. I headed back through the bush, across the rice fields of Jumutung, and was now rushing back across the plain, desperately worried that I might be missing something. I saw a red shirt approaching.

'Jarra Njai's kafo?' said the woman, when we met up. 'They're still in the village. They haven't left home yet.'

When I was within a hundred yards of the village, I saw a group of women standing under a tree. I headed towards them.

They watched me suspiciously as I approached, and I suddenly felt nervous. What if they didn't want me there?

They crowded round me. And it was as though I'd never met them before. These women, many of them very much bigger than me, their faces thrust towards me, all shouting at once, animated – though whether with anger or amusement it was impossible to say. I just stood there, feeling very pale and very vulnerable, wondering what would happen next. A small and very pretty woman in a cream-coloured nylon petticoat stood at the front waving her hands in my face and counting in English: 'Twenty-one, twenty-two, twenty-three . . .' Behind her, another short woman, who seemed to be somehow two-thirds head, was talking even louder than the others. Her name seemed to be Janno, and the others roared with laughter at everything she said. Finally Jarra Njai called on a small boy who was working in the next field.

'They say they are not all here. Thirty-seven women are going to come here.' At this point the pretty young woman started counting on her hands again. 'They say the sun is very hot, and you should sit under that tree till they are all here.'

'Tell them I'll wait with them.'

He told them, and there was a further clamorous response.

'They say they are your grandfather.'

As the women arrived, each with her own hoe, they joined the line of women that was moving quickly forward over the earth. There were the older members of the kafo: Sunkang, tall, dignified and very fair in complexion; Jeynaba, bright-eyed and wiry, who was called 'mother' by the younger members out of respect; Tumbulu Sise, a quiet, gentle woman.

There was Jarjei, a brawny woman of twenty-six, who had already had three husbands. There was Janno, the small woman with the big voice. There were Djankering Minte, Ida Sanyang and Nafi Saho. And there were young women: Fatounding and her co-wife Isatou. Sajonding Minte; Karamo, Kintending and Karafanding; the big Binta Sise; and Arabiatou, whose husband Kemeseng Sanyang had lent the kafo the land for his farm. There were Tutu, Menata, Mokuta, Momunko and Majula. There were Ami Marong, Binta Manjang and Sally Kanteh, who were not citizens of the village, but wives of the MRC staff who had joined the group.

Until last year they had been two kafos. But so many of their members had left to join their husbands in other parts of the country, they had decided to join their kafos to form one big group. They called it the Saniyoro Kafo – the golden chain.

They raised their hoes in time, and there was a great hissing, slicing sound as the blades bit hard into the earth. Jarra Njai went ahead, cutting down the taller weeds and leaving them in heaps at the edge of where the farm would be. But she kept a sharp ear open for the conversation of others, frequently adding comments of her own, and laughing a throaty, cackling laugh. It was a fine day. Everything was very green, and the hot, damp earth gave easily to their eager hoes.

'Tell him to go and sit under that tree. Some of the members are not yet here.'

'No. Let him stay here, so that the heat of the sun will touch him and us.'

'Who asked him to come here?'

'It was Jarra Njai.'

'Listen, this man is going to be our tubab.'

'Why is he here? Has he come to replace the Professor?'

'No. He has come for his own reasons.'

'What are they?'

'Nobody knows.'

'He's like a detective. He's come here for something.'

'He's been sent by the government to look for people who are backbiting. He's going to tape them and find out who they are.'

'He is well prepared. We will not hide anything from him.'

'Let everyone be careful not to use insulting words today. This man will play the tape, and everyone will know about it.'

'Are you saying that no one is going to backbite anyone else here today?'

'That's right. It's not safe.'

'He once came with us to the fields. He worked very hard. We asked him to rest, but he said no. He worked up till it was time to go, then we went together.'

'Even if you tell him to rest, he will say no. He will never agree to rest. When he came to my field an old woman said, "You are killing the tubab with work". So I asked him to stop. Then I asked him where he was going, and he just said, "I am going to Dulaba".'

'He must be searching for something. You will never see a tubab doing that for no reason.'

The sun was at its hottest, and the details of the surrounding landscape, the scrubby disorder of trees and bushes, seemed to fall away into the brilliant, shimmering light. We were aware only of ourselves, a group isolated under the sun, and the next few feet of earth to be hoed.

'Sona,' said Jarra Njai, to the small, pretty woman. 'Mr Sambali said that if we need the school drums, we should just ask and we can borrow them.'

'Did he?'

'Let Sona go for the drums. Mr Sambali is someone she knows well. He is her lover.'

Everyone laughed.

Djankering was the first to start singing. She had a light, sweet voice, slightly nasal in the manner of the region, but with a clear, almost crystal purity.

> 'The world is like this;
> Things are not any other way:
> I said, you repay kindness with kindness,
> And you repay wickedness with wickedness.

> 'I will not forget you, Kemeseng Sanyang.
> I've come to repay the kindness,
> For us to be united.'

The other women joined in the chorus, a bit raggedly at first, but growing in strength and unity as they refamiliarized themselves with the old song. 'We came to repay the kindness,' they sang. 'For us to be united.'

Djankering carried the other women, changing the choruses and adding more verses to this paean of praise and thanks to the man who had lent them the land for their farm. She praised his wives and his children, and called upon the leaders of the kafo and all its members to repay his kindness. Then she began to sing about the people of her own compound, Danso Kunda, subtly altering the intonation of the chorus as the fancy took her, her voice rising breathily as she crammed more and more words, more and more names into the verses, but always returning to the chorus, which the other women repeated after her in a low, hymning chant.

When at last the song came to an end, they thanked her. 'You have tried well,' they said.

'Hey, Fatounding,' said someone. 'Your child is crying.'

'The child is like that,' said Fatounding. 'You will never see the end of its tears.'

'Leave it to cry till its head breaks,' said Binta Sise.

She and Sona had returned with the drums, which lay on the ground waiting for the moment when they would be played. They were made of cowhide stretched over two large tins with green plastic string. They were so battered they had taken on an almost palaeolithic appearance. But if you looked carefully, you could just make out the words 'Blue Circle Cement' on the side of the tins.

'This is a very big farm,' said Kintending. 'We will have to work very hard if we are to finish it today.'

'We're working very fast. Aren't we going to get tired?'

'We have to work hard. We've just had lunch,' said Fatounding.

'Hey, Fatounding!' said someone else. 'Don't talk! Your group is lagging behind.'

'How can we keep up when Tutu and the others are so lazy?'

'We are not lazy,' said Tutu. 'Look at the space I am having to work and the space Fatounding is taking. How can you compare them? Mine is much wider.'

'It is only Tutu, Majula and Fatounding who are behind.'

'Let them stay there,' said Binta Sise.

'If I start at the same time with someone, I never leave them behind,' shouted Janno, from the other end of the line.

'I had forgotten you were here,' said Binta.

'Tutu is just standing there,' said Fatounding. 'How can she do anything?'

'Fatounding is provoking people, and he is taping it.'

'Then he will take my words. For whatever I feel I will say it.'

'Fatounding couldn't wait to start talking,' said Sona. 'She dumped her child under that tree, and came over here and started talking.'

'If anyone wants to say anything, let them stand close to the tape recorder,' said Janno.

'Why don't you stand close to it?' said Binta Sise. 'Then everyone will know how you keep shooting your mouth off.'

'It's true,' said Janno. 'I do shout my mouth off at times.'

Binta and Sona picked up the drums and tied them to their waists, Binta helping the smaller woman, who had the bigger drum. Then with the stick in one hand, and the other bare, they began to beat – a simple thudding, deep beneath the rhythm of the hoes.

I stood there with them all day, under the sun, taping the conversation and the singing. They sang about the village and its people. They sang about the MRC, the doctors and the staff. They sang about the school and the headmaster. They sang about marabouts, heroes and politicians. They sang the songs of their children, and the songs of their grandmothers. They sang songs that were just meaningless collections of words strung together for effect, and they sang songs which were so private that only they knew what they were about. They sang songs about each other, and they sang about themselves.

People wandered off to the village, returning with buckets of water which were passed up and down the line for people to drink. At the far corner of the farm was a big tree under which some of the women had left their babies with their nursemaids. Every so often they would go over to feed them.

When they came to the end of a row the women would stop and stand for a few moments. Behind them a large area of tilled ground was opening up – the dark violet of the earth standing out against the untidy mass of weeds, as though the women were rolling the bush back like a carpet. When they had decided which direction they would take next, they would bend and raise their hoes in one movement. Yet there was nothing regimented about their way of working, they just moved to the natural rhythm of their arms.

They seldom stopped singing, and when they did the air was filled with argument, laughter and discussion. Djankering shared most of the singing with Binta and Sona, though Menata and Sajonding sang songs too, and all of the women joined in with the choruses – throwing in verses, or cries of praise and encouragement whenever they felt like it.

As the afternoon wore on, the two drummers varied and intensified the beat. Binta, huge and ironically benevolent, towered over the smaller woman, as she rolled backwards and forwards up and down the line, thwacking casually at the drum hanging at her thighs, the strap of her dress hanging louchely from her shoulder. She didn't stop smiling all day. Sona by contrast moved in a slow, measured strut, looking very proud of herself as she slapped on the deep-voiced drum. She was neat – neat in her appearance, neat in her movements – and she sang in a sharp, clear, rather knowing voice. She was someone who would have wanted to have been a star, if she'd known what one was. But in Dulaba you could only be a star in your own age group, and she was that already.

> 'Hear the sound of these drums,' she sang,
> 'Our own drums!
> Hear the sound of these drums,
> Our grandmothers' drums!

> 'Hear the sound of these drums,
> Bambo Jarjou's brother – our own drums!
> Mabintu's husband –
> Sanu Njai's husband –

> 'Hear the sound of these drums,
> Our grandmothers' drums!'

'Yo!' said Binta Sise. 'Pour out the songs.'
'It's time for Binta to sing,' said Jeynaba.
'My songs are very difficult. You will not be able to help me sing them.'

'The ne'er-do-wells of the kafo are here,' said Jarra Njai. 'They will help you sing.'

> '*Aiya, Aiya-o! Hey Aiya!*' sang Binta Sise.
> 'You all know I like dancing to the drums.
> As soon as I arrived at the dancing place,
> A small girl accused me,
> And they took me to the police,
> But when I spoke to the commissioner,
> I didn't need a marabout to get me released
> – *Hey!*'

And all the women joined in the rousing chorus:

> '*Aiya, Aiya-o! Hey Aiya!*
> *Nyancho balanta sukwolai la moyi – ay!*'

> 'Listen to what the griots are saying about
> the great champion!

> 'You, the fishermen of the dancing place,
> Who cast your nets for love
> – Move back!
> I'm going to start work.
> If I don't stop to think I'll clear the bush,
> With my big skirt.
> – *Hey!*

> 'Oh, this world!
> I said the laws of the religion have defeated me.
> But I will say it, Jarra Njai Sise,
> That if someone does you a kindness,
> You have to repay it.
> The kindness, the repayment of the kindness;
> God created all of it
> – *Hey!*'

'*Nimbara! Nimbara!*' shouted Jarra Njai, coming before the others, her hoe raised in the air. 'May God make us to be one! May God make us stay together! Let us work hard, so that we can finish this farm today. The sun is going down.'

> 'Hey, you people of high rank!' sang Janno.
> 'Have you seen my Mark?
> I'm searching for him,
> And the sun is going down.

'Hey! My darling Mark,
I haven't seen him,
And the sun is going down.

'Hey! Mark the white man,
The tall man with lines on his neck,
The sun is going down.'

Binta Sise beat her drum faster. 'Hey, look at Mark, the champion!' she
sang.
And all the other women took up the chorus:

'Hey, al Marky joobay jambaro!
Hey, al Marky joobay jambaro!'

. . . over and over again, till the air rang and vibrated with their voices;
the drums beating faster and faster. Two or three of the women threw
down their hoes and, dashing forward, began to dance around me –
swinging their arms, stamping fiercely on the newly tilled earth. The
other women broke out into a syncopated clapping, so hard and sharp it
seemed to split the very air.

Then, as the tempo of the clapping and the dancing and the singing
became almost unbearably wild and frenetic, it suddenly stopped, and
everyone fell about in fits of laughter. The women took off their head-ties
and came forward to wipe the dust and sweat from my face.

'*Nimbara! Marky, Nimbara!*' they said.

4

THE SEASON OF GENERATION

Islam has existed in that part of the world since the twelfth century – introduced through conquest by the Moors, the traditional enemies of the blacks. It had become the religion of trade: a 'universal, egalitarian' faith that promoted a sense of fraternity between merchants of many tribes and many races, thus greatly facilitating the movement of the caravans – of gold, ivory, salt and slaves – over the vast tracts of savannah and desert between the forests of Guinea and the Mediterranean in the north. The rulers of Mali and Songhai, the great medieval empires of the savannah, which had grown rich on this trade, had become Muslims – though they held sway over the countryside through their manipulation of traditional religion, and were themselves believed to be divine.

By the beginning of the previous century, these empires had long since fallen into decline, to be replaced by others, which were themselves only vague glimmers in the collective memory. The Mandingkos, who had come to the lower waters of the great river at the time of Sunjatta, the founder of Mali, had divided its banks into thirteen kingdoms. The ruling families, and the majority of their subjects, were pagans, though there were others who claimed to have 'found their ancestors in the Muslim religion'. They were known as *marabouts* – the name commonly given to a holy man, a maker of jujus. They lived in their own separate villages, where the laws of the religion were rigorously observed, or in hamlets attached to the pagan courts from which they used their 'powers' for the kings. For, while these traditional rulers refused to give up the gods of their ancestors, they attributed great power to the spells of the marabouts. So the people had lived in relative harmony for many hundreds of years.

By the early nineteenth century most of the trade along the great river was in the hands of the marabouts, but they were precluded from owning land or participating in government, and had to pay punitive taxes to the pagan rulers. At the same time, the ruling families, who had traditionally lived from plunder and tribute, had been weakened by dissipation and dynastic rivalry, and many of the ancestral cults had fallen into desuetude.

The *jihad*, the wars of conversion, had begun far in the interior, in what is now northern Nigeria, where certain militant clerics of the Fulani, a pastoral people who had settled in the cities of the Hausa, had led risings against the decadence of the traditional rulers. There were further, almost simultaneous overturnings of traditional power in Fulani-speaking areas much closer to the Gambia. South of the river, the fighting had started in Fuladu, a hundred miles to the east of Dulaba, where the Fulani herdsmen and farmers had risen against the Mandinka kings of Kaabu.

There the Fulani were also pagans, but their war leader Alpha Mollo had been converted by Alhaj Umar Tal, the great marabout from the north, and it was the new religion that had given them the courage to rebel.

Shortly afterwards, the marabouts rose in Badibu on the north bank. They were led by a Koranic scholar named Maba Diakhou Ba. It was his intention to establish the Dar al-Islam – the rule of God – from the Gambia river to the Senegal, three hundred miles to the north. On arriving at a pagan village, he would write a *safo* – a juju – for each of his warriors. Thus protected, their bodies drenched in Holy Water, they believed themselves impervious to the bullets, swords and arrows of the pagans – and even if they died they would go straight to heaven. The village would be burnt to the ground. All those who would not accept the word of God were put to death, and their wives and children sold into slavery. Maba was eventually defeated after intervention by the French, but the struggle spread south over the great river as new leaders emerged: Fode Kabba, Syllaba, Alboury Njai, Moussa Mollo.

Dulaba had been a marabout village from the beginning. The Sise family, it was said, had been marabouts since they came from Manding, their ancestral homeland. So the village had been bypassed by Fode Kabba, the most famous and the most feared of the marabout leaders in the vicinity of Kiang and Fonyi. But the people had helped his forces to cross the Bintang Bolon, among the mangroves south of the village, and many of the young men had gone to join him. The children they captured were brought back to the village as slaves.

Mankono, however, the village to the west of Dulaba, was the seat of the king of Kiang. He and all his people were pagans. There had been a great battle there, and many people were killed.

Fearing the emergence of a unified, theocratic state in the interior, Her Majesty's representatives on the coast had supported the pagan kings with whom their trade treaties had been made, although, in line with their government's policy of minimizing involvement in the region ('No governor would be justified in attacking any of the natives from a preference for the adherents of one rather than another of two barbarous creeds'), this support was often moral rather than physical. Confused by these spasmodic interventions, the conflict dragged on for decades, ending every rainy season, and beginning again as soon as the harvest was gathered in.

By the end of the century, the land was exhausted. Groundnut production had all but ceased, and famine was widespread. Large areas of the country were overrun by the warring bands of rival marabout leaders, making travel and trade impossible. It was at this point that Britain and France decided to partition the region, in order to protect the trade interests that had brought them to that part of the world in the first place.

The memory of this prolonged trauma remained strong in the collective

consciousness. Even more than colonialism, it had shaped their conception of the world of external human affairs. For the racial and cultural
integrity of the tribes had been massively and irrevocably disrupted, as
whole communities moved to escape the fighting. People changed their
religion, their name and even their tribe in order to save their lives. The
Bajo family of Dulaba were said to have originally been Bajie – one of the
most common surnames of the stubbornly pagan Jolas – and the Dibbahs
of Joli were really Jibbah, another Jola name. Isolated among the
Mandingkos of Kiang, they had changed their names to avoid the
attention of the invading marabout bands. And there were other people
in the village, whose grandparents – Jolas – had been bought for a piece of
cloth.

Nowadays such things were almost never spoken about. All the
marabout leaders had been killed or exiled, and under the system of
indirect rule instituted by the British, many of the kings' descendants
retained a measure of privilege as district chiefs. But satiated and
exhausted by horror, the whole of the countryside accepted peace – the
peace of Islam – submission to the will of God. There were no more kings.
Each village made its own decisions through a council of compound
elders, since all Muslims are equal in the sight of God. The maintenance of
the collective harmony was to be the primary aim of society. People were
to stress their unity rather than their differences.

Even today, however, although the people of Mankono are now
Muslims, they never marry with the people of Dulaba.

Sarah Innes and I continued our lessons in Mandinka. We had got as far
as, 'M'mang koddo soto' – 'I have no money'. Early each evening we would
meet in the Inneses' living-room, a large square room decorated with
discreet African artefacts, and framed prints of Newcastle-upon-Tyne,
the city in which the Inneses had worked before coming to Dulaba, and
where they would return when their two-year tour was over. It had
windows along three sides, and fronted directly onto the compound, so
that at night, when one saw its lights through the trees, it had the
appearance of some exotic pleasure pavilion. As one drew closer, and
picked out the details of the tubabs moving in the golden light beyond the
mosquito netting, sitting, talking, or having drinks, it had the effect of
making their lives look even more exalted than they really were.

I sat in this room with Demba Tamba, our teacher, waiting for Sarah to
finish bathing the children, the heavy darkness of the rainy season
stealing through the trees, seeping through the mosquito netting,
thickening the air between the furniture and the art-objects. Demba, clad
only in a pair of red football shorts, lay slumped inert in one of the Habitat
armchairs.

He was about twenty-five, a small man with a big smile, his violet torso,
which at that time of year was naked most of the time, extraordinarily
neatly and finely made. Apparently the pleasantest and most forthcoming of the fieldworkers, the more I had to do with him, the less I felt I
knew him. He seemed to go through sudden and incomprehensible

changes of mood. One moment he would be cheerful and ebullient, the next apparently inconsolably depressed, and then completely blank, as though he'd completely forgotten who one was or what was happening.

Certainly his behaviour towards Sarah and his behaviour towards me was utterly different. As soon as the lesson was over and we left the house, his winning smile would disappear, and he would seem to retreat inside himself. I got the impression that for him I didn't really exist; that Europeans were for him like his job – they were important because they were necessary to his survival, but they, like their work, were essentially artificial. His job was a performance, and the Europeans, like oversized puppets, were part of that performance. I was not directly connected with his work, but I had somehow appeared in his life. I was a confusing factor.

After the Professor left I carried on living in his house. It was called House One as it was the first house to have been built in the compound. Now it seemed very big and empty.

In the days following Helene and the Professor's departure, Natoma and Ousmane each returned to the house, as though to the scene of some appalling emotional misfortune.

Natoma just stood there in the entrance, looking round at the living-room, empty except for the Habitat furniture. Then, without a word, she left.

Ousmane came on the Sunday evening. He sat down in one of the armchairs, clearly ill at ease. He had worked for Helene and the Professor for three years, and they had been puzzled and rather distressed to observe that at the end he had not even come to say goodbye. I offered him a drink.

'It's OK,' he said. There was a long pause. 'I want to go to airport with them. But it's not possible.'

'No.'

There was another long pause.

'I'm working for them for three years. It's a long time.' He went on, but his words became lost in his hoarse mumble. Then he sat back in his seat. 'I'm not happy,' he said at length. 'I'm confused.'

The other visitor was Jere Jarjou. He lay sprawled in one of the chairs, staring off at some indeterminate point in the far corner of the room. 'Oh, that Professor . . .' he said. 'He was very strict and hardworking. This is why some people hated him. But they were useless people, who could not do anything. But I like people like that: who are very strict and hardworking.' He sighed. 'I feel lonely now.'

After that very few people came to the house.

The problems that the Professor had foreseen with my project had never materialized. In fact Ted Whiteman, the Cass's director, had enthusiastically approved it. I was told I could stay in House One till the end of the rainy season, when the roof would be taken off for repairs. I had reckoned I would easily be able to complete my work by then.

Now that I was left there alone, however, I found I had even less idea of what I was supposed to be doing than when I started. And now that the Professor's survey was over I had no excuse for going into the compounds. I became shy of going into the village – of intruding on the lives of the people I had come there to observe.

It rained a lot, and when it wasn't raining it was often overcast. I spent most of my time sitting in House One trying to draw up lists of questions to ask the women. But the words dried on my pen, as I anticipated the reluctance they would feel at having to answer them. It wasn't just that they were busy with their agricultural work. The questioning process itself made them uneasy in some way. All I would receive would be bland assurances of well-being. Or they would simply say that they didn't know. And it was the same with the fieldworkers. Even casual questions thrown into conversations would be greeted with a slow, glazed look.

Late every afternoon I went for a walk. And often I would go into the heavily cultivated area to the north of the laterite road known as Wali Kunda. The groundnut fields and the stands of millet and sorghum went on for miles. These cereals, *sanyo* and *kinto* in Mandinka, were known collectively as *nyo*. While maize was called *tubanyo* or *tubabo nyo* – white man's corn – millet and sorghum were referred to as *morfing nyo* – black man's corn. They were the original crop, the food the blacks had known long before maize, or groundnuts, or even rice. The plants were indistinguishable from maize, except that the head of the millet stood up like a long bristly cigar to which the minute seeds clustered, while the head of the sorghum was floppy and feathery.

Everything was flourishing in the plentiful rain, the nyo plants already standing eight feet high. But the effect of the gloomy greenness was far from exhilarating. The monotony of the untidy patchwork of fields – some already starting to disappear beneath the weeds – studded with dead trees and areas of uncultivated bush, was deadening, almost numbing. There was no sign of contour or relief in any direction – just an endless sameness. When at last the roofs of the MRC compound came into view among the dead trees and tall stands of millet, I always felt a sense of relief. But they seemed always to be somewhere slightly different from where I had expected, and I was left with the mildly frightening thought that if I had somehow missed them by mistake, I would be condemned to wander forever across this relentless scruffy flatness, whose cultivation, whose ownership by man had a nominal feel to it, as though it had been only temporarily borrowed from the wilderness, and might be reclaimed by it at any time – which was of course exactly the case.

At other times I would go south of the village, through the bush to the salt flats, the only place in the environs of Dulaba where one could get any sense of space or openness. They had at that hour, as the shadows started to fall across them, an atmosphere of doleful serenity. Large clouds of violet or grey hung in the sky – big vaporous rectangles, upended, blown into the form of a letter T or a mushroom. If there were to be a nuclear war in Europe, I wondered, how long would it be before we knew about it here?

At the rice fields on the edge of the salt flats, the women knelt and stood in prayer on the dark earth, before starting on the walk back to the village. They were there. And I was there. But at that time I felt almost as remote and as isolated from them as I did from events in Europe.

Every evening I went to eat at the Quarters, the long blockhouse where most of the Staff – the technicians, fieldworkers and drivers – lived. I ate with the 'bachelors', the other young men of my age-group. We each paid a monthly fee to Daouda Jarjou. His wives, Sirrah and Ndey-Touti, who took it in turns to cook, two days on and two days off, would serve up a bowl of food for us. We always ate in Demba Tamba's room, a small box-like space painted to a turquoise dimness. It was a serious business.

We would arrive at a quarter to eight, to find a large enamel basin – one of the brightly patterned Chinese ones that have filtered through to every corner of the known world – standing in the middle of the floor. On top of the basin was a lid. On no account should that lid be removed until everyone was present. Lifting it to sneak a look at what was beneath was *mang betia* – it was bad. It was also forbidden to jump or step over the bowl.

When everyone had arrived we would pull our chairs close to the bowl, the cover would be removed and we would begin eating – quickly and intently – and whether with our bare hand or a spoon, it had always to be with the right hand. Those without chairs squatted beside the bowl, but as one of the older people there, I was always given one of the wooden armchairs.

The food was almost always plain, steamed rice with a sauce of fish and oil, known as *chou*, or a sauce of pounded leaves, called *kutcha*. The latter was the traditional alternative to *durango*, the groundnut sauce people ate almost every day during the dry season. We seldom ate meat, and when we did, we divided a typical European portion between us. For although there were large herds of cattle attached to the village, the bony, docile beasts were kept as a symbol of wealth, and were normally only slaughtered if one of them had an accident – it being difficult to find enough people who could afford to buy the meat. Sheep and goats were saved for prayer days and naming ceremonies. Apart from the kutcha leaves, there would be no fruit or vegetables for several months.

There were seven of us: Demba, Yaya Bojang, Jere Jarjou, Ousmane Koujabi, the assistant mechanic, Malamin Bajie, and Daouda's nephew, a skinny, shaven-headed slither of a person called Alhaji. He squatted close to the bowl, and if there was any meat or fish he would remove the bones and flick pieces of it to the various diners. He was twelve years old, and when he wasn't at school, he seemed to spend his entire life running errands. He appeared to walk at a tangent, his eyes perpetually lowered, as though avoiding the gaze of people who might send him to buy cigarettes.

Visitors also joined us, but unless their arrival had been announced well in advance, no extra food was provided for them. So if there were a lot of visitors we didn't get much to eat. Anyone who entered the room, or was heard to pass while we were eating, would be loudly exhorted to join us. These invitations were obligatory, and it was thought good manners to respond by taking at least one handful. If you were only passing you could shout *Bissimilai* – in the name of God – but if you were a stranger, it was offensive to refuse food or anything else that was offered.

When you were satisfied, you were supposed to sit back with your spoon or your hand between your legs to show that you didn't want to eat any more. But most people just stood up and left the room the moment they had finished. As I was almost always the last to finish, it was incumbent upon me to 'clean the bowl' – eat the last morsels. If I tried to sneak away Ousmane would grab me by the leg and pull me back to my seat. 'Eat,' he would say. 'It will make you strong.'

'And don't leave any,' Yaya would say sternly. 'God hates that!'

'Now you are a real African,' said Demba Tamba, as I sat with them round their communal bowl. But I didn't feel like one. These meals were so brisk, I didn't feel they involved me in their society in any way. What conversation there was, was in Jola or Mandinka, and spoken so fast I could scarcely tell the difference between the two languages. And sometimes they seemed to communicate in a way that was almost subliminal. Sitting there, a stranger in the middle of their communal life, amid all the comings and goings between their various rooms along the length of the Quarters, I felt utterly bewildered.

They were all Jolas. They had been the last of the tribes to submit to Islam. In the forests of Fonyi and the mangrove swamps of Blouf, they had fought long and hard to retain their traditional way of life – not only the men, but the women, who followed their husbands into battle, finishing off the marabout dead with their pestles. Even today, many pagan practices persisted among them, and the observance of the ties of blood and obligation was said to be even stronger among them than among other African peoples. I could feel them around me, tightly-knit, like the fingers of a clenched fist. They endured my presence only because Daouda, their elder, had asked them to. I was like a lump of grit that had become lodged between them – irritating and unaccountably difficult to remove.

It was the season of generation. One night, in the light from the laboratory window, I saw a lump of matter rise suddenly like a fist out of the mud, and roll away over the ground. It was a pair of toads, and the male, having mounted the female from behind, held her in a fierce clench as they bounced along the ground. Then, collapsing against each other, they rolled onto their backs, the belly of the female swelling mightily and rhythmically, before they righted themselves and bounced, still coupling, into the undergrowth.

The termites which hurled themselves against the windows of the house were getting bigger. But before they got so big that they broke the glass, their wings dropped off, and they tumbled to the concrete path where they lay wriggling and rolling, attempting coition amid the translucent debris of discarded wings.

Two students had arrived from England: Jane from Edgware, and Joanne from Derbyshire. They were nutrition students from Imperial College on their 'summer elective', though why they had elected to come to Dulaba was not clear. House Four, where they stayed, was only twenty yards from the laboratory, and they seldom deviated from the path between the two buildings. During their first fortnight they had entered the village only once. They were pale – paler than me – and they scarcely spoke, each apparently waiting for the other to speak on her behalf. They were never seen apart, but then they were scarcely seen at all. Soon their presence was all but forgotten.

One evening, however, when I was sitting at the Quarters, someone said, 'I think they are hiding in that place.'

'Who?'

'The two students. They are hiding in House Four.'

'Maybe they're shy.'

'This is what I thought,' said Lamin Jarjou, Daouda's cousin, who was the head fieldworker. 'That they are shy.'

'It is not necessary to be so shy,' said Bakary Sanneh airily.

'And they're young,' I said.

'This is the impression I had formed,' said Lamin, 'that they are young.'

We were in Yaya Bojang's room – people were lounged in the wooden armchairs, and sprawled over the bed.

'They will not be shy with me,' said Ibou Sanyang. 'I will ask them many interesting questions. Soon they will be very talkative.' His eyes sparkled.

'Mark,' said Demba. 'I want you to help me.'

'In what way?'

'That girl. The one with the big hair.'

'Joanne?'

'That one. Joanne. I want you to speak to her for me.'

'What about?'

He smirked. 'Well . . . You know, she is nice.'

I thought about it for a moment. 'You want me to ask her to have sex with you?'

They fell about – rolling on top of each other, hugging each other as they howled with delight. Bakary Sanneh leaned over Demba's shoulder towards me. 'In a nutshell, that is what he is saying.'

I tried to explain that it might upset or annoy the girl.

'But in Africa this is what we do,' said Jere. 'If you want to have a connection with this girl, I will just go and ask her for you.'

'And she'll agree?'

'Of course.'

'What if she doesn't want to do it?'

'No, no. They don't do that.'

'But it is very sad,' said Demba. 'This Joanne; I like her too much. But whenever I approach a woman I feel very nervous and shy. I can speak to them but I *cannot* ask them. It is a big problem for me.'

'I don't see why it is necessary to be shy,' said Bakary. 'You can just chat to them, take them out, use them, and leave them. It's not a problem.'

'I will *have* one of these students,' said Sanyang. 'At least one.'

'I don't think you will,' I said.

'Mark!' he said, hurt. 'Why do you say that? Are you praying that I will not have one of them?'

'No,' I said. 'I just don't think you will.'

'But why? There must be a reason why you are saying this.'

'He is using psychology,' said Bakary. 'This is why he is saying it. As for me, I like these students, but I don't love them.'

They were trying to make a country – along three hundred miles of riverbank, never more than fifteen miles on either side, and sometimes only eight. The river remained tidal for the first hundred miles from the sea and, unlike the Senegal to the north, it did not flood its banks to create a second agricultural season. The land was dry and hard. It contained no minerals of any value. So apart from some effortful irrigation, the inhabitants were entirely reliant on the one rainy season to grow the food necessary for survival.

The Europeans had had trading posts along this great river for centuries, but the unhealthy climate and the wildness of the inhabitants had deterred them from expanding their territory until the end of the previous century. Even the slave trade was never as developed there as it had been further along the coast.

From the surrounding territory of Senegal the French had administered their West African empire, and they had developed the colony more fully than any of their other territories south of the Sahara. But apart from the strategic importance of the river, the Gambia had been of little value to the British. In an attempt to find a profitable alternative to slavery, they had encouraged the cultivation of groundnuts as a cash-crop at the expense of the traditional staples, millet and sorghum. Otherwise, their impact on life in the greater part of the country had been negligible. In the interior, British law was enforced by only two 'travelling commissioners'. Of the first twelve appointed, three died while on duty, two were killed, one was invalided home, and one resigned.

The people of the Gambia and the people of Senegal were the same – of the same tribes, and in many cases the same families. None the less, it was at the insistence of the Gambian people that the two countries were not merged at independence.

Most of the political parties that had emerged in the period of internal self-government leading up to independence had been based among the people of the capital – the Akus, the descendants of slaves freed from Europe at the end of the eighteenth century, and the Wolofs, survivors of the old families of Saint-Louis du Senegal, the first 'European' city in Africa, who had fled French annexation in 1804. They had been augmented by refugees from the jihad in central Senegal, craftsmen and traders, two thousand of whom had arrived at the British fort one night in 1863, to the consternation of the one constable on duty. They saw themselves as a race apart from the people of the interior, and prided themselves on not being able to speak their language. People of other tribes said that the Wolofs believed themselves to be superior, that they thought they were 'next to the tubabs'. In fact, the Wolofs thought they were better than the tubabs.

The party which had won the country's first elections, however – the People's Progressive Party (PPP) – had sought its constituency among the people of the interior, particularly among the largest tribal group, the Mandingkos. Its leader, who became the country's first prime minister, and its president from the declaration of the republic in 1970, was a forty-year-old veterinary surgeon – a Mandingko, the son of a prosperous trader from the upper reaches of the great river. A shrewd and, even by the standards of our own politicians, an extremely modest man, it was popularly supposed that he had converted to Christianity in order to marry his first wife, Augusta Mahoney, and that he had reconverted to Islam only to marry his second, the glamorous Chilel Njai. He was known to the people of the interior as Kairaba – 'the Father of Peace'.

After independence, the importance attached to the growing of groundnuts increased. The revenues from this single export were almost the only source of the foreign exchange necessary for the country to function as an independent state. The government bought the ground-nuts at a fixed rate from the producers – the individual farmers – and sold them through its Produce Marketing Board.

It was a country of farmers. In the rural areas, every man – the merchants, the artisans, the marabouts, and even the musicians, as well as the vast proportion of the population who had no other occupation –would clear an area of land to grow groundnuts at the beginning of each rainy season. Even in the towns, many would walk to the bush early in the morning to tend their groundnut fields. Even Kairaba himself was a farmer.

Until 1981 the country had no standing army, only an irregular 'Field Force' of five hundred men. It was one of the few countries in Africa to have no political prisoners, and official figures for murder and suicide were virtually negligible. The Gambia was considered an appropriate venue for the Organization of African Unity Summit on Human Rights in 1980.

Samba Sanyang, a former Roman Catholic novice, a Jola, had studied briefly in Moscow, and in Guinea, where he had become an admirer of the 'left-wing' dictator Sekou Toure. He had given himself the name 'Kukoi', a Mandinka word meaning 'to sweep clean'. He stood as a candidate for the official opposition, the NCP, in the 1980 elections, but lost his deposit. He was twenty-eight years old.

One day he met Simon Talibo Sanneh, a driver, a Mandingko, and they decided that as the ministers and senior civil servants were corrupt, and each owned several cars and many houses, they would organize a revolution. In a house in Talinding Kunjang, a poor suburb of Serekunda, they convened a twelve-man Revolutionary Council. Its members included three drivers, two Field Force members of low rank and a dope dealer. They were nearly all in their twenties. One was a teenager.

On the night of July 29, 1981, when Kairaba was in London attending the wedding of Prince Charles and Lady Diana Spencer, they broke into the Field Force barracks using a pair of wire cutters. The following morning, the Dictatorship of the Proletariat was announced over Radio Gambia.

At first the rebellion was met with widespread jubilation, particularly in the urban areas. The country was exhausted by the effects of the drought. Groundnut production had fallen to a third of its former level. And although tourism was booming, the trade was controlled by foreigners and most of the profits left the country. The young men who came to the coast at the beginning of every dry season, searching for work, found only despair. The European-educated élite of the Kairaba regime had lived in luxurious houses. They had behaved like Europeans. They were more like tubabs than the tubabs themselves. The new leaders, however, were 'boys' – just like them.

Many of the Field Force officers, and many rich and powerful Gambians who saw opportunities for themselves in the new order – as well as thousands of ordinary decent citizens – flocked to the rebel side.

High-powered automatic weapons seized from the armoury were handed out to the unemployed, to mutinous policemen, to prisoners freed from the gaol, and to anyone who wanted one. Most of these people had never seen such things before – except in films – and many were killed by accident. Even people who didn't want guns were forced to take them.

The looting was started by prisoners released from the gaol. Field Force officers on the rebel side had shot at them in attempts to keep order. Hard liquor taken from the supermarkets -- normally the preserve only of the élite and European expatriates – was consumed in vast quantities. Soon the guns were being used to settle old scores. There were reports of people going into houses and discharging their magazines at random.

The radio kept up a continuous barrage of propaganda broadcasts. Capitalism would be abolished. Corruption would be abolished. Even traffic jams would be abolished. But the effect of these pronouncements, delivered by Sanyang in a highly charged, almost hysterical manner, was far from calming. Many were frightened by them. Soon the streets of the coastal towns were deserted except for gunmen and looters.

The western powers observed the situation with growing alarm. At the hub of sea and air routes between the northern and southern hemispheres, the Senegambian region was of vital strategic importance. Kairaba flew to Dakar, where, invoking a mutual defence treaty, he asked Senegal to intervene. Senegal was virtually bisected by the Gambia, which divided the centre of government in the north from the most fertile region, the Casamance, in the south. The Trans-Gambia highway, the main road from Dakar to Ziguinchor, the capital of the Casamance, passed through Gambia for only thirty miles, but it was reliant on an antique, rusting ferry to get the considerable traffic of lorries and containers over the great river. The nascent breakaway movement in the Casamance had so far been effectively supressed, but with a radical Marxist-Leninist regime in the Gambia, who knew what might happen?

The Senegalese authorities agreed to Kairaba's request, on the under-standing that when order was restored, a confederation would be formed between the two countries. Meanwhile, the SAS were sent from Britain to rescue the President's wife and children, who were being held hostage by the rebels.

Realizing that he had almost completely lost control of the situation, Sanyang emerged from the radio station with the intention of telephon-ing Colonel Gaddhafi for assistance. But on arriving at the exchange, he found that the equipment had already been destroyed by his own forces. 'I never told anyone to kill!' he is alleged to have exclaimed on seeing the bodies heaped in the mortuary.

It is thought that as many as two thousand people were killed during the week-long rebellion and in the fighting with Senegalese troops that followed. The returning government blamed the insurrection on foreign – presumably Libyan or Russian – agents, but no evidence was ever put forward to support this theory.

Kukoi Samba Sanyang escaped to Guinea-Bissau, but over a thousand others were arrested, including his right-hand man Simon Talibo Sanneh, and Sherif Mustapha Dibbah, the leader of the official opposition, who was accused of high treason. Twenty judges were brought in from Ghana, Nigeria, Sierra Leone and Sri Lanka to ensure impartiality.

After nearly a year in prison, Sheriff Dibbah was cleared of any involvement in the coup, but thirty-six others were sentenced to death. Within days of the coup, Mustapha Danso, already under sentence of death for the murder of the Deputy Field Force Commander, had been hung. He was the first person to be executed in the Gambia since independence in 1965. All other death sentences arising from the coup were subsequently commuted.

That year Kairaba was returned to power with an increased majority.

> 'Kil' Njai's husband,' sang the women of Dulaba.
> 'I'm referring to Lady Njemmeh's husband.
> Sir Daouda Kairaba Jawara –
> God gave him the king's seat.'

5

MIND YOUR BUSINESS, SAVE YOUR LIFE

One afternoon, I was sitting working at the dining table when a small figure peered round the corner of the mosquito netting.

'Sona,' said the figure, by way of introducing itself. 'Jarra Njai's kafo and Fatounding's kafo have gone to the field. They want you to come.'

By the time I had fetched my shoes, she had disappeared. But Samba So, the gatekeeper, told me they had gone to a place to the west of the village, close to their own farm.

The field belonged to Jarra Njai's husband, Kemoring Minte. He had given them the use of his donkey to plant their groundnuts, and he had got his nephew to do it for them. Now they were returning the favour by weeding his groundnut field.

It was already raining by the time I arrived. The nursemaids, clustered close to the tree where the women had left their sandals, climbed up onto the roots, as they tried to shelter from the watery gusts which moved horizontally across the fields. Undeterred, the women continued with their work, slicing off the top two inches of soil, their small, curved weeding hoes dexterously avoiding the groundnut bushes which now stood four or five inches high. The weeds were left lying on the ground to be dried by the sun.

Again the women moved in a line, their arms moving roughly in time – as though in Africa nothing could be done without rhythm.

My arrival was greeted with shouts and guffaws. I took a hoe and started working.

'Mark,' said someone. 'Give us money.'

'I have no money.'

'He-e-e! You have money in your house.'

'No.'

'It is there!'

'I have no money,' I said. '*M'mang koddo soto.*'

They fell about. 'Did you hear the way he said that? *M'mang koddo soto!*' They threw the phrase backwards and forwards amongst themselves, in grotesquely gruff cockney accents.

'Mark,' said Binta Sise. 'Where's my boyfriend?'

'Your boyfriend,' I said, my mind going back to my last Mandinka lesson, 'is in your house.'

'*Whai!* My boyfriend is in my house!' She began to sing. '*Hey, Al Marky joobay jambaro! Hey, look at Mark the Champion! And Mariyama, his wife, is in Europe!*'

I was already beginning to regret having invented this mythical spouse. 'I'm not married,' I said.

'*And Mariyama, his seri, is in Europe!*'

'Who's Mariyama?'

'His *seri*.'

'Where is she?'

'She's in Europe,' said Binta. '*A be tubabidu!*' she sang, languorously drawing out the vowels in her deep voice.

The rain was now harder, slicing over the fields in icy shards. The women decided to give up, as the plants were now almost completely submerged beneath the grey water. The nursemaids had long since gone home, and the women's sandals were starting to disappear into the mud under the tree. They picked them up, and stood huddled around the roots, their sodden faneaus matted around their shoulders. Jarra Njai's husband had arrived, and he led them in a brief prayer to show that the work was finished. They stood there shivering, their lips moving in a semi-audible murmur, cupping their hands to receive the blessing, as they tried to hold onto the corners of their faneaus.

Then as the rain began to subside, they scampered away over the fields to the village, sloshing their way along the water-filled furrows. Some of them wore their calabashes and bowls over their heads like helmets to hold off the rain. Some of them jokingly danced along the furrows, splashing, and flapping their arms like sodden ravens. As they arrived at the outskirts of the village, they divided to go to their different compounds. The rain had almost stopped. In little groups they tripped along the water-filled gulleys that ran along the lanes between the gardens. How green everything was! The drenched colours of their faneaus looked wan beside the brilliance of the weeds and grasses that rose everywhere along the lanes. And on the other side of the fences, the maize was already standing ten feet high.

'Mark, when you go, are you going to have a party?'

'I don't know.'

'Just have a party for our kafo . . .'

'After all, you are the kafo's boyfriend.'

They had started their kafo when they came from the place of circumcision. No one had told them to do it, but they had seen their elder sisters forming kafos, and they decided that they would do the same – so that everyone would know that they were *one*. At first they had called themselves the Ku'lo Kafo – the Secret Group – and they had elected Jongkong Sise, known as Gunjur, a woman fifteen years older than themselves, to be their 'mother'. For they were young, and this woman, though she was not so much older, at least knew more than they did, and if they met together she could advise them not to argue.

When they were children, anyone could be the leader, and they had chosen Karamo Sise, known as Karamo Tombong. When they finally transferred to their husbands' compounds, however, when they were in their early twenties, the leader had to be someone whose surname was Minte, since in their village the Mintes were always the leaders. The person did not necessarily have to be a Minte herself, but someone whose husband's surname was Minte. Jarra Njai was chosen, simply because her husband was older than the other husbands who were called Minte. It had to be said, however, that of all the members of the group, she was the obvious person to be the leader. If she was in a group it would be very difficult for anyone else to be the leader.

When they joined with Fatounding's kafo, they had taken the name of the younger group – the Saniyoro Kafo. It was a beautiful name, and everyone claimed that they had thought of it.

On the corner of the avenue that led from the bantaba at the bottom of the village towards the mosque, opposite the entrance to the compound of Fili Kunda, stood a square, solid-looking house with a well-cemented verandah, that would have given straight onto the street, except that the door and casement of corrugated iron were nearly always kept locked. Another door, in the corrugated-iron fence beside it, opened into a small enclosed yard, with a verandah running along the right-hand side. At the far end was a cooking hut, from the smoke-blackened interior of which bowls, calabashes and other cooking utensils spilled out over the compound floor. Between these objects, hens picked their way among pools of ash, bits of straw and stick, scraps of paper, old tins and other bits of refuse that the children had been using to play with. Someone had been trying to tie bits of reed into circles to form the wheels of a car, but these now lay forgotten in the dust.

The walls of the buildings had been whitewashed, but it was chippec. and worn, the excavations of insects erupting from the plaster like pustules of red dust. A wooden settee stood, or rather lay on the verandah, many of its slats broken or mislaid, and like the *bentengo*, the bench of logs that stood before the main house, it was strewn with rags and bits of cloth that had been used to tie children on backs and wipe their streaming orifi. Everything below waist height was covered in a vague and slightly greasy grey veneer – a patina that indicated the constant passing of children and animals. It was here that Fatounding lived.

She was the colour of wild honey, a dull, slightly greenish brown, which in that part of the world was called 'fair', and considered most attractive. She had a broad, rather boyish face, whose initial appearance of almost Mongolian placidity was belied, particularly on first meeting, by the expression of heavy, thug-like suspicion in her slanting eyes. She favoured an English girl's smock when working, and although it had been let out in several places, her breasts still swelled massively beneath the line where the bust should have been.

It had originally been intended that she and Jarra Njai would be the joint leaders of the kafo. But although she had a strong sense of natural justice, particularly where her own interests were concerned – her voice, hoarse from having bellowed across the rice fields from an early age, was often to be heard booming out over the compound fences in defence of her rights – she was uneasy in authority. She had a tendency to let people off too easily, and it had soon become obvious that Jarra Njai was the real and only leader.

Fatounding betrayed similar tendencies in her upbringing of her three sprawling, squawling sons (the daughter was as yet too young to cause any serious damage). When they were nine or ten, they would be taken to the place of circumcision, after which they would be under the control of the men. In the meantime, they stayed with her in the house of the women, and she rather enjoyed their company – issuing frequent hoarse commands in their direction, but rarely bothering to see if they had any effect. Thus their 'creative play' was a major contributing factor to the state of disarray in which the compound was almost always to be found. She wanted them to go to the tubab school, to learn the tubabs' language, because that, as she was fond of saying, was the language that she liked; though, as she was also fond of saying, she could not understand a word of it.

Her co-wife Isatou was a small, dark person, with bright eyes and a big nose, like a good-natured goblin. Even by the standards of a society in which formal greeting was obligatory on every meeting, she set great store by this procedure, giving out the traditional salutations, always very earnestly and deliberately, in her deep, slow, melodious voice, as though she hadn't yet got over the novelty of using language. Although a few months older than Fatounding, she was the second wife. But the two women got on well together. For in their society it was almost as important that a woman should honour her co-wife as that she should honour her husband. God had brought them both to that place, and as the Mandingkos said, *'Duniya mo le ti'* – 'The world is just for helping each other.' So they shared their tasks – cooking, fetching water, washing clothes, collecting firewood, looking after the children – as they shared their husband's bed.

Their yard was part of the larger compound of Kafuli Kunda, the main yard of which lay on the other side of the avenue. Jarra Njai had lived there till recently, her husband and Fatounding's husband both being sons of the late compound head: Jarra Njai's husband, Kemoring Momodou Minte, by the second wife, and Fatounding's husband, Momodou Kalamatta Minte, by the fifth wife. Momodou Kalamatta, Fatounding's husband, who at thirty-seven was the younger by two years, had once managed to accrue enough money to buy an extra bag of rice from the government store in Mankono, which he had then sold to the other villagers by the cupful. He had managed to maintain an intermittent trade from the cemented verandah at the front of the compound, and was now one of the wealthiest people in the village. But although both men now had their own compounds, they still had to obey the words of the compound elders – their uncles – whom they referred to as their fathers.

Momodou Kalamatta's mother, Mba Bintanse, lived with the two wives in the house of the women. She was a tall, very upright, cheerful person, with few teeth and pale, rather gluey eyes. She helped out with many of their tasks, and was known simply as N'na, Mother.

In the evenings, as the occupants of the house of the women lounged on their beds before sleep – some of the children dozing beside their mothers, others careering between the four beds and the floor – the air was full of stories, speculations and guffaws, N'na adding her own interlocutions from the darkness. The atmosphere resembled that of a dormitory in some downmarket and particularly rowdy girls' boarding school, Fatounding seeming less like a mother, and more like a reluctant prefect. The one person who was missing from this scene of domestic intimacy was their husband, the father of all these children. He was a lean, dark man, whose prominent teeth gave an impression of constant wolfish hunger, though he hardly ever said anything, or showed any expression about anything. At first I thought he resented my presence in the compound. But I soon realized that this extreme indifference was just his way. He moved in and out of the compound almost soundlessly, paying little attention to his wives, and largely ignored by them. It was difficult to imagine that he was out there close by in the darkness, or that his existence could be at all necessary in this apparently self-sufficient female society.

At first there appeared to be little difference between the incipient rice and the vast army of weeds crowding in around it. I had to ask Fatounding to help me identify any number of green stalks. *'Nyaamo . . . nyaamo . . . nyaamo . . .'* All weeds. She kept pulling away at the grasses for some time. 'Rice is not there,' she said cheerfully, and left me to it.

After a time it became obvious which was the rice – the slender, golden-green stems shooting straight from the ground into long spear-like leaves. These, the desired, the precious object, acquired a kind of glow as one spied them among the ranks of the tough, vigorous nyaamo.

It was mercifully cool at the rice field of Tambana, the air perfectly clear and still. The fields ran into each other among the trees at the edge of the salt flats, interconnecting, like a succession of cool, green rooms. Above, through the false ceiling of the branches, we could see a layer of dark, violet cloud.

'Rain,' said Fatounding.

We had a hasty lunch of rice and leaves. Fatounding belched violently, then we returned to work. Soon the freezing rain was upon us. Fatounding put the battered enamel lunch basin over her head. She grinned from beneath it.

'This rain is very good,' she said.

I wondered if it would be possible for there to be too much rain; if a point would come when they would prefer it to stop.

'I pray that God will never give me that idea,' said Fatounding.

My shirt was soon so heavy with water I could hardly move my arms. I took it off and threw it down in the mud. Then I was so cold I had to put it back on again. Fatounding laughed. 'He-e-e, Marky!' she said. Then the rain stopped as suddenly as it had begun, and soon there was no sound save for the low humming of Fatounding singing to herself.

Eventually the field was almost completely cleared. Only the fragile rice stalks stood out from the black earth – though sometimes they were as much as a foot apart.

I had noticed a different sort of dung beetle – an iridescent blue-black.

One saw them burying themselves into green mounds of the fresh dung only to emerge a few moments later having hewn out a perfect sphere four times their own size. If one looked into the undergrowth at the side of the pathways, one would see convoys of them trundling these spheres through the forest of roots. I had heard that they would hatch their grubs on them.

The termite hills were starting to disappear, their castellated turrets dissolving into the earth, leaving the entrances of the internal passageways gaping like anthropomorphic orifi, around which swarmed thousands of tiny brown grubs.

The village itself was now like a great, green garden, the compounds hustling for space between the stands of tall viridian maize that crowded up to the fences, over the roofs of the houses, and even up to the back of the mosque. On the other side of the pathway the burial ground was completely smothered by weeds; only a couple of grave markers written in Arabic poked out above them. And between the massive trunks of the baobabs, their branches now densely covered in leaves, one could see through to the pattern of neatly tilled fields on the south side of the village. The lines of *suno* – the 'early' millet – seemed to come pouring from the earth like green fountains, while the millet and sorghum were now so tall they reached to the lower branches of the mango trees, which stood in a long snaking line around the southern edge of the village. Birds of magenta and turquoise – hard, heraldic colours – darted in and out of their thick foliage. A farmer sat asleep under a tree. It was a scene that had the clear-cut, emphatic quality of a landscape in a medieval calendar of hours – everything in its place in the passing of the seasons, and the time-honoured order ordained by God. It was difficult in a landscape of such richness to imagine that hunger could exist. But that was what was happening in the village, at that very moment.

Since they had existed, they had known hunger at that time of the year. But in their parents' time, they had transplanted their rice to their field at Tankular, on the banks of the great river. As soon as the seedlings began to 'open' in the fields around the village, they were uprooted and taken to Tankular, where they were replanted under the water. This replanting made the stems multiply so that the yield would be greater. Sometimes it was replanted twice.

Tankular was more than seven miles away. But that field was theirs, because their ancestors had been the first to clear that area of land. Going to and from that field had created a lot of work, but the rice they got from there had lasted them almost to the beginning of the next rainy season. When it was finished they would eat the last of the millet. Then they would go into the bush and collect leaves, berries, wild mangoes, wild cassava root, and the baobab fruit – which they called 'monkey bread'. If they lived like that for weeks at a time, they would become ill. They would not die, but they would become very weak. Then when they began to eat normally again they would revive.

Later, imported rice – what they called 'tubab rice' – became available for sale. So when they were children, it was unusual for people to go a day without eating. Even in the rainy season, they would eat once a day. Relatives would help each other, so that everyone could have this one meal.

Even thirty years ago, groundnuts had been a relatively unimportant crop. Millet and sorghum, the crops their ancestors had known, were what they planted. Groundnuts were for bartering, and later for selling. But as people realized the importance of having money, more and more of the village's land was given over to this crop. In those days it would rain almost continuously for three months. It would pause briefly, then, after two or three hours, it would begin again. Or at least that was how they remembered it. In the last fifteen years, however, the rainfall had been less and less. And it was while they were adolescents, working in their mothers' fields, that the salt from the great river had entered their field at Tankular. After that nothing would grow there.

The rice they were able to grow in the fields around the village would be finished long before the dry season was over. Last year there had hardly been any rain at all, and the women had harvested only a quarter of what they had expected. It had been a mystery to the Europeans in the camp how the villagers had managed to survive at all.

The men now concentrated their efforts on groundnuts. In the last three years, the millet and sorghum had been almost completely destroyed by locusts and beetles. People were becoming scared to plant them. Findo, a fine grain, which had once been their favourite food, had now disappeared altogether.

So they had become more and more dependent on the tubab rice, bought with the profits from the groundnut harvest. It was broken rice from South-East Asia – the fragments left over from the milling process – and cheaper than the whole grain. But now there was no rice, broken or whole-grain, in the entire country. People were surviving on what they had stored. If they had none, they would beg from relatives. And if their relatives could not help them, they would go to the bush to get leaves, or simply go without.

I had been living in the camp for nearly three months. For more than half of that time there had been a desperate shortage of food in the village. People had been physically suffering from the effects of hunger only yards from where I was living, and I hadn't even been aware of it. I now knew, from Susan Lawrence's dietary reports, that most of them were surviving on one meal a day, and some weren't eating at all. This knowledge did nothing to lessen my sense of emotional isolation from the people of the village. Indeed, it heightened my sense of the village as a place from which I was destined to remain forever a stranger, even while I was surrounded by its inhabitants for most of the time. I wanted to understand their experience of hunger, to know what it meant to them. But it is difficult to spend time socially with people who will not eat for another twenty-four hours – if then – when you yourself are about to return home for an extremely adequate meal.

At the Quarters, we never went without. Daouda stockpiled rice against such shortages. The sacks were piled up the back staircase of Barbara Smith's flat. Even the leaf sauces that we ate, usually mixed with pounded groundnuts, bits of fish and even oil, were rich in comparison with those of the villagers, which were thin and watery even at the best of times.

I could, of course, have simply gone without, and felt the effects of hunger myself. But I felt that since the emotional impact of a voluntary and essentially academic exercise would be quite different from that of a sustained and unavoidable deprivation, it would be an absurd and even hypocritical action. And as I had never missed a meal in my life, I would probably have made myself extremely ill. I decided that it was definitely not a good idea.

But the strangest and, to an outsider, the most disquieting thing about this hunger was that its effects were not easy to see. Having been exposed to pictures of starving people from an early age, one assumes hunger to be an inherently dramatic phenomenon. In fact, it takes a human being a very long time to starve to death. The people were becoming thinner, but it wasn't happening so quickly that it was evident on casual observation. If hunger was tiring them, it had no apparent effect on their health. And it certainly didn't stop them from working. It was the time of weeding – *bindeyo* – when people fought with the land to prevent their precious, fragile crops – their only means of ensuring their survival on this earth – from being swallowed up by the burgeoning bush. They left the village early each morning, returning only as the last rays of the sun were disappearing over the plain to the west of the village. And they still joked; they still sang as they worked.

'What do you do if there is no dinner?' I asked Fatounding one evening in the house of the women.

'Have a bath, pray, go to bed.'

I realized the fatuity of the question. What else were they supposed to do? They could have gone to the camp, murdered the tubabs, and stolen their one kilogram packets of Uncle Ben's 'Easy Cook' rice. But that wouldn't have got them very far.

'We will rely on God,' said Fatounding. 'And we will eat green leaves.'

Was hunger depressing?

'I'm crying,' she said, pouting and rubbing her cheeks with her knuckles. They all roared with laughter.

It was always difficult at this time of year. But this was the most difficult year so far. She didn't know what was causing it. 'Ask the government,' she said. She only knew that there was a lot of rain. It was the best rain they had had for five years. And when she looked at her crops she felt very glad.

It was pointless to ask the people what hunger 'meant' to them, because for them it was not really a thing. It was an absence of something, and therefore it had no meaning. It was hard – *akoliata* – and that was all there was to say about it.

A European could not live in Dulaba without servants. Anyone who took on less than three would be condemned as *ajawiata bake* – very wicked – and pestered ceaselessly by aspirant gardeners, cleaners and laundry women. So I had Turo, the Professor's old gardener, to sweep the paths around the house, Mabinta, a world-weary but canny woman in her late thirties, to wash my clothes, while Natoma cleaned the house two mornings a week.

She was often accompanied by Mariatou, her twelve-year-old niece, who looked after Natoma's baby daughter Binta and Fatou, an orphaned child who was being brought up by Natoma's mother. Mariatou was a handsome child, so black she was almost blue, but at that time of year she always looked very drawn and exhausted.

I tried to prevail upon Natoma to take her salary early, so that she could buy bread for her family. But she told me to keep it for her. She was saving to buy bowls and basins and bedsheets. I found this attitude extra-ordinary, almost unbelievable. I said that if she took it now, she could use it to buy bread. She said that bread was very expensive. It was one dalasi (20p) a loaf. Her salary was forty dalasis a month. There were eleven of them in her compound. Even forty loaves wouldn't go very far. If she saved that money she would at least have something to show at the end of the season. But if she took it, it would be gone in a couple of days, and then they would be hungry again.

Generally, the Africans seemed to have a low opinion of the nutritional value of bread. They said that bread would never satisfy; that it was only powder, and when you drank it would be washed away. But rice was heavy. It would stay with you for a long time. For them eating *was* rice or millet.

I felt I had to do something. But what? One person could not feed a village of one thousand, four hundred people. Even if one had the money, there was nothing to buy with it. One could not even support one family. For one could not give help one day and withdraw it the next. And why support one family and not another?

Finally, I decided that I would buy bread and take it to Binta and Tumbulu – two of the poorest women in the village – and damn the consequences. 'If you do that,' said Fabakary Manneh, 'everyone will say you are wicked, because you gave to them, and not to others.'

'Will they tell people?'

'Of course.'

'Maybe they won't.'

'They will.'

I dropped that idea.

Darbon Jammeh was a slim, copper-coloured woman of twenty-three; obviously personable, but not markedly different from any number of other women who might be seen daily, wandering in the MRC com-pound, trailing their children behind them. She had, however, been closely involved with the Europeans from an early age, first as a nursemaid to the survey mothers, then to the children of various Europeans in the compound. These people had thought highly of her, and had given her a watch so that she could arrive on time.

Her own mother had died when she was young, and as the eldest daughter she had had to look after her brothers and sisters. At twelve, she had been married to a young man from one of the compounds with which her family traditionally intermarried. But before she had even been given to him, he was killed in a fight with a member of his own age group. This incident was never revealed to the authorities, but her husband's 'murderer' left the village and never returned.

There had been a history of instability in her late husband's family. A sister had died insane in hospital. Another brother had been kept chained in a house in the family compound. Bill, the doctor, had found him, naked and unintelligible, his body covered with sores. He had him sent down to the hospital on the coast before he was starved to death. He had been kept like that by his own elder brother, and it was to this man that Darbon was given when her husband died, because in that society, a woman was inherited by her husband's brothers when he died.

He lived in Serekunda, where he worked as a driver. But when he came to Dulaba, he would summon her to his compound. Often she would refuse to go. Or if she went she would refuse to sleep with him, and he would beat her. If she went to the coast for her own purposes, she would never go to his compound if she could help it. Once she turned up for work at the doctors' house, her face swathed in cloth. When she removed it, her face was swollen and bruised, her lips cut, and one of her eyes was blacked. The same day, Bill had treated her husband in the clinic. His genitals were bruised and covered in scratch marks. He said his wife had tried to tear his penis off.

After four years, she decided to divorce this man. Her father said if she tried to do that, she would be flogged by the elders of the compound – the traditional punishment for a recalcitrant wife. She immediately fled to the district chief at Mankono, who acted as the local magistrate. Her family, fearing that it might go to an even higher authority, immediately forgave her. She called upon her husband to release her and, astonished by her boldness, he agreed.

Many men had sought her – men of the village, old and young, several of the MRC staff, including Lamin Jarjou, the chief fieldworker, and even Daouda, it was said. The person she chose, however, was another of the MRC staff, a young man who was said to be the father of at least one illegitimate child in the village. Her father said that she would never marry this man, that he was not a good Muslim. He had made his own choice, a man in early middle age from one of the neighbouring compounds. He had even gone as far as accepting this man's kola nuts – the elders of the two compounds meeting together to pray, to strengthen the bonds between them. But when he called his daughter to him, she told him that she would never accept this man.

She had heard it said, on the nights when the Koran was interpreted to the people, that a young girl should marry the choice of her parents, because she would not know what was good and what was bad for her. But a woman marrying for the second time, whether through death or divorce, should be able to choose her own husband. And she should choose someone that she loved, so that she could serve him as God had asked her to do. For marriage does not end in this world. It is for the sake of the second world – *Alahira* – which is heaven. She told her father that she did not love the man, and she would never marry him. She was even prepared to die over it.

Her father told her to leave the compound. She spent a short time at the doctors' house in the MRC compound, then she returned and stayed with an old woman in her family compound. She could not stay in the house of the women where she had grown up, because her father's wives were against her. But she did not care what they thought. They were just people her father had happened to marry. They were nothing to her.

She stayed like that for many months: refusing to marry the man of her father's choice, and he refusing to let her marry the man of her choice. Then she found that she was pregnant with a third child.

Almost no one had gone to the naming ceremony, but she had given the child, a daughter, the surname of a young man who had been working in the village as a schoolteacher. He had been moved to another village, on the north bank of the great river, and he denied all knowledge of the child. But recently, since the beginning of the rainy season, it was being said in the village that he had asked for Darbon's hand, and that soon she would be going to live with him.

She was glad. A woman could not stay without a husband. If ever since you had been born you had seen that every person was married, you would believe that you too must be married. Marriage was like death – and every individual must die.

'Do you know this girl?' asked Demba Tamba, pointing at Natoma's niece, Mariatou, who sat nervously on the edge of the Habitat sofa, the child Fatou on her back. 'She's going to be very beautiful,' he said, sitting back in the armchair. There was a wistful sound in his voice, and the child, though she could not understand what he was saying, blushed, going a shade darker if that was possible. 'Oh! I saw my wife this weekend,' said Demba. 'We stayed up till early in the morning – not doing anything, just chatting. Now I miss her very much.'

Two years before, his mother had told him that he must marry his father's sister's daughter. Feeling he was not yet ready for such a step, Demba had gone to Helene and borrowed a month's salary in advance. He had taken this money to a marabout, who had given him a potion. His mother had inhaled this potion and immediately forgotten about the marriage.

Now apparently the marriage was going ahead again, and this time he wasn't doing anything to oppose it. But although according to the traditional law the couple were now married, they would not sleep together for another three years, because his wife was still at school.

Pregnant women were not eligible to attend school. So if a schoolgirl became pregnant, the person 'responsible' would have to pay back to her father all the money that had been spent on the girl's education. This recent convention had taken on the force of a traditional taboo, and while many men chased married women with avidity, there were few who would dally with a schoolgirl.

Demba's wife, who was eighteen, was taking O levels at the Gambia High School, a step equivalent to taking a degree at Cambridge.

'Barbara told me that if my wife comes here I must have Family Planning. But I told her, "I will restrain myself. That will be my family planning."'

'She loves me very much,' he said. 'And I know that if I asked her she would leave the school. But she must be very intelligent to have got so far. So I must let her have her chance.

'When we are properly married, our marriage will not be like some marriages you see, with the husband always shouting at the wife. She must obey me. But I also must obey her.'

Was he still interested in the student, Joanne?

'I am not interested. I want to be able to trust my wife. So she must also be able to trust me.'

Yaya Bojang was also engaged, but unlike Demba, he had arranged his own marriage. 'Three years ago, a girl came here for the summer holidays, to stay with her aunt, who was working for the MRC at that time. During the first week, I was just observing her. Then I sent a letter inviting her to have Chinese green tea with me in my house. She came, of course. After that, when she was washing clothes she would send someone to fetch me so that I could come and chat with her. And when I was going to work in the village, she would ask if she could go with me, and I would buy her fresh milk to drink.

'When she went back to school, I would send her eggs so that she could eat them during the break – sometimes three eggs, sometimes four eggs, sometimes six eggs.

'We have not had sex. We haven't even discussed it. But when we are married, I will not expect her to be faithful to me. Sometimes I must be away from her, and I cannot control what she does at such times. So it is her business.

'When we die, we will lie in different graves. Hers will be over here and mine will be over there. So what each of us has to answer to God is our own business.'

We were approaching Tobaski, or *Bang na Salo*, as it was called in Mandinka – the Prayer of Riches – the most eagerly awaited feast of the Muslim calendar. On that day, the pilgrims who had arrived in Mecca on the Haj, the pilgrimage which every Muslim should try to make at least once in their lifetime, would each sacrifice a sheep, to commemorate the day when God spared the life of Isaac, son of the prophet Abraham. Throughout the Muslim world, each family would try to kill a sheep, or at least a goat. Every child would receive a new suit of clothes, and in the

Gambia, everyone would return to their home village to be with their family on that day.

Nearly all of the Staff had bought a sheep, and some two. People bought them well in advance, as the price of animals rose steeply at that time of the year. They were to be seen grazing all over the compound. Demba Tamba had bought a big ram. He took it for walks around the compound, letting it wander off on a long lead, staring all the while into space, with an air of disconsolate solemnity.

I now saw him as someone quite different from the person I had first met. In his dealings with his employers, the other Europeans, he accentuated, indeed he played on his boyishness, his easy, natural charm. But in the society of the Quarters, his movements seemed slower and more ponderous, like those of someone of a different generation. His light beard, otherwise scarcely noticeable, added to a sense of dignity, a sense almost of authority, that stemmed from his central position in that society. It was not by chance that we ate in his room every night rather than in any of the others. For although he was only twenty-five, he was respected for his steady and essentially responsible nature, and now, of course, he was a married man.

Yet these days he appeared to be troubled for much of the time. For though he had been working in Dulaba longer than any of the other fieldworkers, he had failed in these five years to achieve any significant promotion.

His friend Lamin Bojang had been sent to study at the Cass Nutrition Unit in Cambridge. And he had heard reports that Lamin had received the second highest grades in his class at the end of his first year. He had a Spanish friend who had paid for him to join him and his family for Christmas. He had sent Demba a photograph of himself standing on the beach at Valencia, the tower blocks of the hotels rising in the background.

Demba had hoped to follow him there. But now that he had heard that he had failed his two O levels, it began to seem less and less likely. Lamin would become a 'semi-tubab', and when he returned, he would not eat some of the things he had eaten before. It disturbed Demba very much to think that he himself would never be anything other than a fieldworker here in Dulaba.

Since the Professor left, however, his work had been somewhat different. There was now less wandering about in the heat of the sun. When he went into the village, it was in a Land Rover that went purely for the purpose of his work. He sat in the front seat. He interpreted this as a kind of promotion. After all, the less he had to do, and particularly the less he had to exert himself physically, the higher his rank.

I had decided that I would make a donation to Jarra Njai's kafo. If I gave money to a group no one could accuse me of favouritism. What they did with the money would be their affair. It wouldn't be so much that it would cause great jealousy and disruption in their lives, but it would be enough that they would feel they had something tangible in their hand. It might cheer them up, and I would feel that I had at least done *something*. I thought that fifty dalasis (£10) might be enough.

I asked Jere Jarjou what he thought.

He was sitting in a wooden armchair in his room. He looked down, and then laughed quietly to himself.

'No,' he said. 'I cannot give you any advice about that.'

'Why not?' I asked.

'One batut cannot give advice to a hundred pounds.'

What did he mean by that?

'Your knowledge is greater than mine. I cannot advise you. I am inferior.'

'Why do you say you're inferior?' I asked.

'I am of low rank. Some of the people I went to school with now drive their own cars. But I am nothing.'

'You have a good job,' I said. 'Compared to the people in this village, you are rich.'

'No,' he said. 'I am inferior. I am of low rank.'

I found him the least fathomable of all the people of the Quarters. The most talented and the most humorous of the fieldworkers, his behaviour veered between an effusive, almost unnatural gaiety, and a leaden, murderous melancholia. For much of the time he was abrupt, monosyllabic, refusing even to greet, which in that society was an unforgivable affront. 'You just forget him,' said Yaya. 'He is like that. Sometimes he is even like that to me.' It was his ambition to be a writer, and on arriving I had assumed that he would be my special friend among the fieldworkers. I had soon realized, however, that this was not going to happen.

Now he sat back in his chair, leaning his head against the wall and staring into space. He was wearing a pair of black-framed glasses. I had seen him wearing them many times before, and noticed that they contained only plain glass.

'Anyway,' he said, 'you do not like me.'

'I don't like you?'

'No.'

'I do like you.'

'You don't.'

'What makes you say that?'

'It is just my feeling according to what I have observed. I have discussed it with other people. It disturbs me very much.'

I thought for a moment. 'Maybe you assume that I don't like you because you don't like me.'

'Well,' he said. 'I can't say anything about that.'

'That will be good,' said Yaya Bojang. 'If you give them five dalasis, they will be able to buy a lot of mints with that, and they will be very happy about it.'

'Actually,' I said, 'I was thinking of giving them fifty.'

'You were thinking of giving them *fifty*?'

*

Fatounding was a diamond. I went to the rice field of Tambana with her and Isatou. The dog came too. It was a long, jackally beast, reddish-brown in colour. It was one of the better-looking dogs in the village, having fewer festering bites than some of the others. But it was still almost skeletal. The idea of feeding a dog was, to the people of Dulaba, absurd. And the curs, who were kept ostensibly for hunting, lived off vermin, occasionally being hurled the odd handful of rice – though when food was scarce they were denied even that. They lay coiled like snakes in inopportune places, ready to be kicked or trodden on, flies buzzing around their sores and their bitten-off stumps of ears. When times got really hard, they would go and dig up the burial ground. And when this was discovered there would be a mass killing of dogs, the miserable brutes hacked to death with hoes.

'Has it got a name?' I asked.

'Yes.'

'What's that?'

'Dog.'

I had brought some bread as my contribution to lunch. It was now the only food I could get. I offered it to them. 'Keep it for us in your bag,' they said.

Tumbulu Sise was working nearby. Her mother and Fatounding's husband's mother – N'na – were sisters of the same mother and the same father, and as rice fields were passed on through the women, their rice fields were naturally close together. She was about thirty, and one of the more senior members of the Saniyoro Kafo. She was fair, almost ginger in complexion, and her lower lip was blue, having been tattooed when she was a girl. It had hurt excruciatingly, but as she had asked the person to do it, she had not thought it fair to cry out. And as when they had finished she had not been satisfied with the extent of the blueness, she had asked them to do it again. Despite this, she was not generally known as someone who was particularly tough. Last year, when Bunja the herdsman had let the cattle wander into the fields and destroy the rice, the women had threatened to kill him. Tumbulu had cried at the very idea of it – to the great amusement of everyone, including the herdsman himself.

She was considered by the Europeans to be one of the 'best mothers', because although she was, even by the standards of the village, extremely poor, her four children had all grown remarkably well. It was said that this was because she put them first, that she would make sure they ate, even if she didn't eat herself.

She had a deep, rich voice, and a full, comfortable look about her, like a well-fed cat.

'What have you got in that bag?' she asked. 'Bread?'

'No.'

'You have.'

'No.'

'Mark! You have bread in that bag! Are you going to give me some?'

'Say "No",' said Fatounding, confident that she would be getting some.

'No.' I said.

'When you have your lunch, I'm going to come over and join you. Are you going to give me some then?'

'Say "No",' said Fatounding.

'No,' I said.

Tumbulu picked up a stick. 'You see this stick? I'm going to ask you if you're going to give me some bread, and if you say "No", I'm going to beat you. Are you going to give me some bread?'

'Say "No",' said Fatounding.

'No,' I said.

'*Mark!*' said Tumbulu, hurling the stick to the ground.

The women's hands flew this way and that, ripping away the weeds at great speed. They were piled in heaps along the narrow banks of earth that separated the fields. Isatou, particularly, worked relentlessly hard, saying little, and always standing, bending from the waist to her work. Fatounding, on the other hand, liked to sing and make conversation. By the end of the afternoon, she sat, almost sprawling along one of the embankments, as she continued to pull away at the almost endless mass of weeds.

Tumbulu's eldest daughter, Salimata, who was looking after the baby, Binta Sise, stood watching us. She was like a smaller, thinner version of her mother, with a cheeky, knowing look about her.

'Mark,' said Fatounding, looking up from her work. 'You want a wife?'

'Yes.'

A gleam came into her eye. 'You want a *morfing muso* – a black wife?'

'Yes.'

'You want Salimata?' she said, gesturing to the girl.

'I want a woman,' I said. 'Not a girl.'

Fatounding laughed, hoarsely but infectiously. 'He wants a woman, not a girl!' Then she had a sudden inspiration. '*Darbon Jammeh!*'

'What?'

'Mark is going to marry Darbon Jammeh!'

'That's very good,' said Isatou with sincerity.

'Mark, do you like Darbon Jammeh?' asked Fatounding.

'Yes,' I said. 'Do you?'

'Yes! She is very good, and *very* beautiful. When you get married, you can go to London together.' She carried on working, she and Isatou chatting among themselves. And as the afternoon wore on, I could hear them repeating the story of how I said I wanted a black wife – 'And then he said he wanted a woman, not a girl' – over and over again.

Now everyone was worried about whether there would be rice for Tobaski. Even Fatounding was depressed at the prospect of starving on the prayer day. Rumours abounded about how and when rice would be arriving in the country. It was said that a boatful of rice from the Catholic Relief Services – a charity active in the Gambia – had docked at Banjul. But whether this was true or not, nobody knew. Meanwhile, the rice that had been irrigated by the fresh waters of the upper reaches of the great river was already being harvested. But rather than being brought down-river to be sold, it was smuggled immediately into Senegal, where it would fetch a higher price. I asked Natoma what she thought about this.

'Those people in Senegal are human too,' she said simply. 'They too must eat.'

I was dumbfounded.

'You the tubabs,' she said. 'Why are you keeping your rice from us?'

I said we didn't grow rice in our country.

'But you have it there,' she said.

We did, of course.

I had the sense once again that for the vast majority of the blacks, the world was something which had been taken and held by the tubabs. They had taken it and laid their law upon it. They had access to everything in the earth – its knowledge and its resources. And now that they could no longer grow enough for their survival, the blacks were more than ever at the mercy of the tubabs – in terms of food as in everything else. For they had heard that the weapons the tubabs had could destroy the world, within the space of a moment.

Since independence they had been ruled by people who were blacks like themselves. But the law those people were using was the tubabs' law, and those blacks who were successful were those who followed the tubabs' ways.

Now everything, as they perceived it, was 'tubab'. The government school was the 'tubab school'. The rice they did not grow themselves was 'tubab rice'. A job, indeed the very concept of paid employment, was 'tubab work'. In their grandparents' time, farming had been an honoured occupation. But now almost any form of 'tubab work' was considered preferable to farming.

But as I spent more and more time at the Quarters, I came to realize that although these people – the fieldworkers, the technicians, the drivers and the mechanics, who had been to the European school and gained employment with a foreign company – had followed the 'tubabs' road', they attributed remarkably little importance to the culture of the tubabs itself.

Their traditional society had been divided into three castes: the *jongo* – the slaves; the *nyamalo* – the praise singers, blacksmiths and leather workers; and the *foro* – the freemen. The tubabs had abolished slavery, but they had created a new class of their own – a 'super caste', that was above all the others – the Class of Civil Servants. And while one could only be a blacksmith or a weaver or a musician by birth, the only thing one needed to enter the Class of Civil Servants was education. So one entered school not to gain knowledge *per se*, but to become part of the Class of Civil Servants. Or as one of the teachers had put it, 'You go to school so that you do not have to farm.' What one actually did when one became a Civil Servant – the actual function of one's work – was of little importance.

Thus none of the fieldworkers who had so assiduously carried out the Professor's study over a three-year period knew what its purpose had been. This was admittedly partly because no one had thought to tell them. But it was also because few of them had any interest in knowing. For them, the Camp was just *there*. That the tubabs had been given everything in the earth was due to the creation of God. And since this camp was in their country, it was only right that they, the blacks, should benefit from it. But its purpose, and the factors that governed its existence, were beyond their knowledge or concern.

English was, for them, not the language of a small, damp island two thousand miles away, it was the language of the Class of Civil Servants. And English as they spoke it – picturesquely, but, from an academic point of view, almost entirely wrongly – was as far as they were concerned proper English. English as the tubabs spoke it to each other was for them an idiomatic dialect, and largely unintelligible. And while they all dreamed of visiting that island, to 'further their studies' or 'improve themselves', they had little interest in learning about the reality of life there. Since few of them would be going there, it had for them a largely mythological significance. It was the place of wealth.

The sociologist Barbara Thompson, who had carried out a socio-medical study of the village in the early sixties, had observed that the villagers believed the Europeans to be 'kind devils', who could give people things and make them wealthy.

Aspects of this belief persisted strongly, even among those Africans who had been educated in the ways of the Europeans. They saw the tubabs as being inherently different. They saw them as existing in a reality irrevocably beyond their own. They believed all Europeans to be fabulously, limitlessly wealthy, and there was nothing anyone could say or do to persuade them that they were not. And since most Europeans kept bottles of beer and soft drinks in their fridges, they believed that all Europeans had them, that it was part of the essentiality of their being. Since I did not have any, they assumed I must be hiding them in some secret, inner part of my house, and that it was only through my wickedness that I was not prepared to part with them.

Sometimes cars would arrive in Dulaba, loaded with bread from the coast, but it was tasteless and spongy, like a mouthful of tissue paper. The best bread, which I ate for lunch every day, was baked in a hut behind Kassim's shop, by Sollu, Kassim's brother. It came in French-style sticks, though it was doughier and had a paler crust, with a real bite to it – like the bread in southern Italy.

Kassim's was by far the biggest and most well stocked of the four shops in Dulaba. And lying as it did on the opposite side of the triangle of waste ground from the compound gates, it was in by far the most advantageous position – in close proximity to all the wealthiest people in the village. Unlike the other shopkeepers, Kassim was not a citizen of the village, but a Fulani, a member of the Jallo family from the Fouta Jallon, who lived in the compound behind the shop. He was an amiable, slightly plump young man, who positively exuded corruption. As he was away a lot, 'on business', the shop was usually looked after by his thirteen-year-old brother Seikou, a tall, thin boy, endowed with a seriousness, an austerity beyond his years. He did his homework seated behind the counter in the shop, an environment which cannot have been conducive to study, as the cramped, dark space was usually crowded with people who had no reason to be there, other than to be there. When I arrived in Dulaba, I would go into the shop, and spend twenty minutes waiting to be served, only to find that the other members of the 'queue' had no intention of buying anything, and the 'assistant' didn't think I had either.

Unlike the other village shops, Kassim's had a screen of chicken wire across the front of the counter for security purposes. But it was quite superfluous, partly because it was broken, and partly because customers simply walked round the side of it to rummage through the merchandise at their leisure.

The shop catered principally to the five main vices of the Gambians: cigarettes, kola nuts, black mints, sugar and Chinese tea. But for those with more refined tastes, Nescafé and Ovaltine were available in small tins, and Liptons' tea bags singly or by the box. A sack of sugar was kept open behind the counter, but oil, the Gambians' other great culinary passion, was rarely available. A large bar of ochre-coloured Gambian soap, made at the factory near Banjul, cost two dalasis (40p). A large tin of 'Walgust' tomato paste (Napoli) was kept open on the counter, with a bit of plastic bag over it to keep the flies off. A spoonful cost five batuts (a penny), and came wrapped in paper – usually part of a 'dietary' form that had mysteriously found its way there from the MRC. Sometimes there were onions – rolling around in the dust on the floor – but they were exorbitantly expensive. There were pens, exercise-books and envelopes for sale, and from time to time there were also the ubiquitous rubber flip-flop sandals and lengths of cloth. Kassim got his stock from the coast, or from the great market that was held every Sunday at Farrafenni on the north bank of the great river. He would leave early on a Sunday morning in the bush taxi that left Kiang daily, and return as it was getting dark with a huge sack full of sandals or kola nuts over his shoulder.

If Kassim was away during term-time, the shop would be closed while Seikou was at school – though you could always go into the compound at the back and get Kassim's sixteen-year-old wife, Fatou, to open it up for you. Payment, however, would have to be deferred, as Fatou couldn't do sums. The shop's epic credit accounts were kept on a number of scraps of paper and old cigarette packets, which were written by Seikou in English and Kassim in Arabic, and kept loosely together in an old exercise-book. Having seen these 'accounts', I found it difficult to imagine how they ever recovered a penny. But they never made a mistake with mine.

That night I went with Yaya to Jarra Njai's compound, to present her with the fifty dalasis for the kafo.

If someone wanted to join their kafo, they would meet them, to try to discern something of that person's personality, to see if they felt they could work with them. If they thought they could, that person would be asked to pay a subscription, and they would be considered a member of the kafo. So far they had not rejected anyone's application.

We found Jarra Njai sitting with her co-wife Salinding on the verandah of their house. Her voice from the darkness sounded thin and exhausted. Her husband sat a few yards away, silent, invisible. After greeting I asked her what they had eaten for dinner.

'Nothing,' she said, quickly.

'We had leaves,' said the husband gruffly from the darkness.

'He-e-e, Mark!' said Jarra Njai. 'This is a hard year. This is the hardest year we have known. We are only praying that soon it will be over.'

What would she do if it wasn't – if by this time next week, they still had no rice?

'I don't know,' she said. 'Unless I come and lie down on your verandah!'

There were loud guffaws from the darkness. Even the husband laughed. I handed her the notes. She counted them, feeling their size in the darkness: five ten-dalasi notes.

'He-e-e, Mark,' she said. 'From now on, you also are a member of our kafo. And when the time comes for you to go, we will know what to do.'

One afternoon, as Yaya and I were sitting in what used to be the Professor's office, transcribing my tapes, I spotted Darbon Jammeh passing the window. As usual she was with her three children, the youngest seated on her arm, the other two wandering along behind.

'Look at her!' said Yaya. 'When I first came here, she was so beautiful. Her body used to shine like . . . what! And she was proud. I was told that if I approached her she would insult me. So I kept away, because I felt ashamed in front of her. But now, she has had so many worries, she has become very thin.'

I asked him if he thought she would agree to have an affair – 'a connection' – with me.

'She will, of course.'

How could he be so sure?

'She must. A woman like that cannot refuse you. She knows she will have some interest from it.'

But wasn't that prostitution?

'It is not that. You know, the religion condemns this jiving. It hates it. If you commit adultery, you have caused that woman to sin, so you must give her something so that she can wash herself. You are a European, and she will have the belief that you will be generous.'

Demba was in a very good mood at dinner time. He had just received a letter from his friend Lamin in Cambridge. 'I'm going to visit him there. He is going to send me the money for the air ticket. I have my passport,' he beamed. 'Everything is ready.'

For a moment I believed him.

Later he showed me the passport. It was in a smart brown leather case.

Inside was a picture of a younger Demba, unshaven, startled by the photographer's flash.

'I'm only joking,' he said. 'I'm not going anywhere.' He took the passport and folded it in his hands. 'I always feel sad when I look at this. It has no use. It's like looking at a picture: it is attractive, but it has no value.

'Before, I was ready. I had saved four thousand five hundred dalasis to go to England. But the money was all wasted . . . wasted.'

'Bob Marley!' said Sanyang. 'That man is a preacher and a prophet.'

'Bob Marley is not a prophet,' said Fabakary Manneh, complacently, as he prepared the Chinese tea.

'Bob is a prophet!' said Momodou Coly, hotly. 'He is talking about things that are happening to the youth *today*!' They referred to him in the present tense, though they all knew he was dead.

'Bob is a liar,' said Faks calmly.

'Bob Marley is a terrorist and a gangster,' said Famara Bajie, who tended the doctor's garden. 'That man is a big mafia.'

A young girl sat in the corner of Demba's room, smirking slightly at the ridiculous conversations taking place around her (ridiculous as they were in part intended to be, to provide people with some amusement). No one paid any attention to her. I asked her if she was Demba's girlfriend. She laughed. 'I am his sister.'

She told me that her name was Mayi Faye. One could tell from her surname that she was a Serer. Demba was a Jola. How could she be his sister?

She was there all evening, saying nothing, and largely ignored by the card players and the conversationalists. Demba was nowhere to be seen. In the morning she had disappeared as abruptly as she had arrived.

Demba was very quiet and moody for some days after that.

'She is part of my extended family,' he said.

He pouted thoughtfully, as he stared into space.

'Is she not your girlfriend?' I asked.

He laughed. 'You are observant,' he said wonderingly. 'Very observant!' He sighed. 'You know my real family is not from Sibanor. They live in a very small village in the bush. My father, my real father, and this girl's father were very close friends. But her father had no sons, only daughters. So he asked my father for a child to bring up. So I grew up in that man's house in Sibanor, and until I was twelve, I did not know that they were not my real family. I believed that this girl was my sister.

'There is a joking relationship between the Jolas and the Serers, because in the ancient time we were one people. We spoke the same language. Then we divided. The Serers went one way, and we went the other. So now we can say anything we want to provoke them, and they to us, and nobody can be punished for that.

'But I never joke with the Serers, because when I was a child, they did everything for me. Even now I feel more for these people than for my own family.

'This girl came here to ask me to marry her. I was very annoyed. I am already married – to my father's sister's daughter. I cannot take two wives.' She had wanted to sleep with him, but he had sent her to stay with Daouda's wives. He said she only wanted to sleep with him so that he would make her pregnant, and then he would be forced to marry her. 'But she is seventeen. She is still at school. Anyway I do not want to sleep with her. In the morning I told her she must leave. She did not want to go. She cried. But I told her she must go.'

What had caused this mysterious desperation?

'I don't know.'

Wouldn't she mind having to leave school, if she became pregnant?

'Maybe she feels she is not very good at school.' He tutted. 'I'm not happy about it.'

The bakery had collapsed during a storm. There would be no more bread till it was rebuilt, and who knew how long that would take? It was with a feeling almost of relief that I stopped worrying about the villagers and began to wonder where my own nutriment would be coming from.

Two days later, rice arrived in the village. It was aid rice from Japan. The President had decreed that it must go first to the interior, so that the people of the villages would have rice for Tobaski. It was brought to the headman's compound, where the sacks were distributed according to the size of each compound.

And strange to say, it had no discernible impact on the behaviour of the people of the village. As hunger had been endured without tears, so it ended almost without comment, like a pain which, having driven one to the brink of death, cannot be recalled the moment it has passed.

In the urban centres on the coast, the time of the Tobaski prayer at each of the big mosques was announced over the radio. In Dulaba, boys were sent to each of the compounds to inform people that the time had come. Then everyone would make their way to the praying ground, led by the elders of their compound – always making sure to return by a different route, because the Prophet Mohammed had been warned by an angel, in a dream, that his enemies were waiting to attack him on his way from the mosque. So he had gone home by another pathway, and lived to tell the tale.

Almost all of the Staff had returned to their own villages for the feast, so it was only Daouda, his cousin Ousmane Koujabi, whom he had commanded to stay with him, and myself, who made our way along the back lane from the Quarters to the mosque. The boy, Alhaji, followed, carrying a large rolled prayer mat balanced on his head. The other two wore jackets and baggy trousers of traditional cut, while I wore a long gown and a curious tall cap, both of a deep bottle green. I looked like some vaguely ecclesiastical figure from the background of a quattrocento genre painting; in a word, I looked absurd.

We arrived to find the men of the village, all in their smartest robes, already filling the praying ground. They sat calmly waiting, some murmuring prayers as they flicked slowly through their rosaries. Several 'automatic' black umbrellas, unraised, stood spike downwards in the earth at the front of the throng. In the burial ground, the area of earth that lay immediately between us and the Holy City, the green weeds stood thick and tall among the baobabs.

The Imam began to pray, and we followed him, not in absolute unison, but each at his own rate, so that the low murmuring seemed to pass over us like a succession of grey waves.

A group of the elders crowded around the Imam and placed a white sheet over him, while he read a sermon from the Koran. Then it was all over, and everyone had risen, and was shaking hands with everyone else. The great kettle-drum sounded twice from the compound of Fili Kunda, and between the milling robed figures I saw a flash of crimson, as the blood came gushing from the neck of a sheep. It collapsed, and lay twitching, as the crimson stain spread over the dust. The Imam's sheep had been killed, and now everyone else was free to slaughter theirs. Everywhere one looked, blood was spilling, necks were being twisted. And then the knives went immediately to work.

'Today is a day when we are definitely asked to give out charity,' said Alioune Sware, the MRC driver, as he sat on the spacious verandah of his house in Sanyang Kunda, hacking up the last of the carcass. He handed pieces of the meat to his wife, an enormous, violet woman, who sat stir-frying them on a tiny charcoal stove. He handed her the head. As it blackened, she languorously scraped off the fur. Soon the outer casing of the horns came off. Alioune held them in front of my face. 'These are the horns,' he said. I wasn't sure how to respond, so I just said, 'Yeah.'

The skin of the animal lay, fur downwards, on the verandah. On its slippery, blood-skeined surface Alioune made up piles of the offal, intestines and neck he was now dividing with vigorous strokes of his cutlass. A boy holding a tin tray leaned expectantly against one of the pillars, watching his every move. Alioune was one of the staff members who owned a house in the village. He was about forty; a broad, vigorous, handsome man. As a child he had been apprenticed to a marabout in the upper reaches of the river, but he had run away to the coast, where he had learnt to drive, and taught himself to read and write in English. In the Gambia, where they held the entire transport system in their hands, drivers had a particular reputation for rapacity. Alioune was no exception. Yet you knew that when he took advantage of you – which he inevitably would – he would do it in a thoroughly amiable way.

'I saw you praying in your gown this morning,' he said, wincing as a fragment of meat went shooting past his head. 'It looked very beautiful. Everybody said so.' I thanked him for this obvious mendacity. In Africa there was no such thing as positive criticism. There was praise and insults, and not much in between.

He gave two of the piles to the boy, who sped off with them. 'These are for people who could not afford to kill a goat of their own,' he said. 'We are definitely asked to do this.'

He led me into the house. We sat down on the bed, and he handed me a large chunk of liver. 'This is the liver,' he said. 'Traditionally it is the first part of the animal to be cooked. I think it is the nicest part.' It was delicious.

In Dulaba, few children had new clothes for Tobaski, but everyone at least ate well. All afternoon boys scurried back and forth along the green lanes behind the compounds, clutching handfuls of raw meat to give to relatives. Young girls sauntered up the streets, basins of cooked food on their heads. And in the compounds, the children wandered around polishing their naked, bloated stomachs with their hands.

Binta Sise's husband could not afford to kill an animal. So as there was no cooking to be done, she spent the morning sprawled on her bed, chatting to neighbours and relatives who called in to see her. In the afternoon she went over to Fatounding's, where she and Fatounding and Isatou and Sajonding Minte spent the rest of the day plaiting each other's hair. The compound was no tidier than it was on any other day of the year. Flies buzzed over the goat's intestines and blood splattered over the floor.

Fatounding's husband Kalamatta pegged out the skin of the goat he had killed to dry in the sun. On this, the prayer day, he had discarded his usual tatty gown in favour of a European shirt and a pair of purple Sta-prest trousers. He went about his work in silence, his movements agile but unhurried, exuding as usual an air of self-containment and indif-ference. Not for the first time I wondered what this man was to these women. What he was even doing there. For his wives and their guests paid no more attention to him than he did to them. Each party carried on as though the other did not exist. And dressed as they were today, in the styles of different worlds, it was difficult even to accommodate them in the same frame, to see them as part of the same reality.

The following day the Saniyoro Kafo went to weed their groundnut field for the second time. The afternoon was well advanced by the time I arrived, but there was still a lot of ground to be covered, and they would stay there till it was all completed. Jarra Njai led me to a bowl of rice porridge lying under a tree. She lifted a small gourdful and handed it to me. I said I was full.

'No, no,' she said. 'Now you are a member of the kafo. We have all drunk. You also must drink.'

There was much fun that afternoon: much laughter and provocation, much slapping and chasing. A rainbow stood over the village in a sky of deep azure. The emerald crops, the gleaming red and green foliage of the mango trees, the brightly coloured clothes of the women; everything took its place in the intense evening sunlight, like parts of an immense glistening tapestry.

That night I was violently sick. Whether or not it was the porridge, I don't know, but as I lay on the bathroom floor I felt as though there was an animal inside me, at least two thirds my own size, that was trying to get out through my throat.

*

It was some weeks later that I began to understand more about Demba's life. We were sitting in his room one evening, leafing through his photograph album. There were about twenty photographs, mostly of people I had never seen, and who seemed to have only a tenuous relationship to him. A few showed him posed with various Europeans who had worked in the camp over the years. Towards the end was a Polaroid snap of a serious-looking young man in western clothes, squatting on a carpet of Islamic design, with a rosary in his right hand. 'This is my elder brother, the one just above me. He was the one in our family who studied Arabic, while I studied English.

'He went to Libya, looking for work. That is where this photograph was taken. Before that he was in Nigeria. He died in Libya. So I did not see him for three years before he died. It was in 1984 – of an illness.'

He pointed to a suitcase on top of the wardrobe.

'That suitcase belonged to him. They sent it for me. That is all there was.

'The wife I have now was to have been his wife. And when he died, I had to marry her, because I am the next in line. That is the way of our culture. I could not avoid it. That girl who came here – Mayi – she was my wife, my intended wife. But when my brother died, I had to give her up, and take his wife.

'But Mayi will not accept it. That is why she came here. I was very upset and annoyed that she came. In the end I had to drive her away.'

He looked again at his brother's picture.

'I had lent him two thousand dalasis of the money I had saved to go to England, so that he could go to Libya. When he died that money was lost – because he could not pay it back. And I had to take his wife, so I decided to build a compound in Serekunda with the money that was left.

'Now everything is ended. Soon my passport will expire, and I know that I am never going to go anywhere.'

I realized then the futility of ambition in such a society – the utter fatuity of attempting to own one's own destiny.

The Saturday evening following Tobaski, I returned to Fatounding's compound, 'to chat'. And when the bowls had been cleared away Fatounding settled herself with the baby on her back. 'Now,' she said. 'I'm ready to chat till morning.' A full moon was rising, throwing a hazy steaming brilliance over the corrugated-iron roofs.

The rice they had just eaten was almost the last of the aid rice. Now what were they going to do?

'When are you going to let us have some of that rice you are keeping in Europe?' asked the mother-in-law, N'na.

I said the rice they had just been eating was not from Europe, but from Japan.

'Where is Japan?' asked Fatounding.

I said that Japan was more than three times as far from London as London was from the Gambia. There were general exclamations of astonishment, and of the greatness of God.

There was some discussion about the great wealth to be found in Europe. I tried to explain that not everyone in Europe was rich.

'But the people who make the money,' said Isatou. 'They are rich!'

I'd heard this argument many times before, even from relatively well-educated Gambians. It was difficult to make people believe that even though the Gambia's currency was printed in England, not all English people had access to unlimited amounts of banknotes.

A young man who was studying English at the coast came into the yard and joined the conversation. He started talking about the Falklands war. 'You beat those people very well,' he said.

'You were fighting!' said Fatounding with alarm. 'Were you killing each other?'

We were, of course.

'Mbe kumbo,' she said. 'I'm crying.'

6

THE BIG PEOPLE OF GOD

In some parts of Africa, the whole of the countryside owes allegiance to a religious leader, each person offering up a share of their harvest so that they can share in the blessings of the great ones. These leaders, marabouts as they are called, have replaced the great kings of Africa, the owners of the earth, who had used their spiritual powers to guide themselves and their people.

The people of Dulaba, however, acknowledged no power – indeed they were scarcely aware of any authority – outside their own village. They had of course heard of Mecca – Makkah, as they called it – but they could no more imagine what it was like than they could imagine what Europe was like. Alahira – the next world – had for them a far more concrete and immediate reality. No one from Dulaba had ever made the Haj, but they would all, they hoped, be going to heaven.

Although they no longer worshipped their ancestors, they retained a sense of their village as the entity that had given them life. They believed that their village was itself important to God. They believed themselves to be purer and more pious in their religion than the people of the surrounding villages – even than their relatives in Karafa Kunda. And they said that Dulaba was a holy place – that God answered the prayers that were offered in its mosque.

The people had accepted the authority of the tubabs. Indeed, they had welcomed it (since what could not be avoided must be welcomed), and they had elected one of their number to liaise with these strangers and the independent government who had succeeded them. He was known as the *alkalo* – the headman – or the 'tubab alkalo'.

There was, however, another headman, the *sate-tio* – the owner of the village – whose identity was known only to the people of the village, and who presided over those matters which were between the villagers alone, and must be kept from all outsiders. Traditionally this person was the oldest member of the Minte family, because at the founding of the village the leader of the Sise family had stood up and said that he did not care who was the headman, but he must be the Imam of the village until the end of the world – because his family had been Imams since they came from Manding. So it was that the Sises led the village in prayer, while the Mintes led them in politics.

The present elder of the Minte family, however, was a scholar of some renown in the region, and he had given the position of sate-tio to his younger brother, so that his own mind would be free for prayer.

For more than twenty years, the elders had refused to allow a government school to be built in the village. They had survived since the foundation of the village through prayer. They had needed no other knowledge, no other learning. And they believed that if the young people were educated in the way of the tubabs, they would leave the village. Their village would die. Their world would die with it, and their children who had followed the tubabs' road would go straight to hell. The scholar, Fa Salifa Minte, was among those who had most vehemently opposed the building of the European school, and since it had existed, no child from his compound had attended it.

He was now the oldest person in the village, and he rarely left his compound, except to go to the mosque, where he would sometimes stay for days on end, praying and fasting. I had seen him once early in my stay, walking not far from the mosque – a tall, very thin figure in an immaculately ironed robe of pale blue, carrying a staff and a copy of the Koran wrapped in cloth balanced on his head. He seemed to me to be a figure straight out of myth – standing there in his long robe against the shimmering landscape. And though he greeted me warmly, shaking hands at the beginning and the end of our brief meeting, in the manner prescribed for Muslims, he did not appear to take in the details of my presence, as though he had not the language to describe them. I was just a tubab, and that was all he could say about me.

His compound was situated in the centre of the village, and his house was situated in the very middle of that compound, its entrance hidden by a screen of millet stalks. The first room was empty, its mud walls unplastered, its earth floor bare and uneven. The second room was filled with smoke, curling in thick whorls from a fire in the middle of the floor, over which the old marabout sat crouched. It was raining outside, and only a thin, grey light from the small window filtered through the smoke, but I could see that this room was as bare as the first, except for a bed of branches in one corner. The marabout peered at us rather blankly through the smoke. What did we want with him, this tubab – this half-devil – and this young black, educated in the ways of swindlers and the drinkers of alcohol? Not that he resented our intrusion. Luck followed people like us. We were rich.

The old man's gown was filthy. The ashes of the fire spilled over onto the worn, brittle sheepskin on which he was sitting. Nearby lay the battered tin kettle from which he performed his ablutions. Crouching, he seemed quite tiny, his limbs almost skeletal. He was a most unusual-looking man. His face was very small, his small but full lips pursing themselves almost fastidiously. It was a feature I had noticed on many of the younger women, and it was strange to think that many of them had sprung in part from the loins of this frail old man. Beside him Sanyang looked almost indecently robust, but he kept his eyes lowered out of respect.

'Will we remain here?' asked the old man, his thin, cracked voice surprisingly loud and authoritative. 'Will we remain on this earth forever? We will not. The world is going to end, and all those who have refused to obey God's words will be thrown into the fire. This is why people are thinking of Alahira, the next world. That is the only place they should be thinking of.

'God has made the universe, and everything in the universe is made by God. He has made seven skies, with seven earths, and each of the seven earths is filled with angels. All these angels and God himself are watching the people and what they are doing. If you refuse to pray, and if you refuse to do what the Muslim religion says, there is no way you can avoid it – you must go in the fire.'

Was there any other purpose in studying the Koran, other than to go to Heaven?

'Only to follow God and Mohammed.'

And what was the purpose of that?

'For heaven – for Alahira.'

It was more than seventy years since he had begun to study the Koran. They had written the name of God on his hand to show that he was now a student.

When he was young, he had gone to the bush to farm, but later in life he had left the village in search of knowledge. That was the way they did it. Anyone who wanted to learn must go out and find a teacher, somewhere away from where they lived – so that they would not be disturbed by the demands of their families, and their minds would be free to learn.

He spent eleven years in Jarra, living in his teacher's compound. Every Thursday he would work in his teacher's field. Six days he would work for himself, and the seventh for his teacher. Then, from two to five, every day except Thursday, they would study. After the five o'clock prayer, they would study again until they saw the red sun. There were more than eighty people learning in that compound. That man was a very great marabout. He had been to Mecca twice.

Twenty years ago he had returned from that place, and that was the time he had become the head of this compound. He had not known he would become the head of this compound. Only God knew.

I wondered what exactly it was that he had learned while he was with his teacher.

'Only to pray and to read the Holy Koran. God has asked us to follow the Prophet Mohammed, therefore we should read the Koran. When we die they will ask each of us what our purpose has been in earth. And I will say, "Only to follow God and the Prophet Mohammed."'

The focus of their religion appeared to be entirely on the next world. When they referred to the earth, they were referring not to the physical environment of the planet, but to the state before Alahira: the state in which they would perform the actions which determined whether they would go to heaven or hell. It didn't matter how virtuous, how kind or selfless or industrious a person had been on the earth, if they had not prayed, if they had not fasted, it was of no use. This is why old people were so pious, why they followed the observances of their religion so strictly: they wanted to have an adequate number of blessings to take to God. And that is why people were so desolate when a young person died: the number of blessings they would have acquired would be relatively few.

The more I observed of the practice of Islam in Dulaba, the less I could see that it involved anything other than the mechanical rehearsing of these formalities. Did it offer no spiritual sustenance for this world?

'Sometimes people come to me and ask me to pray for them. People come even from Kombo so that I can pray for them.'

Did he mean that he was a marabout?

'God will never speak to a human being. We will never sit and hear God talking to us. He will only give you signs. It is in these books that he has given us to use that people will find these signs. The Koran will tell you how the sign comes which will tell you whatever you need to know.'

Some people came to him for *lastakah*. If they were in two minds about a problem, they would tell him, and before going to bed, he would read certain prayers from the Koran, asking the Almighty God to help him find the answer to this person's problem. During the night it would come to him in the form of a dream. 'If you want to marry a certain woman, I will be able to tell you whether or not you will be in peace with her. And I will tell you the charities that must be given. If I see something good in my dream, I will also see the charity you must give to make it happen. And if I see something evil, I will tell you the charity you must give to prevent it.'

The Imam of Dulaba was naturally also a marabout, but although he had studied for twenty years with a famous teacher in the eastern part of the province, he was modest about his powers. In the adjacent yard, however, there lived a much younger man, who, it was said, was being visited by people from all parts of the country. He spent most of his time in Serekunda, but when he was in Dulaba he was often to be seen at the thatched bantaba near Binta Sise's house – a tall, burly figure, very black, with a broad, almost babyish face, and a ringing, confident laugh.

'The marabouts,' he said, 'are the scientists of the blacks. The knowledge and the intelligence of the Europeans have been given to them by God. So God has given us certain symbols that we can use. He has even given us his name in the Holy Koran so that we can solve the problems of the world.'

Now I understood what they meant when they talked of 'using' the Koran. They weren't reading it in the hope that through perusing its truths they might imbibe some vague sense of moral or spiritual well-being. They were taking parts of it and tying them to their bodies, that they might avail themselves physically of its powers. For there were certain secrets in the Koran that could be used to effect anything, good or evil, that a human being might need or desire on this earth. But it was only the marabouts who knew what they were; it was only they who knew how to use the different texts and different names of God. They would write upon a piece of paper, a *safo* – from the verb *safiro*, to write – which was then taken to a shoemaker to be sewn into a piece of leather. Sometimes the signs would be washed from the paper with holy water to prevent an enemy from knowing the purpose of the safo. A *na-so* – a liquid juju – was made by writing on a wooden board with a mixture of soot and water. The text was washed from the board, and the patient made to bathe in the water or drink it. When people travelled, they often carried these potions in bottles to protect themselves.

Herbalism was a science quite different from the knowledge of the marabouts. But in Africa, pieces of leaf or root were often incorporated into safos, and the herbalists themselves would often use prayer as part of their treatment. Other objects which were believed to have 'power' were also used by the marabouts: certain shells, stones, horns, furs. To make a *balantango*, a juju to prevent a bullet from entering the human body, it was necessary to use part of the shroud of a virtuous woman. Different parts of the body were believed to have different 'functions', and in some parts of Africa, murder was not unknown to obtain the relevant members. The people of the Gambia, however, were afraid of God, and while there were certain names of God that could be used to kill a person, they believed that any marabout who used them would go straight to hell.

'Everyone in this country, whether Christian or Muslim, is wearing a juju,' said the marabout. 'This is because God's medicine and the tubab's medicine are not the same. There are certain sicknesses that the marabouts cannot cure. There are certain diseases also that the tubabs cannot cure. If a person is attacked by a witch or a devil, they cannot be cured by the tubabs. They have to find a marabout who knows the name of God to call that devil to come out.'

Likunda was the largest of the compounds, and the richest, by virtue of its herd of cattle, which was far larger than any of the others owned by the village. These animals were hardly ever killed, and their milk was kept and sold by the Fulani herdsmen who tended them. So the people of the compound saw very little benefit from this wealth. Nonetheless, it was one of the more salubrious compounds in the village, and there were now more than twenty houses within the compass of its main yard. Its head, Fa Sunkary Sise, was one of the most influential people in the village. He could be seen unfailingly, five times a day, leading a little group of the other compound elders to and from the mosque, wearing almost always the same gown of a dull pale orange, his hands clasped behind his back, fingering the beads of his long rosary. He was a tall, spare man, his gaunt face dominated by a large, almost proboscoid nose, down which he peered at one, his slanting eyes gleaming readily, his thin lips stretching into a smile of beatific amusement. Of all the people I have ever met, he was one of the most gracious, and the one who exuded the greatest sense of confidence in his own masculinity.

He was the second oldest man in the village. He did not know his age in years, but he knew that he had been born three years after the white people had been killed at Sankandi. Sankandi was twelve miles away, at the junction of the red laterite road and the main tar road. There in 1901 Travelling Commissioners Sitwell and Silva were killed, along with Sergeant Cox and five constables of the Gambia police force, while attempting to intervene in a dispute over a rice field between the local marabouts and the pagans of Jattaba. They had been invited to a meeting at Sankandi, and as they approached the bantaba, the marabouts opened fire. In the subsequent reprisals, the village was levelled to the ground by the authorities.

Sitwell's successor, Captain Leese, was the first European to enter the hinterland of Kiang. By that time Fa Sunkary was a young man.

'When he came to the district, all the young men of the villages from here to Tankular would hold a meeting to say that Captain Leese was coming. Then in the morning we would go to him, and carry his loads through the district from village to village. When he reached Tankular, the people from that end of Kiang would carry his loads to the other villages: Brong, Karantaba, Janneh Kunda. Then when he was returning through Mankono, we would meet him and escort him back to the road. That was how we did things in those days. We went everywhere by foot, and we carried everything on our heads. If we wanted to go to Kombo, it would take us four days.'

He had been the compound head for only four years, but as his uncle had been of feeble mind, he had been the effective head of the people for over a quarter of a century.

When he awoke, early in the morning, he would go from house to house, telling them that it was time to pray. When they returned from the mosque, the elders of the compound would meet in his house, and they would pray to each other – not kneeling, but raising their palms towards heaven as they exchanged blessings. Then the women of the compound would all come and greet him.

It was the duty of the compound head to advise the compound people about what they should and should not do. If he heard that anyone was doing anything they should not do, he would call them to his house and talk to them. And if anyone in the compound had a problem, they would come and tell him, and he would take on the responsibility of trying to solve it. If they wanted to marry, for instance, he would send a message to the girl's parents.

During his childhood, and even twenty years ago, the young men would work for the head of their compound. They would plant a large groundnut field and a large millet field for him, and they would spend one day every week working on it. The young men would work always as a group, working on each other's farms in rotation. But now this never happened. Each man concentrated on his own problems, and if the compound leader was old, his son would have to feed him.

In those days, if you disobeyed the elders you would be beaten till you thought you were going to die. Now, if you beat a child, you would be taken to court. It was hard to bring up a child in this generation, because although the world itself had remained the same, the people – the generation – had changed. In his time, they had never gone anywhere. Now the young people were leaving the village during the dry season. And when they returned, they wanted to hold dances. Since their ancestors' time they had not held dances in that village. But now the young people wanted to do it. And they wanted to wear European clothes.

I wondered why that was.

He laughed. 'It is because of you. The children have seen you people, the way you act and the way you dress, and they have tried to follow you.'

Was that good or bad?

'It is good. Because it cannot be avoided. And if you people keep on coming here, they will continue to do it. Because they cannot avoid it.'

The people of Likunda had been strong supporters of the school from the beginning. Before it was built, Fa Sunkary had sent his younger sons to the school at Joli.'And in the end it had been built because the elders had seen that if it was not, even more of the children would leave in search of education.

Fa Sunkary's younger brother, Momodou Karamo, a short, tough-looking man in his early sixties, was the president of the Parent Teachers Association. If anything in the school was damaged, he would organize the villagers to mend it. Recently he had been at the centre of a great controversy, when the Department of Community Development had proposed to build a Community Centre in the village.

There had been many among the elders who had vehemently opposed the idea of such a centre. They said it would be used only for harlotry and the drinking of alcohol. But Momodou had seen that this development would be a great blessing. As a citizen, he had to make sure that this blessing came to his village.

The argument had gone on for some months. Finally the opponents of the centre had called upon the local MP, who also happened to be the Vice-President, to intervene. The ITC, another foreign organization, were planning to build a veterinary centre on the edge of the bush beyond the MRC compound, which would be another great blessing for the village. The Vice-President said that if the Community Centre was not built, the ITC camp would also not be built. The opposition had not felt able to say anything more on the matter.

They had, however, buried jujus on the site of the Centre, to prevent it from being built. But Momodou had not been afraid. He knew there was only one God. Now the Community Centre was built and nobody could say anything about it.

Mba Jongmar Sise was the oldest woman in the village. She knew that because all the people of her age-group, all the girls who had been given in marriage at the same time as her, were now dead.

She lived in the compound of Sanyang Kunda, in a yard belonging to her son. She had had four husbands, all from that compound, and now, in extreme old age, she could rest. She spent most of her time sitting on the verandah of the house of the women, her face set in a mask of extreme bleakness. It was right for an old person to feel fear. Soon she would die, and no one knew what she would face there. Whether she'd led a good life, or a bad life, only God could say. For no matter how steadfastly a person had held to the observances of the religion, they could not know whether God had accepted their prayers and their fasting.

'When I was a girl, we did not know about these tubabs and their medicines. If we were ill we would be taken to the marabouts. The first thing I can remember is that I had a fit, and I was paralysed down one side of my body. I was taken by my parents to a marabout in Karafa Kunda – at that time there was a great marabout living there. He covered me in leaves. He bathed me with them, and then I drank it. I stayed there for three months. Then I recovered and I returned to Dulaba. I was in my eighth year.

'In those days we did not know about the tubabs at all. If they had colonized the country, we did not know about it. And even if they had come into the interior, they never came here.

'In those days people did only what their forefathers had done. If your father had not been a blacksmith or a weaver, you could not do those things. And in this village we know only farming. If you see a blacksmith you will know he is from Karafa Kunda or Tankular. This is because there were no blacksmiths among the people who founded this village. And we will never marry them. They will marry only another blacksmith.

'Then, people respected their parents. They believed what their parents told them. But now they say they want to learn to drive a car. They want to learn to build a house. Everyone is saying they want to do it. And they refuse to farm. How can such people be brought up? How can they be blessed by God, if they refuse their parents? It would be better for those people to stay and farm, and pray to God with their parents, rather than everyone going away.

'The first tubab to come here was Captain Leese. He was the leader of the tubabs at that time. When we saw him, we would all run, shouting, "Tubabo fele! Tubabo fele!" – "The white man is here! The white man is here!" You had to run because it scared your heart. For you had never seen such a person before – his colour and his hair.

'When the tubabs came again, they came with lorries. Makriko came. He was a doctor. He was the one who built this camp here. By that time we were not afraid of them. We were fully grown up. We just stood and watched them, and wondered how they made their skins that colour. Did they pour hot water on their bodies? We stood by that baobab tree opposite the gates, and watched them building the camp. We saw them putting in their machine [the generator]. But we did not go any closer because we were told that rays came from it, and if they touched you, you would die. In those days, if a child stood too close to a tubab, its parents would tell it to move away, because still we did not know what they were. And women never went into the camp. It was not like now when people are always going in and out of that place. If Makriko needed the women, he would come into the village.

'Every year we transplanted our rice to Tankular. That place is a long way from here, but at certain times of the year we would have to go there every day. We would get up in the middle of the night to cook lunch, and we would leave before the first cock crowed. Sometimes we would arrive there before it was even light. We would leave there late in the afternoon, and arrive back here as it was getting dark. And during the harvest time you would be carrying a big basin of rice on your head.

'Since I was a girl I worked hard. What I could not do, I would not do. But what I could do, I would do it. Even now, what I can do, I will do it. The work I have done has been very hard.

'Women work harder than men because they can pound, they can sweep the compound, they can draw water, they can cook, they can go to the rice field. Women should work harder than men. From the day you are transferred to your husband you should work hard so that when you die God will bless you. If you make your husband happy, God will bless you. That's why women work hard.

'I had eleven children. Some died. I was left with three. Some died immediately after they were born. Some died when they were five, some when they were six. Three of them were women and they died with their husbands after they had been transferred. One of them had three children, the other had eight children before she died. I felt sad. But the sadness had a limit, because it was God who gave me those children. And when it was time, it could not be avoided.'

She had been married for four years before she finally transferred to her husband's compound. Had she been happy about that?

'If I tell you I was happy, what will you do? If I tell you I was unhappy, what will you do?'

Nothing.

'So! My husband was handsome. He was fair in complexion. So I was happy.'

Would she have been happy if he'd been ugly?

'If they give you an ugly wife, will you be happy about it?' She gave a wheezing laugh, and it was as though another force had entered her – as though it were painfully wrenching the muscles of her face into the image of someone completely different: the face of a young, impish girl, someone who had once been extravagantly, irreverently humorous. Then she winced, and the image vanished as quickly as it had appeared. The husband, she said, had treated her very wickedly. He had beaten her, not with a stick or with his hand, but with a rope made from baobab bark. Now, however, it was time for her to pray.

The following day we returned, but she told us that she would not be able to answer any more questions. It made her laugh, and when she laughed, her chest hurt terribly.

House One was being eaten by insects. Termites were burrowing up the insides of the walls, their trails of brittle, red dust spreading out from fissures in the plaster like veins. Ants poured out of holes in the concrete floor, leaving heaps of dust to mark their excavations. These were frequently swept away, only to reappear half an hour later. Every few years, a portion of the house that had become particularly fragile would be replaced. So the house was constantly in the process of being rebuilt.

It was the oldest house in the compound; McGregor had stayed there when he first came to Dulaba. In those days there was no air-conditioning. During the dry season, the Europeans threw buckets of water over the floors to try to cool the atmosphere, and in the rainy season the humidity made it difficult to sleep at all.

Like all of the houses it was crawling with animals. Sometimes I would get up in the middle of the night, and find the interior walls covered with lizards and toads. Susan Lawrence had complained of an odd taste to her water, and had later found three monkeys dead in her water tank. And the roofs were full of rats – of considerable size judging by the amount of noise they made. Sometimes it sounded as though there were several young children crashing around up there. Richard had seen a monitor lizard two feet long crawling from the eaves of his house, and thought the din that came from his ceiling at night was caused by the rats and the lizard fighting.

Then there were the 'blister beetles'. These were olive green, with narrow bodies an inch or two in length, and large round heads. The whole organism was modelled with exquisite clarity, like a monster from a 1950s sci-fi movie. They flew very slowly and were constantly crashing into things because of their poor vision. On contact with human skin they caused blisters which could reach to up to a foot in diameter. One had to knock them onto the ground without touching them, and then crush them with the sole of a shoe – which made a loud crunching noise. These were the insects which had been eating the village's millet and sorghum crops for the last three years.

At the beginning of September the maize harvest began, and the period of hunger came to an end. The maize was much harder than European and North American varieties, and unsuitable for boiling. Instead it was roasted over braziers, and everywhere the young children could be seen sinking their teeth into the frizzled cobs.

When I went into Natoma's compound, I found her mother and all the children of the compound sitting deseeding the raw cobs into a huge enamel basin. It was difficult work, as I discovered when I joined them, and soon my nails were bleeding. But they worked with great enthusiasm. Mariatou, the niece, was sitting on the opposite side of the basin. She smiled. 'Kongko a tata,' she said, gesturing off into the middle distance. 'Hunger has gone.'

The raw grain was pounded into a fine flour which was steamed to make *futo*. Some evenings we would gather round our basin in Demba's room, and lift the lid to find it full of this futo, which in this state reminded me of the granular substance used to fill cracks in window frames. To the excitement of all, water would be added – not too much and not too little – and mixed into it. Then Sirrah or Ndey-Touti would come in with a bowl of thin leaf sauce – like algid pond slime – or a thin, hot groundnut sauce, and pour it over the mixture. We dug our hands into the sludgy mass, piling it into our mouths with our fingers. There was something marvellously satisfying and reassuring about this food, and we ate it with a sense of exultation, for the appearance of the futo signified the end of hunger – the end of suffering.

Since Ibou Sanyang's return from leave my life at the Quarters had become easier. His presence seemed to lighten the mood of the place. He had returned more bumptious and voluble than when he went away – or so it seemed to me. He had had his head shaved, which made him look gnomishly, almost threateningly thick-set, and at the same time it was all of a piece with his clownish antics. He was forever getting up to make speeches on Rastafarianism and 'Africanism', designed to provoke and amuse his pious Muslim companions. He would dance grotesquely and sing along to the songs emanating from the cassette player. One couldn't help laughing.

I began to find that place, in which I had once felt so unsure, a warm and welcoming environment; the people gathering in the friendly glow of the electric light on the edge of the immense, implacable blackness of the bush. It was a society in which anyone could get up and dance whenever they felt like it; their action would not be condemned as exhibitionism, but welcomed as adding to the 'sweetness' of the environment.

Often I would arrive at the Quarters to find what looked like violent arguments taking place, with everyone shouting at everyone else at the tops of their voices. But I soon realized that these discourses were held purely for enjoyment. *Kacha* – chatting, gossip, discourse – talk for the sake of the way it sounded rather than what it meant – talk as pure entertainment was the television of Africa. And it was perhaps this physical pleasure in the use of words that made it relatively easy for people to learn new languages. For everyone at the Quarters spoke at least three languages, and some as many as six. A good talker was highly valued socially, and Sanyang naturally considered himself an expert.

He was fond of saying that no witch could kill him because he didn't believe in them; though he was also fond of saying that his father was a *kunfanunte* – one of those who had the power to see witches, who had been given second sight by God so that they could protect themselves and their families. Like many I met, he was full of stories of the supernatural – of lorries that drove by themselves, of disappearing penises, of creatures that were half-man, half-hyena – and indeed of witchcraft itself. In Africa witchcraft was a physical propensity, sometimes hereditary, always malevolent. Witches killed their victims by stealing their souls, then ate their flesh. And while I met relatively few people who claimed to have actually seen such things, it was pointless to ask people if they believed in them. It would be like asking a European if they *believed* in atomic power.

The preparation of Chinese tea – *attaya* – was, to those who could afford it, an essential adjunct to any social occasion. Indeed the lengthy, not to say laborious process was highly valued as a social ritual in its own right. The tea – 'Green Gunpowder' was the favourite – was brewed up strong in a tiny enamel teapot with vast quantities of sugar – the dark liquid endlessly poured and repoured, heated and reheated, until it was finally decanted into three tiny glasses, always from a great height, so that it maintained a good head of yellow froth. These were passed round on a tin tray to the first three people present, who would swipe them abruptly, so that the glasses made an arrogant clanking sound on the edge of the tray. The tea was sucked swiftly and noisily, and the glasses placed back on the tray with a resounding crash. They were then washed and further servings distributed. All in all, the leaves would be brewed up three times, a process which could take as long as two hours; the brew becoming progressively weaker and, to my mind, more palatable. Sometimes fresh mint was added, which was quite delicious, or the leaves would be boiled a fourth time with evaporated milk, which was less so.

People attributed all kinds of physical and even philosophical benefits to this beverage. The young men said they could not go a day without it, and seemed to regard it as a kind of moral and cultural 'right', rather as certain Englishmen view bitter beer, although it had been brought among them by the Moors only relatively recently.

And all the time a game of cards would be in progress – never for money, as gambling was forbidden by the Koran, but the play couldn't have been more serious if millions had been at stake. 'Crazy Eight' was the favourite, and almost the only, game. It was fast and, as far as I could gather, extremely monotonous. The shuffling was brisk, and the cards, an old French pack which had become thick and unpleasant to handle, and from which the images were quickly disappearing, were hurled down onto the table with an almost violent flourish. There was a great deal of banter and psyching of opponents, involving the frequent use of English proverbs: 'The proof of the pudding is in the eating,' 'He who pays the piper calls the tune.' Someone else would be keeping the score, often adding a commentary of his own, to the irritation of the players. Reggae and Senegalese pop came jangling from the cassette player. Cheating was allowed if you could get away with it.

Daouda's rooms were in the middle of the long blockhouse. A thick iron door had been set up as a seat beside the verandah in front of it, and this provided a focus for the social life of the place. If the insects were not too numerous, the attaya, which at the Quarters was a nightly ritual, would be prepared there, in the company of the women – the staff wives.

Sirrah Bajie, Daouda's first wife, was naturally the first lady of the place. She was a tall, strapping woman, commanding by virtue of her size, but ironically and benevolently humorous in her manner. She was from Daouda's father's village, in the Gambian area of Fonyi, while Ndey-Touti, the second wife, was from his mother's village in the Casamance, the village from which Ousmane Koujabi also came. She was so slender, one would not have thought her arms capable of lifting the great basins of water she carried on her head, and she was, as the poem says, 'beautiful, as a dream in stone', her features having that quality of smoothness and stillness, that immemorial placidity one sees in certain Egyptian sculptures – a quality that each of her three children also possessed to some degree. She described herself as an *arajana muso* – a woman who was living for heaven. Yet she was far from docile, and if you said or did anything to offend her, you would soon know about it.

As for the third wife . . . Daouda's third wife was Barbara Smith, the midwife. But that is a different story.

It seemed that every Monday during the rainy season, someone died in the clinic. The patients were brought in from Mankono and Karafa Kunda by Land Rover, every Monday, Wednesday and Friday. And because of the gap of the weekend, Monday was always the busiest day. During the rainy season, the queue stretched out of the lab, along the front of the building, down the side of my garden, and almost to the compound gates. Those that could manage it sat slumped against the walls and fences; those that couldn't just lay on the ground, cloths spread over their heads. When they reached the lab, their notes were taken from the filing system, and they were initially examined by Barbara Smith. Adults with serious complaints and all children were sent through to the doctor, who sat at the far end of the last room.

One child was standing unaided when he joined the queue. During the course of the morning he got closer and closer to the floor. When he reached the doors of the lab, he was sitting down. Beside the filing cabinets he was prostrate. He died only a few feet from the doctor. Cerebral malaria was a major cause of mortality among young children, particularly during the rainy season, when the *anokoles* mosquitoes who carried it prospered in the damp conditions.

Others died because they were allergic to the drug chloraquin. They would literally die on the end of a needle, there in the lab, in Barbara Smith's arms.

By the time Bill, the previous doctor, had left Dulaba, he was treating 22,000 patients a year. On a typical Monday morning, there would be more than two hundred people waiting to see him – which represented nearly ten per cent of the population of the three villages.

These figures worried Ted Whiteman, the director of the Cass. When the clinic had first opened on a full-time basis, in 1974, the villagers only came with major ailments. But as these had become rare under consistent treatment, people began to come with their coughs and colds and headaches. The people of Dulaba were becoming physically dependent on a system of health care modelled on a British general practice – a system that existed virtually nowhere else in black Africa, and certainly nowhere else in the Gambia.

If, for whatever reason, the Cass suddenly had to withdraw, leaving the villagers dependent on the skeletal system of health care the government was able to provide, it would be disastrous. Leaving aside the question of the soaring drugs bill, Ted felt the Cass had a moral duty not to allow the villagers to become over-dependent on the clinic. So before Richard Innes left for Dulaba, he was instructed that the amount of drugs used in the clinic should on no account rise.

Although she thought it was a good thing for a woman to love her husband, Tumbulu Sise did not love her husband. It was not because he was wicked, or cruel; he was kind. But he had nothing, and because he had nothing, he was unable to provide the things that a husband should provide for his wife: soap or clothes or anything else. If he could have provided these things, she would have loved him. But he couldn't, and that was the way it was.

When she was married to her husband, she didn't know him. After she was given to him, she got to know him, and when she finally transferred to his compound, she felt sad. Not because she knew him to be bad, but because her life would change. Before she was transferred, she was free to go wherever she wanted. But now she would have to ask her husband's permission if she wanted to visit someone, and he might refuse. Before, if she needed something, like clothes, her mother would get it for her. But her husband would not get it for her. You can force your mother, but you cannot force your husband. This is why she was sad.

After she'd gone to bed on the night of Tobaski, Tumbulu was awoken by her daughter Salimata crying. The girl was covered in blood. She had gone out with the other girls of her age-group, looking for salibos, as they always did on the prayer days, and she had quarrelled with the girl who was taking the money. They had fought, and the girl had bitten Salimata's finger, until the end of it was hanging off the bone.

Tumbulu went to the house of Fa Lanjy, the dresser-dispenser from the MRC, but he wasn't there. She thought of going to the camp herself, but she was afraid. It was too late. She didn't sleep that night, because the child did not stop crying.

First thing in the morning, she took the child to the MRC. Richard said she would have to go to the hospital in Banjul for treatment immediately. A car would take her that very day. Tumbulu cried, she was frightened. She didn't know what difficulties she would face in Banjul.

She had not had time to cook lunch for the other children before she left them with her mother. Then she had taken all the money she had, and gone with Salimata, and the youngest daughter, Binta, who was still breastfeeding.

By the time they arrived at the hospital, she was already exhausted, but the doctor, although he was black – a Mandingko like her – showed her no sympathy. Indeed he had shouted at her, asking her why she had not gone to the Chinese health centre at Karantaba.

'I don't know,' she said. 'Why don't you ask the doctor who sent me here? I didn't bring myself here.'

But he still told her she should have gone to Karantaba.

Then he gave her a form so the girl could have a bed. Tumbulu picked up the dressing he had taken from the child's wound, and put it back. And later she was glad that she had, for it was a long time before the doctor looked at the girl's hand again.

The bed was a bunk. The top bed had a mosquito net, but the bottom one did not. Salimata had the bottom one. If the hospital was not too crowded, Tumbulu would lie the younger daughter beside Salimata, but when it got busy they would put another patient in the bed, so Tumbulu would have to hold the baby on her lap. They were in that hospital for two weeks, and Tumbulu sat beside the bed the whole time.

She never slept at night. She would wave a cloth over the baby to keep the mosquitoes off her. Sometimes, if only Salimata was in the bed, she would lie down and sleep in the afternoons. She had used her money to buy food on the first day – a loaf of bread and a cup of sugar. When that was finished they just waited. And all this time the child's hand had not been treated.

On the fifth day, she saw the doctor passing, the one who had given them the form for the bed. She called to him, and told him that today was the fifth day, and he had not even examined the child's hand. He told her he had been too busy. After that, the nurses came and dressed the child's hand every morning, and they gave her tablets.

On the eighth day they brought a bowl of macaroni for the child to eat. They had not brought her any food before, because there was no food in the hospital. Even so, the macaroni was just a little. You could have held it all in your hand. After that, if there was food in the hospital Salimata would eat, and if there wasn't, she wouldn't. Tumbulu herself had nothing.

The father of the girl who had bitten Salimata's hand came to visit them. His child had done wrong to them, so he felt he had to come and see them. He had brought ten cobs of maize which Tumbulu's husband had sent for her. Her husband had also given him two dalasis to give to her. But the man explained that he had had to use it for the taxi fare to get there. Then he told her he had to go to the market. She realized that he had used her husband's money so that he could come to Banjul to buy rice.

It seemed like a long time they were in the hospital, because it was the working time, and at night she would think about her crops, how they would be spoiled or delayed, because she could not weed them. If she failed to harvest any of those crops, she would blame that man and his daughter, because they had done wrong to her, and they had never even apologized.

And she worried about what would happen if the child was discharged before the driver came from Dulaba. They would be all alone in that city, with no money.

She didn't use the ten cobs of corn. There were charcoal pots in the hospital to roast it on, but you had to pay to use them, and you had to pay the person to roast it for you. She could have sold the corn, but she didn't know you could do that.

She noticed that the baby was developing a fever. She went to one of the nurses and asked her for some medicine. The nurse told her she would have to go to out-patients, but to be treated there you needed a ticket, and the ticket cost one dalasi. Fortunately, the child got better anyway.

On the Wednesday two weeks after she had arrived, Alioune Sware came with the MRC Peugeot to see if she had been discharged. At that moment the doctor was examining the children in the ward, and Tumbulu was waiting with all the other mothers in the foyer downstairs. Alioune told her to go and find out if the child was ready to go. But when she entered the ward, the nurses shouted at her, and told her to mind her business until she was told by the doctor. A few minutes later the child was discharged, but by that time Alioune had already gone.

Tumbulu stood at the hospital gates wondering what to do next. A policeman came up and asked her where she was going.

'I'm going to Dulaba,' she said.

'The driver has already left,' said the policeman. 'What are you going to do?'

She told him she had relatives in Bakau she could stay with if she could get there. He gave her a dalasi and told her to take the bus.

*

'Some people,' said Alioune Sware, 'believe that God is in the sky. Because when the rains come they hear strange sounds coming from the sky. Other people will tell you that God is in the ground. Because the world is very big and no matter how deep you dig, you will never come to the end of it. But the real place that God is, where God should be, is in the heart of every person on this earth. God is someone who cannot be seen. He is someone who cannot be described, you can only say what he is *like*. He is like a watchman who never goes to sleep. He is like a hunter who never loses his prey.'

Alioune had been apprenticed to a marabout, until he ran away to follow the ways of the tubabs. None the less, he could still read and write in the Arabic script, and he knew far more about religion than any other member of the staff. And like many who considered themselves to be progressive, and at the same time to be pure Muslims, he had a low opinion of the marabouts.

'They are trying to put themselves above God. They are taking different parts of the Koran and putting them together in a way that God has not asked us to do. They are using God's words to try and change what God has created. You see this girl who does not love you? If you go to a marabout, he will work for you, to make her love you. And that is not right. That is not pure Islam – making these things to change what God has decided. It is the same as what the idol worshippers are doing. What God has decided, no human being can go against that.'

Every woman and every man had a devil husband or a devil wife. The great marabouts – the *woleos* – the chosen people of God, would make love with their devil wives, so that they could obtain their help in their work. Some even allotted a particular night of the week, usually Friday, the prayer day, to these demon spouses. Generally, however, these spirits remained dormant, and it was only if they loved someone very much and became possessive or jealous of their human partner that people were aware of them.

A man might be visited by strange figures in his dreams, pointing away from his wife or his lover, telling him to keep away from her. The devil might visit the woman herself, telling her not to sleep with her husband. If she did, any child she bore would die within one month of life. She might begin behaving strangely. The devil might lead her to the brink of a certain well, or to the topmost branches of a very tall tree. The devil would be heard speaking through her, telling the husband to keep away. If he approached, she would throw herself into the well, or from the tree, and kill herself.

Menata was one of the youngest members of the Saniyoro Kafo. She was slim and very pretty, but so quiet and withdrawn that for a lot of the time one scarcely noticed she was there. She was a citizen of Karafa Kunda, and had transferred to her husband in Dulaba only three years before. Even as a child she had been famous for her beauty, and her age-mates would sing about her when they went to the field for work. During the period of seclusion following circumcision she had fainted, and remained unconscious for two days. Her father had consulted a marabout, who told him that a devil was in love with the girl and was trying to take her. He must put a silver bangle on her wrist and make sure that she wore it at all times, or she would simply disappear.

When Menata came to Dulaba, her husband's family knew nothing of this. Only her father knew. Then one day, when she was in the middle of her third pregnancy, she saw something when she was at the well, but she didn't tell anyone what she had seen. Later, when she was cooking, she was found by one of the older women of the compound, standing with her hands over her face. She said something was passing backwards and forwards in front of her face. They had to escort her to the washing place, because she was afraid to go on her own. And that night she went to bed without eating.

When everyone in the house had been in bed for some time, they were suddenly awoken by the sound of her shouting. When they lit the lamp, they found her standing beside the bed with her hands over her face, moving her head from side to side. 'Don't you see this man?' she said. 'Moving his face towards me. His hair is so long it touches me. And I don't want him to touch me.' The next day she had stopped talking completely. She didn't talk for one month. Her father came to see her. She was lying on her bed, and he noticed that she wasn't wearing the bangle. 'Have you lost it?' he asked. She nodded.

He went to a marabout in the village of Dasilame, not far from Dulaba, on the other side of the Bintang Bolon. This man was a Sirif – a woleo – famous throughout the region. It was believed that God spoke to him directly. He told the father to wait till the following day, when he had seen what was revealed to him in his dreams. 'Did your daughter have a silver bangle?' he asked the father the next morning. 'Did she lose it? You must replace it, or you will lose her for ever.' He also told the father three charities he must give: porridge and sour milk to the children of the compound, the girl's head-tie to be given to a woman, three candles to be left in the mosque on a Friday.

The bangle was replaced, and slowly Menata began to recover. Three months later, however, it disappeared again. The people of the compound searched everywhere, but with no success. It was obvious that the devil had stolen it. Then on the evening of the third day, when the husband made his ablutions, it appeared suddenly, lying on his prayer mat. All was well for some weeks, until she began to complain of a headache. No one could sleep in the house of the women because she shouted all night. This time they took her to the MRC. Bill had given her sleeping tablets to calm her down at night. Shortly afterwards she was referred to the hospital at Fajara for treatment. After that she never shouted in the night. She was just very quiet at times.

'I was looking for you for three years. But now I've got you.' This was what Menata had said the second time Bill had examined her. This remark was not addressed to anyone, and she did not reply to any of the questions he asked. She had been brought in two days before, 'not speaking'. He had given her three aspirin. Now he diagnosed 'probable acute schizophrenia. Try calcuprin for one week and review.' Two weeks later she was discovered to have typhoid, and the psychosis was assumed by Bill to have been a product of typhoid fever. She was sent to Fajara to have a mysterious rash examined. But this soon improved under treatment – 'probably a drug rash' – and she was soon back in Dulaba. All was well until a month later, when she was brought into the clinic one evening, 'acutely insane, dumb – trying to run away'. Treatment with largactyl for schizophrenia continued for a further six months, with improvement consistently followed by relapse. She had been pregnant through most of this period. On 11 March 1985 she delivered safely. The file ended ten days later with the words, 'No problems'.

Such women often became marabouts. For when the devils left them, they left them with certain gifts. There was a woman in Joli, who was famous as a fortune teller. People came from all over Kiang to consult her. But she would only see them on Mondays and Fridays.

'I think this is the woman you are looking for,' said the translator.

A tall, thin, rather severe-looking woman had entered the compound, and stood watching us, quite calmly. She wore large, battered, golden earrings that curved round in the characteristic leaf shape. When the translator had explained the purpose of our visit, she unlocked one of the doors, and we followed her inside.

The room was small and neat. The walls were unplastered, but the floor was swept and the bed neatly covered. It was her husband's room. There was nothing in it but the bed, and a wooden armchair, in which I was told to sit. She closed the door to the main compound, and the only light fell from the doorway that led through to the washing area at the back.

She sat opposite me, and told me to take a fifty-batut piece (10p), and ask what I wanted to know.

'To her?' I asked the translator.

'No. You ask the fifty batuts.'

Clutching the coin in my palm, I cupped it to my mouth, and silently mouthed my questions into it.

Then she took the fifty batuts and placed it in a small, chipped enamel basin, filled with violet sand from the compound floor. She took a bangle between the thumb and forefinger of her right hand, and began casually but rhythmically twisting it so that it swung backwards and forwards. The bangle itself was simple and undecorated. I assume it was of silver, as the 'power' of silver was highly regarded among the blacks, because of its supposed purity.

One moment she was chatting quite casually to the translator, the next she was absorbed in her task. She was looking down, so I couldn't see whether her eyes were open or closed. And she was murmuring to herself – something audible but indistinguishable. I had felt a thrill as I spoke to the fifty batuts, and as I handed it to her, I had abandoned myself to events. Now my attention was entirely focused on her hand as it flicked the bangle backwards and forwards in a continual, rhythmic, vaguely masturbatory gesture. Her fingers, long and slender, a silvery lilac in colour, seemed all of a piece with the burnished metal. I was mesmerized by the movement of the hand, bending at the wrist as it bounced the silver bangle in the semi-darkness.

Then suddenly, she dashed it against the side of the enamel basin. It was a sudden, violent, apparently unconscious movement. I started at the clatter. The bangle bounced away onto the sand. Then she picked up the coin and half-buried it in the sand in the bowl. She picked up the bangle and repeated the swinging movement, this time with the left hand, still murmuring to herself. It was the suddenness and the unconscious violence of the way she threw the bangle against the basin that made me realize the intensity of her involvement in the proceedings.

She placed the coin on the sand beside the basin, and drew a circle round it with her finger. Then she began to swing the bangle between the fingers of her right hand, before dashing it against the basin for the last time. How long the whole process had lasted, I had no idea. But as quickly as she had slipped into it, she had come out, and was telling me what she had seen.

'What you are looking for is not an object, or money, but a person. You are not expecting to find them in this country. You weren't expecting to come to this country. You were expecting to do something else, but that has been postponed until you leave here. You can stay here for four years in peace. But I don't expect you to stay that long.

'You are afraid of wickedness. Do not be afraid of it. You will be in peace. You want money. Don't worry. You are going to be very rich.

'This person you are looking for – you will find them. And when you find them, you will be in peace.'

The charities to be given, so that what she had foretold would come about, were two packets of candles, to be taken to the mosque by one of the elders so that he could pray for me, two bottles of milk, one to be given to an elder, and one to a marabout in Dulaba, and a pair of sandals to be given to a particular old woman in Dulaba.

She had the pinched, strained features of a nervous, irritable person. But she sat patient and serene as I questioned her. In the light falling from the back doorway, she had a kind of glow about her, almost of exaltation. She told me that it was a devil that had taught her to tell fortunes in this way. She had been a young woman, with only two children, when she had first seen this devil. She had been on a journey to Tankular, and it had appeared to her in the shape of a marabout, his face wrapped in cloth. This devil loved her, and it had followed her back to Joli. She had never seen a devil before. She had never been a kunfanunte. But every Monday and Friday, that devil would be close to her. And on those days she would be very ill. Her head would ache so much she would have to lie down with a cloth over it. For five years she did no work on those days.

Nobody could see this devil but her, and at first her family thought she was suffering from a mere headache. They had taken her to a marabout in Dulaba, Fa Salifa Minte, who explained that this was the sickness of a devil. He said that the devil must love her very much or it would have killed her. And he made her bathe in a liquid juju. After that, the devil still came to her on Mondays and Fridays. It would be with her from sunrise to sunset. But it told her things – things which she used to benefit herself and her family.

As she twisted the bangle between her fingers, she had spoken some prayers in Arabic, and the devil had answered her in Mandinka, telling her the problems that had brought me there. She had heard it with her ears. For this being a Monday, the devil was with her. It was there in the room at that very moment.

'Where is he?' I asked.

'He is at that end of the room.'

The mud walls were dark, but they and the bed and the floor of dust all looked reassuringly solid.

'Is he standing or is he sitting down on the bed?' I asked.

'He brings a white sheepskin, which he sits on. There, just in front of the bed.'

'What is his name?'

She said she didn't know.

'That is not true,' said the translator. 'She must know his name. But she does not want to tell you.'

7

THE LANGUAGE OF THE GRIOTS

From outside the house of the women, we could hear the high-pitched nasal singing of the women griots. Soon they emerged, the first carrying the child, the second with her own child tied on her back, beating rhythmically on an iron cylinder so that it chimed melodiously with their strained but evocative singing. The child was handed to one of the elders, who after splashing it cursorily with water, began to drag a safety razor across the raw, unformed scalp. The child added a thin whine to the wailing of the women. *Ku'lio* – shaving of the head – was the word used to describe this naming ceremony, which was performed on all Muslim children when they were one week old.

We were in Ibou Sanyang's family compound in Serekunda, near the coast. Maimouna Jatta, the child's mother, and Fatou, the eldest of Sanyang's sisters, sat on a bamboo mat facing the house, their heads draped in light-coloured shawls. Behind them, in rows of armchairs, sat the elders, and beyond them, crowded onto the verandahs and the bentengos, the young men and boys.

The singing stopped while one of the male griots announced the name of the child. It was to be called Yussufa, after Maimouna's father. There was a brief prayer, and then the singing began again, as the child was passed around for each of the marabouts present to bless by spitting upon its forehead. Kola nuts and *munko* – raw rice pounded with sugar – were distributed.

The male griots moved through the throng accosting the younger members of the compound's male line. The biggest of them, a tall, imposing fellow in a voluminous beige robe, homed in on Sanyang, the child's father. His grizzled hair was cut short over his broad head, his eyes hidden by large horn-rimmed shades. He spoke at length in a rich, deep voice, punctuating his speech with grand and emphatic gestures between drags on a Rothman Kingsize.

The griots were the praise singers, the keepers of the genealogies of the ruling families, the founding lineages of all the countries of the blacks. They could sing of the doings of each person's forebears: of their great deeds of bravery, their miraculous acts, their inspired cunning, of their generosity, their wisdom, their piety. Traditionally, they were attached to particular noble families, and would accompany the members of that family at all the key moments of their lives – stimulating their confidence and courage with their songs, advising them on correct modes of behaviour according to their fund of archaic knowledge. They were the keepers of the history and the traditions, the oral heritage of these families. And as these families were believed to be at the centre of their respective communities, so the function of the griots was central to that

society. And great and public generosity being essential to the maintenance of dignity among the blacks, many of the griots became very rich,
some even richer than their patrons.

The laws of shame and discretion which governed the rest of society
did not apply to them. They could be as outrageous and outspoken as
they liked in the pursuit of their arts. They had thus become the political
commentators of the traditional society, exposing hypocrisy and misrule
– not directly, but through their own richly complex vernacular of
metaphor and analogy from nature, history and religion. They were,
however, far from revolutionary, or even subversive. Their function was
fundamentally and essentially conservative. They were there to remind
people of their duty – of their obligation to the tradition and to their
ancestors.

Nowadays their patrons were more likely to be cabinet ministers than
kings. Some travelled the world demonstrating their prowess on the *kora*
– the harp-lute – and the *balafong* – the xylophone. But even today, a griot
could only ever marry another griot. And because people were afraid of
their 'powers', their bodies were never buried in the earth, but were left
standing upright in hollow trees. Among the Wolofs, particularly,
singing and the playing of musical instruments was the exclusive
province of the griots, and consequently there was in the eyes of those of
'higher birth' a certain disgrace attached to these arts.

But if the griots were known by their surnames – Jobarteh, Kouyateh,
Konte and Suso among the Mandingkos – so they could just as easily
identify their prospective patrons. Sanneh and Manneh were the
nyanchos, the descendants of the kings of Kaabu. And a member of one of
these families, even if he or she were wearing vinyl trousers and a Michael
Jackson T-shirt, would still be expected by the griots to behave in a
manner and, particularly, with the generosity befitting a king. Sise, Toure
and Janneh were the marabouts. The griots would say, '*Sise nga na
Manding more!*' Sise nga na Manding more! It is difficult at this remove to
convey a sense of the evocative power of those words on the lips of a griot;
the sense of the individual located against the immemorial greatness of
his or her ancestral tradition. They meant literally that the Sises had been
marabouts since they came from Manding. But they also implied that this
person's immediate family were descended directly from those original
Sises, and not from any other people who had changed their name at a
later date.

Sanyang's family were not part of the founding lineage of anywhere.
They were not even from that country, Sanyang's grandfather having
come from a distant part of the Casamance more than fifty years before.
They had, however, a name that was honoured in that part of the world.
The Sanyangs were the *koringos*. In the empire of Kaabu they had been
deputy kings, provincial rulers, but were ineligible to be emperors. The
griots said, '*Jattafa Koringo*' – 'They who go first into battle.'

It was in this manner that the griot spoke, as he stood over Sanyang,
spilling cigarette ash onto the young man's trousers as he summoned
forth images of his ancestral greatness. Sanyang stared disconsolately

into the middle distance, as though he were trying not to hear the man's words – as though he were trying to block out their power. It was an unequal struggle, however, and Sanyang suddenly thrust his hand into his pocket and pulled out a five-dalasi note which he thrust petulantly into the man's hand.

'Yo!' shouted the griot. 'Jattafa Koringo!' And he fired off a further salvo of praise before moving on to his next patron.

'These people just like to disturb you,' said Sanyang, physically desolate at having parted with so much money.

In the gloomy, overcast days of the rainy season I had heard music coming over the gatekeeper's radio such as I had never heard before: it sounded like orchestras of balafongs, their notes tinkling like raindrops, accompanied by choirs of young girls, their voices raised in a joyous, incandescent wailing; a mature woman, accompanied only by a single drum, crying out, her voice seeming to reach out – effortful, almost agonized. It was a sound compelling, even a little chilling in its intensity – a sound that seemed to have come from *outside*, from *beyond* – from beyond any emotion I could easily put a name to. It owed something to the call of the muezzin, and something to the keening for the dead. But even more, in the way the phrases were pulled urgently, impulsively out of the air, the extreme, almost inhuman sense of possession, it drew on the rites of the traditional religion – the invocation of the spirits. But at that time I knew nothing of this. Indeed I was not even sure where these programmes were coming from. I would look out into the bush and wonder what sort of landscape could produce sounds of such complete otherness.

And there was also a sense in which one heard these sounds from beyond a divide not only of emotional comprehension, but of time and space. For this, it was said, was the music that was heard at the courts of Mali, the great empire that was established around the homeland of Manding in the thirteenth century. No European ever reached Mali, but its towns were described by the Arab chroniclers as great centres of culture and Koranic knowledge. The Emperor Moussa was said to have given away so much gold as he passed through Cairo on his pilgrimage to Mecca that the value of the currency had dramatically fallen.

But apart from these anecdotes and the words of the griots – who still sang the epic of Sunjata Keita, the 'Lion of Manding', the cripple who had healed himself by spiritual means, and founded the empire of Mali – virtually nothing remained of this splendour. The epoch of Manding lived vividly in the minds of Professors of African history. But there among the Mandingkos, speaking the Mandinka language, on land that had once been under the suzerainty of Mali, it was difficult to imagine that it had ever existed. Looking round at the elders seated stately in their most splendid robes, I wondered whether the singing of the griots represented a survival of a lost glory, or if the court of Mali had not, in fact, been remarkably like this naming ceremony; although it was said that young women had walked naked in ancient Mali, and I certainly hadn't seen evidence of anything like that.

*

It seemed to me that Africa was a continent created by women. One day, I went to watch the women planting sesame in a field just outside the village. Sanyang came with me as translator, though exactly what he was going to translate, neither of us was quite sure.

It was about half-past two in the afternoon, and extremely hot. As we made our way along the lanes between the gardens on the north side of the village, we could hear a distant roaring, like the buzzing of millions of swarming insects. And every so often, above the green millet, we would catch glimpses of brightly coloured clothes flashing in the sunlight. Sanyang bit his lip. He had not been keen on this expedition from the outset. I had assumed it was because he didn't want to venture into the bush in the heat of the afternoon. But now I could see his eyebrows knitting anxiously.

Suddenly the red laterite road came into view, and beyond it a great mass of women milling over the land.

'Jesus Christ!' said Sanyang. 'How many people are there?'

'Six kafos,' I said.

'That's a lot of people,' he said. Now we could hear their voices, and differentiate their hoots of laughter. The school drums were being leisurely beaten. 'That is why I didn't want to come,' he said. 'I don't like to be where there are so many women.'

'Are you afraid of them?' I asked.

'Yes,' he said.

The women turned *en masse* as we approached.

'Oh no,' said Sanyang.

As we reached the area where the Saniyoro Kafo were working, the beating of the drums became faster. The women came dancing towards us, the stamping of feet resonating deep into the earth, the air shaking to the hard, syncopated clapping. Then, as the rhythm of the drums built to a climax, the women of my kafo, as one, went down on one knee before me. Then laughing, they rose to their feet, and wiped the sweat from my face, neck and arms with their head-ties.

Sanyang looked desperately miserable, as though he wished he could retract his head into his shirt collar. 'It seems you are well known here,' he said, his eyes narrowing.

Only a few years before, the village would now have been entering a second period of hunger, between the finishing of the maize and the ripening of the rice. But the rice seed that had been distributed by the government in recent years ripened much quicker than the traditional varieties, and much of it was now ready to be cut.

Just beyond the grove of large mahogany trees on the right-hand side of the old bush path to Karafa Kunda was a narrow pathway that led into the rice field of Sukoto. A few yards along it, as though at the entrance to a mosque, lay dozens of pairs of plastic and rubber sandals. For the women always went barefoot into the rice fields, for fear of damaging the crops. Then one turned a corner, and ahead opened up the great glade of

Sukoto, the rice brimming between the trunks of the tall trees, shimmering and gleaming in the glare of the sun like a sea of golden-green, stretching away into the distance till it became indistinguishable from the glittering haze of the salt flats. One could see the women by ones and twos and threes, only their heads and shoulders and breasts visible, cutting the heads of grain which hung heavy from the golden stalks.

On the far side of the field, where the bush became denser, there was another path which led to the field of Kadamah on the other side of the salt flats. But getting to it wasn't easy. The narrow, twisting paths made from the earth and weeds piled at the edges of the individual plots didn't really lead anywhere, and after a great deal of toing and froing, I still wasn't a third of the way across. The women called directions to me. But I'd no sooner begun to follow one woman's instructions than another sent me back in the opposite direction. Finally I emerged onto the hard grey sand, beyond which the mangroves shimmered, immaterial, almost ghostly in the haze of heat. Here and there pools of brackish water sparkled and flashed as they reflected the silver sky. I wasn't absolutely sure where I was going, but I pulled the brim of my hat down over my eyes and wandered off into the dazzling glare. Already I could feel a kind of numbness settling over my brain.

When I was half-way across I heard someone calling to me from among the trees. It was Nafi Saho, one of the members of the Saniyoro Kafo. She was a big, black, fleshy woman with a tinkling laugh. She was also going to Kadamah, so we walked together. She led me through the bush along the edge of the salt flats till we came to a point where the trees and the mangroves were so close they were almost touching. Beyond this, we could see the rice actually growing in the bush itself. Here there were no paths, and we picked our way carefully among the tall stems till we came to a small clearing where there was a sort of encampment. The orange earth had been completely flattened, and a platform of branches with a canopy of palm fronds had been erected. An old iron cooking-pot stood among the ashes of a dead fire. Several young children sat on the shaded platform, while beside it two pubescent girls were energetically pounding. Nafi left her things then led me off into the bush. Jarra Njai's eight-year-old daughter, Markady, tagged along. Here the rice was growing under and among the low trees – those that had survived the burning, and the twisted, febrile remains of those that had not – their branches throwing a lattice of thin shadows over the crops. By now I had no idea where we were. Then we saw Jarra Njai and two other women half hidden among the trees.

It was easy to spot the ripe heads, they were golden-brown at the edges and at the tips, and they hung heavily, bending the whole of the stem. With a small iron blade, a scrap of cloth tied to form a handle, the stalks were cut against the thumb leaving a shaft of five or six inches encased in a long green leaf. When a bundle of about twenty had been cut, the leaves were ripped away with one expert movement. And when the bundle was too large to be held in one hand, it would be taken and piled up under a tree, where they would eventually be tied into fat sheaves.

We were constantly on the move, trying to keep within the meagre shade, leaving the green, upright stalks to be harvested at another time. Occasionally we'd walk yards before we found anything that was ripe; in other places we'd find hundreds of heads packed densely together, and in many cases the thin stalks were already half trampled into the dust, so we had to bend low to cut the heavy, fragile heads. At these places we'd stand working for what seemed like hours before moving on to a new place. All around there was a whining and a whirring and a screeching, as though the undergrowth were full of alarm clocks, digital warning devices and electric saws all going off at minutely different intervals. Despite the unbelievable loudness of these sounds one quickly became used to them, so that it was only when one of them stopped that you noticed it had been there at all.

My nose was running ceaselessly, and having forgotten to bring a handkerchief I had to use leaves, an inadequate substitute. The Africans didn't use handkerchiefs, preferring to blow it out onto the ground. But observing my plight, one of the women, Mba Filije, Jarra Njai's mother, tore off a corner of her faneau and handed it to me to use. She was in her fifties. Her daughter's tallness, her narrow, slanting eyes and her fleshily smiling lips had all come from her. But Filije was more subtle, more feline in her manners and her movements. Jarra Njai was her eldest daughter; her youngest, Isatou, was scarcely older than Jarra Njai's Markady. The third woman was Nafi Saho's mother-in-law, Mama Sise, a small, disgruntled-seeming woman, who said very little.

Kadamah was the furthest of the fields from Dulaba. It belonged to the people of Karafa Kunda, but until recently it hadn't been used for many years. Last year, Mba Nene, an old woman from Karafa Kunda married in Salum Kunda, the compound where Mba Filije was married and where Jarra Njai was born, had said that since none of them had their own fields, they should try to make use of that land. So Mba Filije, Jarra Njai and a group of other women from that compound and some of their husbands and children had gone out with axes and cutlasses, and cut the largest area they could. That was why the individual plots at Kadamah were so much larger than at the fields closer to the village. They were also much less clearly delineated. Jarra Njai's field appeared to sweep right up the low incline that levelled out into the dense, uncultivated bush. Stretching beyond it towards the creek and the end of the cultivated area was Mama Sise's field. Filije's lay below Jarra Njai's, beside the salt flats. Nafi Saho's field was back towards Sukoto, and beside that was the field of Nembali Sise, Jarra Njai's cousin.

Between these plots the women held bellowed conversations which were often passed on for miles over the fields, so that everyone could join in the drama or the amusement. They would howl and hoot to scare away the wild animals – bush pigs and monkeys – and the birds. This was really the job of the young children, but they tired early, and preferred to play or just loaf about.

Towards the end of the afternoon we stopped work and the harvested rice was all gathered under one tree. The appearance of the innumerable grains clustered together in their fat sheaves, all neatly stacked in alternating rows, was something truly beautiful to the women. Carefully, and with great satisfaction, Jarra Njai lifted them by the stalks by which they were tied. Miraculously they held together, hanging from her hands like bells. They were piled into basins and left to be carried back to the village.

The shadows were lengthening, but it was still extremely hot. I slumped against the trunk of a tree, by now virtually insensible, and watched as the women began to prepare *dempetengo*. First they found wood for the fire, then Jarra Njai pounded a small portion of the new rice and shook away the husks. It was then heated in a cracked old cooking pot, until it began to jump out. Then it was pounded again. All three women took part, pounding in rotation into the one mortar, building up speed till the thudding of their pestles sounded out across the salt flats like the beating of a great drum.

The resultant substance was considered a great treat. The grey flakes still warm from the pot were agreeably crunchy and dry, enlivened by charred bits and the slightly rubbery green flakes of the grains that had not been fully ripe. It was extremely laborious to prepare, as it involved a great deal of pounding, and only a little could be roasted at a time. Its ostensible purpose was to provide a treat to entice the children to stay longer at the fields, keeping the animals and birds at bay. But in fact this pounding was a small ritual in its own right – something by which this time of year could be identified – that was done at the end of each harvest day, because it had always been done. And of course the women liked to eat it as well.

Jarra Njai was becoming very irritated with her children. Markady was chasing Nafi Saho's daughter round the clearing, to everyone's annoyance, and her son Lamin was attempting to mend his mother's sandal. It had been mended so many times that there was very little of the original structure left, and this time it was beyond hope. But Lamin's whining excuses only served to make his mother more annoyed. She paused in her pounding, her voice rising to a frenzy. Lamin cringed under the barrage, while Markady went and hid in a tree. But I had the impression that Jarra Njai shouted at her children so much that it had very little effect.

The golden light of the sun fell towards us over the darkening emptiness of the salt flats. We were only three miles from Dulaba, and not much further from Karafa Kunda, but there was an extraordinary feeling of remoteness about that place – perhaps more so than anywhere else I've ever been. And the company of the people I was with – the sound of laughter across the rice fields, the thudding of the pestles answering each other back from the innumerable little encampments dotted away along the edge of the salt flats – did nothing to lessen this feeling. There was a sense of great ancientness about that purely female society of the rice fields. It was *their* place, and they would often strip down to their *be-chos* – the under-faneaus which covered only their haunches and upper thighs – for no man would see them there. I had learnt that it was at one of the rice fields that the women's circumcision took place, and that it was there that they were taught the secrets that their grandmothers had been taught, and their grandmothers before them. I wondered if this sense of ancientness that I felt in the company of the women in that remote place in any way approached the atmosphere of that mysterious and appalling ritual.

I had been told early in my stay that the circumcision was secret and that even to ask questions about it would create anger and distress among the very people whose goodwill was so important to me – and might even place me in physical danger. Yet the longer I spent in Dulaba, the more convinced I became that I would have to know at least something about it, if I were to ever come to a real understanding of that society. As I watched the children rolling together in the dust of the compounds – the girls fighting as vigorously as the boys – I would wonder how it was that later in life they came to perceive of themselves as being so completely different from each other. And in the evenings, as I sat with the Civil Servants, and listened to them talking, entranced but utterly mystified by the sound of their languages, physically so close but emotionally so remote, I would wonder what it was that bound them together; more intimate than friendship, closer even than the ties of blood. I would feel instinctively that as the circumcision was the one area of their society that was definitively barred to me, it must be there that the key to their culture lay.

As I looked out across the salt flats, I wondered if I ever would know very much more about the nature of that event. I must say I didn't feel at all optimistic about it.

It was October – the 'palaver month' – when, according to the lore of the colonialists, 'the strain of the constant humid heat, both day and night, was felt by both blacks and whites alike'. It was a time of irrational arguments, when longstanding tensions came to a head. It was at this time of year that murders were committed. Darbon Jammeh's husband had been killed in October.

The light of the sun was not as fierce and direct and burning as it was during the dry season, but the whole of the grey sky radiated a hazy, generalized brilliance, which, as it approached midday, became heavier and more intense. It was like living all the time in a great steam bath. And all across the bush to the west of the village the long, shining grass undulated like waves on a pale green sea.

The women went to their fields early each morning, leaving the village often before seven, and returning at nightfall. As we sat outside the Quarters before dinner, we would hear them passing through the darkness on the other side of the fence. And as the season advanced inexorably towards its conclusion, and they saw the sheaves piling up in the store houses, we would hear the sound of joyful, agitated clapping, syncopated with beating on plastic water containers.

The shadows of the bobbing heads of the kinto, which now stood almost twenty feet tall, were cut onto the rocky sides of the village street, as though drilled into granite. I had never seen the moon so bright before.

The people sat chatting at the bantabas and the bentengos, and the children ran in gangs, laughing and shouting along the streets. When the moon was full, people would leave their children to play until far into the night. For no one would think of devils on such a night, and it was believed that if the children were seen playing among the crops in the moonlight, the harvest would be a good one.

I sat on the verandah at the Quarters, chatting with the staff wives.

We were discussing our ages, and unlike the village women, they all knew how old they were. Sirrah was twenty-eight. Jori Sanyang was twenty-two. Isatou Bajie, Momodou Jarjou's wife, was twenty-one. Ndey-Touti was twenty-four.

'I'm a very old woman,' she said, hunching her shoulders and drawing a beard on her chin with her fingers. She held up one of her breasts for my inspection. 'Look, I'm a very old woman.' And she almost collapsed with laughter – a high, brittle laugh one heard all too rarely. Her back and shoulders were spectacularly smooth and shining, but as she said her breasts were those of an old woman – or what a European would have considered the breasts of an old woman.

I went for a walk on the laterite road towards Karafa Kunda. On the right-hand side of the road, the ITC – the International Trypanosomiasis Centre – were planning to build a research centre. There they intended to breed a new species of cow that would be immune to sleeping sickness. The villagers saw this development as a great blessing, and already the ITC had installed three pairs of shining brass taps along the village street as a token of their good will. From now on, it was said, there would be no problems with water in the village, for these taps would never dry up.

The two avenues that led to the site of the new camp were clearly visible against the tangled sprawl of the bush, like mysterious runways, their neatness unexplained, the warm earth frozen like everything else into a cool, luminous stillness. Above, the Milky Way traversed the sky from horizon to horizon, like a great wheel of white dust.

A few yards into the bush, a herd of cattle belonging to the ITC stood silent and immobile, only the occasional lumbering movement showing that they had life. The huge tree by which they were tethered threw its great shadow over the road. As I stepped into the deep, bell-like shade, hopping light-footed between the glimmering chinks of light, I felt that sense of elation that secrecy can bring in childhood – as though I had discovered another, private world.

Soon I was back at the Quarters in the glow of the electric lights which with the flick of a switch had extinguished that parallel world; the warmth of conversation drowning out the eerie screeching of the insects and the coldness and the loneliness of the bowl-like firmament.

But it was not safe in that other world.

'Where did you go?' asked Daouda.

'I just went into the bush a little way.'

'You should not go there at night. There are hyenas about.'

'But I kept to the road.'

'They don't mind to go there. A few weeks ago they ate a cow from just beside the road.'

'Yes,' said Demba. 'That night they came right up to this tree at the end of the compound.'

Some nights their howling could be heard, even inside the lab; a desolate, unearthly sound.

On the evening of 5 October, there was a solid downpour for two hours. It would not rain again for several months.

'Have you ever eaten dempetengo with sugar?' asked Sona.

'No, I never have.'

'It is very, very sweet.'

You would say that, I thought.

She was a short woman, one of the youngest and most obviously attractive members of the Saniyoro Kafo, and I could tell she was someone who would appreciate the sweeter things in life. Having initially found her one of the most difficult of the women, I now found her one of the most amenable. 'I like everyone,' she had told me. 'Except thieves, pagans, devils and wild animals.'

Her husband, Braima Sise, worked as an odd-job man at the MRC, while the elder wife, Njonji, cleaned Susan Lawrence's house. Perhaps because of this, she seemed more at ease with the tubabs than did some of the women. I felt that the barriers between us were not as great. 'Everyone is my friend,' she said. 'Even you.'

We were squatting on top of a steep mud bank, digging with our fingers into a bowl of rice into which durango – groundnut sauce – had been embedded like a pool of sludgy, peppery gravy. It was warm only from the heat of the sun, having been cooked several hours before. Njonji's eldest daughter Binta, who had carried the food to the field, and her friend Salli, ate with us. I handed round some bread. Sona hid hers carefully in the folds of her faneau.

Below us lay the rice field of Bananako, where the great glade of Jumutung narrowed towards the Mankono road. An immense tree trunk lay across it, from which Sona's field stretched across and down to the narrow path that ran through the middle of the glade. The rice stood tall and thick, a satisfyingly dry, golden colour.

At one of the fields back towards the village, a young man was beating a kind of wooden slit gong to scare the birds and insects from the millet. The notes of the tingling, tumbling rhythm drifted across the glade, hanging in the dense, heavy air, as the earth disgorged the moisture from last night's rain.

The rice was so tall one didn't have to bend, and it was so dense one could pick a thick bundle within minutes without moving more than a foot or two. But it was very hot, and I tried to stay in the shade.

Sona looked up after a time.

'Do you like futo?' she asked.

'Very much,' I said.

'Do you want some? It is there.'

'Thank you,' I said. 'I am full.'

'Well,' she said. 'I'm going to have some.'

So I went too.

One of the older women had brought a dish of maize futo with red pepper. The women from the surrounding fields gathered round to sample it. Sona added the remains of the rice and durango. I'm never going to refuse food again, I thought. I'm never going to refuse it because I think I 'shouldn't' have it. These people had starved, and now that food was before them they were going to eat as much as they could. They would never have considered that eating a lot might be somehow bad for them. Food was good; it was only good.

Afterwards the other women went off to pray, but Sona didn't follow them.

'Aren't you going to pray?' I asked.

'No. Are you going to pray?'

'No,'

'Why not?'

'I'm a pagan.'

She laughed. 'You're not a pagan,' she said.

'I'm a great pagan,' I said.

She looked at me curiously for some moments. Then she said, 'Repeat these words after me, Bissimilai . . . Araham . . . Arahim . . .' And she went on through all the words of the al Fatia, the Muslims' daily prayer, with me repeating them after her.

She had large, rather grave eyes, with prominent eyebrows. And when she smiled two curious dents appeared at the corner of each nostril. She might otherwise have been almost too pretty.

'There,' she said, when we'd come to the end. 'Now you're not a pagan any more.'

Binta, Njonji's daughter, had covered her head with a piece of rag and tied it under her chin in the manner of a prayer shawl. With an expression of self-conscious piety she knelt down and began smearing her face with dust, as the Muslims are instructed to perform their ablutions when no water is available.

Sona and I looked at each other, then we both burst out laughing.

Yaya Bojang had told me how to approach a woman in the Mandinka language. One had to say, 'I would like us to meet each other.' At which the woman would say, 'What sort of meeting is that?' And one would reply, 'I would like us to have a "connection" – if you wish.' The reply would simply be yes or no. He had assured me that no woman would ever divulge it to anyone if such an approach was made. Now, as Sona stood working only a few feet from me, these words ran constantly through my mind. How easy it would be to say them . . . How much I liked her . . . And what an adventure it would be . . .

Then as I listened to her low singing, I realized that she was singing about me, praising me in the language of the griots.

'Tubabo Mark is here to make us happy.
Since he came, all the members of the Saniyoro Kafo
Have been on good terms,
He is here to make us happy.

'Mark puts me on his back.
He has taken banknotes, and tied me very tightly.
He has bound me with gold.
Mark always sleeps with fifty dalasis in his pocket.
I'm not referring to all the tubabs
– only to Mark!
He is here to make us happy!'

She looked up and grinned.

It occurred to me that if I had approached her, she probably wouldn't
have been shocked or angry. But she might not have sung about me any
more. I decided to keep my mouth shut.

When the shadows began to lengthen, it was time to stop cutting, and
the lengthy process of pounding dempetengo began. Mabinta's daughter
Bana and her friend Homonding were pounding at a clearing on the other
side of the glade. We went and joined them. Many women, old and
young, came to that place, and helped each other with their pounding
before starting out for home. I lay down on a log and listened to the
chatter and the thudding of the pestles. At one point I heard a gruff voice
calling through the trees from a long distance away.

'It is Mamanding Janno,' said Sona. 'She wants you to go and visit her
at her field. Tell her, "A hojo koto hojo a keta nyadi?" How is that which
we discussed in secret?'

I shouted out the words as loudly as I could.

Ribald guffaws came back from all over the rice field.

Sona stayed there for some two more hours, pounding with ceaseless
energy. I wondered at the purpose of this effort. How much dempetengo
did she need? But it seemed to be almost a point of honour – particularly
among the younger women – to stay as long as possible at the place of
work. Finally she prayed, looking almost groggy as she rose to her feet.
She said she was very tired and very hungry, from the heat of the sun and
the effort of all that pounding. She shovelled the remaining handfuls of
rice and durango into her mouth, then I helped her lift the huge basin,
piled high with sheaves of rice, onto her head. It was almost half as tall as
she was. We joined the other women, and made our way in a line up the
slowly rising path, across the plain to Dulaba. Sona went first, the great
basin bobbing gently, unsupported by anything but the folded cloth that
cushioned it on her scalp. The golden sheaves lightly tinged with green
glowed in the light of the evening sun, beneath a pale blue sky on which
the clouds had formed rippling patterns like the sea makes in the sand on
a beach. It echoed the patterns on her faded indigo faneau, which
twitched this way and that from her shuffling walk.

'Mamanding Janno invited you to her rice field when you'd finished work. Is Mamanding Janno your seri?'

'No.'

'Who is your seri?'

'You are.'

And so the news travelled up and down the line.

8

DAYS OF THE HARVEST

On the verandah of the Safari Nightclub in Brikama, those who could not afford to enter stood in the thin grey light listening to the music, though the sounds of funk and reggae could be heard for miles around. There were occasional self-conscious scuffles, with kung-fu style kicks used to no great purpose. Others danced by themselves, their movements abrupt, somehow violent, as though challenging others to mock them. From time to time young women in short, tight skirts, their long hair elaborately plaited, made their way onto the verandah and into the club. The young men stood and stared in silence.

Fabakary Manneh, the young fieldworker who was hosting me in the town, said that drumming was taking place nearby. With our two companions, we headed off along one of the unlit back streets. Occasionally we could hear vague clicking sounds, then an almost metallic 'panging', which sometimes became momentarily louder, then disappeared altogether. Then, suddenly, the darkness was filled with sound – a grinding, pummelling avalanche of rhythm, loud as a great machine – and we rounded a corner to see a flurry of shadows moving against a single light.

The street was blocked by a crowd of women, and between their milling bodies we could see the drummers seated before the corrugated-iron door of a compound.

The tallest, a rangy, muscular fellow in a red shirt and black beret, gripped the bass drum, the *kutiriba*, between his knees, his massively broad hands slapping hard onto the heated skin. He sucked furiously and rhythmically on a cigarette, bouncing and twitching constantly in his seat, as though the throbbing, bumping rhythm would at any moment launch him forward into the crowd. In the shadows beside him a smaller man sat hunched over the treble drum, the *kutir'ndingo*, staring always straight ahead, his mouth slightly open, as though held by the rhythm in a state of trance-like possession. They set up a brisk, urgent rhythm, the on-beats and the off-beats colliding so that all around the women twitched and writhed in anticipation.

As the rhythm mounted, the third member of the group stepped from the shadows, the lead drum, the long, narrow *sabaro*, sounding like a mass of jangling nerve-endings. A woman darted into the centre of the circle, and the rhythms of the drums, while each remained different, seemed suddenly to cohere into a single pounding, pulverizing on-beat. The woman swung abruptly round, then, with a flourish of her arms, she seemed to throw herself against the rhythm, as a great storm of clapping, hard, syncopated with the rhythm, broke out all around her. Her feet, pounding into the dust, moved faster and faster, her body thrust forward, so that her knees rose almost to her chin, her outstretched arms flailing against the light.

This was *lenjengo*, the dance of the Mandinka women. It was often referred to by Europeans as the 'bird dance', as the movements were thought to resemble the first desperate attempts of a bird to fly. But if it had any totemic origin, it had long since been forgotten.

As the rhythm rose to a climax, the individual appearance of the woman, the details even of her movements, seemed to disappear. One was aware only of the whirling, thrusting limbs, the patterns of her faneau flashing against the darkness. Then, as the climax of the rhythm broke over her, she fell back laughing into the crowd, and another woman took her place.

One after another the women threw themselves into the circle: some not waiting for the other to finish before seizing her shoulder; and she, as though frozen by the gesture, would stand stock-still to support her. Others came in by twos and threes; skinny, agile girls whizzing like fireflies; substantial matrons who shook the very air as they moved. Sometimes the drummers would stop in mid-beat, and let the dancer be carried by the frenzied clapping of the crowd. Then the bass drummer would rise to his feet and, facing the dancer, hammer out single shots as hard as he could. Spurred on by this attention and the vehemence of his beating, the dancer would take on a new lease of energy, and the whole place would be in uproar as more of the women threw themselves into the circle.

It was only in Africa that I had seen such complete unreservedness, such total abandonment to rhythm. And unlike in Europe, where such abandonment seemed to lead inevitably to violence or self-destruction, there was no element of aggression. On the contrary, this dance was an expression of affection and joy, called to celebrate the naming of a child. And there was, even in the wildest dancing, an element of control. For there was a technique to dancing lenjengo, which every woman would attempt to master from an early age. The best dancers were those who could invest this furious unleashment of energy with the greatest fluidity and elegance. And it was only the women who danced. The men stood, watching silently from the shadows.

A drum, particularly in Africa, is never a wholly silent object. Even if it is only sitting in the corner of a room, its capacity to create noise and excitement and emotional disturbance gives it a power which goes beyond its potential as a decorative object. If someone had died, you would not walk around carrying a drum. You would hide it.

I had bought two drums from Karamo Saho in Joli. He had cut them from local trees, and each of them followed the shape of the original trunk, so that they leaned slightly, but in opposite directions. Wherever they were, they would remain part of the landscape from which they had been taken. The skins had been dried onto the heads only the day before, and they gave off a rich animal smell.

These drums had to be in Africa to be fully alive – to fully achieve their potential. If you took them to Europe, the skins would become flaccid and lifeless. You would have to heat them a long time before playing them. But here, in Africa, if you as much as touched the skins, you would feel a kind of shock passing along your arm, and you would touch the skin very carefully and with slight embarrassment, because of the thrilling, resonant quality of the sound that emerged. None the less, when the people were going to beat their drums, they would heat them anyway. They would leave them all day in the sun, or put them by the fire till the skins made a 'pang, pang, pang' when they were touched. Then, when they beat these drums, they would not finger them gingerly, they would beat them as hard as they wanted, and you would be able to hear them for miles. As you held the drum between your knees, you could feel the heat of the wood against your skin, and the way it seemed to mould itself against your thigh, and the way it vibrated when you hit it, gave it the feel of an almost living organism. Like the beating of the pestle and mortar, its sound was part of that landscape – like the dust, the hard earth and the trees from which it had been made. And like the mortar, which it resembles in shape, and from which it may have evolved, who can say how old it is, or when people first started to use it?

Dulaba was one of the few villages in Africa where the beating of drums was forbidden. Twice during their ancestors' time fires had started while dances were taking place, and large parts of the village had been destroyed. This had been interpreted by their ancestors as a sign that God did not want drums to be beaten in the village. And it was believed that if they were, some disaster would immediately follow.

This seemed appropriate, for Dulaba was a Muslim place, and the Prophet himself had disliked dancing and the sound of drums. Even in villages where drumming was permitted, the energy they released had to be contained. Drumming was not allowed during Ramadan, or in Gammo, the week following the Prophet's birthday, when a white flag would fly from the mosque. Drumming was also not permitted on Thursday or Monday nights, for the days following were the most important of the Muslim week. Strangers, however, often joked that this tradition had been maintained in Dulaba only because the men of the village were jealous and did not like their wives to go out at night.

The school drums had been made for the Scouts. When the alkalo heard that they were being made, he had come to Sanyang and asked him what he thought he was doing. Sanyang explained that these drums made from tin cans were quite different from the *seyuwrubaa*, the wooden drums of the griots, to which the women loved to dance. Even so, the school drums were never taken into the village itself.

When the leaves of the groundnut bushes began to droop, one or two would be uprooted. If the shells were black on the inside, they were ripe, and they had to be harvested immediately. Many of the more affluent villagers hired kafos to do this work for them. For a kafo would do in a day what it would take one man weeks to do. But they would have to be paid, and they would have to be fed while they were working.

I went digging groundnuts with Tumbulu Sise and Fatounding. We arrived early, as the women did at that time of year, so that they could leave early and escape the worst of the heat. It was by no means the hottest day, the sun occasionally disappearing into a grey haze, but I took some punishment as there were no trees, only the meagre shelter of the tall screens of sorghum that ran between the avenues of groundnuts. By the end of the morning the blisters on my hands were already split open. We worked our way along these avenues, taking one each, pulling the plants to one side, exposing the nuts clinging to the roots, before hacking through the thick root that extended deep into the earth. The plants were then left lying on the earth to dry out in the sun. As we worked we munched constantly on the moist, pink-skinned nuts, straight from the ground and still tasting of roots and earth.

The field belonged to Fatounding's husband, Kalamatta. She was digging it for him as he had got a job looking after the ITC cattle. Tumbulu was there not because Fatounding was her friend, but because her mother and Kalamatta's mother were of the same father and the same mother.

She had returned from the hospital to find that two of her rice fields had become completely overgrown. They should have been weeded a second time while she was away. But she had no co-wife, and no one else to help her. There was a third field at Sukoto that she had weeded a second time, but if someone had told you that that piece of land had been weeded, you would never have believed them. She had got nothing from any of these fields. She had had to rely on the yield from her three other fields, which they had been eating for lunch and dinner since the beginning of the harvest. Now it was finished. The *suno* – the 'early cous' – which her husband had planted, had nearly all been eaten by the blister beetles, and neither she nor he had harvested any groundnuts. When she got her seeds out before the start of the rains she found that they had all been destroyed by maggots, and they crumbled to powder in her fingers as she shelled them. Not all of her husband's groundnuts had been eaten by the maggots, but those he planted had failed to produce anything. There was no reason for it. It was his luck. Now they were surviving only on the raw groundnuts they got working in other people's fields.

She had many relatives. But those who should have been very quick to help her – those of the same father and the same mother – had all died, or gone from the village. There was one boy, who was of the same mother, but he was still very young.

So when she had seen Kalamatta passing, she had stopped him and asked him if he could help her. He had told her that if she went to help at his farm, whatever rice he was able to buy in Mankono he would give to her. She hoped it would not take him too long.

One evening I went into Demba Tamba's house to find a substantial and very beautiful young woman sprawled on the bed. She didn't say anything, but just lay there, a certain gleam in her eyes. As we ate, the others chatted to her, in intimate but always respectful tones. Then, when we had finished, she lay back on the bed, and though her eyes remained wide open, she seemed to drift into a kind of reverie.

She was, I was told, a friend of Yaya Bojang. But as he had not known she was coming, he had left the village till the following morning. The next day was a Saturday, and in the evening there was a dance at the Community Centre. Yaya was always to be seen dancing – never with her, but never far away. The next morning she was gone.

For the next few days Yaya was present in body only. He said virtually nothing, and at mealtimes he ate little as he stared ponderously into the bowl.

'Oh!' he exclaimed suddenly one evening, as we sat in his house. 'I am dying for that girl. And I know that she is dying for me also. We lay here side by side, on this very bed. But we did not do anything, because she is still at school. Is that not correct?'

'It is correct.'

'So!'

'What about your fiancée?'

'My fiancée? Chah! It is complicated.' He stared at the floor as he pondered this complexity. 'You know, if you are to marry someone, it is better if you do not see them too often. Once every nine months or every year. In that way they will never know you. And when they come to marry you, they will treat you with great respect, and they will take great care not to offend you. Because they will not know what you like and what you do not like.

'It is likely that my fiancée has a boyfriend. In fact, I know she has a boyfriend. But I don't care about that. I don't even want to know. So long as she doesn't try to be clever in a way that will make me look foolish.

'Last year she invited me to spend Tobaski in her village. But from the time I arrived until the time of the dance on the evening of the prayer day, she did not address one word to me. So I guessed that something was happening, and at the dance I observed that she was seeing a boy who she had known before she met me. So I decided to find a girlfriend for myself, to show that I too can play. I did not say anything to Fatou. I just let her carry on with what she was doing. And I carried on with what I was doing.

'Then she came to me, very angry, and asked me what I was doing talking to other girls. So I said to her, "You may think you are someone who, when you walk down the street, every man will look at you and want to have you. Well, let me tell you that I am also someone who is very attractive, and if I want to have a girlfriend here, it will not be a problem for me. Everything that you do while I am here, I will know. Even now you are seeing a boy. And don't say that you are not, because I can even tell you his name!"

'So that is how I came to know this girl. She told me she would come here, but I did not believe her. Now she has come, and I know that she loves me with a natural love.

'I am still on terms with my fiancée, but it is not as sweet as it once was. So you see that things are complicated.'

It had at last been confirmed that Darbon Jammeh was to marry her teacher. He had come to the village to claim her, and soon she would be going to live with him. This news had brought to an end my idle speculation about the possibility of having an affair with her.

'Don't be so sure,' said Yaya. 'It is still some weeks before she goes there.'

But she was about to marry the father of her third child, the person she had wanted to marry.

'That does not matter. Here among the blacks, no matter how much we love someone, it does not mean that we will not want someone else. Your wife, even if she loves you with a natural love, she may betray you on the day of the marriage ceremony itself. If she sees someone among the guests who she feels something for, she will have sex with him there, on that very day.'

The harmattan had begun to blow. It came from the north-east, filling the sky with the dust of the desert. When the members of the Saniyoro Kafo arrived at their field to harvest their groundnuts, the world was still shrouded in a fog-like haze, the forms of the surrounding trees and the nearby village reduced to vague, ghostly silhouettes. As they worked, the sun began to filter through, but people were constantly coughing and spluttering, as their hoes, banging into the dry earth, sent up clouds of dust that clung to their arms and faces and hair.

'Let someone go to the camp and collect Mark's drums,' said Sona.

'I will get the drums,' said Jarjei Sanyang. 'I will beat one and Sona will beat the other.'

'Leave it,' said Nafi Saho. 'We are very close to the village, and if the elders hear it, they will not like it.'

'Yes,' said Senabu. 'If the elders hear it, it's going to cause a big argument.'

'All right,' said Sona. 'But when we have finished work we will escort Mark to his house.'

'If we do that,' said Nafi, 'the drums will be beaten. Sona and certain others are very strong-headed, and I know that if they see those drums they must try to beat them.'

'We will not do that,' protested Sona. 'We will beat on a basin like we did at the Professor's party. Nothing can be sweeter than that.'

As they worked they argued ceaselessly about how many people should be in each row, about who was simply picking up the fallen groundnuts and eating them, and about whether people should be allowed to leave early so that they could go home and cook lunch. Jarra Njai was ill, so it was up to Fatounding and Nafi Saho, who had divided the leadership in her absence, to make the decisions.

In the pauses between arguments they sang 'style' songs. These were the songs one heard at dances as the drummers were beginning to warm up. A young woman would step forward from the crowd, hand on hip, and give out a selection of these songs, which provided a satirical and sometimes cryptically insulting commentary on current events, and even on those who were present in the crowd. They were often so gnomically phrased as to be almost meaningless. But if they had sufficient rhythmic interest, people would pick up on them. And while the tune varied from region to region, they were sung always in the same arch, sing-song voice. They were known as the songs of the young women, and they reflected their concerns: love, friendship, loyalty, dancing and clothes.

> 'Sitting beside the white tar road,
> A taxi passed me at terrific speed.
> If you buy a faneau for a hundred dalasis,
> It will look good with a gold chain.

> 'Sibo Mariyama Djankeh – Wo!
> Mother of the civilized people.
> This "Chinese" woman has defeated you all
> – in the game of beauty.

> 'I said, Sibo Mariyama!
> If I am allowed,
> I will have my photograph taken with her.

> 'I'm going to dance the *venti latir*.
> I shook my hips till they nearly split.
> *Venti latir – Wo!*
> I'm not doing that dance again!

> 'My cassette player is very big!
> Since I told the boy I could not solve his problem
> He keeps bothering me with it.
> Hey! I said I cannot solve your problem!'

Now there was even a style song about me:

> '*Tubabo Marky la be ke*
> *Koddo tang lulu nila mbe wola*
> *Ning Marky se ta ya*
> *Miro be nte sassa la.*'

> 'Tubabo Mark is the cause of it all.
> I'm referring to the giver of fifty dalasis.
> If Mark should go,
> People will become ill through thinking about him.'

The women entered the house quietly and seated themselves on the Habitat sofa, the armchairs and the wicker-backed dining chairs. All eyes were on the drums, which stood in the middle of the dull green carpet. They were not very large drums, but they seemed to exert a peculiar hold over the women, as though they were generating some invisible electromagnetic force which drew their attention whether they willed it or not.

Eventually Sona crept forward and tapped gently on the edge of one of the skins. A faint 'pang, pang, pang' rose up into the room.

'Please!' said Nafi Saho. 'We are now close to the village. People will hear us.'

Sona retreated.

We sat there in awkward silence for some moments.

'Come,' said Jarjei Sanyang. 'We have come here to dance. Let us not just sit.'

'Yes,' said others. 'The village is far. They will not hear us.'

Jarjei began to move around the circle of women in a kind of swaying shuffle, clapping softly. I went to the kitchen to fetch water for them to drink. Suddenly there was a great burst of clapping ringing out through the windows and across the compound.

'Hurh!' said Fatounding. 'Today will be very sweet!'

Sona picked up the bass drum, the kutiriba, and holding it experimentally under her arm, she sat on the edge of the coffee table, her fingers playing lightly over the skin. Then she lowered it, and gripped it between her knees in the manner of the griots. Jeynaba took the smaller drum, the kutir'ndingo, and began tapping in sympathy

I found a packet of black mints I had been keeping to give to visitors, and gave them to Ami Marong to dispense. A great whoop of approval went up from the women, and Sona and Jeynaba, who until then had been only tentatively tapping on the drums, began to pound vigorously on the skins. Soon the mud-brick house was shaking to its foundations with the stamping of the women and the shattering, cataclysmic clapping, as one after another they leapt into the circle to dance. A haze of grey dust rose from the carpet. And at the centre of everything was the booming and the clattering of the drums, reverberating through the house and out into the colourless light of midday.

Unlike in the West, where the beating of drums is used largely as an accompaniment to melody, in Africa it is not seen as music as we understand the word. The rhythms are inextricably bound up in the rituals and processes of the people's lives. And like these processes, their forms are precise, and prescribed. Two rhythms which, to a European, may sound equally precise, meaningful and satisfying, may be, to an African, as different as a well-honed sentence and a stream of gibberish. If it is not one of the traditional rhythms of their culture, it is nothing. They don't even hear it is a rhythm.

There were the rhythms of the men, and there were the rhythms of the women. And needless to say they were different. Yaya Bojang tapped the edge of the skin. Then he touched the centre of the skin with the forefinger of his other hand, holding it there to flatten the sound, as he struck the edge of the skin again. He speeded it up into a steady and even stream of sound.

'This is the way they beat called *kumpo*. It is a Jola dance where they cover themselves with leaves.'

It was difficult at that speed to see precisely what he was doing. I tapped the skin twice with one hand, then once with the forefinger of the other. I speeded it up. It sounded pretty good.

'No, no,' said Yaya. 'The way you are beating is the way the women beat when they are in the bush.'

The first time I tried to beat a drum was with Fabakary Manneh. We had gone into the big, cool bedroom where Helene and the Professor used to sleep, and the windows and doors remained firmly closed, because I had been warned that if the villagers knew we were beating drums they would come to the house and break the skins.

Faks showed me the rhythms quite precisely, 'Not this, this and this. Twice with the left hand, once with the right then twice with the left.' Once I speeded up I found I was starting to leave bits out by mistake. I had to do it slowly until my arms did it by themselves, and then speed up. Faks would watch me and wait till he was sure that I had caught the rhythm, then he would start beating out cross rhythms, apparently at random, and with considerable vigour and energy. He had the kutir'ndingo, the small treble drum, which had been tightened to an almost metallic hardness. In the big empty room it sounded unbelievably loud – as though a train were passing through the room. After a time I began to notice new permutations in what I was playing. Was I subtly changing the rhythm without noticing, or was I hearing it differently? It was as though I were inside the rhythm, and new doors were opening in its structure. Whatever, it didn't change the overall pattern, and the volume seemed to increase as we built up speed. I felt sure we must have been audible for miles around. I was facing the door, and at any moment I expected it to fly open, as villagers armed with axes burst into the room. Eventually Faks signalled to me, and he raised his hands, and we both brought our hands down together, in a single resounding beat. Then we fell back exhausted.

'Hundred per cent,' said Faks. 'That is the way the boys beat the drums when they go for circumcision.'

'Do they dance to that?'

'Of course.'

'How do they dance?'

'Any way you like. Just jumping. They will be beating drums there day and night. They will show you certain rhythms while you are there. Then they will tell you to play them. If you cannot do it, they will beat you. That is why every African knows how to beat drums to some extent.'

I held my breath, wondering if he was going to tell me any more.

'On the last day we prayed that whoever told what had happened to us there would die. So I don't think I can say anything else.'

*

New Civil Servants had arrived in the village. And they were quite different from the ones I had already met. Father J was a tall, cool young man of my age, a member of the royal family of Nyumi on the north bank. He spoke English far better than any of the other Civil Servants, and I discovered that this was because his father had also been educated in English.

His friend Pa Konte was a little older; shorter, but equally handsome. He was an intensely proud and extremely volatile character – he claimed he had once shot a man in the leg in a fit of pique. He was a Bambara, one of the pagan branch of the Manding family, who lived largely in Mali. But he had been brought up among the Mandingkos in Fonyi. He had, he said, a great understanding of European women, for he had lived for six years with an American woman, a Peace Corps volunteer. We immediately became firm friends.

They had come to make certain tests on the ITC cattle, and they had been provided with red Honda motorbikes, on which to follow the peregrinations of these bony beasts through the bush. These machines were the envy of the MRC staff, who made any excuse to borrow them and go tearing around the countryside at insane speeds.

Everywhere the young toads lay dead. Their dried corpses littered the pathways – some hunched defensively, others frozen in the attitude of leaping, like Jeremy Fisher in the Beatrix Potter story. Many survived, and at night their massed, symphonic croaking continued. But in the morning I would find more of their bodies rigid on the living-room carpet and the bathroom floor.

With the newly-harvested rice had come tiny triangular insects called *funkwinero*. They didn't harm it, but just sat on the stacked sheaves, covering them and the beams of the surrounding buildings so thickly that they appeared like a solid encrustation. The only way to get rid of them was to smoke them out, though this had to be done carefully. Recently, while trying to remove them from Jarra Njai's cooking hut, they had managed to set fire to the thatched roof, and now only the charred beams stood out against the pale sky.

'Every afternoon since we went to Mark's house, I have heard the boys beating the drums at the school,' said Senabu.

'Soon drumming will be allowed in this village,' said Mokuta. 'Because the school is in the village, and the elders have not said anything about it, though they have heard them.'

'When we went to Mark's house and started beating drums, we were very afraid that they would come and stop us. But they didn't.'

'In Mark's house you can beat drums and no one will hear you. Only the people who are nearby. Even the people at the Quarters cannot hear you.'

Six days after the harvesting of the groundnuts, the Saniyoro Kafo assembled early in the morning to gather the now dry plants together. The elder members piled the plants into heaps, while the younger ones used the biggest basins they had been able to find to carry them to a great stack on the other side of the field, where they were packed tightly together in a round, low mass like a huge, grey cake. This task soon completed, the women squatted under a tree to discuss the kafo's outstanding business.

Momodou Sanyang and Jarra Njai's husband Kemoring both wanted the group to thresh their groundnuts. They had each sent packets of black mints to the group as tokens of their seriousness. Balamin Sise and Luntang Bel, the shopkeeper, also wanted the group to help them. Meanwhile, the owner of the bull that had ploughed the sesame field wanted them to go to his field as well.

There was a clamour of agitated voices. Everyone said what she felt, and nobody listened to anybody else. Jeynaba said emphatically that she could not get involved in any more work for the kafo, since her husband was now working for the ITC and she had to work at his field as well as her own. Ami Marong said they must not get involved in favouritism. 'Let us choose all or forget all. But let us not choose one and leave one.'

'As far as Jarra Njai's husband's field is concerned, we will do whatever the kafo decides. If the kafo says no, we will not go.'

'It is not fair to work on Kemoring's groundnuts while others are not going to have theirs threshed,' piped up another voice.

'During the rainy season we went to help Kemoring weed his groundnut field,' said Menata. 'We just did it for the sake of unity. Kemoring is hand in hand with this kafo.'

'Before we go, let us choose a date for helping the owner of the bull,' said Fatounding. 'He did not charge us for the use of his animal. So we must help him, since one good turn deserves another.'

'Yes, all others we can forget, except this last one.'

'So take these mints back to Kemoring, and tell him that we do not accept them.'

'And tell him we have brought shame on our kafo,' said Jarjei. 'After he gave us his boy for the whole day to plough our field, thinking we would help him.'

'I will not say anything,' said Jarra Njai. 'If the kafo decides to send my husband's mints back, they must send them back. But these people must remember how much Kemoring has supported us.'

There were women who had lost many children – whose children had been born dead, or who had died shortly after birth. And there were women who had never become pregnant at all. And they had the belief that if they behaved in a way that was very shameless – as if they had no pride – that God would help them to have a child. This was known as *kanyelengya*. A *kanyeleng* woman, it was said, would stand naked in front of you – and she would not care.

In Dulaba there were several kanyeleng kafos, but the most notorious was the Kurung Kafo, a group of women in their early forties. Its leader was Safi Mama Sise, a short, stocky woman married in the compound of Kafuli Kunda to an elder brother of Jarra Njai and Fatounding's husbands. She was one of the most notable personalities among the women, not only because her husband was a Minte, which entitled her to be a leader, but because she was one of the hardest workers, one of the biggest talkers, and one of the loudest laughers. She called herself a *jaliba* (a griot) and a *fangbondi*. A jaliba, because if she attended a marriage ceremony she would be the one who led the singing. And a fangbondi because she would sometimes attend meetings she had not been invited to, and speak on her own behalf. For the word 'fangbondi' referred to a demon that appeared during the men's circumcision – which, according to the meaning of its name, 'goes out by itself'.

Daouda's first wife, Sirrah Bajie, had remained for six years without a child. Ndey-Touti, the second wife, who was four years younger, already had a son. But each time Sirrah became pregnant she would miscarry. So she had gone to the Kurung Kafo, and asked them to help her. They had given her Safi Mama's faneau, and her be-cho, her under-faneau, to wear, because Safi Mama had had ten children, many of whom had survived. Then, when the kafo went to Sirrah's groundnut field to work, she had cooked for them. They had eaten the food and prayed for her. Now Sirrah had two strong, healthy daughters. And although these kanyeleng women were much older than her, she stayed with them because of what they had done for her.

'They are after food,' said Yaya Bojang. 'That is what they talk about, and that is what they sing about. If they see you with food, they will just come and take some of it from you. They can come into your kitchen and take food, and you cannot do anything about it. You will find them always together. And if something happens that will benefit them, they will tell each other, and soon they will all know. For example, if they believe that you are taking an interest in them they will tell each other, and they will come together to see you, to see what they can get from you. And if you invite them, they will assume you are inviting them for food. And they will steal things – not big things – just small things.'

Not all of these women were shameless. But they forced themselves to do these things because of the benefits it would bring. Others continued in the way of the kanyelengo, even though they now had many children, simply because they enjoyed it.

Recently, one of their number, Mabintu, who had lived to her forties without ever becoming pregnant, had given birth to a son. This child was greatly prized by the women, and they called him Saibeto, 'the follower of God'.

There were many other people in the village who were known by unusual names. One of the elders, the head of one of the largest compounds, though his name was Lamin Sise, was always called Fadyeiko. His mother had lost many children, so after he had been named officially by the head of the compound, she had held a separate party for her kafo at which she named him Fadyeiko – a name that came from the sound the baboons made when they spoke to each other in the bush. For it was said that the pregnancy of a baboon was always successful, and traditionally this name was said to indicate that God had been merciful.

That woman had never had another child, but it was believed that it was because of this name that this man had lived to such a great age.

A dispute was brewing between the Saniyoro Kafo and the Kurung Kafo. The kafos were preparing to go together to thresh the groundnuts of the men who had lent their bulls for the ploughing of the sesame field. And Fatounding had apparently heard one of the members of the Kurung Kafo saying that they would not work with the Saniyoro, as there were so many rude people in that group. Mr Manneh, the agricultural demonstrator, on hearing that the Saniyoro Kafo would not work with the Kurung Kafo, because of what had been said, had threatened to fine them.

The Saniyoro Kafo were furious. They said that a Civil Servant should not involve himself in such village disputes, and that the insults of the Kurung Kafo must be paid back to them. Finally, however, they decided that as these remarks had been motivated only by jealousy – since I had given money to them and not to any other group – they would help these 'old women', even though the old women did not respect themselves. They would not show the Kurung Kafo any malice as individuals, since they were their sisters, their mothers, their aunts and their co-wives. But as groups they were now enemies, and they would wait for a chance to pay them back.

When I went to ask Mr Manneh and Safi Mama about this, however, they both denied all knowledge of it. I sometimes thought people invented these monumental palavers to pass the time through the long afternoons of work; though there was no doubt that younger people were remarkably neurotic in their attitude towards their elders. A young person could not deny the words of an elder – even a person only two or three years their senior – and an elder had to maintain a sense of dignity in front of the youth. So it was always awkward when people of different age-groups came together, and people preferred to mix socially with people of their own age. If younger people competed with their elders, it was bound to lead to trouble. Each school holiday, the village boys who were studying away would challenge the Civil Servants to a football match, and each time there would be fights, because of the shame the boys felt at losing to their elders.

As I was leaving Safi Mama's compound I thought I did notice just the faintest trace of a smirk at the corner of her mouth. Perhaps it was, after all, one of her jokes that had gone a little too far.

The moon rose huge and red, through a haze of vermilion dust, and shortly after midnight a wrestling competition was convened for the small boys in the centre of the village street.

Each bout began with the two wrestlers grappling each other round the waist. From then on it was simply a question of one forcing the other onto the ground – in the case of these juveniles, simply by pushing each other over. Thus the little circle of spectators and aspirant champions was constantly moving across the street, as people leapt to avoid the ferocious shoving of the wrestlers, who went shooting backwards and forwards, until one of them collapsed under the vehemence of his opponent's assaults. Seen from above, the match must have resembled some unstable microscopic organism constantly slithering this way and that as it formed and reformed.

A group of young men in their mid to late twenties, including Momodou Minte, Sullu Sise and Sambujang Samate, attempted to maintain some semblance of order. Sambujang Samate was a person of extraordinarily dense physique, who had himself been well-known as a wrestler until his brother had ordered him to stop. He had once invited me to go for a walk with him in the bush. I assumed he meant a mere stroll, and I had returned in the evening, my feet bleeding, having walked seventeen miles through the heat of the day. He, though complaining of tiredness, had nonchalantly gone off to play football. He spoke little English, but had an intense desire to go to Europe; though unlike the Civil Servants, he would go not by aeroplane, on a scholarship, but overland, via Libya – 'hustling' as he put it. Tonight he was nominally in charge but he seemed remote from the proceedings. He held a radio to his ear, twiddling with the dial as he attempted unsuccessfully to tune it in. 'In Europe everybody's sitting drinking coffee,' he said to me. 'Here we're doing this. This is local life.'

All across the fields to the north and west of the village, the groundnuts lay on the threshing floors, the work of threshing and winnowing in various stages of completion. Some stacks were still intact, covered with polythene or surrounded in fences of mesh to keep the marauding sheep, goats and donkeys at bay. Others were half-threshed – reduced to a crumbling mess, like huge, grey cakes ravaged by a drunken diner.

In other places the heaps of groundnuts and fragments of broken stem waited only to be winnowed. A tall forked branch would be dug into the threshing floor, to create a high seat on which the farmer would sit as he shook the nuts and chaff into the wind – his wives and sons having gathered them into baskets for him.

It was a time of hard work, for the nuts had to be got into their sacks as quickly as possible before the animals ate them all. But it was also a happy time. For the rain had been good, and the people were seeing the reward for all their months of hard work. And as the season raced inexorably towards its conclusion, there was a feeling of excitement in the air. Every night it seemed that at one or other of the surrounding villages there was drumming, or a disco, or a wrestling match. And at the great gatherings in the bush, where the kafos of the women banded together for work, the singing and the dancing and the laughter were almost without pause.

On the Sunday, a naming ceremony was held by one of the most influential families in Karafa Kunda, and many members of the Saniyoro Kafo had gone to attend. The next day, most of these people had still not returned, but had gone on to further ceremonies at Kulli Kunda and Joli. The event at Joli promised to be particularly lavish, the child being the first male heir of one of the most important families in the village. The child's grandmother was a member of the Kurung Kafo of Joli, so the Kurung Kafo of Dulaba had gone there *en masse* to honour her.

That night I went with the Civil Servants to see Massamba and his group performing in the square in front of the mosque in Joli. The nights were by now very cool, but a girl gave me her faneau to wrap around my shoulders.

It was the early hours of the morning before the dancing began in earnest, the figures of the women glowing as though golden in the light of the hurricane-lamp, as they came running towards the drummers, spinning around only at the last moment to dance. This was what they liked more than anything else – the extremity of this total bodily exertion, this fervent, almost ecstatic unleashment of energy, in which every muscle, every last atom of their energy would be used. It was as though the rhythms of the drums, the pummelling on the taut, heated skins, were touching something actually inside the women themselves, to which their frenetic shaking was an involuntary, though wholly pleasurable response.

They called it *dia* – sweetness – and the more they danced, the sweeter it would be. But if any woman danced for more than about a minute, her friends would laughingly seize her, and drag her from the circle. 'I went to a party,' went the lyrics of one of their songs. 'I enjoyed myself so much I nearly died.'

Suddenly the girl whose faneau I had borrowed was standing in front of me, and placing her head-tie around my neck. There was a roar of approval from the crowd.

'Go on!' said Yaya Bojang. 'You have to dance. Whoever wears the scarf *must* dance!'

I tried to remove it, but hands reached out to put it back, and to place more scarves over it. The next thing I knew, I was standing in the glare of the hurricane-lamp, a buffoon-like figure festooned in scarves, all about me the beating of the drums, the frenzied blasting of the whistle, and the clapping of the women rising to a crescendo. I began to dance – stamping desperately on the hard ground, thrusting my arms into the air in imitation of the women. It had little to do with the rhythm, which was far too fast for me to follow, but I felt suitably shaken as I staggered from the circle, to the howling and crooning of the crowd. It felt as though all the blood in my body had rushed to my feet and hands. Yet I felt oddly elated, and ready for another attempt.

Yaya Bojang seized my hand as I came lurching from the ring a second time. 'Well done,' he said. 'The second time was *definitely* better than the first.'

When I got home I stuffed myself with everything I could find in the fridge, and went to bed feeling strangely happy.

That day the women who had remained behind had gone to thresh the groundnuts of the owner of the first bull that had ploughed the sesame field. So the following day, all the women who had been to Joli went to the field of the owner of the other bull. There were women there from every kafo, the members of the Kurung Kafo easily identifiable by their strings of red, yellow and blue plastic beads – like lengths of plastic drinking straw – and their whistles, which they blew at the first hint of frivolity. There was no sun, but the air was thick and hot, and the work uncomfortable and chaotic, the women of the different kafos jostling each other for position around the great mound of roots and nuts, into which they beat with pairs of long, pick-like sticks. The air rattled with their clatter and the crackling of the groundnut roots breaking under them. Everyone was coughing, wrinkling their noses and screwing up their eyes against the dust that rose from the heap into the branches of the trees that overhung the place. On the outside of the ring more women sat picking through the discarded stems. People began to sing to try to bring a sense of unity to the occasion, but the heap was so big that those on one side could not hear what those on the other were singing.

Around the middle of the afternoon there was a break for lunch, the women squatting in their groups around huge basins of porridge and futo.

The Kurung Kafo moved in groups among the diners, their head-ties discarded, their faces covered in porridge. They sang as they moved, digging their hands into the basins of the other kafos, some heaping the damp futo into the fronts of their shirts.

Soon everyone was back at work, and the clapping and the blowing of whistles from the Kurung Kafo's side of the heap was becoming louder.

'Hey, please,' said a woman called Nyiranding, a member of the Sembendo Kafo. 'We decided that no one will sing today as there are so many people here.'

'Yes,' said another woman. 'You kanyeleng people, please don't disturb us. We've already decided that we shouldn't sing.'

'We have the right,' said Jongkong, known as Gunjur, one of the leaders of the Kurung Kafo, a short, plump woman, very black in complexion – the great friend of Safi Mama. 'Don't you know that wherever the kanyeleng are there should be no silence, only disturbance?' And standing up she blew her whistle in the other woman's face.

Soon a full-scale argument was in progress, with both women refusing to back down. Safi Mama, who had been quietly picking over the stems, came scurrying between the women. 'Come on,' she said. 'Everybody sit down. If you keep on arguing people will say the Kurung Kafo only came here to argue.'

'Whenever we meet this other kafo we always quarrel,' said Gunjur. 'The elders have told people to work together and listen to each others' words. But this other kafo, they didn't hear that. They only came here to quarrel.'

'Come on. Please, Gunjur. Nothing good will come of this. There are a lot of people here.'

'Yes, Gunjur, you are a leader. Forgive!'

'No. I shall never forgive.'

'Getting annoyed with people,' said Nyiranding. 'This is something that we have found with this kafo. You said we're hopeless. So leave us to our hopelessness.'

'Leave it,' said her companion. 'It's finished.'
'Now let us dance!'
'Yes,' said Gunjur. 'We must dance always. It's what we have to do. There must be singing, dancing, clapping and blowing whistles – anything that will make people laugh.'

As soon as the threshing was finished, the Kurung Kafo picked up their sticks and moved on to the next stack, leaving the other women to pick over the roots in relative quietude.

At the second stack the work proceeded quickly to the accompaniment of tumultuous singing. The sun was going down, and a faint golden glow began to filter through the dust. Safi Mama took the lead, strutting slowly into the middle of the heap of groundnuts and smashed stems.

'The villagers have tried to put a stop to it –
But they couldn't!'
'*Hey!*' sang the other women.

'The whole country has tried to put a stop to it –
But they couldn't!'
'*Hey – Hey – Hey!*'
'Even Sir Daouda Kairaba Jawara has tried to put a stop to it –
But he couldn't!
They will try to remove it, but they will not succeed!
Because this kafo does whatever it feels is right.'

The other kafo members rushed in around her, raising their threshing sticks in the air. Some picked up branches of groundnuts, holding them aloft like triumphal wreaths, as the whole group moved in a stately shuffle around the heap. The onlookers let out whoops of hilarity and joy as they began to sway their bodies to the rhythm of the song. And in the centre of the group, Safi Mama continued her narration with the same effortless, guttural gusto with which she did everything in her life.

'If you give it to me – I will not be ashamed.
If you give me the leadership – I will not be afraid.
So don't be afraid, don't be ashamed, to give it to me.
For without leaders this kafo cannot go forward!
We, the great ones – we don't know what it is to be afraid.
You, the people of high rank – we are not afraid of you.
And we don't know what tiredness is!

'I am praying for the future well-being of this kafo!
Come, let us go forward together!'

It was a moment of great warmth and intimacy between a great many people. But Safi was someone who could pull people together in that kind of way; the same as she could beat them with her fist if they annoyed her –

even those of her own age-group. She was, as a leader, even more formidable than Jarra Njai. And this charisma was all the more impressive for being apparently unconscious. It didn't prevent her from merging into the crowd if she felt like it.

Those who had coins came forward to give them to her. 'Nimbara!' they said.

'Nimbara!' she returned, calling their surnames in the song.

It was six years after they transferred to their husbands that they had decided to become a kanyeleng kafo. When they had seen how many of their children were dying, they had had a meeting, and decided that they would take the way of praying that their mothers had taken before them. For a person's prayer could take many forms. She could repeat God's words. She could read the Koran. She could even pray by singing and dancing and smearing porridge on her face. All these things were part of prayer.

They had taken the name Kurung Kafo – the Wicked People. They stole things. And wherever they stole they would dance. If they took food they would clap and sing as they ate; not because they were wicked or stupid, but because they begged God that those who were pregnant might deliver in peace, and that their children might live.

And God had answered their prayers, for now the children of their kafo were many. But they continued their activities for the benefit of those who were coming after them – the younger women who would ask their kafo to pray for them. Sirrah Bajie and many others they had helped were now in peace. The faneau of Kungkung, one of the other elders of the kafo, had been given to Manlafi Darbo, the wife of the fieldworker Seikoubah Sanneh. She was not pregnant yet, but they were expecting it to happen at any time.

After the women of the kafo had been given to their husbands, and even after they had been transferred to their husbands, Gunjur had failed to conceive. So she had been taken by her mother to the kanyeleng kafo. They had done everything for her. It was they who had given her the name Gunjur. But to this very day she had never become pregnant.

The people of the kafo were not upset by this; nor were they even surprised. Whether God answered their prayers or not was His decision. And what He gave He could also take away. It would be a sin to resent it.

That night, as I sat on the verandah of the Quarters, I could hear the sound of clapping, so faint you had to listen hard to catch it. 'Dancing,' said Jori Sanyang. 'In Sanyang Kunda.'

In a dark corner of the great compound, a calabash was being beaten onto the top of a mortar, and in the centre of a small group of figures, I could make out the brawny figure of Jarjei Sanyang, apparently dressed only in a towel, dancing vehemently. 'Njambaro!' she shouted on seeing me. 'My Champion! Come and dance!' And she seized my hand. 'A new wife has arrived in our compound!'

'The new wife is beautiful!' she sang as she moved back among the group of figures around the mortar. 'The new wife is beautiful. The beautiful new wife – *Hey!*'

And she began to dance as the clapping broke out again, the hard sound beating against the warm night air.

'Come and greet the new wife,' she said when she'd finished, and pulled me by the arm into a nearby house. In the large room, which was lit only by a tiny paraffin lamp, a teenage girl sat on the edge of a bed with her arms folded, staring at the floor. A semi-circle of children stood around her singing style songs – most notably *'Tubabo Marky la be ke'*. Who the hell is Tubabo Marky, the girl may well have wondered?

Outside, more people were joining the circle. Jarjei went in to dance again, this time throwing all of her not inconsiderable weight into it. She seemed to be able to dance longer and harder than any of the other women, and she would sing while she was doing it. Whenever I saw her performing – 'demonstrating' as they called it – the word 'incorrigible' came into my mind. She was only twenty-seven, but she'd already been married three times.

Her first husband was a young man, a citizen of Dulaba, who had moved to Brikama, where he had a shop. She had stayed there for two years, until her family sent a message to her husband asking when he was going to pay the remainder of the bride-price. When no money was forthcoming, her grandfather had gone to Brikama to seize her. And though her husband had made an offer of payment (six dalasis, an Ovaltine tinful of sugar and some mousetraps), it was not considered nearly enough, and Jarjei was brought back to Dulaba. Shortly after her return she was married again. But it lasted only for a matter of weeks, and then she was back in her parents' compound, where she stayed, without a husband, for seven years.

On the opposite side of the compound was the house of a man who worked as a driver for the government. He was a stranger to the village, but he had been there for some ten years. And it was well known that he was the father of Jarjei's youngest child. She had loved him very much, and had expected that she would become his second wife. But in the end he had chosen a much younger woman.

She made no attempt to hide the bitterness she felt towards this man. Indeed she loudly publicized the fact that he had never provided any clothes or shoes for the child. But though they lived virtually side by side, he paid no attention. He could be seen at that very moment, in the light of his verandah, sitting drinking Chinese tea with his friends. But she treated both his wives with great respect. And they respected her. She and the first wife were both members of the Saniyoro Kafo, and when the kafo went to the fields to work, she would sing songs in praise of both their daughters, acknowledging their common parentage. Some people might have considered such behaviour shameful. But Jarjei didn't care. Such things needed to be said.

Now she had another husband, a well-digger from Jarra. He travelled all over the country with his work, so she spent only part of the year in his village, and had now come to help her mother with the harvesting of the groundnuts. She realized that she didn't have the full love for this man – that she had only accepted him because her first choice had been disappointed. But she would stay with him, not only because she had heard that when a woman died no one would attend her funeral if she was not married, but because when everyone else was married, it was just not possible to be without a husband.

Ever since the Saniyoro Kafo had come to dance in my house, there had been a fierce debate among the women; between those who believed that the kafo had been right to go there – that the sound of drums beating, at the school or at the camp, was making the life of the village sweeter, that soon drumming would be permitted in the village, that it must happen, that it was part of the changing of the generations – and those who believed that these people were going against the traditions of the village, that their ancestors had observed these restrictions and they should hold to them whether they benefited them or not.

Co-wives, sisters, mothers and daughters were divided on the issue, with the older women sometimes taking the more 'liberal' stance. Few of the women believed that disaster would strike if drums were beaten in the village. But they were all afraid of the divisions it would create in their society; the arguments it would cause between them and their husbands and their fathers – arguments they could never win. And it was this latter consideration that would ultimately determine the course of their action. But though they were prepared to hold to the strictures of their husbands when they were in the village, when they were in the bush, particularly when they were only among those of their own age group, they would behave only as they wished.

It was the day of the threshing of the Saniyoro Kafo's groundnuts. The women had brought my drums to the field. But they had put them to one side until the threshing was completed. It was another dull day – the sun hidden by the dust.

'Please,' said Janno. 'Let's be in haste. We are going to beat these drums soon! Whoever doesn't want to join us can go home. But let me tell you that if we get money for our groundnuts, and we buy cloth and wear it, we're going to feel very happy and we're going to dance and forget all about this hard work we did in the bush.'

'Yes, when we get our cloth, we're going to have a big party in Mark's house.'

It had been their intention, ever since they planted their groundnuts, to spend the money on *ashobi* – 'a very fine piece of cloth'. They would all have faneaus and shirts and head-ties of the same material. It would look very beautiful, and everyone would know that they were *one*.

'There are a lot of groundnuts here.'

'It's going to be ten donkeys.' (A donkey was two large sacks of groundnuts – the load that one donkey could carry.)

'Four donkeys.'

'Four donkeys and one bag.'

'Six or seven donkeys,' said Sona.

'Fifteen donkeys,' said someone else.

'Hey,' said Jeynaba. 'If you're going to say something, say something reasonable, and not just stupid things.'

'Five donkeys.'

'OK.'

When the threshing was completed, and the women sat in a circle picking through the stems, Jarjei and Sona took the drums and sat on top of the heap, slapping the skins in a leisurely fashion.

'*Dolefoy*,' boomed Jarjei.

'*Diiiiii!*' went Sona, making a sound like a tinny motor horn.

'*Koringkoy!*'

'*Di! Di!*'

The women began to clap in time, as the drummers took up an easy loping beat, such as was heard at wrestling matches.

'You people are from Karafa Kunda. We are from Tankular. Let us call each other and wrestle.'

'Get up! Get up! Get up!'

'Are you afraid of each other?' shouted Jarjei.

'Come on, clap, clap, clap!'

Everyone began shouting as Mamanding Janno ran out onto the heap. '*Atcha*,' she shouted. 'Let your wrestler come out and get ready to fight.'

'Is there a wrestler on your side?' asked Jeynaba.

'I don't think there is anyone there.'

'Come on wrestler,' called Janno. 'Please get up. Are you afraid?'

Ida Sanyang got to her feet.

'Yo!' said Janno. 'The Supplement Centre is ready with its wrestler.'

'*Anfamasbih!*' sang Jarjei. '*Ko-sbo!*'

Ida ran over to where Janno was standing, and assumed a combative posture.

'*Ko-sbo!*'

Janno darted backwards, and the two women chased each other over the groundnuts for some moments. Then Janno leapt onto Ida. The bigger woman was laughing so much she collapsed immediately. Janno sat astride her, waving her head-tie in triumph.

'*Mamanding Janno – Yey!*' shouted the women.

'Mamanding Janno is very quick to fell her opponent.'

Janno ran around the circle of women crowing. 'Our group have beaten your group!' she cried. 'You people are nothing.'

The next day it was the turn of the Dinding Kafo – the so-called Children's Kafo – to take the drums to the bush. They had gone to the field of Sambujang Samate and his elder brother Nfaali, which lay to the north of the village, deep among the fields of Wali Kunda. The girls had completed the threshing the day before, and now everybody sat picking through the great banks of stems that surrounded the heap.

The younger girls – the Yaisset Kafo, who were reaching puberty but had not yet been given to their husbands – sat on one side of the heap, while their elders – the My Brother Kafo, many of whom were pregnant and some of whom even had children – sat on the other. And as they worked, a competition began to see who could finish first. The leaders of the older kafo, Bana Sise, the eldest daughter of my washing lady Mabinta, and Homonding Minte, a tall and rather serious-looking girl from the same compound, assumed authority over the group as a whole.

'Whoever has come here to work will work. No one will look after their child,' said Bana, who did not have a child herself. 'These people with babies are just having a joke with us. As soon as they hear their child crying, they say "Hey, my child is crying!" and go and have a sit-down.'

'Our kafo wants to be in unity with Mark,' said Howanding, the second wife of Momodou Jallo, the night-watchman at the MRC. She had a broad mouth, bright eyes, and was known as someone who had a lot to say – and little of it of any consequence.

'Huh,' said someone else. 'Mark has his own people: the Saniyoro.'

'We expect you to follow us wherever we go,' said Howanding.

'If you do that you will be leaving the Saniyoro,' said the other.

'Hey Mark, in our kafo everyone is extremely beautiful,' said Sibby. She was one of the oldest of the girls, a tall woman with a slow, languorous voice. 'There are so many beautiful people in this kafo. We are more than the Saniyoro, and we are also more beautiful than them.'

The others laughed.

I had gone there to find out what sort of things the young girls talked about. But I was surprised to find that, in these sessions of group work at least, their conversation was largely indistinguishable from that of the older women: the constant urgings to harder work, the vilification of latecomers and those who had supposedly come only to play or to eat, the question of whether to sing or not to sing. And like the Saniyoro, this kafo had its clowns, its prigs and its natural leaders. It even had a Fatounding, a Binta Sise, a Jarra Njai and a Sona. If I closed my eyes I could imagine that I was listening to the conversation of my own kafo when they were that age. And when the Saniyoro Kafo themselves had gone on to become the elders of the village, these girls would be what the Saniyoro Kafo were today. People would replace each other, and the village would remain what it had always been.

As they worked, they sang style songs ceaselessly – the two sides of the heap competing to try to drown each other out.

> 'The boy said I'm not beautiful.
> But I'm more beautiful than he is.
> He has a flat nose, a thick neck.
> And a tongue like one pound of meat.
>
> 'The boy went to Libya.
> Didn't you see the knickers that he brought?
> Sexy knickers!
> My buttocks shake when I wear them.'

'Touti Njai, the Wolof – Wo!
Have Touti's breasts come out yet?
If they don't grow,
She's going to miss out on the handsome men.

'There is a boy with small buttocks.
He has nothing but one pair of jeans.
If we are to laugh at him,
Let me be the one to begin the laughter.

'The boy with small buttocks passed me.
The boy with small buttocks did not greet me.
He has nothing in his pockets.
Except when his mother gives him twelve batuts.

'The big girls are all dressed up.
They say they want passports to go to Europe.
Hold everything!
Not everyone will be able to go!

'Planes going to and fro . . .
Plane, come here!
I want to tell you something in secret.
Today let love be far away – my father is around.

'I joined the queue.
The teacher-boy called me from his doorway.
But I just turned a deaf ear.
The teacher-boy has bad breath!

'Our brothers are useless!
Drinking alcohol and smoking ganja.
If you are to give me a husband,
By all means give me a weaver!

'The underwear of My Brother Kafo.
Beautiful young women are all united.
Begged underwear, bought underwear –
All of them are very beautiful.'

Nembali Sise had arrived with Jallo's first wife Mariyama. Nembali was
Jarra Njai's cousin, a stocky, fair-coloured woman in her mid-thirties. She
and Mariyama were the mothers of the two kafos. When the work was
finished, everyone sat down on the heap of nuts so that Nembali could
address them.

'Before you go any further, you have elected us as your elders, so
whatever we have seen that will help you to be one, we will tell you, so

that we can discuss it. We, the elders, we give respect to each other. We don't argue with each other. And when it is time for work, we work. Work never killed anybody! And when we are paid, we will forget all about the hard work we encountered before.'

Somebody laughed.

'Hey, please, don't laugh! We are not here to laugh. I'm not very happy about the way you shared the work today. You older girls shouldn't give all the work to the younger ones and then sit back. That is very bad! You should all mix together: an older girl and then a younger girl, an older girl and then a younger girl.

'When we were young we also elected an elder to tell us what we should do – to tell us to stop backbiting each other and behaving foolishly. That is the purpose of this meeting. We are here to instruct you people to be united. Do you hear us?'

'We hear you!' said the girls.

'Give them a very strong warning,' said Jallo's wife. 'Because sometimes they are very rude about us in their songs.'

By the time the older women had gone, it was late in the afternoon. The lunch, three basins of magenta futo, with slices of brilliant yellow pumpkin poking out of it, still lay waiting to be eaten. But without the addition of water, the futo was inedible. So it was decided to hold the eagerly awaited *tulungo* before heading back to the village to eat.

Sambujang's younger sister, Fatou, a nervous girl, very fair in complexion and wispily slender, beat the larger drum, her mouth hanging open, her eyes bulging with the intensity of holding to the rhythm. One of her age-mates, darker, more substantial, but equally shy, had the kutir'ndingo. They held the drums now under their arms, now between their legs, now on the ground; now beating them with their hands, now with bits of millet stalk – for they were not used to real drums. But though the older ones would sometimes take the drums, they would always quickly give them back, for these young girls were obviously so much better.

The singing of style songs and the beating of the drums continued as they marched briskly along the rough track back towards the village. They laughed and shouted, and their marching picked up speed, until they were almost running. Some of them picked sprays of green leaves, and waved them above their heads as they leapt and sprang along the path; others danced as they went. Then they began to sing a different song, a kind of anthem, and their young voices massed together, ringing out over the bush:

> 'Hey! Rimbo moyi bang!
> Ntolu la rimbo!
> Hey! Rimbo moyi bang!
> Nfa ba la Rimbo!

'Hear the sound of these drums!
Our own drums!
Hear the sound of these drums!
Our grandmothers' drums.'

The people they passed along the pathway did not greet them. They looked away, or they looked straight ahead. But the girls just laughed. They laughed at themselves, they laughed at each other, and they laughed at me. They passed a woman, one of their elders, sitting bareheaded, eating porridge at the side of the pathway, and they laughed at her too.

And always the other voices, the voices of the drums, could be heard resonating beneath the singing and the clapping, as they leaped and danced towards the village.

As they reached the point where the track crossed the red laterite road, Homonding and Bana told the drummers to stop beating. 'We are now almost in the village.' So the two leaders, in whom the care of the drums had been entrusted, put them carefully on their heads and we proceeded on our way. As they entered the village, the intensity and the volume of the girls' singing increased. And they held the drums upright, high above their heads – triumphantly, defiantly – like objects of devotion. Everywhere people ran from their compounds to see what was happening. And the men sitting at the bantabas, the young men and the old men – their fathers, uncles, brothers and husbands – looked on in astonishment, their expressions of disapproval mixed with admiration and a slight sense of fear.

Bana's mother, Mabinta, met them at the entrance to the compound, a look of horror on her face. 'What do you think you're doing, bringing drums into the village?' she shouted. But she couldn't be annoyed for long. They'd done it, and who couldn't feel happy to hear people singing like that?

A great crowd of children gathered around the girls and followed them into the compound, the scores of feet kicking up clouds of dust. Everyone was moving everywhere at once, and the children underfoot added to the confusion. The futo was liberally doused with water, and in less than a minute it had all been eaten. The young children tried to grab handfuls of it, and the tiredness of the girls showed in the irritation with which they drove them away.

Then the drums were picked up once again. The group of girls, joined by other young women and swelled by the great crowd of children, filled the village street, as it made its way towards the MRC compound. The air was filled with their singing, and the drums, held high, could just be seen, towering out of the cloud of red dust raised by their feet.

As we approached the MRC compound, a figure in an olive green uniform could be seen standing in front of the gates. It was Samba So, and he held a long, thick millet stalk horizontal before him.

What's the old maniac going to do now? I wondered.

There he stood, grim-faced. And as the crowd drew nearer, still singing, he began swinging the pole wildly in front of him. The crowd advanced, but paused when it became apparent that he meant to use it. People tried to dash through, but he rounded on them at once. I decided that under the circumstances it was better to leave it for today. If we all tried to go in there would be an 'incident' for which I would be blamed. Homonding and Bana helped me carry the drums into the house. I tried to explain to them that it was for the best. They understood, but I'm not sure that they agreed.

9

A SEALED PLACE

It was in the heightened atmosphere of the harvest time that something happened that was to bring me much closer to the people of Dulaba. It did not make me one of them – for that would have been impossible. But it did give me a stake in the life of the place. From then on it was no longer possible to be a mere observer. And like many changes, the importance of which is apparent only in retrospect, it happened within the blinking of an eye.

Sute Minte, known as Sute Jalo – Sute the Singer – had arrived in the village. He was not a griot in the conventional sense of the word, for he had none of the ancestral qualifications for the profession, but wherever the people spoke Mandinka, he would go to entertain them. And from Dakar to Guinea-Bissau, there was no jaliba like him. He was known as the *karante jalo* – the 'guaranteed jalo' – and wherever he went, the children would sing his song: '*Hey – Hey! Karante jalo!*' But perhaps the most unusual thing about him was the fact that he had been born in Dulaba – a village where the beating of drums was forbidden – in the compound of Kafuli Kunda.

It was the first time he had been in the village for three years, and the women were very excited, for jalibas almost never came to Dulaba.

On the Friday evening, after the Saniyoro Kafo had at last finished packing their groundnuts into sacks, I was invited to Kafuli Kunda, where, I was told, Jarra Njai's husband would be dancing. I tried to imagine the dignified and rather diffident Kemoring dancing in front of the huge crowd of women, but it was very difficult.

After dinner I went to Fatounding's compound, where by the light of a torch I saw two enormous calabashes floating upside down in basins of water. They were carried along the street to the small bantaba in front of the alkalo's compound, where Isatou began to beat on them with sticks – to signal that the dance was about to start.

Soon a great crowd of children had gathered, all singing style songs. I could tell from the clapping that people were dancing, but I could see nothing, for though the air was cool, the darkness was as thick and close as fur. And beneath the raucous singing and the hard, brittle clapping was the sound of the *kijo* – the calabash drums – soft, but resonant, and as the same time as bright and clear and buoyant as water itself – its rhythms insistent, but almost subliminal, underlying everything, driving people to movement, urging them to dance.

I turned on my torch to see dozens of little legs dancing in the beam. Then we were plunged back into darkness. I was densely surrounded by

people, but I had no idea who any of them were. 'Who's that beating the
calabashes?' I asked.

'Sona,' came a voice from the darkness. 'Sona . . . Sona . . .'

Suddenly a hurricane-lamp was lit and placed on a small table beside the
bantaba. The women of Kafuli Kunda, including Jarra Njai, Fatounding
and Isatou, began to clear a big circle around the bantaba, using long
millet stalks to disperse the children. There was quite a crowd – children,
girls, and women of all ages. Safi Mama, who was seated at the table,
began to lead the crowd in one of Sute's songs. The 'husband' of Jarra Njai
who was going to dance was not Kemoring, but his uncle, the jaliba
himself. He sat beside the hurricane-lamp, a scrawny, grizzled figure in a
woollen hat, chain-smoking and staring listlessly into space. Suddenly he
got to his feet and began to roar hoarsely into the night:

> *'Bissimilai – Wo! Kaira – Hey!*
> *Mbe luo fo lola kemo wola – Bissimilai!'*

It was his most well-known song, one of the characteristic tunes which
he endlessly improvised. And the women repeated each line after him,
the voices of the different generations rising together in one great chorus,
sounding curiously anthemic against the harsh, gravelly tones of the
jaliba.

> 'I'm starting the dancing in the name of God!
> The jaliba is starting in peace and in the name of God!
> So everybody pray! Everybody pray!
> It's nearly midnight.
> The crocodile can go and sleep.
> So enjoy yourselves! Everybody, enjoy yourselves!
> The devil has danced!
> So enjoy yourselves!'

As he sang, he advanced round the circle, punctuating his recitative
with wild gestures which greatly delighted the crowd. Crouching one
moment like an animal ready to spring, he would suddenly round on
another section of the crowd, pointing dramatically into the giggling
ranks of the girls. And he began to sing about the people in the crowd,
beginning with the women of Kafuli Kunda, who were his hosts:

> 'Fatounding! You have kept me waiting a long time, Fatounding!
> But it's difficult to be generous, Fatounding!
> The generous old woman . . . Fatounding!
>
> 'Jarra Njai, Hey! It's true, Jarra Njai!
> If you're beautiful you can rest . . . Jarra Njai!'

Laughing, the women rushed forward to press coins into his hand, and
soon more and more people were going into the circle to give him money.
And he devoted a line of his song to each of them. He had something to

say about all of them, because they were all his relatives – the little girls pushing between the legs of the adults, the matrons thickly wrapped against the cold, the young men lurking in the shadows on the edge of the crowd.

The young women began to dart into the circle to dance, their shadows flickering like moths around the lamplit figure of the jaliba.

'The way I walk – Wo! The way I walk!' sang the Jaliba.

There were roars and cackles from the crowd, and the rhythm of the kijo became faster:

'The way I walk annoys people.
The way I walk annoys people – too much!'

And he began to dance, flapping his arms at his sides like stunted wings, his feet pounding rhythmically into the dust. There were whoops and howls of approbation from the crowd, and a great storm of clapping broke out.

After that the circle broke up as everyone fell about in delighted laughter. How they loved to see him dance!

Re-forming the circle proved difficult. Children and even adults were constantly wandering in and out of the dancing area. The clapping and the singing were only half-hearted as arguments started to break out among the women. The jaliba became so irritated he threatened to stop, but the women of Kafuli Kunda managed to restore order and the dancing continued.

Finally, when it was almost time for people to go home, the jaliba turned to me, his face inches from mine as he bellowed out: *'Here is the tubab . . .'*

'He – Hey!' chanted the women, as they clapped in time.

'*The big drummer . . .*
But before you buy drums, let me ask you where you are
going with them . . .
Do you know how to beat them? . . .
If you're not going to say anything . . . You can come and I will teach you
. . . And singing also . . . And when you go to Europe . . . You can sing
there . . . If you don't believe me, you can watch me while I'm doing it . . .
I also will watch you . . . For the sake of tomorrow . . . My own tubabs . . .
Today will be very sweet . . . Turn on your tape recorder . . . Turn on
your tape recorder . . . '

And he began to dance again.

On Sunday morning, the village was almost deserted. The Civil Servants were resting, and most of the villagers were in the bush, winnowing the last of the groundnuts. Only the old men remained, plaiting long stalks of elephant grass into screens of a criss-cross design, with which they would fence off the washing areas at the back of their compounds. They sat in the streets, absorbed and intent over their work, the dust hanging in the air, creating a silver filter for the light of the sun. I was sitting on the verandah of Momodou Coly's house, chatting with Pa Konte and the Headmaster, when a woman, one of the members of the Saniyoro Kafo, came walking by, an enamel bowl wrapped in cloth balanced on her head. I asked her where she was going. 'I'm going to my groundnut field,' she said, and passed on up the street.

I was the only one who had greeted her, but Pa Konte began relating an anecdote to the Headmaster. It was in Mandinka too deep for me to understand, except for the English word 'frustrated', which Pa enunciated with great force, two or three times. But it was obvious that it pertained to this woman, and as I listened, I recalled that a few days before, when we were at the kafo field, I had looked up to see her staring straight at me. She was sitting quite close to me, and I realized that she had been looking at me for some time, the black pupils bright between the layers of grey dust that thickly encrusted the lashes. She had continued to stare at me, and smiled slowly, as though testing me in some way. I recalled how often in the months that I had been following the women's kafos to the fields, I had found myself standing close to this particular person. It was hardly surprising. She was one of the liveliest and most talkative members of the group, and would always have something amusing to say. She sang a lot. She shelled groundnuts for me to eat. She tried to provoke me. And after a while, as the rhythm of the season quickened, and I saw a great deal more of the women, I would often find myself just gazing at her – in much the same way that she had been looking at me. I hadn't given this much thought. I had scarcely been aware of it. But as I listened to this anecdote, I realized not only that I *had* to know exactly what was being said, but that I wanted to know everything there was to know about this woman.

That afternoon, all was quiet in the compound, and I felt suddenly rather lonely. I stood in the empty kitchen of House One and chewed on a piece of bread for lunch, staring out at the thin haze of dust hanging over the deserted football pitch. I wondered whether, if I went to the woman's field, I would find her there. I wondered if I would even be able to find the field. I would be too shy to ask, even though it would be considered within the normal sphere of my work.

After hesitating for some time, I headed out onto the laterite road towards Karafa Kunda, following the general direction she had taken. When I had passed the maize gardens beside the road junction, I looked out for signs of cultivation on the left-hand side of the road. But there was nothing. This was the *wulokono ba* – the real bush, the territory of devils – an apparently endless wilderness of weeds, termite hills and the charred wreckage of dead trees. I struck out into it in the hope of passing through to some of the village's more remote fields. It soon became obvious that the citizens of Dulaba would never cultivate an area this far away, so I cut back towards Wali Kunda, the densely cultivated area to the north of the village. After a time I saw a line of cattle crossing the bush ahead of me, and then a ramshackle shelter of branches and thatch, beyond which the groundnut fields stretched away into the distance, the dust suspended like webs of gossamer between the sparse stubble of dead trees. In the middle distance I could see three women threshing. After the loneliness and desolation of the bush, the sight of normal human activity, even in this bleak environment, was reassuring, almost homely. I was even more pleased to see that one of the women was Jarjei Sanyang. She was with her mother, and her mother's co-wife, Musakeba, who was only two years older than her. The mother gave me her threshing sticks, and sat down to pick over the stems.

'Tubabo Mark is the cause of it all,' sang Jarjei, as we worked.
'I'm referring to the giver of fifty dalasis.
If Mark should go,
People will become ill through thinking about him.'

That song had been on everybody's lips during the days of the harvest. It had even been heard as far afield as Serekunda. A woman had arrived from that town, wanting to know the identity of this Marky.
'Who wrote that song?' I asked.
'Sona,' said Jarjei.
Finally I stumbled off across the fields – having asked for the field by the name of the husband rather than the woman herself. I was accompanied by Jarjei's dreadful son Lamin, who was supposedly showing me the way, though he didn't appear to have any idea where we were going. The dead leaves crunched and crackled under our feet. Here and there the sorghum stalks had been gathered into bundles, but elsewhere they remained strewn over the land, and over large tracts they were the only sign that the dry, grey earth had ever been cultivated. Only the tall stands of millet remained to be harvested. The long yellow leaves, only weeks before a deep, rich green, cracked and rattled against the stems, as the harmattan blew over the world.
I could see another group of figures some way off. They stopped working and watched, as we approached the threshing floor. Famara Bajie, the Inneses' gardener, squatted, picking over the stems, as his wife Nyimansitou, a tall, statuesque woman, passed baskets of nuts and chaff to his friend Sullu Sise, who sat atop the winnowing post. They regarded me with some alarm – as though they had never seen me before; as though I were some devil or lunatic who had just wandered out of the bush.
'Where is Braima Sise's family?' I asked.
There was a pause.
'They have gone,' said Famara.
'When?'
'A long time ago.'
I trudged off back along the path to the village.

*

I sat on the verandah of Father J's house on the main street of the village. One felt rather than saw the people coming and going in the darkness. They passed without greeting, their dark masses momentarily stirring the air, the faint slapping sound of their sandals against the sand, and then they were gone. Now the figure of a woman – just enough information from the movement of the walk to determine the gender. The shoulders, made bulky by the shawl wrapped to keep out the cool of night, leant slightly forward. Her hands folded behind her back, she walked with a sense of ease, freed from the burden of having to carry a child on her back or a vessel on her head. That is the way she would walk, if she were out walking at this hour, I thought. But where would she be going?

Up until two days ago, I would, if I had noticed the presence of this woman at all, have attempted to have drawn some sort of sociological inference from it. Or I would have sat back, and merely enjoyed the exoticness of the setting. Suddenly everything I saw before me took on more urgent and unsettling meanings. The unforeseeable had happened. I was implicated.

The figure of a man in white appeared, walking slowly, gently swinging a lantern. He paused, greeting briefly, then he held the lantern up, and peered into the centre of our group, mildly curious at my presence. Then he continued slowly on his way. He had come from conveying his friend back towards his compound near the camp. It was her husband, and it seemed he passed this way every night at this time.

At night the wind blew through the mosquito netting, filling the living-room with dust. And in the mornings the school disappeared as the wind blew the sand across the football pitch in great gusts. At that time of year people felt filthy almost immediately they stepped from their baths. The wind scoured their bodies with its grey, gritty fingers, giving the exposed parts of their bodies, the shaven heads of the children and the men, and the women's feet and calves – what one could see of them – an oddly worn appearance, as though someone had been doing abstract-expressionist etchings over them. Everyone was looking for 'oil' (vaseline) to restore the lustre of their blackness.

I was tired. I had a cold. I was fed up. The mood of carelessness, even amusement with which I had realized the nature of my feelings towards that woman, had evaporated almost immediately. She was married with three children and though adultery was said to be endemic, the consequences if one were caught, particularly if one were a stranger, could be fairly drastic. A man finding his wife with another man, I had been told, would kill him, without even pausing to think about it. And even if he didn't go quite that far, it was difficult to imagine that he would be particularly pleased about it.

But it seemed to me that even if these overwhelming material obstacles had not existed, she would still have been a far from suitable partner – indeed even from among the women of the village the choice would have seemed almost laughably inappropriate.

She was known to the other Europeans as someone who could be difficult, who was likely to be rude or abrupt. I had sensed myself that she could be selfish, perverse and even treacherous, and yet she was at the same time somehow fatally endearing. Since I had become a member of the Saniyoro Kafo, she had treated me with great honour, and in the moments when we had been alone together, I had noticed a sense of intimacy, a rapport, an ease of communication, that I had not felt with any of the other women. To what this was attributable I had no idea. Yet when I thought about her, which I now did almost all the time, I was still not clear what it was that I wanted from her – since physical involvement seemed out of the question. I knew only that I wanted to extend that feeling of closeness, to explore it, to see where it led.

However, like all of the people around me, she seemed to go through sudden and incomprehensible changes in mood and attitude, and recently I had noticed a cooling in her attitude towards me that was as inexplicable as her earlier warmth.

One day, tired of sitting in House One failing to work, I decided to pay her a visit.

The opposite side of the street rose steeply away from the entrance to her compound, creating a gulley into which had poured the rain and the water from the nearby taps. It had been partly filled with rubble, and the tall foundations of the surrounding buildings had been shored up with cement to prevent them from being washed away. Between two of these buildings, a narrow passageway, also filled with rubble, led through into a narrow yard, around which crowded the verandahs and doorways of the houses of the men, where they were wont to sit and pass the time. Beyond that, the rocky floor of the compound rose past a battered screen of millet stalks into another yard, along which stood a row of corrugated-iron doorways. This was the house of the women, and behind the last of these doors was the room she shared with her co-wife and their seven children.

The day was neither dull nor bright. There were no shadows, but there was a curious glow to the milky, lukewarm air. I was relieved to find that the first yard was empty. I had dreaded having to pass under the eyes of the men – having to answer their joking enquiries which might prove more accurate than they supposed.

The second yard was equally deserted, except for a tiny, ancient woman who sat hunched on the bentengo, an expression of grim resignation on her face. I asked for the wives of Braima Sise, but the old woman knew who I had come to see.

'She is not there,' she said, gesturing to the row of padlocked doors. Feeling the need to explain my visit, I told her I had come to find out how many bags of groundnuts the husband had harvested. 'He is eating lunch,' she said, pointing past the screen of millet stalks to the door of a house that backed into the street. Three or four steps led up to it. A blue curtain was swinging in the doorway. 'Go there,' she said.

'It's all right,' I said.

I wondered if he had been able to hear what we were saying.

*

Late in the afternoon, I returned. The old woman was still there, as iron-faced as ever, and the door of the last house remained locked.

'She has gone to a funeral,' said the old woman. 'In Kulli Kunda.'

As I turned to go she held out a short, black pipe. 'Next time you come, bring some tobacco.'

The following morning I emerged shivering from the bedroom to see a short figure standing on the other side of the mosquito netting. She was wearing a voluminous waramba printed with large, photographic images of Mitterand and Abdou Diouf, the president of Senegal. It belonged to her co-wife, a tall, strapping woman, and she looked quite lost in it. She had just been to the clinic as her insides were paining her, and she looked very exhausted and morose.

'I want breakfast,' she said. 'I want hot water [tea] and bread.'

Turo, the sweeper, was standing under the arbour, chatting with Ramatoulai Jallo, the Fulani woman from Fili Kunda.

'Come to the kitchen,' I said. 'If you stay here they'll all want some.'

But she sat solidly on the chest of drawers just inside the living-room doorway.

'They do not want any.'

'Is my kitchen not pleasant?'

'It is pleasant.'

I brought her a cup of very sweet tea.

'Where's the bread?' she asked, as she began slurping the tea down as quickly as possible.

'I have no bread.'

'Go to Kassim's and buy some.'

'Kassim's is far.'

'Then give me fifty batuts and I will buy some.'

'I have no money.'

'He-eh, Mark,' she said sadly. 'You don't like to give out money.'

'I like it,' I said.

I sat in the Habitat armchair looking at her. She looked back at me, her eyelids heavy, as though it were an extreme effort to keep them open. Then she looked away, and out through the mosquito netting into the grey morning, as she continued to drink her tea. I remembered what Yaya Bojang had told me to say: 'Nlafita ni ye nyo je' – 'I would like us to meet each other.' But the words dried on my lips. Try as I might, I could not get my jaws to move. I just sat there.

She looked at me for a moment, then she put the empty cup down on the sideboard and got to her feet. 'Thank you,' she said, and went.

In the afternoon the women went to complete the harvesting of the sesame. The plants had opened out into tall bushes, many the height of a person, with long, thin, straight branches. Towards the end of the branches were lines of green pods about half an inch in length, and if they were split open one could see the dark seeds neatly arranged in rows.

The women moved over the field in their respective kafos, so I was never far away from her as we worked. It was by now extremely hot, but she seemed to have revived considerably since the morning. The thing that struck me most forcefully, as I sweated away under my straw hat, was that she was actually very beautiful. And when she paused in her work, clasping her hands together as she stretched her arms languorously above her head, I had to look away.

The ends of the branches were cut off in eighteen-inch lengths and tied together in bundles with strips of bark. Then they were packed together in a great mass and placed end upright on the ground to dry in the heat of the sun. Everyone worked hard, and by the end of the afternoon the whole field had been harvested, apart from a few bushes that were not yet ripe.

I wanted to see her, but when I did I was thrown into such a state of consternation that I dreaded it. It was a condition that betrayed all the symptoms of a schoolboy crush. It recalled that time when one's feelings for the opposite sex were so new, so unrecognized, and so alarming in their intensity that they seemed to threaten one's very reason; a time when the opposite sex – their thoughts, their responses, their very physical existence – were so mysterious they seemed a species apart.

But of course the Mandinka women were still a mystery to me. I had been brought up to believe that there were certain 'universal' human emotions, which transcended language and all social and cultural barriers; now I was not so sure. Ted Whiteman, the director of the Cass Nutrition Unit, who had visited Dulaba at least twice a year for the last fifteen years, and who was a hard-headed rationalist in all other than sexual matters, was fond of speculating that there must be many men and women in the village who had fallen in love but who had been unable to marry, and how tragic it must have been for them to have to spend the rest of their lives in close proximity without ever being able to express their feelings. At first I had been fascinated by this proposition. But the more I observed of village life, the less convinced I was that many such cases had ever existed, or that such individualistic conceptions of tragedy even came within the villagers' world view. Indeed, it seemed to me that even to entertain the notion of tragedy, one must believe one had some influence over one's destiny. The people of Dulaba did not believe the individual had the right to any choice over what happened in his or her life.

Late one night I discussed the situation with Pa Konte.

He sipped meditatively at his coffee. 'Do you know her well? Do you chat with her?'

I told him I was nervous of going to her compound, because I would have to pass under the eyes of the men.

He laughed a dry, wicked laugh. 'They make it like that on purpose. They put the women's quarters behind the quarters of the men, so that there is only one way in and one way out – so that a stranger cannot enter without being seen. They call it *sorongkono* – "a sealed place". But if you love someone, you will go there. Even if there is a lion in that compound, you will enter the sealed place.'

I gulped.

'But it is not going to be a problem,' he said. 'She will do it just because you are a European – because for her it will be a "big thing".'

What would it be like? I wondered. Would I kiss her?

'These people do not know kissing. But nowadays some do it. If they have been with someone from the urban areas they will know about it. But you know, these women do not have orgasms like European women. It is because of the circumcision. Some of them can do it, but it is very rare. Maybe those women, they don't cut them so much. But most of them, if you ask them about that, they will not even know what you are talking about.

'The women in these remote areas, they just lie there like a penny. Some of them will lie down and open their faneaus for you, just like that.' He chuckled. 'They couldn't care *less* about it.

'But this woman you have mentioned, she is not like that. She is decent. She is clean. And she is intelligent.'

She was indeed. She was sharp. She remembered things. She could work out what you were trying to say, while others just looked blank. She was cool, shrewd and alert. I thought how much more suitable a partner she would be for Pa Konte than for myself. They spoke the same language, both literally and morally. They knew how to conduct themselves in that society. I was completely out of my depth.

Late one Saturday afternoon, I came out of my house to see her emerging through the glass doors of the lab, a child on her back. She greeted briefly, then scuttled off towards the quarters. People were making their way towards the football pitch, where the Dulaba Civil Servants were about to play the Civil Servants from Kallaji. I lingered near the tree by the Quarters, where a group of people sat playing draughts. I glanced surreptitiously along the length of the building, to where she stood talking with Ramou Jagne.

As she strolled back past the tree, I strolled casually towards her.

'What are you doing?' I asked.

'The child has a fever. I went to fetch medicine – aspirin. But Ramou hasn't got any.'

'I also don't have any.'

She speeded up her pace. Father J appeared and clasped my hand.

'Come to the game,' he said.

He himself was not in the team, but was one of the 'supporters' – a role he took quite as seriously as the players took theirs. From the corner of her eye she watched as we strolled beside her hand in hand. Or rather, she watched Father J. For he was tall and handsome, and exuded an urbanity, a sense of prestige, which was to the villagers even more impressive than that of the tubabs – for he was a black like themselves. And no doubt she also saw him as a man in a way that she didn't see me. I told him I'd follow him over to the pitch.

She was walking slowly, her arms, rather long for her small stature, swinging gently at her sides. I also walked slowly, and tried to appear casual, as though I just happened to be going in the same direction. But I didn't get too close. She turned and looked at my trousers.

'You have money in your pocket,' she said. There were indeed a few coins there.

'You love money too much,' I said.

'Certainly I do.'

She did not pursue the matter, so I let her drift off, and wandered into Sanyang Kunda, where I had the idea of chatting to Jarjei. But Jarjei wasn't there. And when I emerged from the compound, I could still see her, walking slowly down the street, now turning into her own compound. I could hear voices, summoning me into one of the smaller compounds along the side of the street. I was detained there for some minutes, and made to participate in the light-hearted banter which in that part of the world passes for conversation. I was grateful to them for entertaining me in this way, but I felt frustrated and rather angry as I left the compound. Wherever she was, I must simply go there.

She was sitting on a mat outside the house of the women, wrapped in a shawl, dabbing the child with gentian violet. As soon as I saw the expression on her face, I knew that I had been right to go there – that it was all going to be all right.

I sat down on the bentengo and we talked; not about anything very much – just idle, disinterested questioning and the exchange of meaningless compliments. The co-wife was at work at Susan Lawrence's house, and the yard was very quiet. I felt suddenly completely at ease – that I was where I should be. Everything I said seemed to be extremely witty, or at least to have a certain poignancy. 'Now you understand our language very well,' she said.

'I understand nothing,' I said.

'You understand *completely*,' she said.

Njonji, the co-wife, had bought a grinder for making groundnut paste, and as she was busy at the camp for much of the time, it was left to Sona to operate it. Whatever she made from this she kept. This was what Njonji wanted. Now they were equal as co-wives should be. Njonji had her source of income, and Sona had hers.

Fatou Sanneh, Pa Lanjay's daughter, arrived with three big cups of groundnuts to be ground. I volunteered to do it, and they both watched amused as I laboured with the heavy rotary handle.

Soon it was time to fetch water.

'Wait here,' said Sona. 'I'm only going to fetch one potful.'

I passed the time with the children who thronged around me, climbing and pushing and shoving each other on and off the bentengo. Njonji's Binta was the eldest, a curiously mature girl of nine, as handsome as her mother, sharp and quick. The second, Arabiatou, was stocky and talkative, with a loud and very throaty voice. Sona's eldest daughter, Aroki, was quieter, with a slow and rather sly grin; her second daughter had gone to be weaned by her grandmother in Karafa Kunda, as was common practice.

The twins from Njonji's first pregnancy had been born dead. The next child, also male, had died before he had even been named. Since then, although Braima's wives had managed to produce seven daughters, neither of them had yet had a son. There would be great honour for whoever did; and Njonji was, even now, heavily pregnant.

Sona returned from the taps, which were just outside the entrance to the compound, and went into the house. In the distance I could hear the sound of the football match – shouting punctuated by rousing cheers. I felt it might be time to go. I went to the door of the house and called her name. Soon she emerged, holding a single cloth to her breasts. Water glistened on her black shoulders. She was black. Blacker than the shadows in the interior of the house. Her hair was twisted into spikes, which having been wrapped under her tiko all pointed upwards. The whites of her cool, unsurprisable eyes glowed clear against the darkness.

I felt suddenly that I must go, that it would be dangerous to stay there a moment longer.

'You Europeans, you wash twice a day,' she said. I wondered where she had got that idea from.

'I'm going,' I said.

'Stay,' she said.

'I'm going.'

'Stay for dinner.'

'Thank you. I'm going.'

I rushed from the compound as though great springs had been attached to my feet.

The following afternoon, the members of the Saniyoro Kafo gathered in Jarra Njai's compound to look at the money they had received for their groundnuts.

They had had the largest yield of any of the women's kafos – four 'donkeys' and one bag. A bag having been set aside to be planted next year, the remaining eight bags had been taken by Nafi Saho to the government depot at Brong, a few miles further into the interior of the province, where they had fetched five hundred and eighty dalasis.

The great heap of crumpled notes, some green, some red, that had been kept carefully wrapped in a piece of cloth, was laboriously counted and recounted several times.

'Money!' said Sajonding Minte. 'The key to the world.'

'Everyone is keeping quiet,' said Sona. 'They all love money!'

'Today we are very big people,' said Fatounding. 'Anyone who sees this money will be very happy to join our kafo.'

'Truly money is the key to the world,' said Jeynaba. 'But money can separate people. It can even separate relatives. And it does not last. It will pass, like the wind blowing through the sky.'

It is often assumed that people in very remote places, like Dulaba, are not interested in money. In fact they were passionately interested in it, and because it was something that was relatively new to them, it didn't have the associations of guilt and corruption that it had for some of the

Europeans. In spite of Jeynaba's reservations, it was, for most of them, something that was wholly good.

As recently as 1960 the sociologist Barbara Thompson had noted that it was quite rare for women to have money. 'Getting money was not important to them at all.' The only way they could acquire money was by selling an animal they had inherited, and even then they never handled it themselves. Their husbands would buy things on their behalf.

But now, since they had stopped going to their rice field at Tankular, many of the women maintained their own groundnut fields – something that was unheard of in their grandmothers' time. They had gardens where they grew vegetables to sell. Some of them had jobs working for the tubabs at the camp. And they kept the money they made for themselves.

Their grandmothers, unless they were married elsewhere, or followed their husbands in pursuit of learning or trade, had never gone further than the next village. But now women were travelling all over the country by taxi; visiting relatives; attending naming ceremonies; going to the markets and buying metal-frame beds, bowls, basins, and the newest and most beautiful clothes. They were sending their children to school, and they could, at their discretion, help their husbands with the problems of feeding the family; which gave them greater influence among the people of their compound. All this was because of money.

'People say we are very foolish to spend all this money on cloth,' said Fatounding. 'But it is our money, and we will do what we want with it.'

'Jarra Njai,' said Janno. 'When you go to buy this material, don't tell them we're from Kombo, or they'll think we have money. Tell them we are from Kiang, and they'll know we are poor and maybe they'll reduce the price.'

'Yes, Jarra Njai, don't go to Farafenni, go to Brikama.'

'You people are saying let's do this, let's do that. But you don't know that even one piece of cloth is very expensive now,' said Nafi Saho.

'Let's just make it a head-tie each then,' said Jarjei.

'Let's share the money,' said Janno.

'No, I swear to God!' said Sona. 'Let us buy ashobi and wear it. It's better than just sharing the money.'

'OK,' said Janno. 'But we're not going to buy an ugly piece of cloth. An ugly piece will not be bought.'

'What are we going to do with the animals we have bought?' asked Sajonding.

'We can kill the animals, eat them, dance and sing – finish,' said Sona.

'We're going to sell the bigger goat,' said Nafi Saho. 'It delivered but they all died. It delivered again and they all died. It has no use, so let's sell it.'

'Then save it for me,' said Janno. 'I'm going to buy it later.'

In accordance with Islamic tradition, one-tenth of the money was taken out to be given in charity – in this instance to provide candles for the village mosque. Then when their existing funds – the money I had given them, and the forty dalasis they had made from selling a goat – had been added, they were left with six hundred and twenty dalasis (at that time £124).

A great discussion broke out, with everyone talking at once at the tops of their voices. People would get up and walk around the compound, waving their arms vehemently in the air to emphasize their points. There was a brief pause, and then Ami Marong's husband Lan Jaiteh, who happened to be passing, was summoned into the compound.

'They say,' he said, 'that what they have will not be enough to buy the material they want. But if you go with them to Banjul to buy it, maybe you can add something to make it up.'

I did a quick calculation to work out how much that was likely to be. Material at eight or ten dalasis a metre. Three metres for the small people, four metres for the large. Thirty-eight members. It was going to be at least 1,200 dalasis. They all looked at me expectantly. It was all I could do to suppress a great shout of laughter. They were expecting me to throw in over a hundred pounds.

I tried to explain the situation through Lan's rather muffled interpreting. But the significance of the huge discrepancy between the two figures sank in only slowly. If I could not put up that amount, they wanted to know, how much could I afford?

'Not much,' I said dismissively.

'*Not much!*' mimicked Jeynaba with eyes of fire. 'He-eh, Marky!'

For the first time in months, I felt the great gulf in culture and comprehension that lay between us. In the excitement of bringing in the harvest, I had naively believed myself to be one of them. Now I realized that I was, and always would be, a stranger – an alien. I listened to them talking about how they were going to get the Headmaster to write letters to the other Europeans asking them for money. It was absurd, even degrading. But I knew I would never be able to make them see that. In the centre of the group, Sona was also having her say. I got up and went home.

That evening, Jarra Njai and Jeynaba came to my house with Faks. They said they hoped I was not annoyed with them for asking for the money. They had just been 'trying their chance', and as it was not possible I should just forget it. They would, they said, be very upset if they thought it had created any division between them and me. 'They realize you have nothing and are a hustler just like them,' said Faks. I endorsed these sentiments, and said I hoped God would lead them to whatever they were seeking.

Sute Minte was still in Dulaba. Since that first night in Kafuli Kunda, he had been summoned to perform in several other compounds, where he had received money, food and clothes. Each of these tulungos had been boisterous, even wild affairs. During the days, he sat at the bantabas, chatting with the other members of his age-group – those with whom he had played as a child. Sometimes he sat on the bentengo at the entrance to Fatounding's compound, chain-smoking and staring into space. He had small, pale, rather gluey eyes, and very few teeth. With his woolly hat set always at the same rakish angle, and his odd loping walk, he cut a distinctive, if slightly disreputable figure. Now he was at ease in Dulaba, but it had not always been so. For it was not easy for a citizen of Dulaba to become a jaliba.

His father, the former head of Kafuli Kunda, had been a great marabout, and had decided that his son should follow in his footsteps. And as in those days fathers were very proud for their sons to be learned in the Koran, he had given his son powerful liquid jujus to drink, so that his mind would be very quick to learn. One night, after he had drunk one of these potions, he had had a dream in which the devils had taught him how to sing. He had woken and sung till daybreak, so that he would not forget any of these songs. But the walls of his house were made only of millet stalks, so everyone in the compound could hear him, and in the morning they all told him he was mad.

Then he was just a boy of ten years, and he sang only for fun. But later, when he was a fully-grown man, he began to sing in public. He had done it twice in the village. The elders were very angry, and Sute's father told him that if he did it again, he would kill him.

Sute fled to the village of Jomar, where he formed a group with a drummer. They began to travel through the villages singing for the people. Since then he had travelled to many distant places. Now the eyes of the jaliba had seen everything.

In the ancient times, when a jaliba came to a village, all the young people, boys and girls, would leave their work to attend to him. They would lodge him, kill a goat for him, and make it their business to entertain him assiduously while he was in their village. The girls would make ashobi to wear when they danced for him, and they would buy clothes for the jaliba to wear. Even when Sute was a boy, there was a very famous jaliba in Brong, and if he asked the people for a cow, the whole village would join together to provide one for him. They would go and clear that man's field and plough it for him. But now this never happened. He knew for a fact that if he asked for a cow, he would never get one. In fact, in certain places he had been treated wickedly.

At the village of Bantanto in the Casamance, he had bought kola nuts and given them to the elders to greet them, and to inform them that a jaliba had arrived in their village. Now, among the Muslims, the kola nut is a sign of peace, and if you accept the kola nuts that a jaliba has given out, you must look after him – take care of his food and lodging. But in that village, they just took them, chewed them, and then forgot him completely.

In Missera, there was a funeral taking place when he arrived. After it was over, they accepted his kola nuts, and told him that he could return after the last charity of the funeral had been given. He came back and stayed there for three good nights. And in all that time, neither the boys or the girls were even aware that there was a jaliba in their village. They ignored him – just like that. So he made a song up about them. He told them that the people on the north side of the village were masturbating while they were listening to him. The women, he said, were all suffering from leprosy, and all the men had a disease which had caused their testicles to swell to a great size – even the Imam. And these people had not been able to do anything, because a jaliba can say whatever he likes. For he will never name anyone directly. You will hear someone being insulted, and you will know from what is being said that it is you. But you will not hear your name, so you cannot say anything.

The village where he most liked to perform, and where he knew he would be very well received, was Njamaa, in Pakao. When he was resting in his house before going to the dancing place he would already be able to hear the women and girls at the bantaba, singing his songs. Those women knew how to host a jaliba. For the jaliba to be happy, the clapping should be sharp, and the chorus loud and active with him.

I asked him if he thought the women of Dulaba were good at hosting jalibas.

'They are not,' he said. 'They have no idea. If you are going to give the jaliba money, do it and go back to your place. If you are going to dance, dance, and go back to your place. That will please the jaliba. But to have people wandering around in the dancing place is something that makes the jalibas very annoyed. Jalibas never come here. That is why these people don't know how to behave. They don't know that for the jalibas the bantaba is a place of work.'

It was the coldest day I had known in Dulaba. In the streets around Kafuli Kunda the people sat huddled around little fires, wrapped in faneaus and shawls. Without the presence of the sun, the rusted corrugated-iron, the crumbling walls and the bits of rubbish lying everywhere made the place look squalid and depressed. As Sute and I talked, the 'Koranic scholars' of the compound stood waiting to wend their way to school. Dressed only in whatever pieces of rag would cover their dusty, grey bodies, clutching exercise books in the last stages of disintegration, they stood in a line, some short and squat, some tall and bony. Although their bodies were hunched against the cold, the faces were impassive to the point of numbness – as though they'd just been dug from the wreckage of a plane crash – and clearly unaware of what a pitiful spectacle they made.

I had agreed to arrange a dance at the Quarters, with Sute performing in honour of Sarah's friend Kathy, who was visiting. The Saniyoro Kafo would organize it. They could put the money they received from Sarah towards their ashobi. It seemed to me to be an excellent idea for a fund-raising event.

I told Sute that the kafo would bring the kijo – the calabash drums – to the dancing place. They would keep children – and adults – out of the dancing circle, and they would sing loudly, clap loudly, and encourage people to do the same.

Sute grunted his assent, but said that if the tulungo was not a success he would hold me personally responsible.

*

Sute arrived at the Quarters almost immediately after dinner. He was furious. 'Where is everyone? Where are the drums?'

People scurried this way and that, fetching calabashes and filling big plastic bowls with water. Soon Nyantang, Daouda's niece, was beating out the summons to the dance, while a semi-circle of kids chortled out the Sute Minte theme. At this the man relaxed, lit a cigarette, and sat down to chat with Sirrah Bajie. But of the Saniyoro Kafo there was no sign.

Time passed and nobody arrived. I went and stood outside the compound gates. Even at that distance the kijo was scarcely audible. I went to my house, and found Jarjei and Jeynaba waiting in the living-room. We chatted for a bit, but as no one else arrived, I went back to the Quarters, to find the tulungo in full swing. But apart from Mama Njai Sise, heavily pregnant, and scarcely the most electric member of that organization anyway, there was no sign of the Saniyoro Kafo. Sute, fuelled by his irritation, was in fine form.

'The Saniyoro Kafo did not come!' he sang, to hoots of derision from the crowd. Never again am I going to organize a social event in the continent of Africa, I thought.

I returned to the house and found the rest of the kafo calmly seated in the living-room. 'What's going on?' I hissed. 'Everyone is *there*, but you're *here!*'

Jarra Njai sensed my irritation, but couldn't quite see its purpose. 'We've brought this faneau to put the money on. Can we take this table to lay it over?'

The Habitat coffee table was quickly carried to the Quarters, where the tulungo came to an abrupt halt while it was set up on the edge of the circle. Jarra Njai had brought with her a sort of skirt of loosely hanging strips of material which she now tied round Sute's waist. Then there was a pause. Those who had been clapping and singing in the full flush of the dance a few moments before, now stood about disgruntled, as the arrival of the people who were supposedly organizing the dance brought it to a standstill.

'Where's Sarah?' asked Mamanding Janno.

'Never mind Sarah,' I said. 'Get the dancing started.'

Janno conveyed my sentiments to the others, and soon Sute was singing again. Then people began to dance. In the pale light emanating from the verandah, it looked as though a great stampede were taking place, in the middle of which stood Sute bravely continuing his narration. The Saniyoro Kafo were doing their best to make the show go with a bang, in the way *they* knew.

I'd never realized how many women of some stature there were in the kafo. They stood around the inside of the circle, towering grim-faced like some elite guard, more than conscious of its ability to dispose of the person it was supposedly protecting. Children who ventured into the circle were dispatched with such vociferousness that Sute was frequently drowned out. Perhaps because they were so closely related to him, and had known him as long as they could remember, they found it difficult to take his antics seriously. The clapping and the singing were definitely on the thin side.

Father J, who stood quizzically observing the proceedings from the verandah, called me over. 'These people are supposed to be making the singing louder. They're just laughing at him.'

I collared Tumbulu Sise, who was standing nearby. 'Tell her that,' I said. There was a vehement exchange between them.

'She says she agrees, but what can she do about it?'

The arrival of the doctors' party was greeted with a renewed burst of dancing. Sute raised his voice to its full croak, and things began to swing a bit more. His narration was somewhat marginalized, but it was an enjoyable event none the less. Everyone danced and a lot of money was handed out.

Finally the moment came when the Saniyoro Kafo saw the opportunity to do what they had come there to do. Sarah and Richard were drawn to one side, and with Father J translating, they were invited to join the kafo. As it happened, Sarah had agreed to join Mabinta's kafo, the Sembendo, not half an hour before, and Richard said he didn't think it would be fair for him to join as he wouldn't be able to make the commitment of time and energy that I had. They weren't particularly impressed by this argument, but they had no option but to accept it. But he would, he said, make a donation to their fund. Hopes were raised. Would it be hundreds?

Every so often I caught a glimpse of her face, before it disappeared among the great crowd of figures milling in the darkness in front of Daouda's verandah. How implacable it appeared, how still amid the commotion – the smooth, rounded brow, the full lips that had known no doubt. From time to time she would come forward to dance. She was a good dancer.

The kijo and the women beating it were largely invisible, but the rhythms continued to bubble and seethe, growing ever more complex and exciting, ever more stimulating to movement. I myself was constantly moving: wandering on the fringes of the circle, clapping loudly, whooping, encouraging others to clap and sing, and pathetically attempting to join in the singing, as I felt it the duty of a host to do. Sometimes I would dance myself, or waltz slowly over to give Sute a coin or a note. These displays were greeted with great howls of mirth and approval, and the momentary exhilaration they provided served only to mask the bleak realization of what should have been obvious all the time – that she had no interest in me whatsoever.

Sometimes she would join the drummers. There would be three of them, and I would just be able to make out her expressionless profile as she added further complex syncopations to the beat. She knew what she was doing. It was her skill. She was a drum-beater, and everyone acknowledged it. But how lost this facility made me feel. How marginal and irrelevant my own skills seemed in comparison with her mastery of this inherently erotic medium, whose rhythmic variations were local, but whose language was universal.

*

I had to talk to someone; someone who would understand how I felt. The dance was over and, their friend Kathy having gone to bed, I went to the doctors' house.

They were sitting having their nightcap. As 'Project Leader', the person in whom the responsibility for the good relations between the MRC and the village had been entrusted, Richard received my announcement with an appropriate seriousness.

'I trust you're not planning to *do* anything about it,' he said, staring mordantly over the surface of his mug of tea.

'What do you mean?'

'Our work here is largely with the women. If it were to be perceived by the villagers that our interest in them were anything other than scientific, the consequences could be disastrous.'

Sarah gasped with impatience. 'But *who* is it?'

I knew I would never be able to tell them; that I would not be able to speak her name without faltering.

'The women often have to spend long hours with both the Gambian and the European staff. It's absolutely vital that the village men should be able to trust us. Can you imagine what would happen if they thought that . . .'

'And what about the woman?' said Sarah. 'Her life might be completely destroyed by it. Which I think would be rather selfish of you.'

'What about my life?' I said.

'You're going to leave,' she said. 'You'll forget it.'

'Will I?'

I told them that before this nothing anybody said or did had really mattered. I was shielded from events by a kind of analytical distance. Now everything mattered. I was involved. I felt part of what was happening.

'I think it's vital that you regain and retain that distance,' said Richard.

'But how?'

'Why not go away for a week?'

I didn't see the point in going away just to feel fed up somewhere else. Anyway, where would I go?

'Well anyway, I'm going to bed,' said Sarah.

'You really must try to overcome this,' said Richard, when she'd gone. 'In an environment like this, such feelings could easily become obsessional.'

'Mmm,' I said.

My recollection of that other world, England, was becoming increasingly vague. I found it difficult to imagine that I had ever been anywhere other than Dulaba. But, as I recalled, I had achieved nothing there. And I was now achieving very little here. I sat in the study of House One, staring at a blank sheet, too exhausted to even think what I was supposed to be writing about. And life would go on like that. When I had suffered sufficiently here, I would return to suffer there. It would not be intense suffering like I felt I was experiencing at the moment. It would be a gradual and languishing disintegration into total failure.

Here I was failing by not being a black – by not having the social and practical skills they had absorbed since childhood; and by not having the physical blackness itself – the deep violet blackness, and the physical sense of belonging it conferred. I loathed my whiteness, felt virtually unsexed by it; I had always been thin, now I was absurdly thin. I was living with people who had recently been starving, and I looked in a worse state than any of them. And I was not even a real tubab. I had not the wealth, the status, or the ready-made sense of purpose of Sarah, Richard and the others.

And yet, paradoxically, I felt for the first time the physical oddness of my position in the Saniyoro Kafo – of being a man among thirty-seven women. Before, it had not mattered. Not that I had not been aware of them sexually – but it had been a distant, almost vicarious interest. Now I felt suddenly intensely, physically awkward among them.

And I was furious with them. Membership of their group was, I felt, something too important for them to sell it off as a gimmick to the Europeans. On the other hand, didn't the concept of the kafo 'father' have a solid grounding in their tradition? Why shouldn't Richard be their father?

Fortunately, Richard saw things from my point of view, and only gave them ten dalasis.

Essentially, though, I was jealous. I felt that the kafo was my exclusive preserve, and I didn't want any other tubab to intrude upon it. More than that, I didn't want them to want any other tubab to intrude upon it. And they knew this. They knew exactly how I felt. They were extremely good at gauging changes in emotional temperature.

Once every five weeks, Dr Bill Snow of the ITC would come and stay in my house for a few days. He was an entomologist by profession, and had spent much of his adult life in Africa: in Kenya, the Sudan and Upper Volta, as well as in the Gambia. He had lived in Dulaba for five years from 1967 with his wife. They had been the only Europeans at the camp at that time, and they had lived in this very house.

He was a stocky, ruddy man, with a sandy beard and thick glasses, at times blokily amiable, and at others almost mystically withdrawn. On these brief trips to Dulaba, he would spend the days following the cattle through the bush, trying to establish the pattern of their wanderings. He went always alone and on foot.

One evening, I told him what I had told the doctors. I asked him what he would do if he were in my position.

'I'd leave,' he said tonelessly. And then just breathing the words: 'But of course, you can't do that. You've got too much invested in all of this.' He pondered for a moment. 'Are you thinking of this as something that might continue after you leave?'

I told him I couldn't imagine leaving. I couldn't imagine not being in Dulaba.

'Yes,' he said. 'I must say I'd be very frightened of such feelings if it was me. . . The possibilities for disaster are just so great. Although I had one chap working with me here once – an Englishman – who would have done it without even thinking about it. He was that sort of person.'

'He had a relationship with one of the village women?' I asked, startled.

'No, but if he'd wanted to, he would have done. That was his attitude towards women. I must say I find it impossible to be casual in that kind of way. He was completely irresponsible. But in some ways that's much less dangerous than being like me . . . or you.'

'I wish I was like him,' I said.

'It would be easier.'

I suggested that my current malaise might be simply a neurotic response to confinement.

'Yes,' he said, breathing through his teeth. He smiled slightly, his eyes narrowing behind his glasses.

'I was once here for quite a long time on my own. I would spend all day wandering in the bush, and in the evenings I would come back here and read Dostoevsky. After a time things started to become rather strange.'

Jarra Njai was now heavily pregnant. She moved through the world, her stomach before her, like a great ship. Farming was now over and she set her mind to new money-making schemes. She and Salinding had only got one bag of groundnuts between them from their field. Her tiko was in rags, her sandals were broken and her eldest daughter Markady had no clothes. Her husband Kemoring was working for the 'betinary', digging sand for the new camp, but though he had just been paid, he was unable to help her with these problems. So she decided to get a job and solve them for herself.

The opportunities for employment were not great. In fact they were limited entirely to the camp; and as far as she was concerned, her most likely avenue to *campo dokwo* was through me. Ever since I had arrived she had nurtured the hope that I would use my influence to secure her employment, and now she came daily to the house to conspiratorially discuss the possibilities. Unfortunately, she didn't realize that my influence in such matters was negligible.

'We will go to Sarah together and ask her,' she would say. I would say it would be better to go separately. 'As you like,' she would say. 'You are my arms and legs now.'

She had a way of approaching one that was both very flattering and very intimidating; in that it carried with it the implied threat of the sheer physical weight of the disappointment that would ensue if the required help were not given.

'Is Sarah not a tubab like you?' she would say. 'If you face her, she must help you.'

When she didn't get a job, she would blame me for refusing to help her, while Sarah would blame me for interfering. But I had by now become so heavily embroiled with Jarra Njai and her family that I was obliged to at least try to help her.

Sarah was reading to her children from a book about Babar the Elephant when I went to broach the subject, and she didn't welcome the intrusion.

'I'm afraid there's absolutely no chance. We *will* be having visitors in February who'll be needing people to wash and clean for them, but I've already got a list of about twenty people who actually took the trouble to come to see me themselves, and we certainly won't be needing anybody else. She *can* come and see me if she wants, and I'll explain the situation to her, but don't give her the impression that if she comes to see me I'm going to be able to help her, because it really isn't going to be possible.'

Jarra Njai received this information with all the grimness one would have expected. She sat staring at the coffee table in my living-room, wincing with disappointment, her hopes of the last six months, fanned to a peak of expectancy over the last few days, dashed to nothing.

Two days later, I saw her sauntering past the house with a huge bowlful of washing balanced on her head. 'There goes Jarra Njai,' said Tumbulu, who happened to be at the house at the time. 'Now she also is working at the camp.'

'She can't be,' I said.

'It's true,' said Tumbulu. 'She has a job.'

Sarah looked rather sheepish when I confronted her with this. 'Yes, well . . . I had forgotten that our friend was coming. And she did come to the house and get Sali Kanteh to show her how to use the iron. So I thought she deserved it really.'

That was the kind of person Jarra Njai was.

It poured with rain all day. Dr Snow said that it was not unusual to have small amounts of rain at this time of year, but he had never seen as much as this. If it continued, the groundnuts left out in the bush would be ruined. I inspected the drum heads. They had gone flaccid – the texture of a damp cornflakes packet – and the sound they made was about as interesting.

In the afternoon, as the rain battered on the corrugated-iron roof of Jarra Njai's house, the Saniyoro Kafo met to discuss their financial situation further. It was decided that everyone should contribute ten dalasis to the ashobi fund.

Sona was in a boisterous mood.

'Mark is going to pay twenty dalasis,' she said, 'because he is a tubab.'

'Hey, he cannot afford that,' said Isatou Bajo.

'He will pay twenty dalasis,' said Jeynaba. 'Don't make things easy for him.'

'You are a tubab,' said Sona. 'Black and white cannot be equal in terms of money. Hey, Mark! You're looking at people with a frown on your face, but if you only pay ten dalasis we're going to kick you out of the kafo.'

I had intended to pay twenty, but as she had put it like this, I decided I wouldn't.

'I'll pay five,' I said. 'You can pay twenty.'

How they laughed.

In a year-old copy of *Cosmopolitan*, I had read an extract from a publication called *The Dirty Weekend Book*, in which a group of Sloane Rangers offered advice to those who might be planning such an excursion. 'On the journey,' they advised the men, 'wear corduroys, trad brogues if necessary, sea-island cotton shirt (avoid stripes), good tie . . . *Don't* wear anorak, lumberjack tartan shirts, American running shoes, flared jeans, grey viscose trousers, duffel coat, cowboy boots . . .' Even in London such considerations had hardly been pressing. But as I read on through the descriptions of days spent in bed, walks through parks and on headlands, languorous meals, I realized that these were precisely the sorts of things I would have liked to have been doing with Sona.

I imagined her making her way through the Friday evening rush-hour crowds on Victoria Station – a slightly dumpy figure in her full best robes, her luggage tied up in a faneau, balanced on her head, a chewing stick skew-whiff in her mouth – slightly awed by the size of the crowd, her eyes none the less cool as she raked the ground for potential obstacles. Then, as the train moved through the darkening suburbs, we'd sit opposite each other by the window. I imagined her face, animated as she expressed her opinions, moving backwards into a landscape of greyness, mist and factories . . .

Sadly I reflected that even if I were to find myself alone with her, the most I could hope for would be a cursory coupling of not more than fifteen minutes; any longer, and she would start worrying about her husband wondering where she was. The structure of the women's lives was not designed to allow lengthy discourse with men. They were simply too busy. In the traditional African society, social pleasures were sexually exclusive. The idea of 'playing' together, of doing all the purely pleasurable things in life together, was unknown. A man and a woman would not walk down the street together, even if they were married.

The next day the world shone beneath a blue sky, and a naming ceremony was held for Ami Marong's daughter. The Civil Servants attended *en masse*, and after the prayers were over they lingered on the forecourt of the compound to chat, play cards and drink Chinese tea, to the sound of reggae from Seikoubah Sanneh's ghetto-blaster. At the back of the house, the Saniyoro Kafo busied themselves with the distribution of the porridge. A stranger, Ami had no relatives in the village, so the kafo had come to help. The child was the daughter of the whole kafo; she was to be called Mariyama.

In the middle of the afternoon I returned to find that the Civil Servants had moved their chairs to the shade of the lane at the side of the compound. There they sat, staring morosely into space, numbed by the heat of the day. In the cramped yard at the back of the compound, the preparation of lunch was nearing completion. Sona, a cloth tied around her stomach to keep her brilliant white shirt clean, was in charge. She had been at it for several hours, and was looking very hot and bothered. People were constantly wandering in and out of the cooking hut; things kept getting mislaid. Tumbulu, Jarra Njai and Jarjei were helping, but it was becoming very difficult to move as more and more of the kafo members were arriving, crowding into the shade along the edge of the compound.

Inside the house of the women sat a group of women from Karafa Kunda. They were all members of the same kafo, and there had been great delight when they had told the Dulaba women the name of their group: the Saniyoro Kafo. 'Sit and wait,' said the Dulaba women. 'When we have eaten, we will all dance together.'

Finally, the great iron cauldron was dragged into the open, and the cooks all gathered round to watch and advise as, using a long spoon, Jarjei served out the *benakino* – the rice, glistening golden with oil – into the various bowls. People retired to the corners of the compound and the houses to eat in their different groups. Another bowl was carried out to the boys in the lane. The brilliant orange pumpkin was melting with oil, and the meat of the goat oozed with peppery juices that made the lips tingle.

As the Civil Servants were still sitting in the lane beside the front of the compound, the women decided to dance in the house of the women. At first they just stood there. Nobody seemed quite sure where to begin. Then Sona, who had been born in Karafa Kunda, and knew the women better than the others, took it upon herself to get things moving. The tight, white shirt shone as though molten in the dimness. With her torso thrusting relentlessly forward, her arms flailing against the darkness, she seemed suddenly hardly human – reduced to a burning, glittering shape, like some fantastic bird, some primordial spirit of energy, constantly in the process of becoming. One of the Karafa Kunda women joined her, and they danced together, synchronizing their movements – staring into each others' eyes as their arms shot outwards.

Again and again she went into the circle, and it seemed to cost her so little effort. She just smiled – a clear, pure smile. She stood and sang style songs, and Lan Jaiteh, the father of the child, came into the room and gave her a dalasi. Then it was the turn of the Karafa Kunda women to sing their songs, and she gave their singer the dalasi. Then everyone was dancing, and the house shook to the echo of their clapping.

Soon it was time for the Karafa Kunda women to leave, if they were to reach home by nightfall. The Dulaba women walked with them along the red laterite road, escorting them towards their destination as tradition demanded. And all the time the clapping and the singing never stopped. It had been decided that soon the Dulaba women would to go Karafa Kunda to greet the kafo there.

When they reached the big tree, where the ITC cattle were tethered, the women squatted down at the side of the road to pray. Holding their palms towards heaven, they briefly murmured the al Fatia. Then they all got up, and the Karafa Kunda women proceeded on their way.

When the Dulaba women had proceeded some few yards back towards the village, they heard a sudden commotion behind them. They turned to see the Karafa Kunda women standing where they had left them, smiling as they sang and clapped in honour of their hosts. The Dulaba women danced back along the road towards them, and they all danced together briefly before the Karafa Kunda women picked up their bags and continued on their way.

We returned to Dulaba in a mood of careless happiness. Jarra Njai and Jarjei pulled sprays of leaves from the bushes at the side of the road, and leaped from side to side waving them in the air. The Karafa Kunda women had given us a dalasi, and when we arrived back in the village, we spent it on black mints at Kassim's shop.

I awoke the next morning feeling as though I hadn't slept for a month. Susan Lawrence had held a pre-Christmas dinner party for the Europeans. But I had found it far from calming. It merely added to the unnatural, almost feverish state of tension in which I now found myself. It was as though the air in Dulaba were becoming more and more difficult to breathe.

I opened the curtains to see Sona striding through the crowd of people gathering to queue for the Monday-morning clinic, her mind elsewhere. I shut the curtains again quickly.

'I've got to get out of here,' I thought.

Dr Snow's Land Rover was leaving for the coast in twenty minutes. I scraped a few possessions together, hurling anything that might incriminate me into the only cupboard that would lock, and clambered aboard.

It was the first time I'd been further than Karafa Kunda for over three months, but I felt no exhilaration or relief at escaping, only an exhaustion that was almost physically painful. My mind could make no sense of the passing landscape, of the haphazard jumble of villages that appeared to have been thrown together at the side of the road. Now the dense areas of cultivation that had virtually buried them during the rainy season had long since been cut down, leaving them standing bare and beleaguered on the parched grey earth. The bush about them seemed just a chaos of half-dead and useless vegetation. I passed the journey in a daze of half-sleep. Whenever I opened my eyes, it was as though we were always in the same place, such was the overall sameness. And always in this world, so flooded with white light that it was almost painful to open one's eyes, people just seemed to be wandering – endlessly and apparently aimlessly.

We arrived at Bill's house in the exclusive 'Pipeline' area of Serekunda to find a well-dressed European couple sitting drinking gin and tonic on the verandah.

'What have you been doing?' asked the woman. 'You both look absolutely ghastly.'

We went with them, and Bill's wife and two children, to a Lebanese restaurant, where Bill bought me the biggest steak on the menu. The restaurant also served as a video library, and Bill's wife Judy took out *On Golden Pond* for the third time. The European couple were old acquaintances of the Snows. He worked for the International Labour Organization, and had just been posted to Ethiopia. They talked about house prices in Addis Ababa, and Judy talked about her performance in an amateur theatrical production the previous evening. My sole contribution to this occasion was to be the person the Snows' eight-year-old son Jonathan spilt a bottle of Coke over. He did this by smashing a plastic model of a spaceship against it. He had to do it twice before the bottle actually fell over. Bill asked him why he had done this, but he couldn't think of an answer.

10

THE CROCODILE

Jeynaba's daughter Jalika and her friend Musakeba Sanyang wandered in and out of the house of the women, chatting and joking and getting in the way, dusty and unkempt as they would have been on any other morning of the year. Jalika was ten and Musakeba, one of the brightest, cheekiest girls in the village, was nine.

When the sun was high but had not yet completely dispersed the cool of morning, two old women arrived in the yard, shepherding a group of young girls before them. Jalika and Musakeba were wrapped in shawls and bustled quickly out into the yard. Then with the other girls they were shooed quickly, almost furtively, out of the compound, across the main street, past a line of enormous baobab trees, towards the bush.

Jeynaba and a group of the other mothers quickly put a few odds and ends into basins and a plastic carrier bag, and followed their children off along the path.

Every three years, when the last of the millet had been cut, and everything that could be taken from the land had been taken and gathered into the storehouses of the village, the children would be taken to the bush. While they were there, something would happen to them. They did not know what it was, for it was held as a secret between all the women who had ever been there. But they believed it would be a great honour for them for it was something that had happened to every woman of their tribe. And it was a necessity. If a woman did not go there, she would not even be considered a woman. She would be nothing. She would be referred to as *solimal* – 'the uninitiated'. She would never be married; if she cooked food, no one would eat it. And although they knew that it was not mentioned in the Koran, they said that a Mandinka woman could not be a pure Muslim until she had been to that place.

What happened there was particularly secret from men. Less than twenty years before, at a village near the coast, a man was discovered hiding in a tree overhanging the *nyakaboyo dula* – the place of initiation. He was beaten to death. Although the matter was reported to the authorities, no charges were ever brought against anyone.

Jalika, Musakeba and the other girls of their compound had been taken to a place only a few hundred yards beyond the edge of the compounds. The other women followed them gradually, slowly wandering off in small groups. Then, all at once, there was not a single woman left in the village.

At one in the afternoon, the village street was silent and deserted in the brilliant white sunlight. Mama Sise and a friend suddenly emerged from a pathway. 'It is finished,' they said.

Twenty minutes later, everyone had returned. Figures drifted across the streets carrying bowls and basins. Normal domestic routine had been resumed as though nothing had happened.

I found Jeynaba cooking lunch. There were very few people around. She led me into the next compound, to the house of Mba Jongmar, the oldest woman in the village. In the cool, dark interior I saw seven of the initiates – the *ngangsingolu* – sitting on the floor, wrapped in new faneaus – cheap ones, tie-dyed with big blotchy diamond patterns in bright colours. Beside them on a mat lay three of the smaller children. And on the three beds in the room lay more of them – sixteen altogether. Each wore a new head-tie, carefully folded, knotted with a big triangular lump over the forehead, and tied at the back.

Those who that morning had been the most incorrigibly boisterous and stubborn now lay almost inert, as though numbed with shock. Musakeba Sanyang lay completely still. I sat on a chest on the opposite side of the room, and she stared at me for a long time, regarding me as though I was a series of abstract shapes – as one often does see the world in the state of brief but utter peace that can follow an event of extreme violence.

The only movements any of the initiates made were of their heads and jaws as they slowly and impassively munched on fresh bread rolls which were handed round from the piece of old denim in which they had been wrapped. Here and there one could detect near their eyes tiny marks, which shone like silver, where the tears had not been completely washed away.

With them sat a few women, mothers, elder sisters and aunts. Some of them lay on the beds with the youngest children. Others just sat staring into space. Very little was said.

One little girl would not sit down. She just stood near the doorway, resisting all efforts to get her to move. She did not say anything. She just looked extremely sad. Eventually one of the older women gathered her up in her arms and laid her down on a bed on the far side of the room.

Another girl started to wander out of the room. A young woman grabbed her by the shoulders, and started to force her back in again. But an older woman told her to let the child go, and then went with the child out into the compound.

> 'Ngangsingdingolu – wo!
> Initiates!
> When you were in the village,
> You did nothing but insult the elders
> – that was your job.
> Now the crocodile has surprised you!'

It was planned that the girls from the compounds in the middle of the village – Mbara Kunda, Minteba Kunda and Mintering Kunda – would be taken to the bush at the time of the five o'clock prayer. In the end, however, it was decided that it was too late and they would wait until tomorrow.

I wandered around the village, trying to get the measure of what was happening. In Mbara Kunda I found Sona sitting on the bentengo with her youngest daughter, Bakoto, barely two years old. She told me the child would be going to the rice field the following day.

'She's too young,' I said. 'She's not ripe.'

'She is ripe,' said Sona, laughing. She pointed to her eldest daughter. 'This one is not beautiful.' She pointed to the second daughter. 'This one is also not beautiful. But this one,' she said taking the youthful Bakoto in her arms, 'is *so* beautiful.' And she held the child to herself, smiling radiantly. I had to look away.

Before coming to Africa, it had been my intention to make the subject of initiation one of the principal themes of my work. Strong feelings of revulsion towards some of the practices involved had led me to feel that it was a subject that *should* be described and discussed. I had soon realized, however, that in Africa there are certain phenomena that are outside the area of rational enquiry, and that to attempt a formal investigation of this ritual was completely out of the question – indeed my male translators refused to even use the word in the presence of women.

I had come to dread the moment when I would finally have to confront this issue. I had more or less resigned myself to the fact that my treatment of it would be at best sketchy and impressionistic, using what hints I had gleaned from other people's research to build up a sense of the mystery surrounding the ritual, which would hopefully mask the absence of real information.

It had never occurred to me that the event would actually happen while I was staying in the village. On learning that it would take place, which I had done quite by chance only a few days before, I had felt a curious mixture of fear and excitement. From the first mention of the word *nyakaboyo*, I had sensed a mood of strange, almost indescribable lightness, elation almost, come over the women. I sensed that what was about to happen would take place in an area of human emotion that was outside anything I had myself experienced – that was beyond anything I had ever imagined I would encounter. Now I was being presented with the opportunity to learn more about it. I resolved to stay as close to events as possible, without physically breaking the taboo.

The next day it was the turn of the children of Kafuli Kunda – the day when the children of Safi Mama and Jarra Njai, the leaders of two of the most important kafos in the village, would be taken to the bush. They would go not to the field close to the village where the young girls from Sanyang Kunda had been taken, but to the main place of the initiation – the nyakaboyo dula itself – the rice field of Faroto about a mile to the south west of the village.

'That is the day when you should try to be as close to things as possible,' Alioune Sware had told me. 'That is going to be a very interesting day.' Jarra Njai had told me that they would take me part of the way along the path with them, and they would meet me on the way back.

I arrived at Jarra Njai's compound at seven-thirty in the morning. She and Salinding were pounding rice for the initiates' lunch. Janno, who lived nearby, had come to help, along with Mbasire, a young woman married in her compound, who also happened to be Salinding's sister. The cold earth looked blue in the early morning light. The big thorn tree at the back of the compound stood out against the sky like a mass of barbed wire. It was only the effort of pounding that was keeping the women warm. In the east the sun slowly rose, touching the women's bare arms with its long yellow fingers.

The women's work, the comings and goings in the compound, continued at their usual unhurried pace. It was as though nothing was going to happen. Then suddenly, at nearly nine, we left the compound, walking at great speed. The streets were full of women, all walking towards the far side of the village.

Past the mosque, past the bantaba at Fili Kunda, there was a narrow path squeezed between the rubbish tips and the compound fence of Old Bajo Kunda. Beyond that one walked straight out into the uncultivated bush. About twenty yards along this path there was a large spreading mango tree known as the *duto koto* – the old mango tree. During the period of the initiation, no man was allowed to go beyond this point. The men who tended the gardens beside the rice field would suspend their activities during this period, and if any man had any reason to move out of the village in that direction, he would use another path.

Among the Jolas, the beginning of the women's initiation was the occasion of great public rejoicing. Friends and relatives would converge on the village from all over the country. Many animals would be killed. It would even be announced over the radio. And on the morning of the children's departure, the men would escort them to the edge of the bush, with drumming and dancing.

It was the tradition among the Mandingkos, however, that the beginning of the initiation would not even be mentioned to anyone not directly concerned.

So the women went together, but never so densely as to constitute a crowd. They walked quickly, but casually, with the minimum of noise and fuss, and dressed only in what they would have been wearing anyway. As they passed the bantaba at Fili Kunda, the men who sat weaving the elephant grass into screens did not even look up from their work. Each side feigned nonchalance.

I was disappointed to find how close the old mango tree was to the village. 'Go home,' said Jarra Njai. 'When the sun is high you can come back, and when we return we will dance for you. But don't go any further along this path. If you go there they will beat you.' And off they went, leaving me sitting on the roots of the old mango tree. Salinding followed carrying an enormous enamel basin on her head, in which had been packed the smaller of my drums, and the skirt of hanging strips that Sute had worn at Sarah's tulungo. Otherwise the women carried as little as possible; though some had babies on their backs.

As the figures got further and further away there seemed such a lightness in their step, such an eagerness in their walking, they seemed about to break into a run. All about them the bush spread into a sea of weeds and grasses from which the last vestiges of greenness were rapidly draining. In the morning sun it shimmered in the silver haze of dust thrown up by the harmattan. In the distance the vegetation grew taller and thicker, with bushes and small trees, and the women abruptly disappeared, as though the bush had closed around them like a curtain.

More and more women passed me; the old women walking sedately, their shawls piled up on their heads, the young girls scampering and laughing. All of them asked me the same questions: 'What are you doing here? Why have you come here? Are you going to go there?' And all of them gave me the same answers: 'Don't go there! Men don't go there! It is not good. If you go there they will beat you.'

I felt a pang as I watched them disappear off along the path. In spite of my feelings about the ritual, at that moment what I wanted more than anything in the world was to follow them along that secret path – to share in the mystery, and the happiness they would feel. I felt that I had been through a lot with these women, and now it was painful to be excluded from something which meant so much to them. It was the expressions of exhilaration and expectation on the faces of the women, who dashed off along the path as though pulled by some irresistible magnetic force, that made it most difficult to just stand there and watch them go.

As I walked back into the village, I passed the last few stragglers: Sirrah Bajie striding along; Ami Marong running past the entrance to Old Bajo Kunda in her eagerness not to miss anything. When I came to the bantaba at Fili Kunda, the men looked up with amusement.

'You didn't go to the bush?'

'No.'

'Why not?'

It was the first time I had heard the joke. I was to be bored with it by the third time, and apoplectic with irritation by the five thousandth.

'If they mock you,' said Nafi Saho's husband, Momodou Fulo, looking up from his elephant-grass screen, 'just tell them, "Mem be koos, wo le be kas!" – "What is with you is also with us."' In this case meaning, 'We also have our secrets.'

There are certain places in the world where the lie of the land gives a disconcerting reminder of the curvature of the earth. The area around the old mango tree near Old Bajo Kunda was one such place. On one side of the path the land stretched over the plain, gently curving away towards the rice fields of Jumutung. On the other side it seemed to bend upwards among the enormous trunks of the baobabs at the back of Fili Kunda, towards the long line of mango trees that encircled the village on the south side. During the rainy season it seemed as though the untidy green profusion of the bush were flooding in on one from all directions, and the great trees were rearing up like ships over the undulating horizon. During the dry season, when the trees had shed their leaves, and the crops had been hacked down, leaving only a whitening stubble to be burnt from the land, it was possible to see clearly for some distance in every direction. But it was as though these perspectives had been imperfectly joined, so that whenever one looked in a different direction, one had to readjust one's vision of the world.

Perhaps this sense of disorientation was one of the reasons for the slight queasiness I felt as I sat under the old mango tree waiting for the women to return. The path where the two horizons met, and along which at any moment the women would appear, stood out like a trickle of mercury, shuddering and shimmering in the haze of early afternoon. It was strange now to recall how many times I could have walked along this path if I'd wanted to, and how few times I actually had. Now, suddenly, it was forbidden. There was no sign to tell one of this. There was no one there to bar the way. The only thing to prevent one from simply getting up and walking along it was the force of the collective belief. Now there was nothing on earth that would induce any man to walk down that path.

The secrecy surrounding the initiation had the ostensible purpose of protecting the children from witches. For in the society of witches, whoever could capture the soul of a ngangsingo – an initiate – would be crowned king. So throughout this period they would be trying to get close to the children.

But it also went much deeper than that. Since the beginning of the event I had detected among the women an enthusiasm close to exaltation, which made the formal devotions they shared with their husbands seem mechanical, almost nominal. And although it was not for them something that was separate from Islam – indeed it was part of Islam as they conceived of it – it was something that was from *before*; from before Islam, from before their sketchy knowledge of their history, from before even their conception of themselves as a people – from before everything. Thus they did not know the purpose of the ritual itself. They knew only that it was something that their grandmothers had done and that they also must do. In turn their granddaughters would do it in exactly the same way, as would their grandchildren. This was one's purpose as a woman – to live one's life as one's grandmother had lived it, and to ensure that one's granddaughters also lived that life. Going to that place, and enduring whatever it was necessary for one to endure there, whether one lived or died, was all part of being a woman.

But the event was not only an ordeal, it was in its own right something beautiful and marvellous – an occasion for the most profound happiness – not so much for the children themselves as for their mothers, and indeed for any woman who went there. To take one's child there was not only a duty, it was an act of tenderness and love.

The secrecy was also something they had found with their grandmothers. It was part of the significance of the event itself. Anyone who invaded it would die – automatically. And it was likely that some of the children who were undergoing the event would also die.

As I sat there on the roots of the old mango tree, a sentence I had read on the first page of a book by Roland Barthes entered my mind: 'Euclid is the eponymous hero of secrecy.' I had no idea what this meant, nor had I ever got any further with that book. But the phrase had lingered in my mind, and as I sat there in a state of rising nervousness, I repeated it over and over, involuntarily, in my mind. I knew that simply by being there on the very edge of the event, by even showing a passing interest in it, I was starting to invade the taboo. I wondered how I should behave when the women arrived, and, more importantly, how they were going to behave towards me.

From time to time I would strain my ears to see if I could catch any of the sounds that would be coming from that place – the screaming of the initiates, the clapping and singing and the beating of drums. Now and then I would pick out thin, high-pitched shouts, but the wind was blowing in the wrong direction. They must have been coming from the few children remaining in the village. The path, shining in the sparkling haze of dust, gave no indication that this day was any different from any other, or of the enormity of the event that was taking place at the other end of it. In the opposite direction, the village, apart from these occasional cries and the braying of a donkey, was almost ominously quiet. The branches of the baobabs towered over the roofs of the houses, like the rigging of steel ships.

Then three figures – three young women – appeared out of the bush, ambling slowly along the path towards me. They had the weariness in their walk of people who have been exposed to the sun for a long time.

'What are you doing here?'

'Nothing. I'm just sitting here.'

'Go home. People aren't coming yet.'

'It's not finished?'

'No.'

'But you're going?'

'We're going to cook lunch.'

They wandered off into the village. Soon more women arrived, singly or in small groups. 'Don't stay here,' said some. 'When the old women come, they will beat you. They will cut your lips off.' 'Don't worry,' said others. 'Wait here a little. Soon they will come.'

There was a long wait. And then suddenly a great dark mass appeared through the gap in the vegetation – a swarming mass of figures, some carrying cloths over their heads to keep off the sun. A woman who had already arrived at the tree turned and watched.

'Your people are coming,' she said. 'The Saniyoro Kafo.'

Nafi Saho had my big drum strapped around her waist. Fatounding was wearing a filthy khaki shirt, full of holes, and on her head a sort of baseball cap, equally battered and filthy. Round her waist hung Sute's skirt of strips. On her face was a smile of exhausted contentment and slight embarrassment. But the embarrassment was at my presence rather than her appearance. She knew why she was dressed like that. I had no idea.

Ami Marong wore her tiko draped over her head and tied under the chin, dalasi notes pinned over her forehead. Other figures passed us: Djembai Minte, with clusters of tin cans strung around her waist; two young women dressed as men, in the guise of navvies.

'Come on. Let's sing for Mark,' said Jarra Njai. 'He's brought his tape recorder here.' It was clear that anything that happened there would be only a pale, pathetic shadow of what they had experienced at that place, and after a few minutes of effortful singing and a couple of nominal attempts at dancing, Jarjei said, 'Mark, everyone is tired. The sun is hot.'

'That's right,' I said. 'Rest.'

Jarra Njai began looking apprehensively back along the path. 'Come on Mark. We're going.'

I said I'd stay and wait for the others.

'No. Don't stay here. Come with us. This afternoon I'll take you to where the children are.'

I was compelled to go.

Jarra Njai sent a huge basin of steamed rice, and chicken cooked in palm oil to the place where the children were staying. Then we sat down and ate rice with the less choice parts of the bird, the head and the legs, also swimming in the yellow oil.

'This food is not nice,' said Jarra Njai. 'I could not get much oil.'

There was plenty as far as I could see.

It was about half-past five by the time we left to go and see the children. I wondered if the singing and dancing I had been told would occur would still be happening by the time we got there. On the pathway we met Jarra Njai's mother, Filije Minte. 'Where are you taking this man?' she asked.

'To the place of the ngangsingolu.'

'Hee-ee!' said the older woman, raising her hand to her face in a horror only partly leavened by amusement.

In the past the children would have stayed in a shelter of palm leaves at the place of initiation. In recent years however it had been found safer and more convenient to bring them back into the village at night to stay in one of the women's houses of their respective compounds, which would be given over entirely to this purpose. This was known as the *jujuo* – the house of the initiates.

The jujuo in Kafuli Kunda was the house Safi Mama shared with one of her co-wives and her husband's mother. As we approached we could hear a muffled banging and crashing coming from within. A group of old women sat outside, and watched us stone-faced; though whether through exhaustion, inertia or disapproval it was impossible to say. We went up to the doorway, and I halted, uncertain as to whether to proceed. 'Come on,' said Jarra Njai.

The atmosphere in that dark, almost cavernous interior was, in contrast to the calmness and quiet of Sanyang Kunda the day before, heightened, excited. Light entered from a doorway on the other side of the room, against which moved the silhouettes of the leaping dancers. And here there was none of the circumspection and self-consciousness that usually attended the young girls' dancing – one person nervously entering the circle at a time. Here they just threw themselves into the circle, shaking their limbs with all their force, oblivious of appearance. In fact to call the dancing place a circle was an overstatement. People would just begin dancing where they stood, the beating of an upturned basin bouncing and echoing off the corrugated-iron roof. For the first time since I came to Africa I felt that I shouldn't have been there.

'Here are the ngangsingolu,' said Jarra Njai. In the corner of the room, the little figures sat in rows, their tikos carefully knotted over their foreheads. But it was so dark in that part of the room that the expressions on their faces were indiscernible. I saw them only for a moment before they disappeared among the milling figures.

Safi Mama was leading the singing, raising her throaty voice effortfully over the din of the crashing basin and the clapping and the constant chatter. Then another older woman took over. Bareheaded like some extraordinary female goblin she leapt this way and that, making strange attacking motions with her arms, as though wielding an invisible spear.

> 'Ai Waali – o!' she sang.
> 'The people I run with are leaving me behind.'

> 'Singkolingkolingsing – Hey!' chanted the girls.
> Singkolingkolingsing!'

> 'The ngangsingolu are leaving me behind!'

> 'Singkolingkolingsing – Hey!
> Singkolingkolingsing!'

Then Jarra Njai took her turn. Facing the children she sang a song in honour of Salingding's Bintu, and her own youngest daughter, Nakeiba, who would be going to the bush in two days' time.

> 'I said the elephant will not fail to make me dance!
> You the head of an elephant,
> Beautiful young ladies,
> We have heard your words.
> Nakeiba said, "When we go to the crocodile,
> Myself and Bintu we're going to bring mints for you."

> 'I said the elephant will not fail to make me dance!
> You the head of an elephant,
> Beautiful young ladies,
> We have heard your words!'

She swayed slowly as she sang, and then as the rhythm built, and the clapping and the beating of the basin became almost deafening, she rallied what energy she had left after the exertions of the morning, and danced for the child – stamping heavily, vigorously shaking her body and arms. Into this dance she put all the feelings of tenderness that she felt for her co-wife's child at that important moment.

Then it was time to go.

'I just want to stay a bit longer,' I said.

'No, no. Don't stay here.'

'Just a bit longer.'

'All right. But don't stay too long. You understand.'

Then I saw Mariyama Sibo Djankeh bearing down on me through the crowd. 'What are you doing here?' she shouted. 'Don't you know we also have our private affairs?'

I decided to call it a day.

The following day the children from the *sate ba* – the middle of the village – went. Once again I sat and waited for them at the old mango tree. Once again they stopped briefly and sang while I taped them. Beyond them I could see a dark flurry of passing figures, among which were the newly initiated children.

Later in the afternoon I went to Kafuli Kunda, where the atmosphere had relaxed considerably since the previous day. The ngangsingolu were seated on mats spread out over most of the floor. They wore strings of white cowrie shells across their foreheads, beneath their neatly knotted tikos, which it was believed would close the eyes of the witches. They seemed to be recovering remarkably well, and many of them leapt to their feet and danced strenuously to the beating of the basin. Throughout the period of the initiation, the clapping, singing and the beating of basins or anything else that was to hand was more or less continuous. The singing was usually led by the young women aged between their early teens and their early twenties who watched over the ngangsingolu. These were the *kintangolu* – the 'slaves' of the initiates. The children of a man's sister were obliged to look after that man's children during the period of the initiation, until they themselves were transferred to their husbands' compounds. They would stay with the child in the jujuo, fetch water for her to drink, escort her to the toilet, and together they would cook the initiates' food. But although this was an obligation, guardian was probably a more suitable word than slave. For they were the ones who taught the children most of the songs, and disciplined them when the old women were not there – and they were not slow to mete out punishment. The initiates were there to learn respect, and the guardians intended to help them learn it.

Also present were a number of girls of the same age as the initiates, but who were dressed in their ordinary clothes. These were children who had been initiated in previous years, but who had been too young to take in the lessons they had been taught there.

Now that the actual day of the children's initiation had passed, there was no great hurry for me to leave. And generally there was a return to normal imperatives. 'Have you got any spare batteries?' asked Safi Mama. 'The children are in my hands, so when you're ready, don't forget me.'

Officially it was the oldest women of the compound who were in charge of the children, and took the donations which strangers made for the welfare of the initiates. But it was Safi Mama who appeared to be in control of what was actually happening – getting the children from place to place, making sure they were fed. Needless to say it was a function she spontaneously and naturally filled.

I walked home feeling very despondent. Over the last three days I had recorded little that would tell me anything about the initiation. I had arrived home from the jujuo the night before to find that one of the microphone channels of my tape recorder had not been working, and what remained was just a garbled, inaudible mess. I'd wondered for a moment if the spells that had been cast to protect the initiation were not so powerful they would prevent me from recording anything of significance. Most of the songs I'd just recorded in the jujuo I'd already heard dozens of times since I arrived in the village. The events were taking place virtually in my presence, but their real meaning, their real significance was slipping past me.

I met Pa Konte sitting outside his house in the high street. He told me not to be discouraged. 'If I went to the jujuo, I would be driven from the door like a dog. It is only because they like you that they have allowed you to enter there.'

As we spoke, a line of little figures appeared out of the twilight – tikos knotted across their foreheads, faneaus tied at the chest – the uniform of the ngangsingo. The child at the front carried a flag of flowered material tied to a stick. They had just come from the bush behind the village, where their wounds had been washed, and they sang as they made their way back towards the jujuo.

As they passed, they curtseyed to us, and to a middle-aged woman who was talking with, or rather haranguing Pa. I hadn't paid her much attention, though I hadn't been able to help noticing the Tupperware box she was carrying. She greeted me, and asked why it was that she knew me, while I didn't know her.

'That woman is disturbing me very much,' said Pa when she had gone. 'We are distantly related, so she wants me to buy her a bedspread.'

'Who is she?' I asked.

He looked at me in disbelief. 'She is the *ngangsimba* – the mother of the initiates,' he said, as though only someone of doubtful mental competence could not be aware of it. 'She is the one who has circumcised all these girls. Did you not see that box? That is where she keeps the bark that she uses to wash their wounds.'

She had come from another village, further into the interior of the province. She was protecting the children from witches. For there was no woman in Dulaba who was kunfanunte – who possessed the second sight. She was the mistress of the nyakaboyo dula, the owner of the jujuo. Nothing would happen during the course of the event without her say-so.

I wondered how she could protect the children at night, when they were all sleeping in different compounds.

'She does not watch them with her eyes. She watches them in her mind. She sleeps in that compound where the teachers live. Her daughter is married to the owner of that compound. If anything is happening to any one of them, she will see it in her mind, and she will fly there to protect them. But no one will see her. She will be invisible.'

His own mother had been a ngangsimba, and sometimes as a child when he was sleeping beside her, he would realize that though her body was there, her mind had gone elsewhere. It was as though she was dead. Then in the morning she would be there just the same as always.

'People in our village say she must have done something very great for me before she died, because I ride my motorbike through Kiang at night, and nothing has happened to me. You know, the people at the coast believe there are very many witches in these remote areas.'

When the children left the village on the morning of their initiation they were taken immediately to the saline pools close to the creek, where they were bathed. They would hear the crocodile moving among the mangroves, and they were told that what was about to happen to them should never be told to anyone. If they told, the crocodile would know, and it would come for them.

Then they were taken to a place close to the rice field, where they would wait, as one by one they were taken to the place of initiation itself. When they reached that place, they would find all the women of the village there waiting for them, and the ngangsimba – the mother of the initiates – seated under a tree. The child would be laid on a mat in front of her, and all the women would crowd round to watch. She would be held down while the ngangsimba took a pin and lifted her clitoris. Then, with a blade sterilized by burning, she would cut off the child's clitoris, and the inner lips of her vagina. It was considered a great honour if she did not cry.

When all the girls had been circumcised, their mothers, their grandmothers, their aunts, their sisters and all of the other women, would dance for them, under the heat of the sun.

On Wednesdays the initiates did not go to the rice field because traditionally that was the day when the women rested. But in the evening I was invited to the jujuo in Kafuli Kunda to hear the *su-kwo* – the religious songs.

It was obvious immediately on arriving that these were not the conventional su-kwo that one would hear sung in the streets and in the compounds on the nights of Kitimo and Gammo. They were in Mandinka rather than Arabic, and their cadences lacked the pious 'falling away' of the Muslim su-kwo. They had an immediacy, an aliveness, an abruptness in their rhythm that referred to no wider tradition. They were wholly of this place – of the hard, unpromising earth, of the 'bush of women'.

One of the guardians would call a long phrase, to which the massed youthful voices would bawl back a brief reply. There would be another phrase, another reply, then the whole thing would be repeated, with the ngangsingolu calling the tune and the guardian giving the responses. Often one of the musakebas – an old or even a very old woman – would take over from the guardian. 'Don't shout!' she would say. 'Sing!' And their voices, shining like cymbals, would rise as one, for the sheer physical pleasure of it, in response to the deep, hoarse utterance of the musakeba.

'*Nale bala kuntung kuntungola*,' sang the musakeba.
'*Arijana dibeng*,' sang the initiates.
'*Itolu tala koring balo la.*'
'*Arijana dibeng.*'

'We who are free to roam about.'
'In the shade of heaven.'
'And you the ones who are forced to go against your will.'
'In the shade of heaven.'

Then the song was reversed;

'You who are free to roam about,' sang the initiates.
'In the shade of heaven,' intoned the deep voice of the musakeba.
'And we the ones who are forced to go against our will.'
'In the shade of heaven.'

This song described the difference between those who had passed through the test of initiation and those who were still in the process of undergoing it. And the contrast was further expressed in the voice of the musakeba, gravelly with experience, and those of the ngangsingolu, brash and clear in their moment of emergence from the aimlessness of childhood into a new world of consciousness and responsibility. Before they came here, they were not considered 'conscious' – they were not expected to know the difference between right and wrong, and were thus not considered responsible for their actions. On leaving the jujuo, they would take their place in society. They must know how to greet people, and to show respect to their elders.

These songs too were a discipline to which they must submit. And with the endless rhythmic repetition, the brief tunes – sometimes rousing, sometimes poignant – took on new and subtle resonances. Like the rhythms of the drums they became structures which the singer could inhabit and explore.

To the mature women who visited the jujuo, the singing of those songs was a physical pleasure in which they, as initiates of the society, could take part. They had not heard them in the three years since the last circumcision – these songs which carried not only the weight of their literal meaning, but a deeper sense of the women's own childhood and the way it fitted into the unchanging scheme of the Mandinka women's lives. For the children who were learning these songs, and hearing them for the first time, they were part of their absorption, of their assimilation and unquestioning acceptance of the rhythms of that life. It was almost mindless – it was meant to be. Yet it had an undeniable beauty and compulsion.

Someone greeted me, and I turned to see a short figure, its head swathed in a shawl, sitting in the darkness beside me. It was the ngangsimba. 'Mark,' she said, laughing silently. 'You never know me.' The initiates also hadn't noticed her. She greeted them sharply, and, startled, they got to their feet, curtseying and saying, '*Jattafa Koringo*' – the praising of her surname; all except one child who ran screaming into a corner of the room, and stood whimpering in the shadows. Safi Mama went after her and dragged her into the middle of the room where, screaming hysterically, she was forced to embrace the ngangsimba. 'Yesterday I beat her,' the ngangsimba said to me by way of explanation. Then she turned to the children.

'I've come to say good evening to you. Today all of you were here, clapping, singing and dancing. And tonight we're going to sing the su-kwo. When I've eaten I'm going to come back here, and every one of you will dance. If anyone refuses to dance, what I will do to that person, only I know. Today I went to one of the jujuos and I found them fighting. I drove their mothers out, and then I beat them. The same thing applies to you if I find you fighting. In the bush, I was the one who stood between you and the crocodile. None of your mothers were there. So I don't see why you should fight in my presence.

'I am afraid of no person except God. The ngangsingolu who I take to the bush never ask, "Where is mother? Where is father?" They have been handed to me. So if they do anything wrong I will deal with them very seriously. I took permission from the fathers and the mothers when the children were handed over to me, so whatever happens to you before you are released will be my responsibility.'

'This is what we are praying for,' said Safi Mama to the children. 'That you should be circumcised in peace and released in peace. And that you should be released without any marks from beating.'

'The ngangsingolu don't know what is happening,' continued the ngangsimba. 'So I'm going to discipline them. If any of the mothers disagree with that, let them come with me to the bush again, and we will solve the problem there. Tomorrow if I come here again and I hear that one of the ngangsingolu has been disturbing people . . . just leave that child with me.'

When everyone had eaten, the doors were shut and the old women sat down together to concentrate on the singing. They were joined by women from the nearby compounds, and by the guardians, who had come in from cooking the dinner. As the evening wore on in the great room, lit only by a tiny oil-lamp, the singing and the clapping which accompanied it became more and more animated. The clapping was not consistent but would break out in syncopated bursts when someone felt like adding to the momentum of the singing.

By now the ngangsingolu were falling asleep. Safi Mama went among them shining her torch in their faces and prodding them awake. 'Come on. Everybody get up. Get up and sing!' But soon they were nodding off again. The call and response was now between the guardians, who sat close to the ngangsingolu, and the old women seated at the far end of the room. At moments of excitement one or other of the old women would get up and dance. Stamping vigorously in time, the old woman, often well over seventy, would wave her arms high in the air, as the clapping of the young women broke out around her. Everyone loved to see the old women dance, and it was only during the circumcision that they would do it, brought to their feet by the collective energy of the moment – what they called 'happiness'.

And so it went on till the girls of all the compounds of the village – nearly two hundred of them – had been circumcised. The last to go were the children whose mothers were married in other parts of the country, who had been brought to the village especially for the ceremony.

In their grandmothers' time, the ceremony had taken place when the girls were in early adolescence, as a preparation for marriage. But they had found not only that the children's wounds healed more quickly when they were younger, but that the children themselves wanted to go at a younger and younger age. It was also true that among every group of girls there would be some who would be kunfanunte, and they might use their powers to resist the ngangsimba. The older they were the more difficult it would be to control these powers.

The youngest children, those who had only recently been weaned, and were barely able to talk, were taken separately, and were kept, not in the jujuo, but at their mothers' houses. One of these was Jarra Njai's Nakeiba, who had gone to the bush wearing a 'Dukes of Hazard' sweatshirt.

Early each morning the initiates would be taken to the bush, where they would learn the lessons of the circumcision. At midday, when the sun was at its height, they would return to the village, where they would spend the afternoon resting, singing and sometimes dancing. In the evening the doors of the jujuo would be closed and they would be joined by their mothers for the singing of the su-kwo.

After a week of rushing from one end of the village to the other in the heat of the sun, trying to be always in the place where the significant events were taking place, while at the same time attempting to feign uninterest, I had ended up with the feeling that that which was of interest had just finished the moment I arrived, or would begin the moment I left. I felt sure that it was from the *ngangsing denkilo* – the songs of the initiates – that I would learn whatever it was necessary for me to know about the ritual. But I was not even sure if the songs I had recorded *were* ngangsing denkilo, or simply religious songs that could be heard by anybody. The moment someone began to sing something of interest, they'd be nudged by someone else, and they'd sing a more familiar song. It all seemed to be taking place just outside my field of vision. I decided to go and see Pa Konte, and get him to use his influence with the ngangsimba on my behalf. After all, she was the 'owner of the jujuo', and whatever she wanted to happen would happen.

I found Pa in the bush attending to a newly-born calf who was unable to stand up. It was the hottest time of the afternoon, and there was no shade. Needless to say he didn't welcome my hair-brained questioning.

'I can't go there, man. She is trying to get a bespread from me.'
A what?
'I told you she wants me to buy her a bedspread.'
What was I supposed to do?
'Just go to her and present her with your problems. Tell her honestly what you want. I'm quite sure that whatever she is able to do for you she will do. She is not a bad woman.'

The ngangsimba was a short woman, in perhaps her late forties or early fifties. She lay sprawled on her bed in a room at the back of her son-in-law's house, dressed only in an old faneau. Her breasts, which were large, rolled over her body, almost past her waist. She was fair in complexion, and though her crust of hair was now grey, she had a roguish, almost lecherous look in her eyes. And when she smiled, which she did a lot, they sparkled, her eyebrows rising like question marks. Yet it was an ambiguous smile, that might vanish at any moment; and what it would be replaced by I dreaded to think.

Between her breasts hung two jujus – one of leather, inlaid with a diamond-shaped piece of mirror. If she was in trouble she would look in that mirror, and she would be able to see what was happening anywhere in the world. The other, which was wrapped in snake skin, would enable her to become invisible. A witch would come in the form of an animal – as a monkey, or a horse, a vulture, a cat, or even a bat – or it might come invisibly. But from her bed she would be able to see them, and then invisibly, or in the form of an animal, she would go to that place. Firstly she would remove the 'sight' of the witches. Then, if she wanted to, she would kill them. But if that juju was removed they would be able to see her, and they could kill her. So she would never ever remove it from her body.

This was the first year she had been a ngangsimba. Before, she had only gone to help. But the previous ngangsimba, who had been a citizen of Dulaba, had lost her second sight. This was easily done. If she took the nintingo – a clay bowl with holes that they used to steam the rice – and placed it over food to cover it, or if she took food from a high shelf and spilt it on herself, she could easily lose her powers. When she heard that, this woman had come to Dulaba, and told the people that, from now on, she would be their ngangsimba.

She had always known she would be a ngangsimba, for she had had the power of a kunfanunte since she was a small child. They were all kunfanunte in her family. If any child did not have the power, they would know that he or she was a bastard.

'You cannot go to the nyakaboyo dula. I have placed a net over that place, a spiritual net – which is invisible. Every knot of that net has been tied spiritually. No one who did not go there on the first day of the circumcision can pass through that net.

'There are two kinds of ngangsing denkilo; the ones we sing in the village, in the jujuo, and the ones we sing in the bush. The ones we sing in the village are not secret. But the ones we sing in the bush can only be heard by people who have themselves been to that place.

'However, as it is you, and this is necessary for your work, I will help you. The day after tomorrow, when the girls come from washing their faneaus, you will meet us on the pathway, and I will get them to sing for you the songs they sing in the bush.

'Today at five o' clock, you will return here, and I will take you to the jujuo in Sanyang Kunda where you can record the songs they sing in the village.'

When I returned at five o'clock, I was told that the ngangsimba had had to attend to urgent business elsewhere, but that I should proceed to Sanyang Kunda, where they had been told to expect me.

The women seated outside the jujuo regarded me with a certain amount of suspicion, but told me to go through to the yard at the back of the jujuo. There, the ngangsingolu came forward one by one, curtseyed and shook my hand. There was a strong smell of urine in the air. I was told the surname of each of them and had to repeat it as we shook hands. They seemed to enjoy the ritual, particularly Musakeba Sanyang, who slapped my hand from on high in the characteristic manner of male friendship.

There was one little girl who sat on a mat apart from the others. She sat upright, wrapped to the chin in a faneau. She sat completely still, an expression of total blankness on her face.

'She was ill,' said one of the women shortly. 'Now she's better.'

I turned on the tape recorder, and the ngangsingolu ran through a brief recital of style songs. At a suitable interval I told them that I really wanted to hear the ngangsing denkilo. There was a horrified silence. The women looked aghast; even the children seemed slightly alarmed.

'Hey,' said Penda, getting to her feet. 'Ngangsing denkilo is ku'lo!'

'Didn't the ngangsimba say I was coming?'

'No.'

'She said I should come this afternoon to tape the ngangsing denkilo.'

'She was joking with you.'

Two days later, on the morning on which the ngangsingolu would be going to wash their faneaus, I felt weak. I had been suffering from a particularly unpleasant form of diarrhoea, and it had occurred to me as I sat hunched on the toilet in the early hours of the morning that maybe someone had 'taken out some means' to prevent me from learning anything more about the circumcision.

I thought I would just about have enough strength to stagger down to the old mango tree, and carefully gathered together my tape recorder, microphone, spare batteries and tapes. I didn't want to forget anything, and miss any of the songs. On my way out, I met Mabinta, my washing lady, who was on her way in to get her fish out of the fridge. I was rather surprised to see her. I would have thought she would have been in the bush with the rest of the women. I asked if today wasn't the day when the ngangsingolu would be going to wash their faneaus. She said it wasn't.

'What is happening today?' I asked.

'Nothing is happening today,' she said.

At the teachers' compound, I found Mr Balde sitting in the yard. I told him that the ngangsimba had told me that today – 'the day after tomorrow' – would be the day of the washing of the faneaus. He laughed.

'You know in these remote areas, when they say "the day after tomorrow", they don't mean that it will actually happen the day after tomorrow, they just mean that it will not happen tomorrow.'

He told me the woman had just left for Sanyang Kunda, where she was attending to one of the children who was sick. I remembered having vaguely heard something about one of the ngangsingolu having been taken to the clinic. Then I recalled the child I had seen sitting motionless in the yard. Balde said he had heard the woman saying that the child had been attacked by a witch. Someone in Sanyang Kunda had been attacking the child. But she had 'seen' this person, and stopped them. He said that the woman hardly slept. When he returned to the compound, or if he got up in the night, however late, he would always see a light burning in her room.

Had the Europeans gone into the village during the period of the circumcision, they would have been surprised to see the streets blocked by women dancing in the middle of the afternoon, or tulungos being held among the piles of ash at the back of the big compounds. But as it was, they stayed well away. Their feeling was that they wanted 'nothing to do with it'. Richard had told me long before that he thought the ritual 'bestial', and it was rumoured among the Civil Servants that he and Barbara Smith were going to try to put a stop to the practice in Dulaba – though this seemed most unlikely.

Thus the heady, at times slightly hysterical atmosphere of events in the village did not impinge on the camp at all. It was as though the camp were retreating in on itself during this period.

One evening, however, when she and her husband Rajiv had come to my house for dinner, Susan Lawrence told me she had heard that one of the children had been brought to the camp bleeding from two arteries, and without Richard's intervention would undoubtedly have died. She said the doctors were surprised at the extent of the child's wounds – that rather more had been 'taken off' than expected – though she wasn't sure of the details. I was deeply distressed by this piece of information. At that time it was understood from the reports of anthropologists and doctors who had worked in the area that only the 'mildest' form of female circumcision was practised in Dulaba – a ritual incision was made in the clitoris, or only part of it was cut off. But even more than the degree of injury, I was shocked by the extent to which, in my haste to empathize with the emotions surrounding the ritual, I had set aside this aspect of the matter. I felt a twinge of guilt, as though I were in some way responsible for what had happened. I was also perplexed and rather irritated that this drama had taken place in the building adjacent to my own house without me even being aware of it. I resolved to get the full story from the doctors the following morning.

*

How many times since coming to Africa had I been exasperated, sometimes almost to the point of tears, by the inhabitants' reluctance to impart the simplest information. In Africa, whatever a person needed to know they would be told in due course by the person in their society, usually one of the elders, who was authorized to tell them. What they did not need to know they need not think about, for that was not their business. Thus it was bad to ask questions. Not-knowing was an essential condition of existence, for there were things that one should not know – which it would be bad for one to know, which would bring harm not only to oneself, but to the person who told, and to those who were the object of the secret. So the people had been brought up to keep secrets from an early age, for in secrecy lay the wholeness of the individual and the society.

Now, during the period of the circumcision, after two weeks of 'ku'lo' – of rushing from one end of the village to the other in the burning sun, of attempting to imbibe something of the nature of the ritual from observing the actions of people who were blankly terrified to reveal anything about it, of recording songs that I wasn't supposed to record, and at the same time not knowing whether the songs I was recording were those songs or not – I felt smothered and exhausted by mystery. I felt as though I were facing it each day like a tangible, physical force. At times it seemed to manifest itself even in the physical appearance of the village – as though it seethed from the very pores of the earth, oozing like a resin from the rough wood of the buildings.

I felt relieved as I walked towards the doctors' house. These people were Europeans, like me. They were from the same country as me; from more or less the same social class. They would understand why I *had to know*. Curiosity was part of our culture.

It was shortly after lunch, Richard had told me he would discuss my enquiry with Sarah, and as I approached I could see them sitting relaxing in the square pavilion of their living-room. Outside the inner door of mosquito netting, I removed my shoes in the customary manner, as though entering a temple or mosque.

After telling me that a second child had been brought to the clinic for treatment, Richard said, 'We have considered your request, and we've come to the conclusion that we can't abuse our position by giving out information which is medically confidential without the permission of the people concerned.'

What was he talking about?

'There is no medical confidentiality in this country,' I blurted out.

'Are you sure of that?'

'Fairly sure,' I said, not sure at all.

'We have to think of our own ethical position,' said Sarah. 'Which as far as we're concerned would be exactly the same whether we were here or in Newcastle. Why don't you ask the girl's parents? If they say yes, fine. If not, you'll just have to leave it.'

What did she mean 'Leave it'? This was my work. How could I leave it?

They both just sat and looked at me. I decided to change tack.

'We're in the middle of the African bush,' I said. 'Miles from anywhere. Who's going to know or care if you tell me?'

'And suppose the child's parents were to hear that we'd given you information that was confidential?'

The child's parents had never heard of medical confidentiality. They had been upset that Bakary Sanneh, the lab assistant, had been present when Richard had examined the girl's genitals, not because they wanted to protect her natural modesty – not because they didn't want him to see the girl's body *per se* – but because she had been attacked by a witch, and if he saw what had been done to her at the nyakaboyo dula, she and all the other initiates would be in even greater danger.

I exhaled sharply.

'Just ask the girl's parents,' said Sarah, 'If they allow it, we'll be happy to tell you.'

'I can't possibly ask the girl's parents. They believe they've already surrendered the information to you – that by coming here they've given up their right to privacy. They would never understand that you wouldn't simply give me information, as one tubab to another.'

Sarah looked out of the window.'I think you should consider very seriously whether you should be investigating this subject at all. They do feel so terribly sensitive about it.'

'But don't you think we ought to know?' I said. 'Don't you think we *should* know?'

'Of course I do. I just think you should consider the ethical implications of how you go about getting your information.'

Fatou Mbaye was the community development worker in Dulaba. It was her job to teach the women how to make soap, how to dye cloth, how to sew, and all the other things for which the Community Centre had been built. But as the Department of Community Development had not been able to provide her with the materials to carry out any of these activities, she had very little to do.

She was in her early twenties; tall, serene-looking, very black in complexion. She was a Wolof, but she had gone to the circumcision, because she had grown up in Serekunda among the Mandingkos.

'All of my friends had been to that place, but by the time I was ten, my sister and I still had not gone. We felt shy and ashamed because other girls younger than ourselves had been there, but we had not. I did not like the way our friends looked at us and the things they said. But when we asked them what was there, they said there was nothing there; only that if you went there, they would give you many different kinds of food.

'But my father would not allow us to go there. He said we are Wolofs, and the Wolof women do not go there, so we also would not go. But the woman next door was a Mandingko, and she said, "Do not worry. When the time comes I will take you there." '

So it was that Fatou and her sister ran away to the circumcision. When they arrived in the bush, all the girls were kept in a separate group, and one by one they were taken to the place of circumcision. It was not far away, and it was when she heard the screams of the other girls that Fatou first began to feel afraid.

'All of the women crowd around you. They press forward to look. You cry. You must cry when they do that to you. And then they dance around you, as you feel as though you are about to die.

'They carried us back to the house and laid us there. When they brought the food for us to eat, I could not eat anything. I just lay there. I was still losing a lot of blood.

'It is difficult. Obviously it is very hard. But you must face it. It is like giving birth. That also is difficult, but you must face it. And you can face it. There is no question of that. You must face it.

'There are three things a woman must face in her life. The first is circumcision. The second is when her husband first enters her. The third is when she gives birth. At those three times she must cry. She will cry, and there is no avoiding it.'

If she cried the first time her husband entered her, would she enjoy it after that?

'Of course.'

She would still enjoy it, even though she'd been circumcised?

'Yes! It is the same as if she had not been there. Though I have heard some men say that it is nicer with a woman who has not been circumcised.'

Her husband worked as a driver for the Department of Agriculture. On the wall were a number of photographs of his and her families and friends. She pointed to one of a white girl with long hair, sitting rather morosely on the steps of a mud brick house.

'My husband had an affair with this girl before he met me. He told me that it was nicer with her than it is with me.'

How had she felt when he told her that? Had she been upset?

'A little. But not as upset as I felt at the way my friends looked at me before I went to the circumcision.'

The Sembendo Kafo held a tulungo under the mango tree at the back of Sanyang Kunda. The Sembendo was the largest of the kafos, comprising nearly all the women in their thirties. The dance was a rowdy, almost violent affair – people pulling, pushing and shoving each other in and out of the circle in their eagerness to dance or sing. Several of the women were wearing the kanyeleng costume – bunches of tin cans trussed around their hips, or extended on strips of cloth from the waist. Everyone behaved exactly as they felt, to the constant thudding and battering of the kijo. If someone danced badly they were met with howls of derision; they would be slapped around the head and dragged from the circle. If someone danced well, the response was exactly the same. If anyone faltered in their singing, someone else would push them out of the way and sing the song *they* wanted to hear.

It was very difficult to record anything, as my microphone was constantly hurled this way and that in the milling crowd.

The Saniyoro was the last of the women's kafos to get round to organizing a tulungo, and to be honest it took a bit of effort to get it started. They were not one of those kafos who were constantly on the verge of a full-scale tulungo. There were a lot of very quiet people in the group; the sort of people who are always at the back of the crowd. Even the good dancers didn't take themselves seriously, and after a few seconds would stop and run laughing to the edge of the circle.

Menata, in an electric pink chemise, beat the kijo while the others formed a rather thin circle around her. 'Come on, clap,' said Jarra Njai. The others responded rather uncertainly. Eventually more people arrived. Sona sang style songs, and a suitable level of uproariousness was reached.

At the same time, the Serious Kafo – the young women in their early twenties – were at Kafuli Kunda, dancing in the street in front of the alkalo's bantaba, and the Sembendo were at Salum Kunda, nearly all of them actually inside the jujuo. As I arrived, the Serious Kafo emerged running from the house, laughing manically. Everyone leapt out of the way as the young women came thundering past. Having finished their own tulungo they had come to invade that of the older women, and were now being driven out. Inside the jujuo, the air was so thick with dust stamped up from the floor, and the steam from the women's sweating bodies, that it was almost impossible to breathe. One had to fight one's way through this grey haze, as though through some dense, toxic miasma. In spite of this, the dancing was some of the most animated I have ever seen.

The woman beating the grinding board onto the mortar stood staring rigidly ahead, slamming the board up and down at fantastic speed to create a frenzied shuddering sound, which, together with the metallic clanging of the basin, almost shook the house. The women danced without any inhibitions whatsoever, as though held and physically shaken by the frenetic beating of the kijo. Suddenly the woman who had been beating the mortar dropped the grinding board and leapt in among the dancers – a short, stocky figure, shaking her buttocks, as if in the throes of some uncontrollable spasm. 'Hey! Hey! Hey!' chanted the crowd in time, as other women crowded in around her, shaking, all caught by the fierceness of the energy. It carried on for some minutes, as the rhythm of the clapping and the beating and the dancing and the singing became faster and faster until it came to a sudden halt, and everyone fell back gasping and cackling limply in the smog of dust and sweat.

One day, in the jujuo in Minte Kunda, I had seen a silver bangle placed upright in the sand so that it stuck out of the ground in a loop shape. One of the ngangsingolu lay before it and, raising the trunk of her body, bent her head right back and seized the bangle with her teeth. She then righted herself and gave the bangle to one of the women.

This was one of the games the ngangsingolu were taught in the jujuo. Some were designed purely to encourage the bravery and ingenuity of the initiates: the silver bangle would be placed in a basin of water. One by one the initiates had to plunge their heads into the water, and pull out the bangle with their teeth. Others had specific lessons for the children: a calabash would be placed upside down on the ground. Wetting her lips the ngangsingo would attempt to lift the calabash by sucking the rounded base, and then right it in a decorous manner. This was virtually impossible; the message of the exercise was that if you saw a bowl with a cover on it, you should not look to see what is inside. Someone has put it there for a purpose, and it is none of your business.

They were taught never to sit on a man's bed when no one else was present, and never go into a man's room without knocking.

They should wear their be-chos – their under-faneaus – at all times. If they had a sexual encounter the stains would not show. And if a man tried to rape them they should pull the garment tightly between their legs to make it more difficult for him to penetrate them.

Most important of all were the *pasingo* – secret signs that would allow them to live more easily in the Mandinka society. When a stranger entered the nyakaboyo dula, she would be tested with a number of these signs, to see if she too was among the society of the initiates. She might be thrown a scarf in a certain way, which meant she had to dance. If she did not it would be unfortunate for her, to say the least.

If a girl saw her mother sitting with other people, so that her thighs were showing, and she didn't want her to be shamed in front of those people, she would make a deft and simple gesture with her fingers, so that no one else noticed, and her mother would be able to discreetly adjust her faneau. Or if a group of elders were talking and a young girl approached them, there was a sign they could make, whereby she would know that what they were saying was not for her ears.

These and many other signs were supposedly secret from men. If a man made one of these gestures to a woman, she would be deeply upset, and would insult that man, and probably his mother too. There were other signs, however, which were taught to both sexes in the jujuo. If a girl's father was sitting at the bantaba, and there was a shortage of rice in their compound, she would make a special sign to call him to dinner, so that he would not have to invite everyone else.

If a man's wife came to visit him and she brought a younger sister with her, there was a certain way he would shake hands with her to let her know he wanted to have sex with her, without upsetting the younger sister. And there was a sign a woman could make to her lover to let him know she was having her period.

During the last days of the circumcision, the ngangsingolu wandered further and further from the jujuo. They were taken to watch the dances that were held in their honour, and they would go round the village in groups, accompanied by their guardians, visiting the various compounds, where, in return for donations, they would pray for people. It was considered very good luck if the ngangsingolu prayed for you. In Minte Kunda a pair of twins were undergoing the ritual, and I was advised very strongly that I should give them money to pray for me – for at least one of twins would be kunfanunte.

One morning the children from Salum Kunda arrived at the MRC compound, their flag flying. They had got a few feet past the gate when the window of Barbara Smith's flat flew open. 'Out! Get out of here!' she cried. 'Samba So,' she called, as they walked back out through the gate. 'I thought I told you not to let those children in this compound.'

It was said that Barbara did not want her daughter to see the ngangsingolu, or she too might want to go to that place.

When everything was over, I sat down with Jojo Bajie, my new translator, and transcribed all the songs I had recorded on my visits to the various jujuos. It was a lengthy process. It was often difficult to pick out the exact words, and we had to be sure that what we were writing down was exactly what was being sung. Finally I had written out the words to all the dozens of songs I had recorded.

> 'I'm ashamed of my guardian, Manding Jala.'
> 'My guardian!'
> 'But turn to the left, Manding Jala, my guardian.
> The date has not yet been fixed.'

'What does that mean?' I asked.
'I have no idea,' said Jojo, sprawled back in his easy chair.
'You must have some idea.'
'None! I would not lie to you. If I know something I will tell you. But I have never heard this song before, and I have no idea what it means.'

> 'The foot of an elephant! The foot of an elephant!
> An elephant can change its mood at any time!'
> 'Momodou!'
> 'The centre of the sun,' said Nyomi Manka.
> 'Momodou!'
> 'Go to the gate. There is a crocodile there.
> I am praying that it will not catch me.
> The light of the sun.'
> 'Momodou!'
> 'Take the light to Momodou's place.
>
> 'Do not let them go near the spring.
> Those who did not fast on this earth will never drink from it.
>
> 'Kill them,
> Kill them.
> Those who did not pray will never see the spring.
>
> 'The leaves of the cotton tree are grass.
> When it dries you can make it into a box,

And the weaver will make it into a faneau,
Which will not itch when you wear it.'

The meanings of some of the songs were obvious:

'Do not ever insult women –
Women bore you.
Do not ever insult women –
Women bore you.
However difficult it was, women bore you.'

Others, however, were just apparently arbitrary conjunctions of names and images lengthened into song with meaningless phrases included only for their rhythmic interest. But certain images recurred: the crocodile, the dried grass, various trees, all of them located in heaven, different species of animals and birds. There were numerous references to water: to the spring, to the well, to the river. The significance of the crocodile I now knew, and I was convinced that each of these other images had an equally potent meaning.

As we worked Natoma would occasionally wander in and out to mop the floor, her usual lugubrious expression lightened by amusement at our frustration. I decided to ask her the meaning of some of these songs. She responded slowly and without looking up.

'We don't know. We learnt these songs from our grandmothers. We have sung them ever since our ancestors first went to the circumcision. But as for the meaning we have forgotten them.'

'Is that true?' I asked Jojo.

'It could be.'

'Do you believe her?'

'No.'

Jarra Njai's mother Mba Filije was also working at the camp at that time. One day she came in and sat with us as we worked. I decided to play her one of the songs from the tape.

'My mother,' said Jojo. 'Does this song have a meaning?'

'Yes.'

'She says yes. The song does have a meaning.'

'Can you ask her what the meaning is.'

'Please, you are not supposed to ask about such things.'

'Just ask her.'

Her eyebrows rose. Her chewing stick nearly dropped out of her mouth.

'Marky! That is a great secret!'

'You are wasting your time,' said Jojo. 'No one is ever going to tell you anything about this. And if you keep on asking it's going to create a big problem for you.'

'Today,' said Mba Penda, 'will be nothing but dancing! Dancing and clapping! Everybody clap!'

It was the *Fani Kuro Lungo*; the day when the faneaus of the ngangsingolu would be washed for the first time since the day of their circumcision. It was the last time they would visit the rice field of Faroto for the purposes of initiation.

The dancing and the clapping began then and there. A pan was seized and beaten in time. It was some minutes before order was restored.

It was a sunny morning, but cold and windy. In Sanyang Kunda the ngangsingolu were becoming more and more difficult to control as the period of their confinement came to an end. They spilled out of the jujuo, dancing and cavorting around the yard. Soon, however, it would all be over.

Accompanied by their guardians they proceeded in single file to each of the jujuos along the main street. At the compounds in the middle of the village – Mbara Kunda, Minteba Kunda and Mintering Kunda – they collected only two or three children. But at Salum Kunda, where fourteen children were being held, there was a lengthy wait while they were got ready. The flags and the faneaus of the ngangsingolu fluttered in the wind as they stood in line waiting. There was an atmosphere of lightheartedness and relief – a holiday mood. The women danced and sang in front of their children, and everybody clapped.

'The ending has come. We will not come this way again. So let us dance. Occasions like this are not common in this village.'

As the girls of Salum Kunda emerged from the compound, the procession moved off, the two lines of girls moving parallel along the street, their flags at the helm.

At Kafuli Kunda there was another long wait, the girls held in their lines by their mothers and their guardians. Everywhere one looked people were bursting into song, and, to the accompaniment of beating on basins, they would begin to dance where they stood. In the midst of this pandemonium, I caught a glimpse between the flags of a small, still figure. It was Sona, and she was staring at me with an expression of unusual warmth, tenderness almost. Her white tiko was draped over her head and tied under the chin in the manner adopted for prayer, which gave her an uncharacteristic appearance of meekness. Her eyes held me for a long moment, then I looked away. When I looked back a few minutes later, she was still looking at me in the same fixed manner. I found this a little unnerving, though not unpleasant. But what, if anything, it meant I was not inclined to speculate. I had long since given up trying to understand her behaviour. For however warmly or coolly she behaved towards me, I could be sure that on next meeting her attitude towards me would be completely the reverse.

Suddenly there was the sound of another song, even louder than the others. I turned to see the Kurung Kafo dancing towards us along the street, smiling gleefully as they added their noise to the chaos of voices already filling the air.

The procession began to come apart as it squeezed along the narrow path between the rubbish tips and Old Bajo Kunda. And at the duto koto most of the women stopped and let the children go forward to the rice field with their guardians and those mothers who had elected to go with them.

The singing and dancing and the beating of basins continued at the old mango tree for some time. Two of the younger women – Nafi Bajo and Satou Jammeh – were wearing men's clothes: their husbands' work clothes – old jackets and trousers of European cut – that they had borrowed without them knowing. It was the trousers that caused the greatest excitement. As the older women danced, one, or sometimes both of these 'men' would leap into the circle, kicking their knees in the air, sidling up to the older women, and suggestively gyrating their hips to great howls of hilarity and delight from the rest of the women. Satou was one of the best dancers in the village, and she moved among the women, her trousered loins twisting and writhing, her legs springing effortlessly from the ground. She moved up beside Mba Penda, urgently thrusting her pelvis against the body of the older woman. 'Oo-Ah!' moaned Penda, to the crashing of the basins. 'Oo-Ah! Bubacar, you have killed me!' From time to time one or other of Satou's breasts would burst from the front of her husband's waistcoat.

The progress back through the village was a lengthy one, there being frequent pauses for songs, jokes and impersonations. The sun shone brilliantly on the dusty streets, and the air rang with the spluttering guffaws of the women. Every so often the procession would come to a complete standstill as everyone collapsed in fits of laughter.

The group got smaller and smaller as people stopped off at their various compounds. Satou and Nafi now wore faneaus wrapped around their trousers. As they reached the middle of the village, however, they met a group of schoolboys returning home for lunch. Satou darted behind a building, reappearing moments later minus the faneau. She pranced out into the middle of the street, where to the astonishment of the boys she executed a few extravagant dance movements, before stepping lightly back along the side of the building. The boys paused for a few moments, as though unsure whether to believe what they had seen. Then they continued on their way.

The ngangsimba had told me that at two o'clock, at the call to the *selifana* prayer, I should begin walking along the path towards the rice field. On the way I would meet them, and they would sing for me the songs they sang in the bush. After I'd been walking for about five minutes, the call to prayer boomed out across the bush from the mosque's newly repaired loudspeaker. My heart raced as I realized I'd left the duto koto earlier than instructed. Everything shimmered and glittered in the brilliant white sunlight, which, combined with the heat and the nervous, rasping sound of the insects, made me feel almost feverish with apprehension.

About half-way along the path I saw a group of old women approaching. I decided to stop and pretend that I was simply waiting on the pathway. I squatted down in the shade of a clump of elephant grass. When they arrived the women asked me where I was going. I told them. 'Go there,' they said simply.

My first sight of the nyakaboyo dula was the crimson and violet and blue of the faneaus hanging out on the garden fences to dry. In the distance, from the rice field itself, I could hear the muted sound of clapping. Young girls were pulling the faneaus from the fences and carefully folding them, then stacking them in basins. It was a scene quite empty of drama – domestic, almost idyllic; shaded by the tall palms, the girls moved without hurry. They started in astonishment, however, when they caught sight of me proceeding along the path towards them. 'What have you come here for?' they asked. I explained. 'Go and sit by that tree,' they said. 'But don't go any further.' I walked along the path which sloped down between the gardens to the salt flats, and slumped down under the palm tree they'd pointed to. At the end of the path I could see dark figures moving against the silver sand of the salt flats; against the shuddering brilliance of this background, the silhouettes seemed to flicker and dance with a shadow-like fluidity. It was a magical scene, giving the impression that everything that took place at the end of that path had a kind of lightness to it, an enchantment – as though because people had gone there for one purpose, and one purpose only, time and morality were different there, and the laws that governed everyday life had been abandoned in favour of a different set of laws. Now I could hear the clapping – coming from just the other side of the gardens.

Suddenly it stopped and people began to come rushing up the path. Those who had been languidly folding the faneaus hurled them into the basins, and putting them on their heads began to dash back towards the village at a quick trot. Mba Filije came running past. 'Quick,' she said. 'The ngangsingolu are coming.'

The ngangsimba appeared. 'Come on. Get up,' she said. 'We're going.' She had removed the net from the nyakaboyo dula, and now all the evil that had been pressing in on that place since the beginning of the circumcision would pour into it.

We arrived at the duto koto to find that bamboo mats had been spread out in the shade. As the ngangsingolu arrived they were seated in rows. Then the ngangsimba, who was wearing a salmon pink, turtle-neck pullover, began to organize the *ngangsimba tulungo*, the dance which would symbolically represent the emergence of the children from the bush. The young guardians stood in a line along one side of the clearing, while on the other stood the musakebas – the old women. It was now the middle of the afternoon, but no one had drunk or eaten since dawn. The musakebas danced and sang, and they even went to the extent of cutting sticks to beat the guardians into dancing. But neither the guardians, the ngangsingolu, nor the musakebas themselves really had the strength to continue. So it was decided to leave the dance until the evening.

In the late afternoon it became apparent that the ngangsimba tulungo would be postponed till the following morning. At Kafuli Kunda, the guardians beat the kijo, while the ngangsingolu danced for their mothers. Some of the older children were quite accomplished, but for others it was their first attempt. The youngest girl of all brought smiles to everyone's faces as she bounced up and down on the spot in time to the rhythm. 'He – eh! She has tried well,' they laughed. Then all the children were brought forward in turn to sing the style songs they had learnt during the period of their confinement. 'Tubabo Marky la be ye ke' was by far the most popular. 'Hey, not that again,' said Safi Mama when the song was repeated for what seemed like the hundredth time. 'Try a different one,' she said, giving me a sharp look.

I arrived early at Sanyang Kunda. It was bitterly cold, so I went and sat by a fire in one of the houses. The tulungo had been postponed yet again. I noticed that the triangular knot in front of the initiates' tikos had been untied. I realized that something had been contained in that knot. But what it was I would never know.

The ngangsingolu were all gathered together in the centre of the compound. Carrying their flag, and together with the ngangsimba, Mba Penda and all the guardians, they walked up the street to the house of Mba Jongmar, the oldest woman in the village. She told them to be sure to remember everything they had learnt in the jujuo. Now they were members of society, and they were responsible for whatever they did. Then they prayed together.

They walked down the street to the big bantaba, where they turned right towards Minte Kunda. The ngangsimba sat down on the bentengo next to Mba Bintanse, the elder woman of the compound, and all the other musakebas, and with the initiates of both compounds seated round their feet they prayed for the future success of the children. The ngangsimba then told the children that they were free.

Immediately they leapt to their feet and ran screaming and shouting out of the compound, and up the lane towards the Arabic school. As they passed, the girls in the school came bursting out of the doorways and followed them up the street as fast as their legs would carry them.

A few days later I returned to the duto koto. The ngangsimba tulungo had still not been held, but the ground under the spreading boughs of the tree had been cleared in readiness. The flat circle of brown dust was darkening by the moment, under the heavy shade of the foliage, which in the fading light looked almost black. The last traces of greenness had drained from the landscape, and the trees seemed almost to be floating over the dry, dusty earth, as the golden light of the sun drew back towards the west. If one looked in the other direction, it was as though night had already fallen. The moon hung over the village in the cold blue sky. In one direction it was day, and in the other night. With the heat and cold of the two states falling on me from different directions, I had again that feeling I had had on the first day of the circumcision, of being in a special place, a place where different parts of the earth met. Under my feet the ground waited for the feet of the women, the sound of their voices and their clapping.

'Ngangsingdingolu – wo!
Initiates!
The crocodile has surprised you,
My children.
Now the crocodile has gone back to the river.'

There were now no crocodiles in Kiang. They had long since been killed for their skins. But twenty-five years earlier, when there were still a few left, the sociologist Barbara Thompson had noted with some surprise that while the men were terrified of crocodiles, the women did not appear at all bothered by them. If they saw one scuttling away into the under-growth near the rice fields, they wouldn't even pay any particular attention to it. But that was not perhaps so very surprising. After all, it was their animal. They had done nothing to provoke it, so it would never harm them.

11

SONA

The building of the new camp was now well under way. From the gates of the MRC compound, the huddle of sheds and container buildings on the far side of the football pitch resembled one of the interminable succession of goods yards that flank the railway lines on the western outskirts of London. The sulphurous yellow arc lights had banished forever the enormous blackness which on moonless nights had threatened to engulf the old camp.

The price of rented accommodation doubled as the spare houses and rooms of the village filled up with carpenters, painters, plumbers and electricians. They lived as 'bachelors', several to a room – Rastamen, Gaddhafi supporters and those who refused to fast – shouting to each other in their own languages, brewing up Chinese tea at the side of the street, their cassette players blaring loudly late into the night. The carpenters of the village worked beside them, and those who had no trade became labourers or watchmen. In the early evening, as the women queued for water at the new taps, and the workers made their way home from the building of the new camp, Dulaba was busy as never before. The village had indeed, as Alassane Drammeh had predicted shortly after I arrived, become 'a city in Kiang West'.

The Community Centre was being put to new uses. In January the heats of the provincial Schools Drama Competition had been held there. The plays had to be on the subject of 'Health', and Dulaba's entry, a play by Mr Balde entitled 'Prevention is Better than Cure', had easily won. A few weeks later, the cast and its supporters had gone on the ITC lorry to the finals in Mansa Konko. They had returned in the evening bearing the trophy for the whole of the Lower River Division, which was processed triumphantly round the village on the back of the lorry.

Yet, despite these appearances of burgeoning prosperity and growth, all was not well. Although the people had received more for their groundnuts than ever before, the price of groundnuts had been falling worldwide for several years. The country was now almost bankrupt. For years the currency had been held at the artificially high level of five dalasis to the pound. But the World Bank had made it a condition of further loans that the dalasi be floated on the world money market. Within days it plummeted to half its former value. The prices of imported commodities, which had risen several times in the previous six months, went up again immediately.

The country's largest market, the Albert Market in Banjul, was destroyed in a mysterious fire, and with it went a sizeable proportion of the Gambia's material wealth. Scores of traders and craftsmen who had stored their wares, their equipment, and even their life savings in the market, were ruined. There were rumours of sabotage. A minor fire led to a story that the country's oil reserves had been blown up.

In Dulaba, this all seemed very remote, but effects of devaluation were felt immediately. The radios and torches of the village were put away, as no one could now afford the batteries to power them. The only people who now had the foreign currency to import rice commercially were the businessmen of the capital, and they charged as much for it as they could. A hundred kilo bag of imported rice, which six months before had cost 98 dalasis, could now be as much as 260. Such a bag would last a medium-sized family for a month. But many of the farmers of Dulaba had received no more than 1,000 dalasis for their groundnuts, and some significantly less.

The government sold aid rice (under agreement with the donor countries, who believed the farmers would cease production if they were merely *given* food) at a fixed rate of 157 dalasis a bag. But this was only rarely available. A hundred such bags arrived at the government store in Mankono late one afternoon. By eight the following morning they had all been sold.

For the villagers, it was all part of the difficulties they believed were now coming upon the whole world; a compounding of the difficulties they had been facing since the beginning of the drought fifteen years before. But while they were secure in the knowledge that it was all beyond their comprehension, let alone their control, they were unimpressed by their government's attempts to face up to these problems. There was widespread resentment against those who were profiting from these times of hardship, and while there were few who would finally make the step, many seriously considered the possibility of going over to the opposition.

The women of the Kurung Kafo remembered what God had said, that He will help those who help themselves. So they went to the Headmaster, and asked him if he would write a letter to the government, so that the name of their kafo could be heard throughout the length and breadth of the country. He told them that the only way they would get the attention of the government would be by forming themselves into a *tesito* – a self-help project.

In the villages all over Kiang, the women – with the assistance of aid organizations – were planting gardens, big communal gardens, spread over as much as an acre, in which each woman had her own area. They were planting tomatoes, onions, cabbages, aubergines, and different kinds of green leaves. One of the biggest gardens was at Karafa Kunda. It had been sponsored by Action Aid, and had wire fences, and three cemented wells actually inside the garden itself. There were no aid organizations working in Dulaba and the women had long since realized that their husbands would never help them in such matters. So they decided they would organize their garden themselves, as their own self-help project.

The Kurung Kafo was not large, so they joined with the Musakeba Sise

Kafo, a group of women in their early thirties, named after its leader, the tall, thin woman of Kafuli Kunda – who also happened to be Safi Mama's co-wife – and they assembled in the Headmaster's compound, where they told him what they intended to do. Three years before, when the new well was being dug close to the school, they had helped to pull the earth and rocks from the ground and carry it away. They had worked hand in hand with the Headmaster, and since then he had taken a close interest in their affairs. He told them that they could use the area of land beside the school for their garden, and they could use the school well to water it. He would also try to get help for them from the Catholic Relief Services, who were involved in many of the gardens in Kiang. But he told them that in order to qualify as a tesito project, they would have to change the name of their group to the Dulaba Young Farmers Club'. This they readily agreed to do.

'I think that for all of them it is the same,' said Fatou Mbaye, 'circumcised and uncircumcised. They all like it. But if you really want to know what it is like with a circumcised woman, why don't you go with one and find out?'

With whom?

'Anyone that you like. If you tell me the name of the person that you like, I will speak to her, and ask her to come to you.'

What if they said no?

'They will not do that.'

Why not?

'Because they like it.'

It hadn't taken me long to decide who I wanted her to ask, though it took me rather longer to get around to asking Fatou Mbaye to do it. She had looked rather surprised.

'Is there something wrong?' I asked.

'No. It is just that she is pregnant.'

Now I was surprised. I'd noticed that she was slightly fatter, but had attributed this to the fact that she was getting more to eat.

'Is that bad?' I asked.

'No. It is good – if it is not a problem for you. In Africa men do not like to have affairs with pregnant women. They think it brings bad luck. But women like it, particularly during the first two months, because they believe it will make their delivery easier.'

Now, however, I was not sure it was such a good idea. In fact I was sure it was an extremely bad idea. It was not only morally wrong, but seemed bound to lead to disaster. Each morning I woke just before dawn, almost feverish with dread. But just as I had made up my mind to go to Fatou Mbaye and tell her to forget everything, I would see Sona in my mind's eye, almost as though she were herself standing over the bed, as she had looked as she came from her bath that evening a month or so before – wrapped only in her old faneau, her shoulders gleaming against the darkness. And I knew that if I could have her, I would have to do it.

*

Each day the fence around the garden beside the school was getting bigger. Stakes had been driven into the ground at intervals of two or three feet. Thinner, more flexible branches were tied horizontally along them with strips of wet bark, and millet stalks, the long, thin, white twigs called *baroum-barow*, and virtually any other vegetable matter that was to hand, were stuffed vertically between them. The women began working just where they felt like it, some concentrating on their own area, others helping out whenever and wherever the fancy took them. The different parts grew slowly towards each other, with new sections sprouting up apparently at random, until suddenly it was finished. It looked incredibly fragile and makeshift. But that was the traditional way of making fences, and at some time or other it must have proved effective.

The following Sunday, the Headmaster measured out the seed beds. They were to be the same size as those at Karafa Kunda – five metres by one and a half – with paths a metre wide running between them. As soon as the marking pegs were in place, the women claimed their areas and began to turn over the soil with their hoes. One end of the garden had been tilled and watered before the other end had even been fully marked out. The Headmaster had considerable difficulty in persuading the women not to extend their beds into the pathway areas. If they were any larger it would make them difficult to weed without trampling on the nascent plants.

More women were arriving all the time to see if they could make use of the spare beds. Most of the women had four beds each, and when you considered there were at least forty women involved, that meant that this was a very big garden. The Headmaster worked on with his tape measure and his pegs, a cigarette poised between his lips. He was not a citizen of the village, so it was very good for him to be seen to be involved in a project of this kind.

At three o'clock, the MRC weekend transport would be leaving for the coast – and I would be going with it. As I packed my bag I suddenly heard a familiar voice ringing out, harsh and declamatory, across the compound forecourt. I peered out through the mosquito netting. All I could see was the glare of sunlight reflected from the dust. Then between the stakes of the garden fence I could just make out her figure, standing by the gate, locked in discussion with Samba So, the gatekeeper. I had been avoiding her – until I knew whether Fatou Mbaye had yet spoken to her. Suddenly I felt an overriding compulsion to go out there.

As I stepped from the shade along the side of the house into the full force of the sun, I saw her walking straight towards me. The brutal sunlight seemed to shatter into a kind of halo against her rounded violet forehead. She was wearing the white shirt. It made her body glitter all over.

She had thirty dalasis, and she wanted someone who was going to the coast to buy her a bedspread with this money. As we spoke I felt once again the sense of intimacy between us, and I noticed an uncharacteristic expression of uncertainty, of nervousness even, in her dark eyes.

Cursing myself for not being able to speak the language properly, I told her I didn't know anything about buying bedspreads.

'Just get the kind wrapped up in the packet. Do you know that kind?'

I said I didn't know it very well.

I could envisage myself wandering through the market at Serekunda, pursued by gangs of apaches all trying to 'help' me, only to bring back something that wasn't what she wanted. I said that maybe Demba Tamba could get it for her.

'Demba Tamba,' she repeated. She seemed very worried.

She sat by the gate until the transport departed. She asked everyone who was going if they would help her. No one would.

On my return on the Sunday evening, I went to see Fatou Mbaye. She was sitting in her room breast-feeding her child. But she sat so still that in the dim light one was scarcely aware of the activity. We sat for a few moments in silence. I could just see her eyes. They were, as always, extraordinarily cool and impartial, as though she had already seen everything on the earth. We could hear laughter coming from the next room. The low ceiling of corrugated iron blocked out most of the noise, but it made the air uncomfortably thick and hot.

She told me that she had seen the woman.

'What happened?' I asked.

'She laughed. She said that she did not believe me. I said, "It is true, and I know that you will not disappoint him." She said that you will see each other.'

She paused for a moment while she transferred her son's mouth from one nipple to the other.

'So she will see you, and tell you when she will come. And you will make sure you are there at that time.'

'Is this not all very wicked?' I asked.

She seemed surprised. 'In what way?'

'From the point of view of the religion.'

'According to the religion, if you love someone, you must face them. Otherwise you will spend all your time thinking impure thoughts about them.'

Now I was working every day with Jojo Bajie in the study of House One. We could not have the air-conditioning on as it drowned out the sound of the tape recorder. So we sat there, and sweated.

Jojo was the cousin of one of the mechanics, and he had come to Dulaba looking for work with the MRC or the ITC. But as neither was available, I had taken him on as a more or less full-time translator. He was a pleasant young man – easy-going, but punctual. He always walked in a very upright and dignified way, despite the ragged and frequently filthy condition of his clothes. I had noticed that he always socialized with people some years younger than himself. 'According to my birth certificate,' he said, by way of explanation, 'I am twenty-five years old. But I do not think I can be that age. My body does not feel twenty-five years old.'

He had trained as a nurse at the clinic run by the German Methodist Mission in Sibanor. He was supposed to attend a birth in the clinic as part of the course, but he had not gone. 'You know, we were told by our elders when we went for circumcision that it is bad for a man to attend such an event.'

Why?

'I don't know. They just said it was bad.'

What if he had to deal with a woman in labour during the course of his work?

'I don't know . . . Maybe it's going to be a problem.'

One day when we were in Mankono for the dance that would mark the end of the circumcision, I took him to meet a woman of my acquaintance in that village. He asked me if I intended to call her to my house so that I could make love to her. I asked him what made him think she would agree to such a summons.

He became annoyed for the first time since I had met him.

'I'm not a child,' he said. 'I've seen the way you move with these women. Any woman you ask must come to you. There is no way out.'

Now every woman in the village had a garden. Those who did not have a place in the Kurung Kafo garden cultivated tiny plots, squeezed into the corners of their compounds, behind the washing areas and the rubbish heaps, or between the walls of the houses and the corners of the streets – always tightly fenced with millet stalks or baroum-barow. Each of these gardens had to be watered twice a day – one pan of water for each seed bed. These pans were not small; they were huge bowls of iron or plastic that held thirty litres each. The women would help each other to lift them onto their heads, but if no one was around they would have to lift them themselves. I tried to lift one once, and could only get it about an inch off the ground. Yet one saw girls of twelve carrying such basins on their heads.

Each morning, as I sat in the kitchen eating breakfast, I could see the constant stream of figures moving backwards and forwards between the Kurung Kafo garden and the school well. They walked very slowly, swaying slightly under the weight of the pans. Those who had jobs at the camp had to rise at four-thirty in the morning to complete this watering before they went to work. And when they'd finished watering in the evenings, they'd have to draw water for their husbands and children to wash with, before they began cooking the dinner. It was the young wives who worked the hardest – those with no co-wife or daughter old enough to help them.

By the evening, the eyes of the women, as they stood waiting at the taps, were dull and heavy, their movements listless and mechanical. The sun, the heat of which grew harder and more intense with every passing day, had only begun to wane by the time of the five o'clock prayer, and it drained and stupefied the women into a state approaching somnambulism.

By seven the darkness was thickening around the bantaba at Fili

Kunda, and the evening sky was stretched taut like a sheet of silk – the lemon-yellow of the sun, which had disappeared behind the thatched roofs of Old Bajo Kunda, gradually merging into a deep and startling magenta – across which, in a great fan shape, small grey clouds were neatly laid out, like pebbles in a Zen garden.

'Is it not beautiful?' I said to Fatounding.

'It is beautiful,' she said. 'What of it?'

As I walked back up the village street, I found myself turning along the alley between the tall buildings into the compound of Tamba Kunda. As I arrived in the yard that sloped upwards towards the house of the women, I saw a number of female figures standing looking towards the end house, from which came the sound of angry voices. I picked out the deep, resonant voice of Njonji, the co-wife, and Sona's sharp, brittle tones rising above it. In accordance with tradition, Sona had had to take over the elder wife's duties during her week of confinement – cleaning Susan Lawrence's house each morning, as well as doing all the cooking, washing and fetching of wood. Njonji had beaten her in the race to produce the first male heir, and it was a matter of some amusement among the other women that Sona had taken her defeat in exceedingly bad grace.

As I stood there, the argument began to spread along the row of houses, more and more voices joining in the unreasoning, unlistening struggle, and I decided to withdraw.

By Friday evening, I decided I would have to speak to her. That morning she had appeared at the window of the study where I was working with Jojo. It looked out onto the thoroughfare along which, on Mondays, Wednesdays and Fridays, the whole world would pass by. She had stood there, and we had greeted each other through the glass. She looked at me intently – her eyes so wide I was afraid I would fall into them. Then she turned as abruptly as she had appeared, and walked away. I sat there shaking, hoping Jojo wouldn't notice.

The old woman greeted me as I appeared in the compound. I realized now that she was the husband's step-mother. With her sat her daughter, the husband's sister, of the same father but a different mother. I had felt, from the first time I visited that compound, that these two women were fully cognizant of my motives, and that while the sister disapproved of me, the old woman gave me her secret moral support.

'She is cooking,' she said, puffing contentedly on her pipe. 'Go and help her.' And she gestured towards the end house.

I sat on a stool in the yard at the back of the house. I felt a mixture of confidence at having finally come to the moment of decision, and the foolishness one inevitably feels at having to sit perched on a tiny stool in the middle of a cramped area through which many people are trying to pass. She emerged from the cooking hut looking hot and harassed. There was a certain heaviness to her movements; she was now very obviously pregnant. She shouted at one of the people in the yard – her daughter –

who ran off into the house, then she shot me a dark look. We greeted briefly, then she went back into the cooking hut.

'I waited at the gates of the camp for a long time,' she called, as she shook a pan of groundnuts she was roasting over the fire. 'But no one would agree to buy my bedspread for me.'

'People were very wicked to you,' I said.

'You also were wicked,' she said. 'You also would not help me.'

'I didn't know what sort you wanted.'

'I just wanted a bedspread,' she said simply.

Then, as all of the people in the yard were children, she came straight to the point. 'Fatou Mbaye said you want to chat with me. My bedspread costs forty dalasis, but the money I have is only thirty dalasis. Bring the ten dalasis here, and then I will come and chat with you.'

'You don't want to chat with me,' I said.

'I want it.'

'You come and chat with me. Then, *maybe*, I will help you.'

'That is fair,' she said.

Her daughter returned with the shirt she'd been sent to fetch. Then Sona went back into the cooking hut.

I was still smarting with annoyance when I set out to walk to the Bintang Bolon, late the following afternoon. I lay down on the tiny landing stage. The tide was in, and I could feel the water lapping against the wood only a foot beneath me. The fibreglass hull of the Professor's dinghy lay on the mud nearby. One of the villagers was still paid to maintain a canopy of leaves over it, though it had not been used since he left. The Professor had enjoyed some of his few moments of peace in Dulaba in that boat. I recalled how on certain evenings we had scudded in wide zig-zags along the bend of the creek, the cranes gliding low over the water around us, their great wings slowly beating the air. What a long time ago that seemed. It was difficult now to imagine that the Professor had ever been there. I suddenly felt very alone.

As I walked back across the salt flats, I saw that place as I had first seen it: as unutterably alien and strange. Crabs like tiny devils crawled into their holes in the dark, stinking mud, and on either side of the laterite causeway the salt flats stretched out, shining dully in the evening sun. On the far edge, the branches of the trees hung down, as though to hide the bush. It was a landscape that didn't answer – that didn't give anything back to the observer. It just lay there, flat and dead and silent. I now knew something about the people who lived in this landscape, and the significance it had for them. But without the presence of the people themselves, the land returned to its former inscrutability.

On reflection, I wondered why I had ever thought the behaviour of the people who lived in this landscape should be any less extraordinary, any less alien to my expectations. In England people didn't love each other for a bedspread, but here perhaps they did. The bedspread! That was where I had made my mistake. I should have taken her money and made the effort of going to the market. If the money had not been enough, I could have made it up. It would have been an opportunity to demonstrate my good intentions, to show that I was someone who was supporting her in her struggles on the earth. It was absurd to suggest that the one I would have chosen would not have been to her taste. Whatever I had chosen she would have thought beautiful; to have it would have been enough.

It seemed to me, looking back on my life, that all my failures had been failures of generosity. That whenever the moment had come to show my hand, I had withdrawn it. This was why I now had nothing.

And if she was trying to exploit my feelings, who could blame her? When one thought that the verb most commonly used by African men in relation to their sexual dealings with women was to 'use', it was hardly surprising that the women should try to squeeze from such contacts whatever rewards they could. Nor was it surprising that they should 'change their direction like the wind'. What other defence was open to them?

12

THE ELEPHANT HEAD

Pa Konte was one of the most physically impressive people I had ever come across. He wasn't very tall or big, but he was all lithe, tigerish muscle. And his features, though fine, had a ruthless, leonine composure. He sat squarely in the Habitat armchair under the dim lightbulb – a dark, majestic presence.

'How can you live like this, man? How many months have you sat here without a woman?'

I mumbled something about an English student who had been there during the rainy season.

'That was months ago. For myself, I have to make love, man. When I feel it, I must do it. There is no way out. If I sit for a month without sex, I'm going to go crazy. I don't agree with that thing, masturbation. So even if it's an old, old woman or a blind person, I have to do it.'

In the village of Jiffarong, which lay beside the red laterite road, a few kilometres from Sankandi, there was a schoolteacher, a tall, slender, but sturdy woman of twenty called Maria-Theresa Gomez. She was a Manjago, a Christian. In a different context she might have made a fortune out of her appearance. Instead she was teaching English among the baobabs of Jiffarong. I had met her at the heats of the Schools' Drama Competition in January, and I well remembered the relief I had felt when she told me she was not a Muslim. She had said it with an appealing definiteness. Maybe it was easy to be so definite in a language that was not one's mother tongue. When one of the village boys went to spend a weekend in that village, I told him to greet her on my behalf. And when he returned he said she had laughed, and asked when I would be coming to see her.

'I know that woman,' said Pa. 'They call her Marri. She is a Christian, and if you go there you will find that her clitoris is *definitely* there.' He thought for a moment. 'We will go there next Saturday on the motorbike. I will speak to her for you. You know, if you go there alone, and just speak to her like that, you are going to fail. But if I go to her as a black and explain everything to her, I will talk to her very seriously, and you will surely have her.'

I wasn't sure this was really my style. Anyway, what made him so sure she would agree?

'I know the blacks, man! It's our culture. If you go, you will speak to her in English. If I go I will speak to her in Mandinka or in Wolof. The things I am going to say to her, you cannot say. Believe me, man. I know the way these things are done.'

But he had said she was a Christian. Weren't they different?

'Hey! In terms of these affairs, it's all the same.'

I said I'd rather risk failure on my own terms than go along with such a plan. It seemed to obviate the whole point of the endeavour. Wasn't one looking for some sort of spontaneous meeting of minds?

'It's up to you,' he said. 'But I can tell you that if you don't get a black to help you, you will sit here alone until you go mad.'

After months without any visitors, the camp was suddenly full of new tubabs. I was sharing my house with Sharon, a woman of twenty-six, with a mane of crinkly auburn hair, a technician from the Cass who had come out to begin a project with Anne Shergold, one of the scientists. Anne and her husband David had lived and worked in Dulaba from 1978 to 1983. When her current brief visit was over, the Staff, many of whom had been employed by Anne and her husband, and who retained strong feelings of loyalty towards them, held a party in her honour.

Large quantities of benakino with goat and chicken were washed down with bottles of Sprite and Coca-Cola. Then a disco-dance was held in the Community Centre. Anne was asked to commence the dancing with Bakary Sanneh. One moment the building was almost empty; Bakary and Anne dancing alone in the middle of the great warehouse-like floor. The next, the whole of the youth of Dulaba were pouring into the building from every orifice, dancing towards them like a tide by which they were immediately swallowed up.

Europeans almost never attended such events in the village, so the ten or so present lent an air of glamour and 'importance' to the proceedings. There were also an unusually large number of married women present. Jori Sanyang and Maimouna Jatta danced together to Super Jamano's 'Oumaro', swaying majestically, their billowing robes shimmering in the dim light. Most of them, however, the assistants from the Supplement Centre, the domestic staff of the Europeans, simply sat in a line along one wall of the building, staring miserably into space, too embarrassed to dance. In the darkness along the opposite wall sat the *samakumbalu*, the 'T-shirt wearers' – the young girls of the village.

Samakungo or *samakumba* – 'the head of an elephant' – was the traditional way of praising a young woman in the Mandinka language: the girls old enough to have the body of a woman, but who had not yet been given to their husbands, and those who had been given, but had not yet transferred to his compound. It implied that that person possessed all the strength, wisdom and ingenuity of the great animal. Anyone held in particular awe would be called *ningkinangkikungo* – 'the head of a dragon'. For the dragon can breathe fire and disappear at will, so anyone named after it must be very special indeed. But if you addressed a woman by any of these epithets she would invariably reply, *'He-e-eh! Inte mang kei samakungo ti. Inte mu challifenyo le ti!'* – 'I am not the head of an elephant. I am the tail of a fish!' For the tail of a fish is never eaten or used; it is just discarded, like those women who are never pursued by men.

Many people were interested in dancing with Sharon, and as in Africa such things are considered best arranged through a go-between, I spent much of the evening failing to assist them.

'Why can't people stop hassling me?' she moaned as she watched the dancers from the relative safety of the verandah.

Father J, who was looking very grave and regal in a fawn robe, looked disdainfully at the samakumbalu. 'Those people are girls?' he asked, incredulous. 'They are doing nothing. They are just sitting there.'

But as the evening wore on, and they lost some of their shyness, they became more active, dancing with each other and with the few men who deigned to ask them.

That night the most noticeable of the samakumbalu were Homonding Minte and Munya Sise. Homonding was nineteen, fair in complexion, very tall and thin – but scarcely fragile. She was the leader of the My Brother Kafo. She had been married to a citizen of the village who lived in Kombo, but he had never come for her. She lived with her grandmother in Bakary Kunda, so that she could help the old woman and be 'disciplined' by her, while she waited to see if anyone else would ask for her hand.

Munya was twenty-two. She had been the great friend of Darbon Jammeh. They were more or less the same age, and they had worked together as nursemaids at the MRC, first in the lab and later for the children of the Europeans. While she was there, she had become very attached to Njundu Sise, who cleaned Barbara Smith's house. They had planned to marry, but her family had not accepted him, because they said that Njundu was not a good Muslim, that he did not respect his father. The visible nature of this affection, the sense of tension that surrounded it, and the consternation that was caused when it came to an end, were seen by the Europeans as evidence that the attitudes of the villagers in such matters were basically the same as their own. They couldn't help noticing, however, that within a week of Munya's parents refusing his suit, Njundu had found another wife in a nearby village. Munya was eventually given to a man sixteen years older than her, whom she did not love. And that, the Europeans all agreed, was 'rather a pity'.

Now Munya was working as the 'maid' of Dr Sabari, a Gambian scientist working at the camp. She had a son, but he was constantly ill. Richard attributed this to neglect on her part. 'She may be beautiful,' he said, 'but she's killing that child.' She was dark, with a large Roman nose, which, set against the overall suavity of her features, gave an impression of exceptional alertness. But she wasn't someone who was always looking around to greet everyone in sight; indeed she seemed often absorbed by her own thoughts, and one would have felt nervous of interrupting them without good reason.

I walked over to the samakumbalu and called her to the floor. Like most African women she did not look at her partner as she danced, but stared at the floor with an expression of stoic grimness. This left me free to stare at her as much as I wanted. What must it be like to be actually purple? I wondered.

When the song had finished, I thanked her, we shook hands and returned to our places. Later, when I was in that part of the room again, she called me to sit next to her. 'Can you dance?' I asked. It was a fatuous question since we had been dancing together only half an hour before – though not quite as absurd when couched in the Mandinka language. 'Of course,' she said. 'Come and dance.' So we got up and danced to another reggae number. When it was over we once again shook hands, and she went back to sit by the wall. Here, then, was the person for me. I decided to seek guidance.

Yaya Bojang, dressed only in a pair of yellow satin boxer-shorts, was dancing fervently by himself in the brilliant light of the verandah. He listened intently to my question. 'You just ask her at what time tomorrow she will have the chance to come to you. She will know what you mean. She is someone who is very quick to understand.'

Not tonight?

'No, tonight is not safe. There are too many people around.'

She stood instantly, as though magnetized, when I called her. The stony, ruminative expression she had worn while dancing returned to her face.

'Around ten o'clock time,' she said.

I looked at my watch as I walked home. It was half-past one. I looked up at the stars. 'And she can tell the time!' I thought.

I emerged from the shower the following morning to find Mabinta, Natoma, Filije and Fatoumata Sise, Sharon's washing lady, all seated on the Habitat furniture drinking coffee. As I stood drying my hair, I caught sight of a purposeful muscular walk on the other side of the mosquito netting, and heard a strident voice calling, '*Salaam aleikum*.'

'Gordon Bennett!' I thought. 'She's *early!*'

I darted into my bedroom, which was still in darkness, the curtains having been kept closed in readiness. What a time to arrive! What was I going to do? To give myself time to think, I shovelled my daily dose of anti-malaria pills into my mouth. Then I went back to face whatever awaited me in the living room.

Most of the company had tactfully departed, leaving only Munya and Filije. As I sat down, Filije got up and went back to her sweeping. I made brief small talk with Munya, then I said, 'What I want to say is secret.'

'Secret,' she repeated, looking thoughtfully off into the middle distance.

'There are too many people here now. The afternoon is better.'

She thought for a moment. 'Between now and five o'clock I will come.'

Then she got up and went.

It was hotter in the afternoon than it was in the middle of the day. For the residual heat thickened over the surface of the earth, and one moved slowly and heavily through it, as though swimming blindly against a current. I sat for five hours on the Habitat sofa, working as I waited. The fan whirred overhead, but it did nothing to cool the air. It simply moved it around the room in great swirling gusts, so that one felt as though one were being constantly blown on by an immense hairdryer. Eventually Mabinta arrived to do the ironing, and I knew that the moment had passed.

*

Nor did she come the following day. So on Friday morning, having made sure that Dr Sabari was hard at work in the lab, I went over to his house.

The curtains in all the rooms were drawn. I knocked on the door, but there was no reply. I tried the handle, and as it was not locked I went in. No one was around in the bare passageway. Then a voice called, 'Mark'. And the living room door swung open. She looked all mouth and nose and cheek-bones – her eyes reduced to slits that glittered as she waited to see what I would do. We greeted each other, then I asked her why she had not come.

'I went there, but Mabinta was ironing. So I did not go in.'

'Yesterday also you did not come.'

She looked down, playing with the besom of palm fronds in her hand.

'Yesterday I did not go anywhere,' she said.

'When will you come?' I asked.

'Today, in the afternoon.'

A month before, when there was still money left from the harvest, the new clothes started to arrive in the village. There were the *simisos* (chemises), a style based on the petticoats of the Europeans, which the Mandinka women liked to wear as a shirt. That year they came in brilliant, electric colours – scarlet and black, a vehement pink, cobalt violet, turquoise, and a particular fluorescent green contrasted with maroon, of which some people doubted the tastefulness. Then there were the vests, tie-dyed with indigo. Many of the women already had them, but since they last came to the village they had faded to a dull grey. In the new ones, the indigo was fresh with a liquidescent, coppery sheen, as though if you squeezed the garment the pigment would ooze out onto your fingers. Against the depth of this background, the thick white rings stood out in startling contrast, like lunar craters. The samakumbalu liked to wear these garments with strings of yellow plastic beads, with which for some reason they looked remarkably good. But it was by no means solely a 'youth' fashion. One saw girls of eight and women of sixty dressed in exactly the same way – in fact they often *were* the same clothes, passed around the women of the compound from day to day.

It was in this way that Munya was dressed when she appeared along the mosquito netting beside our living-room that Friday afternoon.

'*Marky dindingo!*' she called at the top of her voice. 'Mark, the small boy.'

'Give me a break,' I thought.

She sat down on the sofa and settled her son Ibraima beside her. I fetched her a bottle of lemonade, then I sat down at the other end of the sofa. Let's get to the point, I thought, before some inane interruption occurs.

'Munya,' I said. 'I would like us to have a connection – if you wish.'

'A connection.' She repeated the word slowly and quietly to herself, and stared thoughtfully off at some point miles away, way beyond the mosquito netting. She took a mouthful of lemonade and thought a bit more. Then she said, 'Perhaps' – languorously drawing out the syllables of the Mandinka word, '*tomando*'.

Now I had to think quickly. 'Is it difficult?' I asked.

'It's not very difficult,' she said.

We talked for a short while longer about this and that. She lived in Salum Kunda, opposite the big bantaba at the bottom of the village. It had once been described by Richard as one of the more Dickensian compounds in Dulaba. 'That is,' he said, 'if a compound in Dulaba can be described as Dickensian.' She told me that her mother was Gunjur, of the Kurung Kafo, which rather surprised me, as I had always understood that Gunjur had never had any children of her own. But Munya seemed very definite, indeed proud of it.

I asked her if her son had been ill. 'Yes,' she said, smiling. 'He was sent to Fajara.' Then, perhaps detecting some element of criticism in the question, 'But only once.'

And all the time I was thinking that I should be saying the things that would persuade her, that would subtly move her, to do what I wanted.

I had had it impressed on me on innumerable occasions since I arrived in Africa that in order to get something from someone, be it a cup of rice or the attentions of the one you loved, it was necessary to talk. You had to tell that person what it was you needed, why you needed it, and why that person rather than anyone else was the one who should give it to you. If you gave up too early in your *dyamo* (discussion) you would fail. I had once heard Lamin Jarjou trying to seduce one of the English students. He had gone on trying to persuade her long after any European would have given up. He just went on and on, as though eventually she must submit out of admiration for his sheer vocal stamina.

I could have told Munya that she was the most beautiful woman I had ever seen, that I loved her 'too much'; both of which, at that moment, seemed to be true. But I said none of these things. I could say nothing. I could only notice how the indigo vest made her skin seem almost iridescent – here violet, here black, here almost green.

Finally she said, 'Thank you,' in English, and got to her feet. There was something about the definiteness and the finality of the way she tied her son on her back that made me realize that she would not come – that she had already decided that she would not.

She went, and I looked at my watch. She had been there scarcely fifteen minutes. I was assailed by an almost overwhelming sense of frustration and disappointment – but not of rejection, for it seemed to me that the reasons for her decision were much deeper and more fugitive than mere physical antipathy. And my frustration was not only that of frustrated desire, but at my powerlessness before the immeasurable and incomprehensible barriers that lay between us.

Ramou Jagne, the lab assistant, was an Aku, the descendant of slaves freed from Europe at the end of the eighteenth century. Her family had emigrated to England, and she had spent the first six years of her life in a flat in West London. Her father still lived there, but she had been brought back to the Gambia, where her grandmother had converted her to Islam.

She had married a Wolof, also a Muslim, though she now declared herself a 'free thinker'.

'A woman from this village will never have an affair with a European,' she said. 'It is not because they do not like them. It is because of the feelings they have about the Europeans, deep within themselves.'

Did they think the Europeans were unclean?

'It is not that.'

Did they think the Europeans were . . . devils?

'It is not that either, though it is something like that. You know the amount of time these people have been in contact with the Europeans is not long. It is really only a very short time. You know they don't think that the Europeans are actually devils, but they feel that they are somehow superhuman. The respect they feel for them is so great that they cannot feel naturally towards them – they cannot get beyond that.'

I walked out into the bush along the old Karafa Kunda road. The moon was already up. I could feel the turbulent vegetation stretching out around me, for mile upon mile. The leaves of the plants glimmered jewel-like in the fading light. The orange rock of the path glowed as though radioactive. Once again I felt the strangeness of that landscape – only this time I felt that it had defeated me.

Around their waists the women wore strings of beads, which hung low, just above their genitals. They were called *jelly-jelly* in Wolof and *jo-no* in Mandinka. They were worn by children of both sexes even before they could walk. In fact they often wore nothing else but their jujus. But the jo-no of a woman was almost never exposed to the light of day. It remained hidden among the folds of faneau around the woman's hips. It thus had great erotic connotations, and was for some an almost fetishistic instrument of arousal.

Even more arousing than the sight of the jo-no was the sound of the beads rattling together as the women swung their hips. The fondling of the jo-no was considered by some to be an integral part of lovemaking. Perhaps when his wife's body had been all but drained of its life by childbearing and manual labour, a man could still get some interest from the jo-no.

Jarra Njai had finally returned with the material for the kafo's ashobi. She had gone to Brikama, where she had stayed with a woman called Satou Jammeh, who had been a member of their kafo as a child, but who was now married in that town. They soon discovered that it was virtually impossible to find cloth at ten dalasis a metre. At all the shops and market stalls it was at least twelve-fifty a metre. Finally Satou took them to a shop run by a Moor of her acquaintance. They were there bargaining for many hours. Finally they got what they wanted: nine 'pieces' of cloth, and five metres, all at ten dalasis a metre. The only problem was that the pieces were not all of one pattern.

'Some people may say,' said Fatounding, fingering a rather thick cloth: washes of crimson, lilac and turquoise, across which cascaded a torrent of bottle green umbrellas. 'Some people may say that Jarra Njai has refused to give them the nicest piece of cloth, and given it to others. I myself won't say it, but some people may say it.'

'The money I had to buy these pieces was not that much,' said Jarra Njai, wearily defensive. 'Which is why I was unable to buy a piece big enough for everyone to have the same.'

'Fatounding,' said someone else. 'That should not have been said. We all know that the money we have contributed was not enough.'

The other patterns were equally startling. One showed peacock feathers of orange, green and blue, their fringes overlapping to create a spidery pattern across the material. This was generally considered the most attractive of the three designs. The third consisted of narrow black and white stripes, broken by motifs of red and green. It was difficult to say exactly what it resembled. It might have been candles rising out of a Christmas cake. It might have been prison bars and a bouquet of flowers. Or it might have just been a pattern.

'Mark,' said Janno. 'When we have sewn our clothes we're going to come to your house to dance, and we're going to Karafa Kunda to greet our kafo there.'

'Listen,' said Jarra Njai. 'When we cut this cloth, some people will have three metres, and some people will have four metres. Those people who don't get four metres won't be happy, but the material is going to be divided according to the size of the body. The big people will have four metres, and the small people will have three metres. For myself, I don't care if I only have two metres, but I want to see that everybody is happy.'

'Jarra Njai,' said Tumbulu. 'What you have said I have heard. You are the leader of the kafo. You cannot satisfy everybody. Whatever you say, we will agree to it.'

While the Saniyoro Kafo were thus engaged, Fatou Kambi Sise was having her hair plaited. She was twenty-three, a stocky, vigorous woman with a disarmingly direct manner. She had two children and was pregnant with a third, but until today she had continued to live with her mother. She did not own anything. If she needed anything, such as clothing or jewellery, she would ask her mother. That night, however, she would be transferred to her husband's compound, in the ceremony known as the *manyo bitto*. So in the afternoon all the women of the compound had gathered together to adorn her in the style of the *manyo* – the bride. Her hair was tightly and elaborately braided to her scalp, and silver coins were fastened to it on long strings of beads which hung about her shoulders, one central *leddo* dangling over her forehead.

She would only be a 'bride' once in her life – any subsequent marriages would take place without ritual – and this ceremony, which lasted three days, was one of the most important transitions she would go through in the course of her life. She would become a *forromuso*. She would have to find and clear her own rice field. And whereas before she had been able to go to dances as she liked, and wander in the village with her friends in the evenings, now she was under the authority of her husband, and she would not go anywhere, or do anything, without first asking his permission.

While the women plaited Fatou Kambi's hair, women came from other compounds to greet them, and to sing and clap for the manyo. All the manyo's new clothes, and the basins, bowls, pots and pans that the manyo would use when she went to the husband's compound, were stacked up in the mother's house. The visitors went there to examine and admire them, and occasionally to pass malicious comment on their quantity and quality.

Between now and Ramadan, all the women of Fatou Kambi's age group would transfer to their husbands. They would wear the regalia of the manyo, the braiding, the coins and the turban that covered it, for six months – until the end of the rainy season. All this time they would carry with them a *kalama*, a small gourd split to form a spoon, a symbol of their new status. It was decorated with the shape of a star, drawn onto it with red-hot metal, and the rim was hung with coins. When the time came to harvest the rice, the manyo would remove the coins and fill the kalama with dempetengo, then give it to her husband. He would eat the rice, then smash the kalama to demonstrate his mastery over her. The bride would then take off her regalia. But until her husband took a new wife, she would still be referred to as the manyo – the new wife.

I found Munya pounding millet in the yard in front of the house of the women. I sat down on a small stool by the wall of the house, and surveyed the scene. She had a long torso, broad shoulders and long arms, so that she leant forward over the mortar as she worked, pounding neatly but with considerable power. Everything seemed to be done in one long, sinuous movement; her arm swinging low to scoop up the calabash, from which she would tip more of the millet into the mortar. I didn't like to stare, but I could hardly take my eyes off her. Working with her was a younger girl whose name was Nyiranding, but who was always called Jhibaila. She was roundish, fairish in complexion, and always giggling.

A bearded, grinning head appeared over the corrugated-iron fence. It began bantering flirtatiously with the girls, who laughed appreciatively. Munya had a deep, guttural laugh, like water going down a drain, and a way of punctuating her conversation with grunts that was almost brutish. The young man, whose name seemed to be Bambo, came round into the yard. He was tall and well-built, and had a way of staggering slightly and waving his cigarette as he talked, which he may have imagined was appealing to women – and may well have been. He greeted everyone in Wolof, which nobody could understand.

Soon another young man, named Yaya, appeared at the gate. He was a citizen of the village, unlike Bambo, who was one of the workers at the new camp. He too was grinning broadly. 'I'm just making some chat with these people,' Bambo said to me in English.

'Right on,' I said.

There seemed to be an unusually high level of intersexual communication in this compound.

'There's a tulungo tonight,' said Munya, looking up from her pounding. 'The manyo bitto.'

As I left, she followed me out of the gate into the next yard, the basin of
pounded millet on her head. She sang gaily to herself a phrase from a
song by Bob Marley: 'A buffalo soldier . . . A buffalo soldier . . .'

I arrived at Bakary Kunda to find the manyo sitting in her mother's house
surrounded by a gang of children, all dancing, singing and beating on
basins. She sat on the edge of the bed, expressionless and apparently
asleep. The old women began to arrive, and formed a circle round the
edge of the room. A bathtub was placed in the middle of the floor. 'You'll
have to go soon,' said Mabinta, who lived next door. 'This is going to be
the *manyo kuo* – the washing of the manyo. It is *ku'lo!*'

Not *more* ku'lo, I thought!

As soon as the room had filled up with people, many of them – the
children, the women who had not yet transferred to their husbands'
compounds, and myself – were driven out. Munya stood before me in the
brilliant, almost frosty moonlight. 'We the children are going to have a
tulungo over there.' And she followed the crowd running out into the
street.

Beside the main bantaba was a curious, kiosk-like edifice with glass
windows and verandahs on two sides. In the early days of the MRC, it
had been used as a dispensary. The children and girls divided onto the
verandahs as they began to clap and sing the songs of the young people –
style songs and *lenjeng denkilo* (dancing songs).

Back in the parental compound, the women were starting to emerge
from the mother's house. It seemed to take them a very long time to get
from the house to the entrance of the compound, which was only about
thirty feet away. It was difficult to work out what was going on, and there
seemed to be a considerable amount of confusion among the women
themselves. There was a lot of agitated discussion. What happened then
had an air of dreamlike unreality about it. A mat was placed on the
ground at the top of the short slope that led out of the compound. The
manyo sat down on it. A man laid a piece of white cloth over the manyo,
so that it fully covered her. Then, murmuring prayers, he placed a thickly
folded faneau on her head, so that it lay flat like a mortar board.
Eventually the white faneau was pulled back, the manyo got to her feet
and the procession moved on its way. It did not have far to go, as the
husband's compound lay only on the other side of the street. Once inside
the compound gate, the manyo proceeded to the husband's house, a
room just wide enough to have a small bed wedged across the end of it.
Once the manyo was seated on the bed, the rest of the women crowded in
and out of the house in groups, an exercise which, needless to say, took a
very long time.

At the old dispensary the singing and dancing continued, while in the
yard of the husband's compound, the women stood talking in groups.

'Mark, it's over. You can go.'

'No, Mark. Stay.'

'Mark, it's late. Go to the camp.'
'Hey, Mark. Don't go. Stay.'
What was I supposed to do?
'Mark, do you want to go?'
'No.'
'Stay then.'

It was not over. The manyo had moved to the house of the women, where she would be living from now on. The white faneau which covered her head was tied across her face, so that only her eyes were showing. She sat on the bed, totally motionless except for her eyes, which seemed to burn with an almost mystical fire, their huge whites glowing like pieces of the moon.

The room was not large, but all of the women managed to crowd into it, and by the light of the tiny kerosene lamp, the corrugated-iron roof seemed suddenly very high. The women began to sing and dance and clap. It was impossible to see who anyone was, and soon the place was a blur of dark figures whirling in the thick dusty air – the beating on the basin pounding relentlessly, like a hammer on an anvil.

> 'The manyo has come – the tail of the fish!
> She met me here with a scorpion's tail.
>
> 'The manyo is crying – *Ai Waali!*
> May God make her like it.
> May she bear –
> What God has done!
>
> 'The one who breaks relationships is on her way!
> She met me here with a scorpion's tail!'

On the verandah on the far side of the old dispensary, Munya and a group of the other young women and girls were singing.

> 'Darling, let's shake hands.
> May God give you a good night.
> The night will not be sweet,
> Because I sleep alone.
> The one who refused to dance,
> He has a special way of walking.
> You stopped me from sleeping –
> You stopped me from sleeping –
> Playing with the jo-no!'

Each time they came to the vigorously, almost viscerally alliterative chorus, they put their hands on their hips and suggestively gyrated their pelvises. They sang it over and over again, each time adding a greater oomph to the chorus:

'Te ne leeuw –
Te – te ne leeuw –
Jo-ni kobaso!'

All of a sudden they stopped singing and went running off along the street in a great shouting crowd – past the bantaba, and off along the street towards the mosque – their voices growing fainter and fainter; all except Munya who remained, standing beside me.

'Where are they going?' I asked.

'I don't know where they're going,' she replied, and laughed her deep gurgling laugh. We stood there side by side, leaning against the wall of the old dispensary for what seemed like a long time. Although the moonlight was now stronger than ever, her face registered only as a darkness beneath the shade of the verandah, and I could sense nothing of her expression. Only one figure remained at the bantaba, sitting motionless in the shade of the mango tree. He seemed to be looking at us, though he might just as easily have been asleep. It seemed that now I should say something, but I had no idea what. Munya made no attempt to move.

At length, I said, 'You're not going to the place of the women?'

'Yes,' she said. 'I'm going there now.'

We walked off in that direction. At the entrance of the compound she asked me if I was going home. I said I was. 'Bye bye,' she said, in English.

All the next day I wandered moodily through the house. 'Marrying someone off at that age,' I thought. 'To someone they don't even like . . . How can that be right?'

Late in the afternoon. I returned to Salum Kunda to the house of Fatou Kambi's husband. She was sitting on the bed; two or three children playing on the floor. She was wearing her manyo's regalia, but without the white faneau – the *fani koyo*.

'Hurh, Mark!' she said. 'You've come.'

'That's right,' I said.

That evening there was to be more dancing. She began to prepare herself. She opened the chest by the wall. It was full of faneaus and other clothes. 'Fifteen faneaus,' said Fatou Kambi proudly. They were nearly all indigo – the colour the manyos had always worn – tie-dyed with lines of little circles that stood out against the dark background like stars or particles of radioactive rock, or with batik imprints of wriggling lines that sizzled across the shining blue material like electric currents. There were also a few shirts, and a particularly splendid faneau in which stripes of red and green alternated with thick bars of gold thread. 'This one cost sixty dalasis,' said Fatou Kambi proudly as she held it up.

Her mother had paid for this trousseau. She had also provided her daughter with six enamel basins for serving food, five big calabashes, two large plastic bowls for carrying water, and two iron cooking pots. The manyo had to be well prepared, or she would be shamed in front of the people of her husband's compound. Often the co-wives would also buy new utensils so they would not be outshone by her.

The cooking pots alone had been forty dalasis each. The basins were twenty-five each, and then there had been the calabashes and the plastic pans. I wondered how the old woman had been able to afford all this, for she had no husband, and she was a leper and had no fingers with which to work. She must have saved for years, or she must have had a relative who had helped her.

The room filled up with women, who stood and watched, laughing and chatting, as Fatou Kambi changed into the most beautiful of the new clothes. Then everyone moved outside towards the old dispensary, and Fatou Kambi sat down by the wall under the verandah. The women gathered around her in a semi-circle, and the folded faneau was again placed on her head. Then there was clapping and dancing for about twenty minutes. All the time I couldn't take my eyes off Munya. She stood holding her son in her arms, wearing a brilliant crimson headscarf, and a string vest that looked as though it had seen better days as a dish cloth. Like most of the women of Dulaba, she was quick to flare up in annoyance and equally quick to fall down helpless with laughter, yet she seemed incapable of making an ungraceful movement. 'I can quite see the attraction,' Sharon had said. 'She's one of these people you've just got to watch. There are certain people like that in the world.'

'Hey you! Munya!' called one of the older women as they began to disperse. 'Wash the feet of the manyo.' Fatou Kambi stretched out her legs, and Munya took a calabash of water, and spilt some of it on the manyo's feet. Then she bent down and wiped the dust from the manyo's feet. Now she was the oldest woman in the village who had not yet been transferred to her husband. Soon she too would have to go. She did not yet know when it would be, but when the time came she would have to go. There would be no avoiding it.

I went to Tankular with Pa Konte, in search of fish. The red Honda motorbike bumped this way and that along the road of pink sand and rock. We sat on the long wooden jetty, over the dark water of the Great River, which slid by as slow and silent and secretive as mercury, and waited for Pa's grandfather, who was one of the main fishermen of the village, as the sun sank lower and lower. One by one the canoes returned. The first was in the hands of a thin, gangling man and a small boy. The man was extraordinarily ugly, but obviously very skilful, for his catch was larger than anyone's else's. The fish made a satisfying thud as they were hurled one by one onto the dusty wood of the jetty. Finally the man moved the boards at the bottom of his canoe to reveal a gleaming barracuda six feet long.

His entire catch had been sold in advance to two young men who had their van backed up to the end of the jetty. They were Serers, like many of the people who now crowded onto the jetty, talking and bargaining among the heaps of silver fish, and like many of the fishermen themselves, and the air crackled with the sound of their guttural language. They had come from Senegal, and settled in the village to pursue their business – the buying and selling of fish. The women were particularly active in drying the fish, and the yellowing flesh lay in acres along the strand, its potent reek hanging strong in the air. Judging by the amount of money that was changing hands, Tankular must have been a very wealthy village.

Suddenly there was a commotion at the end of the jetty. A group of small boys who had somehow managed to secrete themselves there had begun to emerge from their hiding places. One by one they ran whimpering towards us. As they passed along the jetty, two middle-aged men hit out at them, the first grabbing them by the shoulders and thumping them across the back with all his strength. Soon all the boys were screaming and bawling at the tops of their voices.

Some were smart enough to run the gauntlet as quickly as possible, but others were so stunned by the first beating that by the time they reached the second man, who was wielding a lump of wood, they just stood there as he thrashed them mercilessly over the head and shoulders, splinters flying in all directions. If the boys were slow in staggering away towards the dry land, he would lean over and give them another resounding thwack around the head, which set them howling even more loudly.

I looked on, horrified, hardly able to believe my eyes. But the crowd of people on the landing stage, who had paused in their bargaining to watch, merely chuckled at the spectacle. Indeed there was no trace of malice, or even of real anger on the faces of the two men; they smiled as they 'worked'. As the last of the boys scuttled moaning into the village, the two men strolled back along the jetty, expressions of satisfaction on their faces. The man who had wielded the lump of wood wiped the dust from his hands. 'Hurh!' he said. 'They won't come back again tomorrow.'

At last Pa's grandfather's canoe appeared. At first it was just a dot, and then all of a sudden the grandfather, who was standing in the canoe, was looming towards us at great speed – a faintly piratical figure in a cloth cap and a dark blue Chinese dressing-gown.

'What makes you so sure he won't have sold all his catch?' I asked.

'Hey, Mark,' said Pa. 'Do you think I am a fool? This man is my blood grandfather.'

The man looked scarcely old enough to be his father.

'In fact, he is my grandfather's younger brother.'

I bought ten fish from him. Ten fat silver fish, each over a foot long. I decided I would give some of them to Munya.

By the time we reached the junction with the red laterite road, it was fully dark. We moved quickly on the more even surface. Suddenly, apparently at the same moment, we noticed a pale streak ahead of us, towards the right-hand side of the road. Something not dead or static, but something living. Pa stalled the bike, sending us both tumbling onto the road. Pa got up unhurt and, breathing heavily, retreated a few feet along the road. I too was not scratched or bruised, but thought it lucky that I wasn't.

'Look at that, man,' said Pa, staring transfixed with terror. It was a snake, about two feet long and fat from eating, heading into the tall grass on the right-hand side of the road. 'We are lucky we saw that. It could have killed us.'

The snake moved very slowly, but Pa refused to budge until it had completely disappeared. 'Can't we just go past very fast on the other side of the road?' I asked.

'What? If we do that, it's going to bite us.'

'Can they move that fast?'

'Yes! These things are very dangerous.'

As we proceeded on our way he told me that he was terrified of snakes because a sister and a brother of his had died from their bites.

Later, Pa related the story of the snake to Father J, who was not at all impressed. 'How big was this snake?' he asked me.

'About two feet,' I said.

'Come on, man! It was *at least* six feet,' said Pa.

It was the day of the long awaited *ngangsingsitindo*, the great dance that would celebrate the fact that the children's wounds were completely healed. Although they had now been at home for nearly a month, they still wore strings of cowries across their foreheads and around their ankles. They were still ngangsingolu, and would have to remain as such until their mothers could afford to buy them the new clothes necessary for this great event. This was the time when the relatives of the circumcised children cut sprays of leaves and danced with them, waving them above their heads. I asked Gunjur if they were going to do this. 'We are going to do that,' she said. 'And we are going to do everything else as well.'

After lunch I went down to Fatounding's compound, where the ngansingolu were being adorned for the occasion. Isatou had taken the necklaces and cloths that she had asked one of the MRC drivers to buy for her at the coast to her mother's house, where her daughter was staying.

In the yard opposite, the other ngangsingolu were being vigorously scrubbed with soap and water. Then began the laborious process of plaiting their hair, a quill being used to achieve the requisite fineness; small beads were threaded into it across the forehead, and a small coin was left dangling below the string of cowries. They were put into new shirts, faneaus and tikos of patterned indigo, and their faces were made up with kohl, pink lipstick and a powder which gave their faces a lighter, coppery sheen. When it was decided that they were all suitably beautiful, they were herded down to the old mango tree by the well near Pa Alkali Minte's compound. It had been hoped that the event could be held in the Community Centre, but a party had arrived from Killaji police station, and the Civil Servants had decided to use the Centre as the venue for a picnic – which consisted of drinking Chinese tea, eating stir-fried meat and playing cards.

By the time everyone had assembled at the old mango tree, it was after five. The ngangsingolu were seated on mats in a great circle, around the outside and in the middle of which swarmed their mothers, aunts, sisters and grandmothers. Every woman in the village was there. The atmosphere was like that of a great market, people milling everywhere in groups; though a market of and for what, it was difficult to say. Nobody seemed quite sure what to do next, and so they just stood and waited for something to happen. Occasionally basins were beaten, but the place was so crowded it was difficult for the rhythmic impulse to carry. Some of the women began to dance. Binta Camara and Njonji Bajo, both women of a certain volume, danced together with great vehemence and energy in front of their daughters. Elsewhere Safi Mama and other stalwarts of the Kurung Kafo were dancing for their children, taking off their tikos and shaking their bare heads at the ngangsingolu, laughing uproariously all the while.

'Aren't the ngangsingolu beautiful?' someone asked me.

They were, of course, but arguments were breaking out everywhere. A group of the ngangsingolu were ordered to their feet and their mat rolled up. What was going on?

'It's over.'

Already?

'It's late,' they said simply. And within minutes the place was practically deserted.

The camp was unusually busy that Sunday morning. There was a constant stream of callers at the house: Civil Servants looking for Sharon, women and girls coming to pay their respects as they went to and from their gardens, children who wanted to play with the drums. None of these visitors were expected; one, however, was less expected than the others.

Sullu Sise was a young man of the village, employed by the MRC as a carpenter. He was a slight, rather enigmatic man of my own age. At first glance one might have said he was weedy. But if you looked closer you could see that his body was just extraordinarily tightly knit. He had a rather blunt face, with slanting eyes that gave nothing away. He had always said that he would find me a girlfriend. I had assumed that he was joking. Now he stood in the doorway of House One. I looked beyond him through the mosquito netting to where a young woman in her early twenties stood holding a child by the hand. She wore a simiso the colour of a London bus. She was black and handsome, and stared back at me with an expression which in another context would have been described as 'dumb insolence'. I had seen her countless times before, but neither her face nor her name had ever really registered.

'Now you have chance,' said Sullu quietly in English.

One group of people had just left, but I could hear another approaching along the path. 'It's difficult now,' I said.

'When?' asked Sullu.

'This afternoon.'

'OK,' said Sullu, turning to go. Then he gestured at the woman. 'Is she all right?'

'Yes,' I said.

She continued to stare back at me unflinchingly. 'Yes,' she said, repeating the English word after me. And then she laughed.

All afternoon I sat working on the sofa. As the shadows began to lengthen

I was struck by the implausibility of the situation; perhaps it was a joke; perhaps I'd imagined it. Anyway, I was getting rather bored with sitting waiting for people who might or might not turn up. I decided to go for a walk.

I returned just before dinner. As I was leaving the house Sullu slipped out of the darkness.

'What happened?' he asked.

'I thought you weren't coming.'

'He-e-e, Mark. We came here twice.'

That night a kora player was coming to Daouda's house, and many of the women would be coming to listen. While the performance was at its height, I would slip back to my house.

'Where is her husband?' I asked.

'In the middle of the village. A long way.'

'*Astafourlai*,' I said. 'May God forgive me.'

Sullu laughed silently and shook my hand, as was the habit of the country.

'She wants to do it?' I asked.

'*Kende ke!* Very much!'

'You're playing with me.'

'It's the truth, I swear to God.'

In the event, someone died and the kora performance was cancelled.

In the middle of the afternoon, the Vice-President, Bakary Darbo, our local MP, came to the village to present the members of the committee who would be promoting the PPP in the forthcoming elections. The meeting was held under the mango trees outside the Community Centre. The elders of the village sat around the Vice-President and his party on wooden armchairs, or on the benches from the Supplement Centre, while in the middle sat the griots who would take it in turns to relay the words of the various speakers – bellowing over the heads of the assembled masses in ringing magisterial tones. It was an ancient tradition, designed equally to enhance the dignity of the great and to give voice to the shy and inarticulate.

There was no other amplification and this, combined with the heat of the afternoon sun and the gentle canopy of leaves overhead, gave the occasion a less formal atmosphere than other political meetings I had attended.

The women stood around the meeting place in a great circle, and from where I sat I could see every woman of the village with whom I'd ever had any dealings – some with faces strained in concentration at the words that were being said, others seemingly blank and indifferent. Again and again I found myself staring into the impassive eyes of the young woman in the bright red simiso. She had a small child tied on her back. Her face was round and very black. That morning I had met Sullu in the compound. He had told me that he would come with 'the stranger' in the early evening. I decided that when all was said and done it was an intelligent face.

At six precisely, Sullu entered the living-room and sat down beside me. 'She's coming,' he said.

I had felt no apprehension about this event, as I couldn't believe that anything would actually happen; I was merely intrigued by the improbability of it all. But now events were upon me, and the intentness, the blunt purposefulness of Sullu's manner made me feel nervous.

What exactly was going to happen?

'After the talk I will go,' he said, looking out over his shoulder towards the compound gates. 'I only come the first time. The second, the third time and the fourth time I will not come.' He started suddenly. 'No one must come here,' he said. 'It doesn't matter about the tubabs, but no black must see her,' he said.

'No one will come,' I said.

Then she arrived, walking slowly along the frieze of mosquito-netted windows. She looked smaller and more vulnerable in a white petticoat.

'Mark,' she said in greeting, slipping off her rubber flip-flop sandals as she entered.

'Come on,' said Sullu, and led us into the office.

It was now evening, but a thick amber light still penetrated the curtains, filling the rather musty air of the room.

'Lock the door,' said Sullu.

'It doesn't lock,' I said.

We sat down on the office chairs. Behind us hung a curtain which obscured the two beds used by visitors.

Sullu began to talk, in even, measured tones, which helped to mask the extreme urgency, indeed the danger of the situation. Always using her first name, he spoke respectfully but authoritatively, like a grown-up brother advising a recalcitrant younger sister with whom he none the less wishes to remain on good terms. I could understand most of what he said, but my attention was so absorbed by the appearance of the woman that I scarcely heard it.

She sat on the edge of her seat, her hands folded on her lap, her feet tucked neatly beneath the chair. She lowered her head, her rather big eyes raised, expressionless, towards the door. She seemed remote inside her extreme blackness, as though she had withdrawn herself from the events that were taking place around her. Her hair, carefully plaited beneath the white tiko, the three tiny scars on each cheek, seemed marks of her differentness, her unapproachability. I suddenly saw her, not as an individual person, but as a 'Mandinka woman' – the sort of tribal, primitive person one sees on a wildlife documentary – a fragile, exotic presence. It would be shameful to exploit such a person.

'Pass through,' Sullu was saying, nodding towards the curtain.

The woman sat on the edge of her chair exactly as before, saying nothing, signalling nothing.

'She doesn't want to go,' I said.

'She wants to,' he said. 'Pass through there. Go on.'

I could only interpret the blankness of the woman as great unhappiness – though she had of course agreed to come. Then it occurred to me that perhaps Sullu had some hold over her that he had used to persuade her to come here.

'Let her go,' I said. 'She doesn't want to come.'

'She wants to,' he hissed.

'This man is an elder,' he said to her in Mandinka. 'Go there. You must not disappoint him.'

There was a long pause. Then, without altering her expression, she got slowly to her feet and walked round to the other side of the curtain. I followed her.

She sat down on the end of my bed, staring straight ahead, a faint smile on her lips. I sat down beside her, and kissed her on the shoulder. Then I put my arm round her and kissed her mouth. Her lips did not yield. I prised my tongue effortfully between them, and felt the touch of something hard and slithery. She pulled her face away from me.

'You're sucking black mints,' I said.

'Yes,' she said.

Slowly and carefully I pushed against her shoulder. This was the action of seduction, the nominal forcing of the woman. She lay back at the touch, and then slid herself upwards so that she was lying fully on the bed. Then she pulled the folds of her faneau apart and lay there, with her arms by her sides, like a patient on an operating table, staring at the right-hand corner of the ceiling, a slight smile on her face. Between the silky blackness of her thighs, I could see the triangle of pubic hair, the jo-no . . .

I raised myself above her, and began mechanically unfastening my trousers. I smiled broadly at her in an attempt to introduce some sense of intimacy between us. She looked back uncomprehendingly. Her own slight smile vanished.

All the time, Sullu was sitting only a few feet away on the other side of the curtain.

I could have just entered her without ceremony, without even thinking about her feelings, as I knew I was meant to. But it would have seemed a callous, almost brutal act – for I could see no evidence from her behaviour that she even wanted to be there. I felt sure that she must have been forced in some way.

I hung over her, wondering what I should do next.

'Is this good?' I asked at length.

'It is not good,' she said dryly.

'Why?'

'The sun is going down.'

She slid past me, and went back around the curtain. I thought she must have been leaving, but then I heard her telling Sullu to leave the room. She came back and lay down on the bed, exactly as before.

By now I was completely confused. I just sat on the bed beside her for a few moments.

'Go,' I said.

She got to her feet, and went to the door. Sullu came back into the room.

'She said you didn't do anything.'

'She didn't want to.'

'She wanted it.'

I took out a ten-dalasis note and handed it to the woman. I felt she should have something for risking herself in this way, but she waved it away. I was astonished. That would have been a lot of money to her. She looked away, close to tears.

Sullu sat down on the sofa with a sigh when she had gone.

'He-e-eh, Mark,' he said, shaking his head sadly. 'You had the chance.'

'I thought she didn't want to do it.'

'What did you do?' he asked, curiously. 'Did you do this?' He mimed the gestures of kissing and embracing.

'Yes.'

He clicked his tongue. 'They don't know that.' He pointed to his groin. 'They only know this.'

I was in a state of utter misery as I walked along the red laterite road towards Karafa Kunda with Sharon. I'd told her everything that had happened. I had to tell someone. The burning of the bush had already begun, and the land at the side of the road was covered in indigo ash. But the flames had moved through the undergrowth with such speed that they hadn't had time to burn everything, and the leaves still hung brown and frazzled from the blackened branches. An orange moon hung low in the grey evening sky.

What a place! And what a landscape! It seemed to me as I reflected on the events of an hour before that the culture of the people was as harsh and as arid as the physical world in which they lived . . . Was that it? It somehow seemed so cruel, so lacking in human feeling . . . that a woman like her should know nothing else.

I had been told time and again that that was the way they did things, and I had not believed them. I had thought that when it happened to me it would be different. It hadn't been.

'Just forget it,' said Sharon. 'You can sort yourself out when you get back to England.'

But I wasn't thinking about England. What distressed me most of all was the thought that I had disappointed the woman. She had gone there for me, and I had failed to appreciate the gesture. Well, if that was the way they did things, that was the way it would have to be.

I passed her in the compound two days later, and she greeted me with no trace of acrimony – simply speaking my name in the same toneless manner as before.

Then, two days after that, as Jojo and I were finishing work for the day, I caught sight of her sauntering slowly past the office window, a calabash balanced on her head. Where could she be going? I wondered. She was heading in the direction of Susan Lawrence's house, where Sullu was working.

How many hundreds of times had I seen Sullu at work in the compound, perched on his ladder by one of the houses or standing intent over his workbench, as through the seasons he attempted to keep the woodwork in a good state of repair. His was a presence that invited no questions – he was so much a part of the background that he had become almost invisible. And the women coming and going in the compound, always on some errand or other – bringing or taking this or that to the houses of the Europeans or to the Quarters – I had grown so used to seeing them that I no longer questioned their presence: they too had become part of the texture of the place. Now suddenly I saw in every passing figure a clandestine possibility. Any one of these people might be on their way to some secret assignation. It was extraordinary to think of the intrigues Sullu might have been arranging from his vantage point in the compound, of all the messages that were being exchanged as men and women passed each other only momentarily in the streets.

I was suddenly aware of a whole new dimension of life in the village – an under-layer: the secret world – and I saw how easily much of the real life of the place had passed me by, even while I was standing in the middle of it. One could have lived in that compound for years on end, one could have spent hours in the fields and even in the houses of the village itself, and still have had very little idea of what was going on around one. The scandals and the disasters of the village came and went, and unless they were medical in origin, they didn't impinge on the life of the camp at all. The sociability and the apparent informality of the Africans made it easy to live among them. The sense of goodwill between the the village and the camp was entirely genuine, but only a certain amount was given out at the superficial level of courtesy. The word ku'lo – secret – was after all one of the most frequently used in their language, and unless one were part of their society, one would never know.

Those first months when I had sat each night at the Quarters, people coming and going all around me, communicating not only in languages that I could not understand but, unbeknownst to me, through the use of secret signs. It was hardly surprising that I felt not only not part of what was happening around me, but that I sometimes felt as though I were not even a solid part of the physical environment in which I sat.

One night, about a week later, I went to the village to look for Sullu. It was very dark. I could just make out the dense masses of the houses and the compound fences along the sides of the street in which Sullu lived. An even thicker area of darkness announced the overhanging eaves of his thatched house. A small figure was sitting in front of it, utterly motionless in an upright chair.'

'Mark.' It was Sullu. 'Come inside.'

The air was thick and hot inside the house. Sullu lit a lamp, which sent a feeble glow up into the thatched rafters. He sat back in an armchair with an air of exhausted satisfaction. We chatted for some time about nothing in particular, then I asked him if he would ask 'my person' to come to my house the following day.

'In the evening?' he asked.

'In the early afternoon. About half-past two.'

'She will come.'

I was once again doubtful.

'Why does she want to do this?' I asked slowly.

'She likes it.'

'What?'

'You.'

The house had two doors – one onto the street, the other onto the yard which led through to the house of the women. His wife was breast-feeding, so he had no sexual contact with her at the present time. If he was expecting company he would simply lock the back door and wait for a gentle knock at the front.

'I had someone here just now – immediately before you arrived.'

'Who?'

'My girlfriend . . .' A smile of satisfaction spread over his face. 'Munya!'

It was early afternoon; the hottest time of the day. The whole world had retreated from the harsh white glare of the sun. I sat on the Habitat sofa, peering out through the mosquito netting at the deserted compound forecourt. The watchman was hidden inside his pillbox, and only one figure sat on the bench beside it, slumped as though in sleep.

Then I saw her walking demurely out of the white heat of the afternoon. She was dressed largely in white – to the Christians the colour of purity, to the Muslims the colour of peace. My heart plunged into my stomach.

As she stepped lightly between the white walls that flanked the compound gates, I saw her bristle slightly as though, like a spy passing through an alien checkpoint, she expected a gun to be levelled at her head at any moment. But it was the attitude only of a split-second, unnotice-able to a casual observer. And then she had passed through, and walked on, inexorably, towards my house.

'I'm going to be sick,' I thought.

I was so happy that evening. As I strode out along the old Karafa Kunda road towards the rice field of Sukoto, I sang at the top of my voice in Mandinka. I hope no one could hear me.

At the rice field, I found an old woman digging up some bulbous, crimson roots. She had a whole sackful of them. Here and there the women had burnt the ground in preparation for the coming season. The place looked like Regent's Park after some dreadful catastrophe.

In the middle distance, over towards the salt flats, I saw a great group of figures moving silently through the undergrowth. It was difficult at that distance to pick out the details of their features, but they seemed to walk almost upright. There must have been nearly a hundred of them, the biggest maybe two-thirds the size of a man. They went first, then the females, their young clinging to their chests. One of the largest of the males leapt onto a hanging branch, as the females passed, and bounced fiercely up and down, sending a hissing, rushing sound across the rice field.

'Baboons,' said the old woman. 'Go there. They will not hurt you.'

I didn't think I would.

13

THE WORLD OF GLASS

In the dry season the world itself was like a husk, like the desiccated, fragile remains of some fabulous flower, an infinitely complex entity, now brittle and drained of life, its every surface porous and rough with dust. The mud walls of the village were now more worn than ever. The rusting corrugated iron looked as though it could be punctured as easily as paper. Yet everything shone and glittered as it reflected the relentless, scourging brilliance of the colourless sky. The garden areas at the backs of the compounds lay empty, like great pools of dust, their fences all but disintegrated under the to-ings and fro-ings of sheep and goats and the gangs of heedless children. In each of these areas two rickety platforms had been erected: one surmounted by a great heap of groundnut chaff for feeding the animals, the other with bales of dry grass that awaited the season of thatching.

At that time of year it was as though the very texture of the air was different; as though it were thicker – as though one saw objects, not through glass, but as though everything were actually within that glass itself. And through this molten lens, the sun burned at your mind and body, reducing you within minutes to a state of numbed dazedness. Stepping from the shade into the heat of the day, you received the light like a dull blow to the head.

Skinny, yellow-headed lizards scampered noisily up the mosquito netting. Birds of orange and black, of iridescent blue-black and turquoise, their eyes rimmed with yellow, darted among the trees of the compound. I was reminded of the sense I had had on first arriving in Africa that I had come to a place where everything was somehow *more* – every flavour stronger, every sensation more extreme, every colour – where it existed – more brilliant.

One evening, as I was returning from Karafa Kunda, I looked out of the Land Rover to see that the whole world was on fire. A hundred yards from the road, the flames rose suddenly from the darkness. And beyond them, the forms of the trees could be seen, outlined in fire – here and there the land erupting, sending great sheets of sparks into the sky. Where the flames had subsided, they left a carpet of glittering embers, stretching for mile after mile into the distance. The edges of this carpet drew ever closer to the road, but it looked rather as though the land were moving towards it, as though the whole world were slowly tipping into the flames.

The next day the whole of the area north of the road had been reduced to a blue, smoking waste, only the largest trees and here and there the odd bush having miraculously retained their foliage. In the afternoon, a great tower of black smoke could be seen rising out of the bush, a few hundred yards to the north of the camp. It soon disappeared, but then the sound of the fire could be heard much closer, the smoke rising in gentle gusts over the trees. And then all of a sudden the flames could be seen less than thirty yards away – quivering, almost transparent, the thin tongues licking into the air. Eagles and other birds of prey hung on the shuddering wall of heat, waiting to pick off the small animals that ran before the flames.

Every year these immense conflagrations oozed like a black acid over the bush. They were against the law, and it was said that, without them, the country could have been a major exporter of hardwood: the bush having become thinner even within living memory. Even the villagers were aware that the smaller number of trees was a contributing factor to the decline in rainfall. But the government was far away, and they knew that when the time came they would set fire to the bush, as their ancestors always had done.

In the past, the flames had come as close as the compound fence; though this year the land north of the village was bare after the harvest, and the laterite road now created a further barrier. But though a brake had been burnt around the new camp, the people seemed to take the dangers of these fires remarkably lightly; only a year before, at a village beside the road beyond Mankono, a man and a boy had been killed when their compound was engulfed.

During the long afternoons, the women sat in the deep shade of the mango trees, plaiting their hair, picking the lice from each others' heads, or just talking or sleeping. But they were used to working, so they liked to do little tasks while they chatted: crocheting clothes for their children or tearing palm fronds into strips to make brooms. Or they went to collect bush mangoes, which they peeled and dried to add to their sauces, and the long black pods of the netto tree, the seeds of which they used to flavour *nyankatango*, a dish of rice and dried fish. Some made clay pots, which they fired in the stumps of burning trees. And almost every woman went two or three times a week to the salt flats to make salt, leaving water from the bolon to evaporate in holes they scraped from the earth with their bare hands.

The cultivation of the gardens continued. While the sun was still hot, the women would start carrying their basins to wait for the taps, which at that time of year were only on for about two hours a day. The new pump beside the school was 'open' all the time, however, and from my house I could hear the grinding of the lever from dawn, through the hottest part of the day, till long after dark.

It was already dusk the first time I went over to help. I felt rather self-conscious as I stepped up onto the podium to shouts and hoots of encouragement. At first I found it surprisingly easy. It was just up-down, up-down, while the interior of the mechanism made a reassuring clanking sound. After about ten minutes, I felt as though I had lost several pints of vital bodily fluid, and the lever seemed to have ceased functioning. It was only with extreme effort that I could make it move at all.

'Mark, stop. You're tired,' shouted the women.

'No, no,' I said. I had to go on, if only to preserve my honour. I fell on the lever with all my force.

The hot, blue dusk was closing in around me like a thick steam. I felt as though I were about to expire into it, but I kept going.

'Stop! Stop!' exhorted the women.

'No . . .' I could hardly get the word out. It was as though some hard, dry object had been stuffed into my mouth. I managed to keep going for another three minutes, then almost fell off the podium. I appeared to have lost the use of both legs.

'Marky, thank you. Now go and rest,' said the women. I managed to find my way back to the house, where I shoved my head under the tap.

After a few attempts, I found it less taxing, and from then on I did a stint on the pump almost every evening.

The women queued for the taps and the pump, but they never seemed to be able to do it without some kind of argument, and whenever one passed these places, one always heard the sound of voices raised in annoyance or laughter and the clanking of basins as people jostled each other for position.

It was at this time of day that my person would come to the house. While the others were absorbed in their arguments and their banter, she would put her iron basin down, and stroll casually towards the camp. She still wouldn't allow me to kiss her. And she made almost no expression, except for a faint half-smile, as she stared up at the far corner of the ceiling. For the women were taught before they got married that they should never show any emotion at these times. As soon as it was over, she would push past me and sit up primly on the edge of the bed. It was only sometimes when we were at our extremity that I would feel something of the person I was holding. Afterwards, when I looked back on such moments, I would want very much to be with her. But I knew that I could not go and chat with her in her compound, as I did with the other women – that she would not have liked it, could not have borne it. When I passed her in the street she would greet me quickly, and in the same flat way as before, only a look of slight nervousness in her eyes giving anything away. When other people were present, she would not even look at me. At first I accepted this as the way of their culture, and more than understandable under the circumstances. But as time went on I found it more and more difficult to bear.

The new agricultural season had already started with the cutting of the *waa* – the tall, thick 'elephant grass' that filled the rice fields. The stems were burnt away, then the roots hacked from the earth and raked into heaps to be burnt with the frazzled crimson leaves that littered the ground. The crackling of the fires, now gentle, now fierce, now quickly dying, could be heard all along the edge of the salt flats, the smoke lingering in drifts among the charred trunks of the trees. I wondered how, when they were burning the grass, they managed to stop the fires from spreading into the parched, brittle undergrowth. 'There is only one place where the fire will stop,' said Jarra Njai. 'And that place has been decided by God. So when the fire reaches that point, even if the grass is very dry it must stop.'

One morning, as I was walking to Kadamah to work in Safi Mama's field, I was called by a boy who was walking along the path behind me. 'A woman is calling you,' he said. I turned to see a short figure, a hoe hooked over its shoulder, hurrying along the path towards me. A scarlet cloth was draped over one side of her face to protect it from the light of the sun, which was becoming more intense by the moment. It was Sona. She was about fifty yards away, and I didn't know whether to wait for her or not. Then she began to run towards me – heavily and effortfully, with short steps. It was only the second or third time I had seen an African woman running. I stopped and waited till she caught up.

She laughed, out of breath.

'I had to run to catch up,' she said. 'But I don't know how to run.'

Once again I had that feeling one has when one is thrust into the presence of someone to whom one is powerfully attracted, that time has suddenly shifted into a different gear, as though the very air is beating to a different rhythm. She was by now heavily pregnant, and I was acutely conscious of her swollen stomach and bloated breasts.

'Soon I will be tired,' she said. 'Now I'm always tired.'

'Why's that?' I asked.

'Nothing,' she said.

'Because of this,' I said, pointing to her stomach.

'There's nothing there. Only food.' Then she said, 'It's your child. It came from you.'

'That's what I want,' I said. 'But you don't want that.'

'Is that what you want?' she asked.

'Very strongly,' I said. I looked off into the tall grass at the side of the path. 'This place is a long way from anyone,' I said.

'Yes, but there's no bed here,' she said.

'That's not a problem,' I said.

'Mark, I told you before to bring money.'

'Hurh! Please! Don't disturb me.'

She thought again. 'That which you carry before you, is it very, very big?'

'Obviously,' I said – not quickly enough.

'But Mark, I think that when you lie with Sona you will not have any strength.'

'Hey . . .!'

By now we had reached her rice field, which lay by the path in the forest, before one came to Sukoto.

'Give me some water to drink,' she said.

I hesitated for a moment.

'Okay,' I said. 'But don't take too much.' My mouth was dry with annoyance and desire and the intensifying heat. Here the trees, now taller, were closing in around us.

'Do you think you're smarter than me?' I asked.

'Yes,' she said.

At Safi's field I worked off my irritation by throwing myself into the work. The ground was hard and dry, and beneath the brittle surface was a layer of clay from which the blade bounced as if from rubber. The earth exploded into my face, filling my eyes and nostrils with dust and grit. I was soon black from head to toe.

As we emerged from the fields onto the salt flats, everyone started at the sight of a great billowing mass of violet smoke erupting from the trees on the other side of the flats. We could hear the booming and cracking of the fire from where we stood. The women watched with expressions of alarm, as about a hundred yards further inland there came another great cloud of smoke, suddenly, in a enormous, rolling gust, unfurling itself and then disappearing into the brilliant sky.

Putting their belongings on their heads, the women rushed off in a scampering line, along the path across the sand towards Sukoto. More women joined us there, and they told us that the person who had done this was Mama Njai.

As we joined the main path we met another line of women also heading back towards the village. At the end of the line was Mama, a curious set expression on her face – an expression of helplessness and also of defiance – the expression of someone who has done something far beyond that which can be apologized for.

The women walked quickly, their voices raised in anger and agitation. Mama had been trying to burn a tree-trunk which lay across her rice field, when a spark jumped into the surrounding undergrowth. The fire was spreading into the area south of the village, which had been set aside for the cattle to graze in, the elephant grass to be saved for thatching. There was now no way of stopping it.

That night the whole of the sky to the south of the village was lit up a fearsome, shimmering orange. At last the men went out to fight the fire before it threatened to engulf the village itself. The way they had always done this, and the only way they could do it under the circumstances, was to burn the land surrounding the village, so that when the bigger fire came raging out of the bush, there would be nothing for it to catch onto.

All around the south edge of the village, on the far side of the women's gardens, there was a circuit of paths, beyond which began the tangled, unruly sprawl of forest. The men, young and old, moved along them in line, some carrying blazing branches, gently touching the brittle undergrowth with the flames. Others carried sprays of leaves with which they swept the glowing embers back into the bush. Quickly the flames leapt, lighting up the surrounding trees and the figures of the men who stepped back from the heat, and quickly they died, as they moved ever backward into the bush to meet the main fire, which we could see glittering and cascading through the trees only a hundred years away.

In places these paths were only a foot wide, and it would have taken only one leaping spark to turn the tall, dry grass on the village side of the path into an uncontrollable mass of flame that would have killed us all. But the men did not seem particularly concerned. They had done this many times before, and they would no doubt have to do it many times again. When they reached the south fence of the new camp, beside which a fire brake had already judiciously been burnt, they set off back towards the village.

The next day Mama Njai was summoned before the village elders and fined one hundred dalasis. She pleaded with them, and the fine was reduced to fifty. The men were very angry over what had happened. But no woman would condemn her. For what God had placed upon a human being, no one could remove. And what had happened to her could have happened to any of them.

Kalamatta, Fatounding's husband, had been ill for some months. He had been referred to the MRC hospital in Fajara, where he was told that he had cancer of the stomach. This had meant little to him or his family. God had already decided the moment of his death, and that a doctor said it was curable or incurable was neither here nor there. Shortly afterwards he had travelled to a village in Fonyi to seek treatment from a marabout there. This also had had little effect, and as the weeks passed and the man grew weaker and weaker, a kind of numbness descended on the compound. The women – his mother and his two wives – continued to go about their tasks. Fatounding still joked – she had even accused Binta Sise and myself of bewitching her husband. But often it was as though they were there in body only; their minds seemed to be somewhere else entirely. 'He is a little better,' they would say simply on meeting.

One Sunday, in the European month of March, the doctor visited the man in his compound. He was alarmed to see how much the man's body had swollen. And he felt mildly irritated that the doctors at Fajara had not made it clearer to the man and his family that he would not recover. But afterwards, the doctor, a young man who had come out from Cambridge while the Inneses were on leave, wondered how successful he had been himself in explaining to the man's wives that he would die very soon.

On the Tuesday evening, I visited the compound at Tumbulu Sise's suggestion. It had been an overcast day, and the grey darkness thickened over the compound in a layer of hot, suffocating cloud. The yard was crowded with women, who each sat for some time, staring heavy-eyed into the violet dust, before moving on to complete their tasks. Others stayed, leaning as though stunned against the posts of the verandah. 'He is a little better,' said Fatounding. Even then I didn't get the message.

The men stood in a silent group in the meagre shade of the spike-like baobab branches. Everyone leant forward, attentive, towards the digging of the grave. There was no sound apart from the murmured comments of the grave diggers, the slicing of the spades into the hard, sandy soil, and the unceasing rattling of the insects. It was early afternoon, and Kalamatta had died two hours before.

The men of his age-group, Seikoubah, Braima, Turo and his brother Kemoring, among others, took it in turns to climb into the hole and shovel out the spadefuls of dust. They worked energetically, but without hurry, completing their task with extreme care – cutting the edges of the grave hard and sharp, into a perfect rectangle. It was a long, narrow grave, like a letter-box into the earth; about four feet deep. An inset had been carved into the base of one of the walls, into which the body would be placed.

A shallow ledge, a foot wide, was cut around the mouth of the grave. The younger men went to break sticks, just wide enough to fit into it and across the grave. Then they were laid in a neat row, until the hole was covered.

The men moved off in a silent group towards the mosque. A long box, poles threaded through loops on either side, lay on the ground in the enclosure. Njundu and Sullu picked up the box by the poles, and carried it towards the compound of the dead man.

As we passed through the corrugated-iron door into the compound, I became aware of a great group of women gathered in the forecourt of the main part of the compound on the other side of the street. I didn't think it seemly to stare, but from the corner of my eye I could see their brilliantly coloured clothes glittering in the sunlight.

Inside the house, the elders were attending to the corpse, and in the small yard, the younger men were cramped into every area of shade, seated on mats on the verandahs, or squatting along the sides of the buildings. Those who had just come from the mosque squeezed in among them, and everyone sat and waited, staring listlessly at the ground, aware of the activity inside the house, where Kalamatta was being sewn into his shroud, and the greater crowd of women, waiting also in silence outside the yard. Above, the sun loomed huge and merciless. Occasionally women passed stone-faced through the gathering, carrying bowls of porridge, which was being given as a charity from the house of the women.

How long we sat there, crouching silently, I don't know. In the intense heat it was easy to lose track of time. But all at once there was a commotion from inside the house, a banging and a bumping, as the man's body was moved in the long box. People began getting to their feet. Suddenly there was a low grinding whine, like the moaning of a child who has continued to cry long after his tears have been exhausted. It came again, building in volume and intensity. Fatounding appeared in the doorway of the house of the women, a cloth draped over her face. Isatou came after her, clinging to her shoulders, and then the mother, almost insensible, her pale, watery eyes seemingly visionless with grief. Pushing forward through the crowd, they began to try to fight their way into their husband's house.

At this agonized display of feeling, the composure of the gathering rapidly disintegrated. The yard was suddenly full of women who had been entering through one of the other houses. I could see the women from the Quarters who had been comforting the dead man's wives, Jori Sanyang standing, staring beatifically into the sky, her eyes filling with tears like those of a saint at a neon shrine. Then I saw the women of the village: Jarra Njai and Tumbulu, their bodies racked, bent double with sobbing, their faces contorted with anguish – making no attempt to hold back the tears. Everywhere one looked it was the same – the people one saw every day, staggering helplessly, their faces broken by tears. It was like one of those medieval paintings of Doomsday, in which the timeless village calm is riven by apocalyptic chaos – when the familiar figures of the everyday world are dragged from their time-honoured positions of security, and held up before the viewer, their faces contorted by a kind of cosmic agony.

I pulled my hat down over my face as I was pulled along in the crowd of men. The coffin was now being passed out into the street, through the front of what had once been the dead man's shop. The drum from the mosque sounded twice, like a gun going off inside my head, and then from the other side of the street, from the direction of the forecourt of Kafuli Kunda, there came a sound such as I had never heard before – high-pitched, urgent, scarcely human – like the crying and sighing animals might make on witnessing some atrocity against their kind. And though high, it was hideously dry, as though it had been dragged from the very depth of the body.

It became louder. As we pushed through the narrow doorway into the street, the men began to cry – moaning softly, the tears pouring forth without control. I averted my eyes from the place of the women, as the howling became louder all around us, and held my hat flat against my face, to hide my own tears.

Death was only death. And no human being could feel resentment at what God had done. But one could at least show sympathy for the people who had been left behind, and sadness at what had been lost. This man had been in his prime; he had left two young wives and seven children. He had been a quiet man who never involved himself in other people's quarrels. He had minded his own affairs. But he had also been a shopkeeper, and when times were hard he had helped many people, without asking anything in return. He was the leader of his age-group, and would in later years have been among the leaders of the village. Barama, one of the Mandinka words for leader, meant literally a pillar. This man of thirty-seven had been at the centre of his community – at the centre of the people themselves – and he had been roughly and untimely pulled from among them. And he was a man; for however much a woman had been loved by the people, another wife could always take her place. A man could never be replaced.

As the cortege approached the mosque, I turned to see the figure of Safi Mama, standing at the corner of the street in a pose of almost heroic anguish, calling out to us to honour the dead man. Then the howling of the women began to fade away, for the women never went to the burial ground, not even if it was a woman who had died.

Our tears began to subside, and silence once again descended as we moved among the baobabs towards the grave. The body was lifted from the box without comment, heavy in its white shroud, and lowered gently into the grave. The row of sticks was placed neatly back over the hole, and a few spadefuls of earth, branches and dead leaves thrown on top. It seemed a fragile covering for a human body. Then we squatted down in the dust to pray, cupping our hands to receive God's blessings; the dull murmurings flowed over us in thick, irregular waves of sound. Then we passed our hands over our faces, and began to get to our feet.

There were further prayers in the enclosure of the mosque, but by that time the women had begun to disperse. The sense of agony was lifting – rising and evaporating into the white afternoon sky.

That evening, as on every other evening, a football match was held at the ground between the camp and the school. The heat still lay thickly over the rock-like earth of the pitch, and the atmosphere was tense and fractious. Even before the game had started, arguments were breaking out. As usual, the village boys complained that when they were picking teams, the Civil Servants would all go on the same side, while the Civil Servants said that if there was any difference of opinion, the villagers would always side with each other, regardless of the rights and wrongs of the situation. Shouts could be heard coming from the cluster of boys in the middle of the pitch. Lamin Jarjou's stocky figure could be seen in the centre of the circle, his big face dangerously intense. Even from the edge of the pitch one could sense the pressure building up inside him. From the pump, the women – the mothers, the aunts, the sisters of the village boys – watched discreetly, and with a sense of growing unease. They muttered among themselves about the wickedness of certain of the Civil Servants.

Now, halfway through the game, the ball was forgotten as the players stood watching Jere Jarjou facing one of the village boys.

One of the most educated, the most able, and ostensibly the most westernized of the Civil Servants, Jere's mind was so bound up in traditional notions of honour, fealty and masculinity that it was impossible to imagine him outside an African context. And it was perhaps because I took these matters comparatively lightly that he disliked me so much. He prided himself on his prowess in all sports, but spurned women and the sexual act. Early on he had told me that it was his ambition to become a writer, and he had asked me about the price of correspondence courses from London. I had given him what little information I had, and told him I would teach him everything I knew for nothing. He seemed to take this as a further insult. He was tall, with a round, shallow face like a tea-plate, and bulging nocturnal eyes. His apparently gangling physique was in fact excessively powerful, like a steel band constantly poised ready to spring. Sometimes I would sense the hatred coming off him like a dark steam, and I would feel afraid.

The other boy was far from puny, but he was half a head shorter than Jere, who with a blow to the chest had felled him. He stood over the village boy, raining blows on his face and body. His friends ran forward to pull him away, and the village boy sprang to his feet, spitting insults and threats. He backed away as Jere was led off by his friends. The darkening air was big with the shouts and advice of the milling people.

Suddenly the village boy was advancing on Jere, a rock in one hand and a stick in the other. I watched helpless and appalled from the other side of the pitch as he drew closer and closer to the oblivious Jere. 'He's going to kill him,' I thought. Then, alerted by his companions, Jere dodged away, and the village boy, now almost hysterical, was disarmed.

But this was not England, where the opposing parties would have been held back by force until they were completely pacified. Their companions touched them only lightly on the arms as they advised them, for they were almost as absorbed in their feelings as the protagonists themselves. As people were leaving the field, I looked up to see Jere bearing down on me at great speed. His eyes were very wide, and his face, which had grown very pale, was set in a determined half-smile. In his hands he carried a large rock.

I felt a rush of air as he passed within inches of where I stood. The village boy began to run desperately. But hands reached out to grab Jere and, shaking his head in disgust, he threw the boulder to the ground. Then, laughing manically, he began to walk back to the camp.

A large crowd of villagers surrounded the boy as he made his way to his compound. They stood outside the fence, watching as he walked towards his house. He went inside but moments later re-emerged, crying with rage and shame, waving his arms wildly in the air.

This was the other side of village tolerance. The people might seem easy-going, even passive; indeed the most heinous crimes were shrugged off as 'an accident' or 'the will of God'. But if they were pushed beyond a certain point, it was as though something inside had snapped – and they would suddenly be beyond all reason. They would, it seemed, even kill, without pausing to think about it.

It was like the mother, normally indulgent, who would suddenly have to be held off one of her children, after the most trivial, even negligible of misdemeanours. It would be a long time before she was pacified.

One had to be very careful in one's dealings with the Africans – much more careful than I usually was.

The pestles sounded like thunder through the compounds. Two days after the funeral was the *munko la* – the distribution of the munko – the raw rice, pounded with sugar, that was given out as a charity at the times of birth and death. During the course of the morning, every woman went to help with the pounding in the forecourt of Kafuli Kunda.

In the afternoon the men gathered at the mosque to offer prayers for the dead man. It was at this time that those who had known him would speak on his behalf; would tell of his good deeds, of his piety. Relatives had come from all over the region, and representatives had come from the villages of Joli, Karafa Kunda and Kulli Kunda, to pay their respects.

Since the funeral, Fatounding and Isatou had scarcely stirred from the area of floor in front of Isatou's bed, where they now sat, their feet wrapped in grubby pieces of cloth. They should, according to their religion, have dressed in white for the entire period of mourning. But this was Dulaba, and even if they had been able to afford it, it was difficult to imagine anything staying white for very long.

Relatives sat with them, and many, particularly N'na – the man's mother – and Tumbulu Sise – his cousin – were still close to tears. Fatounding and Isatou, however, just sat staring at the floor. They would reply politely but monosyllabically to the greetings of their visitors, and then lapse back into blankness. It was as though, because this period was too painful to bear, they had withdrawn from it. They were not allowing themselves to feel anything, and had thus almost ceased to exist; as in a way all women did for the period of mourning.

Now the room was filling up with the elder women of the nearby villages, who had come to sit with them while the men were at the mosque. They sat on the beds around the room in silence, though on entering each newcomer would offer prayers for the wives and mother, with murmurs of 'Amen' from the assembled gathering. Each of them gave a small sum of money to N'na; partly from courtesy, partly from sympathy, but also because death was an auspicious time to give.

Fatounding's Nyimansitou, now a strapping child of eighteen months, but oblivious to the import of the moment, clambered onto her mother to feed. Mechanically the mother pulled her shirt aside to let the child to the nipple. Then Isatou's Haminata, still barely four months old, following the example of her sister, began to pull at her mother's shirt.

Jarjei like to socialize with the 'strangers', the young men, most of them from the coastal region, who were building the new camp. A group of them lived together in a house in the corner of her compound. She would sit drinking attaya with them far into the night. She would joke with them, provoke them, play cards and ludo with them, dance with them, and even fight them. If she felt tired she would go into their house and sprawl out on one of the beds. The only thing she wouldn't do was smoke their *tai nyamo* with them.

Whenever I passed the taps beside her compound she always seemed to be in the centre of some almighty row, of which the only words I could understand would be 'fuck off', said in English, which naturally were used by her alone. The younger women were greatly amused by her. She was a character! God had made her that way. They admired her courage and her wit, even though they would never behave like that themselves. And they were also rather wary of her, for she was very strong, and while she didn't mind making a fool of herself, she wouldn't allow anyone else to do it.

Many of the older women, and even some of her own age-mates, looked askance at her behaviour. A married woman, going into the houses of the young men like that! And they discussed it at great length. But she was now so far from being the submissive, dutiful wife she had been brought up to believe she would be that she no longer cared. And who were these people to criticize her? Had they never sinned themselves? God had not given it to her to marry a man that she loved, so what could she do?

For all her bravado, she was in truth a sad person. She still felt great bitterness towards the man who had disappointed her. Even as she caroused in the house of the strangers – which was next door to that man's house – she would have his child with her. It was his child; everyone knew that. But he had never given out one single batut for it. That was why it had no shoes, no dress, no shirt – only a pair of knickers to shield it from the world.

She did not like this child. It had a small mouth, and mean eyes, like its father. And it had a dry voice – all it did was whine. The older child – 'the small boy' – she liked, but this 'baby girl' was *mang betia* – she was bad.

For a week after the funeral, Fatounding and Isatou were confined to the house of the women. People came to sit with them – sharing their sorrow, as they would have shared their happiness at a marriage or the birth of a child. But as the weeks passed, visitors became fewer and fewer, and the three women – Fatounding, Isatou and N'na – were left alone with their thoughts. They had been in peace together in that compound. They had moved together like the moon and stars. But whether they would stay together, they did not know.

After the first week of mourning they could go out of the compound, but they would go only to the taps, or sometimes to the fields, and they would come straight back. In the coastal regions, the period of mourning lasted forty days; in Dulaba it lasted five months. During that time they would not plait their hair; they would not go to dances or involve themselves in any form of levity. Nor would they speak to men. They tied bands of white cloth around their tikos so that men would know they were widows and would not approach them. Round their necks they wore large, square jujus of white cloth. For in this period of uncertainty they were particularly susceptible to attack by witches.

They would remain living in their late husband's compound, while his family waited to see if they were pregnant. Then, when the five months were over, they were free to leave. And they would be open to offers of marriage.

Kalamatta's youngest brother had come from Serekunda and was staying in the dead man's house. He was, if anything, even less communicative than his brother, and scarcely spoke to the women. For their part they regarded him as something of an intruder, flashing him suspicious looks as he slipped shadow-like in and out of the compound. While he was no doubt pleased to have inherited this well-appointed, self-contained compound, he seemed less than thrilled at having to spend time in Dulaba. It was possible, indeed it was likely, that he would be compelled by the elders to propose to Fatounding or Isatou, or even to both of them. For the people of the compound were obliged to provide a husband for the women. And while the women were free to accept or refuse as they chose, the pressure on them from their own families to honour the bond – the badiya – between the two families would be very great.

If they left, they would be allowed to keep their daughters. But their sons must eventually return to the late husband's compound. When the time came for them to go to the place of circumcision, their 'step fathers', their father's brothers, would come for them. For they were men. They bore the name of that compound. They were part of it, and the people of that place did not want to lose them. The daughters also had that name, but they would in any case eventually leave to get married.

And so most women would remain in their husband's compound, simply so that they would not lose their children. But even if a woman and her son were parted, it was likely that he would still be a frequent visitor to her compound. For in that society, a man's mother was his best friend. She alone had borne him, and she alone would put his interests above all others.

I had not seen my person for some time. I missed her, but there was nothing I could do. Our paths never seemed to cross, and though I got Sullu to ask her to come to the house several times, she never did. Occasionally I would catch a glimpse of her at the end of the street, disappearing into one of the compounds. Or early in the morning I would see her crossing the football pitch, heading off into the bush with her two friends of the same age. But although I would sometimes go into the bush in the hope of seeing her, she was never anywhere to be found. She was a young wife alone, with many tasks, and a young child to take care of. Maybe it was difficult for her to find the time. Or, more likely, she had simply grown tired of me.

For the first time I thought seriously about this person who was now withholding herself from me physically, as before she had withheld her personality, even as I held her in my arms. And I realized I knew virtually nothing about her.

'They just behave like that because that is how they have seen their elder sisters behaving,' said Pa Konte. 'They did not get the idea that they should feel close to you because of what they have done with you – that they should open themselves to you because they love you. They will feel shy. They may just feel that they could not look at you. They don't want anyone to know what they have done, and they are afraid that if they look at you people will see how they feel.

'They believe it is a spirit – what they call a *satano* – that is making them do this thing. They know that it is wrong, so they tell themselves it is a satano that is making them love you and come to you. Some days they will not be able to resist that thing, and they will come to you. This is our belief, that any bad thing you do, a satano has caused you to do that. Even if you kill someone you will go and apologize to their family and say that it was a satano that made you do it.

'But don't think that because this person has behaved like this towards you that she does not love you and she will not come to you again. She will. She must. I am quite sure of that.'

It was time for me to start to bring my project to a close. During the long afternoons I would sit on the Habitat sofa and draw up long lists of questions, as I had done at the beginning of the project, which I hoped would give me the answers I felt I needed to complete my understanding of the village and its people.

It was a tortuous and self-defeating business – trying to reduce whole aspects of a culture to the glib formulae of a questionnaire – but I felt it was a formality that had to be undertaken, even though I knew that most of the questions would be met only with the bland platitudes they deserved: 'We are all in peace . . .', 'It is just due to the creation of God . . .', 'It has no meaning . . .' And who was to say that these were not the 'true' answers?

There were certain queries about the economic and human structures of village life which required only one-word answers. But there were other subjects – such as the inner feeling of the women – which would remain impervious to such questioning. And that, I reflected finally, was probably a good thing. When they could rationalize their feelings in the terms of 'me generation' psychology, they would no longer be the people I had gone there to write about.

During these interminable afternoons, when it took so long for the shadows to lengthen, when the only things that stirred beyond the verandahs of the house were a few foolish children, or the women who, heat or no heat, had to continue their tasks, one understood the overwhelming loneliness and boredom – the terrible sense of isolation – that had been felt by those European women who had been left there, often for years on end, with nothing to do.

In order to try to clarify my thoughts and give some sense of shape and direction to my questioning, I spent many hours poring over those two documents that had already proved so useful in my research: the 'Dulaba census' and Barbara Thompson's thesis. As I turned and re-turned the rumpled pages of the census – assembled with what effort, and all so carefully typed on some massive office machine, the script of which now looked so primitive – and tried laboriously to piece together the parts of the great family tree so that I could understand more clearly the relationships between the various compounds, further secrets emerged: the details of divorces not mentioned, of short-lived marriages conveniently forgotten, of children dead, whose memory was too painful to mention.

The whole village lay before me in this map of humanity. I could now see more than ever how closely the people I had been observing were related to each other. As I looked, this web of relationships seemed to thicken, to mesh more tightly together. As I looked at that abstract plan, I saw more clearly than I had even from living among them the bonds of flesh and blood that united them as though they were physically joined – as though they were all only part of one person.

It was like an immense jigsaw, and when all the parts had finally been found everything would become clear. Life in Dulaba had often seemed like a novel – and not just because I had gone there to write a book. In Europe life was irritatingly inconclusive. One felt that the telling incident that would bring all its various strands together would never happen, that the earlier sub-plots would never be paid off, that the mysterious stranger, the harbinger of one's destiny, would never arrive. The communities that had given us life had been shattered and their pieces could never be reassembled. People lived their lives in a maze of abstractions. But in Dulaba, the people were still one. And one felt that, finally, everything would fall into place; that all debts would ultimately be settled. Blood would, as the griots said, return to its source. Life would add up, because the people themselves added up.

On the edge of the football pitch tiny plants were starting to appear, their leaves a shiny, brilliant green. They were called manonkaso, and they were said to be a sure sign that the rain would come.

14

THE BUSH OF MEN

The village of Kasumai was spread over a broad, park-like plain, on which, in the rainy season, millet, sorghum and groundnuts were cultivated. Like all Jola villages, its compounds were situated some distance from each other, for in the traditional Jola society there had been no authority above that of the compound head, and by maintaining this physical distance, each family asserted its independence and autonomy. Among the many trees dotted over this plain, some standing singly, others clustered together in spinneys, there were several that were sacred, that represented the houses in which the ancestors were living. Sacrifices were made to them before each rainy season and at the birth of every child. And through them, the ancestors gave signs by which the people guided their lives.

Once every ten years, one of these trees, a baobab, would bear fruit in the dry season, and the people would know that three years later, the children – the young men of the village -- would have to be taken to the bush for the great initiation ceremony known as *bukutop*. It was for the Jolas one of the most important observances of their culture. And the order of its events was laid down precisely, day by day, according to the tradition. On the Saturday evening, the initiates would depart for the bush, and in the days before, relatives and friends would arrive from all over the country to help convey them towards their destination. All these people would have to be fed and housed. Scores of animals would have to be killed. Sack upon sack of rice, and barrel upon barrel of oil, would be cooked and eaten. So for three rainy seasons, every unmarried young man in the village would go and work as a farmer in another village to earn money so that his father would feel proud on those few days.

During these days, the initiates would be taken to worship at each of the sacred trees – the *jallangos*, as they were called. And the trunks of the trees would be painted with the blood of the animals that were sacrificed.

Kasumai lay in the hinterland of Fonyi, on the south side of the Bintang Bolon, only a few miles from Dulaba. Earlier in the week, I had heard distant rumbling sounds carried on the breeze. At first I thought it was thunder, but I was told that it was the sound of the guns going off in Kasumai to mark the beginning of the initiation.

Early on the Friday morning, I had crossed the Bintang Bolon with a group of young men of my age-group, and we had stopped in the first compound we had come to. Box-like shelters of branches and leaves had been built onto the houses. But these, like all the buildings, were deserted. We had no *jatio* – no guardian – there, so we had no position and no rights in the village, and – most importantly – no one to provide for us during our stay. So we sat down on the dusty earth of the verandah, huddled into the meagre area of shade, and waited, helpless, until someone came who would use their own rights on our behalf.

There were eight of us: Turo Sise, a tall, kindly, though rather grave young man; Sambujang Samate and his best friend Momodou Minte; Mbemba Sise, a carpenter from Fili Kunda; Lamin Sise, a boy of few words – saturnine, almost demonic of countenance; Nuhar, the thickset and almost morbidly macho husband of the young Duwar of the My Brother Kafo; and of course Sullu.

Through a gap between the fences of the compound, I could see through to a broad expanse of land, open beneath the immense white sky. Beyond it the trees dissolved into the haze of heat. I could hear a distant grumbling, roaring sound, which as it grew nearer distinguished itself into shouting and singing and an indeterminate rhythmic throbbing. Then suddenly a shape appeared on the right-hand side of the gap. A great group of people was moving over the land – a darkly seething mass, which, as it grew larger, began to glitter in the sunlight. The distant crowd moved with infinite slowness across the gap and then finally disappeared behind the left-hand wall. The others watched too, but no one made any expression or comment.

It just so happened that the compound we had entered was the compound of Abdoulai Bajie, where Daouda and his wives had been staying during the previous week, and where all the Dulaba Civil Servants would be staying when they finally arrived in the village.

It was the custom of the Jolas that a woman should return to her own village when the initiation was taking place there, so that she could help out with the cooking and so that she could escort her brothers to and from their ordeal in the bush. In this period, which occurred only once every ten years, she was considered to be free. For she was back among her own people, and thus outside the authority of her husband. Sirrah Bajie, Daouda's first wife, was related to Abdoulai Bajie. She was clearly not his actual sister, but the principle remained the same.

Now Sirrah came striding across the yard towards us.

'Are you all in peace?'

'Peace only.'

'I hope there's no trouble.'

'No trouble.'

'Do you have a jatio?'

'No,' we said with one voice.

'Yo! Come with me.'

We picked up our possessions and followed her. The sound of the singing became suddenly louder and I could hear the rhythm, not of drums, but of dozens of pieces of iron being rattled together in a tingling, jangling syncopation.

The next thing I knew I was moving on the edge of a chaotic mass of people. There were men dressed as women – in shirts and faneaus of flowery patterned material, their hair plaited, but their beards left unshaven – and women dressed as men in voluminous baggy trousers, or shorts, tight over their robust haunches. They were all festooned in long strings of beads, draped criss-cross over their chests, and many carried wands painted in bright primary colours, which in Fonyi were the sign of the kanyelengo, and small wooden troughs in which to put the food they stole. Some had coloured their faces white with powder, others red, others blue. And everywhere swords, cutlasses, and even guns were being brandished with great gusto.

It was difficult to tell how many people there were, they moved so turbulently over the uneven ground to the relentless beating of the irons. And where were we exactly? We seemed to be somewhere at the back of one of the compounds, among the rubbish heaps and the wreckage of last year's gardens.

In the middle of the crowd, the bonnets of the ngangsingolu, the crests made from rams' beards, could be seen bobbing in time to the rhythm of the irons. But it was impossible to see any more, for their guardians, the kintangolu, clustered closely around them, hiding them from the gaze of the witches, of whom there must have been several in the crowd. There, in the centre of the shuffling mass, I could see Ousmane Koujabi, moving close beside the initiates. He too was one of the guardians.

Suddenly there was an immense thundering crack – so loud it seemed to cut to the very centre of one's being. And it was almost immediately followed by another, even louder. I stood hunched with shock. I turned to see Sambujang behind me, his eyes darting in terror. The rest of the crowd danced on oblivious to the terrifying explosions that rent the air at unnervingly irregular intervals. There would be a pause for some time, and then 'Bam!' – and I'd again be shaken rigid. Looking down over the fields that sloped away from the compound I could see young men in massively baggy trousers, their hair plaited like women's, dragging huge, home-made guns over the earth. They would lay the guns – which appeared to consist only of a thick barrel and an enormous trigger – on the ground, then hit the trigger with a stick. 'Bam!' The recoil would send the gun shooting twenty feet backwards over the ground, setting fire to the remains of last year's crops as it went. Then the transvestite incendiarists would nonchalantly drag it away to set it off somewhere else. They moved, these young men, in curiously stylized leaping strides, their immense trousers flapping behind them like wings.

They're mad, I thought. Someone is going to get killed. I had to get out of the way. But where was I going to go? The brain-splitting bangs came from first one direction, then another. I might as well stay where I was, I decided. They would hardly fire into the crowd.

I looked up to see Sullu watching me with some amusement. 'It's only gun-powder,' he said.

I breathed a sigh of relief before I was shaken by another deafening retort.

In front of us a young man in a sweat-stained safari suit moved unsteadily among the dancers, his bloodshot eyes unnaturally wide and staring. Round his neck he wore a number of jujus – thick collars of twisted leather and fur. He suddenly lurched and tried to grab hold of the cutlass another man was holding. The man resisted and they struggled over the thick blade. The young man made no attempt to fight – his attention was focused entirely on the blade, which he began to try to wrench round so that he could impale himself on it. People clustered round and with some effort managed to prise away his hands. He staggered off and began dancing close to the ngangsingolu, jumping high into the air with the men who led the singing. Then moments later he again had to be restrained from getting hold of a knife, with which he tried to cut himself. And all the time the guns were going off, with a great 'Bam!' that seemed to shake the very earth, and the irons were jangling the same endless, insistent rhythm. I felt frightened and confused. I didn't know where to go. Sanyang appeared at my side.

'Is that man drunk?' I asked, pointing to the young man, who was dancing again, his face flushed with an unnatural exhilaration, his eyes staring wildly into space.

'No,' said Sanyang. 'He has put on jujus that are too powerful for him.'

The crowd had now more or less come to a standstill, though the beating of the irons and the dancing around the ngangsingolu continued. A few yards away another circle had formed. A young woman wearing only a faneau sat on the ground, her legs splayed towards a row of five wooden posts and a number of ants' nests that had been dug out of the earth and laid in front of them. A gourd of palm wine hung from one of the posts. One of the ngangsingolu, the girl's brother, also clad only in a faneau, sat on the ground immediately behind her, his legs stretched out along either side of hers. Then a second ngangsingo, a younger brother, assumed the same position behind him. An elder took the gourd of palm wine and moved it in the air, weaving a complex loop shape over their heads. Then he spilt some of it over the posts. He took a cock and, partially cutting its throat, dropped it onto the first boy's head. It bounced off and collapsed in the dust beside him. Then it rose up and began a kind of manic fluttering dance. People moved back to give it room to move. They hurled coins, which showered jangling and clattering into the faneau between the girl's legs. All the time the women shouted at the cock, 'Tell us that he will be safe. Yes, tell us only good things.' They waved their arms, vehemently pointing at the cock. It fell over and writhed, its wings twitching, for a few moments. Then it slumped into stillness. The old man picked it up and cut it open. He examined the entrails, then held the body up to the crowd. A great cheer went up. The women whooped, and began clapping and stamping vigorously in the dust. It was good news. The ancestors had said that the boy would be safe from witches while he was in the bush. The body of the cock was thrown onto a pile of similar corpses at the base of the posts, and the whole process was repeated for the second boy. Again the ancestors said that the boy would be safe. There was more cheering, clapping and dancing. Then all three got up and made way for another girl and her brothers.

A sprawling network of palm-leaf shelters stretched back over the kankango from the main buildings of Abdoulai Bajie's compound. These shelters had the same name as the house in which the initiates would live in the bush – *jujuo* – and they were built to the same design. Scores of people would be staying there until the departure of the initiates, and Abdoulai was feeding all of them. I wondered how many of them he knew as little as he knew us.

As the sun reached its zenith and the excitement temporarily abated, he led us to the back of the kankango, and helped us build a jujuo of our own. It took about half an hour. Then we all crawled inside to rest. I asked Sullu if he would be following the initiates to the bush. 'No,' he said. 'The Jolas have too many ways.'

Later Ousmane Koujabi took me to where the ngangsingolu were being kept – in the end room of a long building. They sat grim-faced and silent, naked except for faneaus wrapped around their loins. In contrast to the Mandinka boys, who were taken mostly before the age of ten, they appeared to be mostly in their late teens. The youngest could not have been less than fifteen. Many of them would have been circumcised without ceremony when they were young. Some had even been taken to the hospital. But the cutting of the penis was of comparatively little ritual importance to the Jolas. For them the very act of going to the bush had a religious significance in itself. None the less, many were still circumcised in the bush, sometimes as many as two or three hundred at one time. Nowadays, their wounds would be dressed with medicine provided by the government, but in the past they were reliant on leaves and powders made from roots and bark, and out of every hundred boys, it was likely that one or two would die. So initiation had come to be closely associated with death. It was seen as an inevitable, even a necessary part of the process.

And, I was given to understand, there were certain other things that happened there, the nature of which I would never know. Whatever they were, it was necessary for the initiate to be 'sexually mature' in order to understand them.

I asked whose hands they were in and Ousmane pointed to a boy of curiously hermaphroditic appearance. I gave him five dalasis and left.

As the sun began to sink, more and more people could be seen moving along the paths over the flat fields, strewn with stalks and stubble undisturbed since last year's harvest. Each of the compounds had a brightly-coloured sheet hanging over the entrance with family photographs pinned to it in glass frames. Inside, traders had set up stalls selling faneaus, cigarettes, sweets, batteries – anything the visitors might need. One of the big shopkeepers from Sibanor appeared to have transferred his entire stock to the village and was doing a brisk trade. The houses and the verandahs and the bantabas were by now milling with people, and more were arriving all the time.

I kept bumping into people I knew – people I had met in Fonyi and Kombo, people from Mankono, Joli and Karafa Kunda, people who had stayed or worked in Dulaba at one time or another; and I bumped into people I didn't know but who appeared to know me, including a quartet of girls from the village of Dasilame. The smallest of them was a very fair girl, almost pink in complexion, called Fanta Toure. I was rather taken with her, and she with me if her behaviour was anything to go by. 'She is your person,' said Sullu. 'You can have her. She's not a child. Now you have a person here. I also must find a person.'

I met a young Jola man of my acquaintance and we sat talking for some time on the bentengo outside the compound where he was staying. There was a large mango tree overhead, and the golden-green fruit hung ripe and heavy.

The young man asked one of the women seated beside us to cut one for me. She pointed to a thin strand of orange bark only about four inches long, tied to one of the lower branches.

'Oh,' said the young man, and he laughed dryly. 'I think it's better that you don't have one of these mangoes. That piece of bark is the sign of the *kangkurang*.'

I had seen the kangkurang during the Christmas festivities at the coast: three young men in skirts of leaves, their chests and heads bound in orange bark of an almost synthetic brightness, all armed with cutlasses and sticks. They went from compound to compound at the head of a great crowd of children, dancing furiously to the beating of drums, demanding money in a kind of African version of trick or treat. This was the terror of the jujuo reduced to the level of masquerade, but even there it provoked among the women a sense of unease that was all too real.

Here in Fonyi there was only one kangkurang, and the leaves with their appearance of festive jollity were absent. The bark was cut whole from a *kaffalatak* tree, and bound around the head, body, arms and legs of one of the kintangolu – the guardians of the initiates. Any of them could be the kangkurang, except that that person had to be kunfanunte – to possess second sight. From that moment that person was regarded not as a human being but as a devil – a devil that was controlled by the *mansa kwiang*, the elder who was in charge of the jujuo. And no one who had not been initiated should know the identity of the person who was inside the bark.

Three months before the beginning of the initiation, the kangkurang was summoned to find the kintangolu – the older boys who would guard and instruct the initiates in the jujuo. The kintangolu were the sons of the initiates' fathers' sisters – which effectively meant every young man in the village. A man had to be a kintango three times before he was free of this obligation.

When they heard the drums beating the women would run and hide, while the young men ran through the streets of the village crying, '*Chori! Kill! Chori Mama Tambawuleng!*' 'Chori' was the personal name of the kangkurang – the hot one, the 'red spear'. They praised him so that he might have mercy on them. But their running was leisurely, almost stylized, for they knew they must be caught, and as the kangkurang approached they would lie down as it ran trampling over their prone bodies. It would then turn and walk back over them slapping each of them hard with the flattened blade of its cutlass. When it had done this twice the boys would roll apart, and the kangkurang would walk between them beating the blade onto the ground beside them. The mothers, watching from behind the fences, assumed that their children were being beaten yet again. 'Ndeysan!' they cried. 'What are they doing to our children?' Many wept openly.

The elders had said that no one must cut any of these mangoes until they were all ripe, and the signal had been given. They had called the kangkurang to protect that tree and anyone caught stealing them would be taken and beaten – 'without mercy'.

All through the heat of the day the beating of the irons had never stopped. The clattering, jangling sound, constantly to the same insistent rhythm, could always be heard from somewhere across the plain. The irons, a shallow V shape, slightly indented in the middle, were beaten with a thin rod, also of iron, by groups of young women who moved in a tight circle in the vanguard of the ngangsingolu.

Now, in the yard in the centre of the compound, the relentless jangling had reached an almost frenetic pitch. Ahead of the young women moved a great crowd of men bearing swords and cutlasses, all singing in the characteristically 'rolling' Jola style. The deep voices rose and fell like the swell of an immense sea, the higher voices of the women seeming to blow over them like the wind whistling above the tumult. If one listened carefully, one could hear them calling the names of their ancestors, the great heroes of the village, saying how much sweeter it would have been if they could have been there on that day. They waved their swords before them as they moved in a stately, shuffling dance around the bentengo in the middle of the compound, which, like the verandahs, was crowded with onlookers. 'Stand back,' advised my companion as the procession drew near to where we were standing. 'These people do not know what they are doing.'

Men would leap forward from the crowd, moving before the others with the same huge, slow strides that the young men with the guns had used, their brilliantly patterned baggy trousers billowing around them. They brandished their swords extravagantly, smiling with exultation, and a certain self-satisfaction that I didn't really understand.

Two young men, their necks and naked muscular torsos strung with every kind of juju, began to saw experimentally at their shoulders with their cutlass blades. But they were told to stop. They should wait till tomorrow. Today was not the real day. Tomorrow everything would happen.

Just after dark, a coach arrived full of people from the coast. Everyone in the country knew what was happening there that weekend. There were already four thousand people in the village, and tomorrow even more people would be arriving to escort the children to the bush. On Sunday there was to be a wrestling match, and it was said that the army was coming to keep order.

Daouda was to present a disco that night and the speakers were already tied to the roof of his and Barbara's estate car. All the bachelors from the Quarters were by now present, and they stood with the Dulaba boys in the light from the car. Now that it was dark I had once again lost my bearings. We appeared to be beside a kind of thoroughfare, for a great number of people were coming and going in the darkness. Under the trees, scores more people sat on mats – just sitting in the darkness, looking at nothing. Nearby we could see the fires where dinner was being cooked in huge cauldrons. Women passed with basins of water on their heads. For some, almost the whole period was taken up with these tasks, while on the other side of the compound we heard other women – visitors – singing and dancing in the jujuos.

Sullu and I went for a walk. We could only just make out the line of the path that led away towards the other compounds, and we could only sense the other people moving around us. After a time we became aware of a short figure moving quickly and intently ahead of us. 'Greet this person,' Sullu murmured in my ear.

'Good evening,' I called. 'Are you in peace?'

'Peace only,' came a woman's voice.

'I hope there's no trouble.'

'No trouble,' came the voice rather defensively.

'What is your name?'

'Mayi.'

'And your surname?'

'Bajie.'

She asked us our names and our surnames. Then she slowed slightly till she was walking only just ahead of us and at the same speed.

We exchanged more pleasantries. 'We're looking for a guardian,' said Sullu. She stopped walking and stood, waiting to hear what he would say next. 'We have no guardian here. We're looking for someone to be our guardian – someone who knows how to be a guardian'. She listened carefully. She said it might be difficult. There were many people. Sullu told her where we were staying. Then she pointed in the direction of her own compound. She was a citizen of the village, she said. She might be able to help us.

The dialogue continued for some minutes, Sullu restating our need for a guardian. It seemed a curious thing to ask for, though I had a fairly good idea as to his intentions. Finally she said she would see what she could do to help us. She would return in a short time. And with that she hurried off into the darkness.

Sullu was jubilant. 'Yo! Now we both have someone for tonight.'

'But you didn't mention that,' I said. 'All you did was to ask her about a guardian.'

'She knew what I meant.'

Nevertheless I was sceptical. It seemed highly unlikely that she was going to come back at some ill-defined future time to this obscure spot to take two complete strangers off to erotic adventures in the darkness, just because they had told her that they had no guardian.

'She will come,' said Sullu.

And sure enough about twenty minutes later two figures approached along the path.

'*Salaam aleikum.*'

'*Aleikum salaam.*'

'We have come. This is my friend.'

'Yo!'

Greetings were exchanged.

As we followed them at a discreet distance through the darkness towards Abdoulai Bajie's compound, I wondered what on earth I was involving myself in. None the less I could feel a queasy, insidious desire rising in me.

Sullu directed them through the compound to the path that led to the Dulaba boys' jujuo. We stopped outside. Sullu shone the torch into the empty interior of the shelter. The two women looked inside. 'Yo,' said Mayi. 'Later we will return.' In the light I could see that Mayi was a stout, agreeable-looking woman in her late thirties. Her companion was younger, less stout, but also somehow less agreeable. Then they disappeared.

'You can have Mayi, the very fat one,' said Sullu.

'All right,' I said.

The disco, which was being run off the car battery, was now set up, and I could hear Jojo Bajie summoning people over the PA system. Admission was one dalasi for boys and fifty batuts for girls. Where exactly was I? I had once again lost my bearings. Apart from the feeble light from Daouda's car, all was utter blackness. I went off to relieve myself and nearly fell down an enormous hole.

In the main thoroughfare of the compound, Sullu stood close to the shopkeeper's light so that Mayi and her friend could use the number on his baseball shirt to identify us.

Then suddenly I heard Jojo's voice announcing that the disco was cancelled. This was a surprise, as it was for many the most eagerly awaited event of the whole circumcision. The elders had forbidden it. This was not a night for such things. Tomorrow would be the night for celebration. The disco was postponed until then.

Mayi Bajie and her friend didn't appear.

'Let's go and find them,' said Sullu.

'Leave it,' I said. 'If they don't want to come it's their affair.'

'No, no,' he said. 'We'll find them.'

Once again we wandered off into the darkness. The compound was not far away, and we found her without too much difficulty. She looked rather alarmed at seeing us. She said they had been afraid to come, as the elders had said that this was a very important night, and any woman who was found alone talking to a man who was not her husband would be beaten.

A dance was held under an immense mango tree, one of its branches curving round like a great arm over the dancers. There were perhaps two hundred women on the front row of the dancing circle – gorgeously dressed, at last freed from their labours. They stood in the glow of the drummers' lamp, solemn and poised, like some fantastic female army of the night, rapping out an insistent on-beat on clappers made from the hard spines of palm fronds, as the rhythm of the drums began to build.

Then one by one they went into the circle to dance, the rhythm of the clappers breaking into an infernal clattering like the feverish scratching of immense insects. It seemed to take hold of the women and shake them as, arms outstretched, their feet pounded the earth. The intensity of the rhythm barely abated – there were never fewer than four or five people in the dancing circle – until the patterns of their dresses began to disappear in the haze of dust they had stamped out of the earth. The initial solemnity had evaporated in the heat of the rhythm and now there were only smiles of triumph and exhilaration. This was the Africa of the European romantic imagination: the throbbing of the drums in the night, the great dancing circle on the edge of the bush, the exuberant, instinctive gaiety, almost dangerous in its intensity. It was a scene from a childhood reverie, and at that moment it was all perfectly real.

As the night wore on, more and more of the men who stood watching in the darkness on the outside of the circle broke through the cordon of women to dance. They leapt shaking from the earth, their feet springing from the ground with an agility and energy that seemed almost supernatural. Yet, being men, they were more self-conscious than the women. They seemed to demand more attention and approbation. And being men, they naturally got it.

I was woken at seven by the sound of the guns. I drifted off again and woke to find myself wedged into a double bed between five others. More people were asleep on the floor and in the armchair. Outside I could hear what sounded like large groups of people moving through the compound. The heat was intensifying by the moment.

Famara Bajie, who worked as a gardener for Sarah and Richard Innes, came into the room and began rummaging under the armchair. The prone Lamin Jarjou slumbered on. From a plastic bag, Famara pulled a thick ring about nine inches in diameter covered in long, bristling fur. Then he took out a pair of rubber gloves and a large plastic bottle full of a beverage known as *bingko*. The colour of chocolate milk, it was made from fermented millet and was only drunk at the time of the initiation. The people denied strenuously that it was alcohol and when I had drunk some I had felt only mildly drowsy. It had an odd, sour taste. Famara drank deeply from the bottle, then he started, realizing that I was awake and had been watching him. But his features quickly recomposed themselves, and he flashed me a confidential smile before leaving the room with his possessions.

People were leaving the compounds in large groups and, to the beating of the irons, were converging on a large flat field at the centre of the village. Each of these processions was headed by a group of sword-wielding men, some so laden with jujus they seemed to find it difficult to move. Though on examination of their red, heavy eyes, this may also have had something to do with the amounts of bingko they had drunk. It was also an aspect of their dance: the slow, stylized, prancing movements – some leaping in long bounds, others moving in a jerky, melodramatic shuffle, their gigantic trousers dragging in the dust behind them. A crowd formed round the edge of the field, while those who wished to participate in what was about to happen moved into the middle. I noticed with horror that some of them were carrying not only swords and cutlasses, but spears, rifles and handguns. They made a strange sight as they leaped and danced over the ridges of dry grey earth, expressions of a curiously remote ecstasy on their faces. One man was dressed entirely in a brilliant red, a sort of Phrygian cap hugging his scalp, another in blue, another in black. Many were so covered in jujus – with strings of safos, collars and belts and bangles of leather and fur, twisted and knotted and sewn with cowries and pieces of horn – that it was difficult to tell what they were wearing underneath. They reminded me momentarily of the super-heroes in Marvel Comics, and I'm sure that is quite close to the way they saw themselves.

'You see this man,' said Yaya Bojang, pointing to a stout, stocky man of a certain age. 'He is my stepfather. He is famous for this throughout the whole country. Where he is now, no bullet can enter his body and no knife can cut him.'

He was certainly one of the most transported of the participants, his face and movements evincing a kind of exhausted exaltation as he half-pranced, half-staggered between the other dancers. Others, however, had come closer to the purpose of the affair. One man was attempting to impale himself on a spear. Another was holding a revolver to his head and was starting to squeeze the trigger. I was beginning to feel very alarmed. Even if it was all only a performance, they might easily maim or kill themselves or one of the bystanders – possibly myself – by mistake. Every few moments one of the home-made guns would go off with a thundering crack in the adjacent field. It didn't add to one's feeling of security.

'O-ho!' said Yaya, as a man pointed his tongue out towards us. He pulled out a knife and ran the blade vigorously across his tongue for some moments. There was no sign of blood. Then he went dancing off in the opposite direction. 'Now do you believe in jujus?' asked Yaya. 'You have seen this man cutting his own tongue with a knife, and there is nothing wrong with him. Now you *must* believe.'

The man with the revolver had by now pulled the trigger as far as it would go. There was a faint click. Then he pointed it in the air and it went off with a crack and a whisper of smoke. Everywhere I looked, people were sawing and gouging at their arms, necks and shoulders with swords and knives, and the skin did not appear to be disturbed in any way.

I had heard about this dance ever since I had first arrived in the Gambia. It was thought to be the ultimate test of the power of jujus. Even the Professor had been impressed by it. I was not, however. There was something altogether too theatrical about the people's movements. The blades might not have been very sharp. Certainly some of them looked less like real swords and more like the decorative articles that hang in suburban living-rooms in England. And I had seen at least one youth use the blunt edge of his cutlass. The sound of the revolver had not been very loud. It might have been a cap gun.

Still, it was difficult to imagine that they could hack and slash at themselves with such abandon without drawing one single drop of blood. And it occurred to me that even if it was all real I probably still wouldn't believe it. It probably *was* all real, and I just couldn't believe the evidence of my eyes. I was probably incapable of accepting such things.

Suddenly a new figure came leaping, as though in slow motion, into the arena. He wore a waistcoat and billowing trousers of a turquoise, flowered material. Round his neck was the collar of bristling fur, and on his right hand a yellow rubber washing-up glove that must have come from under Sarah Innes's sink. Famara's normally amiable, almost sleepy smile was replaced by a wild grimace. He went up to the first person he saw and began trying to seize his cutlass. The man resisted and Famara went off in search of another weapon. He finally got hold of a kind of stainless-steel dagger, and, clutching it with his yellow washing-up glove, he began slashing furiously at his forearm. I felt rather sorry for him. There was an air of slight desperation about these antics. I didn't know why he was doing these things and, unlike the young man the day before, who had seemed genuinely crazed, I don't think he did either.

Nearby an old man was attempting to shoot himself in the stomach with a hunting rifle. He was having some difficulty, as people kept making nominal attempts to stop him, and the trigger was always just out of reach. Whether he finally succeeded or not I never found out. And to be honest, I didn't really care.

After lunch, I went to the Dulaba boys' jujuo to rest. The palm-leaf shelter was empty, and I lay down on the sheet of plastic that had been laid down on the floor, and sank into a dazed stupor of half-sleep. Some time later I became aware of the sound of drumming in the intermediate distance – though whether in the muggy middle distance of a half-dream, or in real space, I couldn't tell. It seemed to be moving slowly around me like an orbiting moon. It had begun about the area of my feet, and was now moving around the top of my head. It was monotonous but rather thrilling.

I shook myself and sat up. It was real drumming, and it wasn't far away. There had been no absence of rhythm since I had arrived in Kasumai, but this one was somehow even more compulsive – the staccato variations constantly underpinned by the insistent and rather ominous booming of the bass drum. I decided to go and see what was happening.

I emerged, bleary-eyed, from the jujuo to find a group of young boys standing by the fence looking down over the field towards the palms that overhung the rice field. 'It is the kangkurang,' said one. Then he giggled. 'Why don't you go there?'

'I think I will,' I said.

He came running after me. 'Please, I beg you, do not go there. It will beat you without mercy.'

'Don't worry about it,' I grunted.

As I walked across the field I caught sight of a group of figures running through the undergrowth on the edge of the rice fields. There was something strange, something oddly frightening about the way they were running. It was unhurried, deliberate, almost balletic. They paused and turned in time to the beating of the drums, and then ran on as though driven by the pounding rhythm.

I was suddenly overtaken by the feeling of shock I had felt on seeing newsreel film of soldiers in some distant country firing into a crowd of helpless demonstrators – the sense of horror no longer held at bay by abstractions, but suddenly held up clear and lucid, and at the same time the sense that finally it was not so very dramatic.

'Shit,' I thought. 'This is really happening.'

Then I caught sight of a great figure, monstrously tall and hairy, rising out of the dust and raining blows on something or someone at its feet. A number of men ran beside the young men wielding long, whip-like branches which they flicked over the heads of the runners. One of them turned and saw me. 'Hey!' he shouted. 'Get out of here! Get out!' I turned and started to stroll back up the field. 'Run!' he shouted '*Run!*'

I did not run, for as I turned, I saw a great crowd of people watching from the safety of the compound fences. Feigning nonchalance, I walked as quickly as I could towards them.

'What were you doing?' asked Sanyang, as I reached safety. 'Who told you to go there?'

'No one,' I said. 'I just went.'

'If they had caught you, you would have been beaten terribly. They don't want anybody to see what they are doing there. When they go to the bush this evening don't even go an inch beyond the line where the other people stop. If you do, they will take you to the bush too. They will not care that you are a tubab. These people do not care what they do.'

Being among the Jolas in Fonyi was curiously different from being with the Mandingkos in Kiang. The people looked the same but they were subtly and indefinably different. It was a little like going on a weekend trip to Boulogne. Certainly they were less overtly friendly than the people of Kiang. But then Fonyi was a little more developed than Kiang. The main road ran through it. It was closer to the cutting edge of the world.

As the evening approached, the bachelors from the Quarters and the Dulaba boys all sprawled out on mats under the trees, and rested, along with scores of other people. Groups of young women and girls came and sat near us, laughing and making gentle fun of us before moving on. And my companions, all of whom had had an eye out for the talent from the moment we arrived, responded in kind. 'This is like a bank holiday on Brighton beach,' I thought.

I spotted Fanta Toure among the crowds of people milling past us.

'You see that girl,' I said to my young Jola friend, who had come to sit with us. 'Is she not very fair?'

'Yes,' he said. 'I also have noticed her. They say she is a Mandingko, but she comes from the village of the Sirifs.'

'But she is as light as a tubab.'

'Have you ever seen a Sirif?'

Now he mentioned it I had seen many very fair-coloured people in Dasilame, but I had assumed they were Fulani.

'They are not from any tribe. They are what we call *woleos* – the chosen ones of God. Whatever prayer they offer, God must answer it. They are related to the Prophet Mohammed through Fatoumata.'

I wondered why the relatives of the Prophet should want to go and live in the tiny village of Dasilame, hidden away among the mangrove swamps beside the Bintang Bolon.

He looked rather miffed. 'You have come here. Why should they also not want to come here?'

As the shadows lengthened, the beating of the irons resumed. Now from every direction an almost feverish jangling could be heard. It was almost time, and in every compound the relatives of the ngangsingolu began to dance in readiness. On the verandahs and the bentengos even more people stood and sat, waiting to accompany them to the bush. Once again the bonnets of the ngangsingolu could be seen bobbing in the middle of the brilliant crowd of kanyeleng women and juju men. The latter seemed utterly drained by the exertions of the morning; it was only the significance of the moment that was keeping them upright. The wands and the swords waved over the heads of the crowd. Flutes and trumpets made of animal horns wailed and moaned above the jangling of the irons. I watched the girls, who stood in close, almost conspiratorial groups ringing out the rhythm – always the same – unchanging, unbreaking and seemingly unending. When Europeans came to these African celebrations they wanted the action to begin as soon as they arrived. They wanted to see up to an hour of the best of what was on offer and then move on to other things. In fact, they might have to wait many hours for things to start and when they did they would go on for as long as they should go on – be it fifteen minutes or fifteen days. These girls, the sisters of the ngangsingolu, had been ringing out the same rhythm on those irons almost non-stop for several days, and one felt they could easily continue for several more.

I felt suddenly exhausted with the monotony of the ringing irons, with the vast milling crowds of people, whose expressions of exhaustion seemed to answer my own. At that moment I understood the frustration of the young men with the limitations of their grandparents' culture. For there was now, and probably only ever would be, one way to beat those irons – just as in Dulaba the women danced almost always to the same rhythm. I understand their longing for something beyond it – something that would change and develop, even if it was only disco music. But at the same time I understood how these things were completely necessary to them. For the things they wanted – westernized music, American clothes, electronic gadgetry – the whole world now wanted, and they had little with which to bargain for them. So it was necessary to hold on, at least for the time being, to the forms of their grandparents' culture. Without these they would have been utterly lost.

I decided I had now seen as much as I needed of this event. I could already imagine the departure of the initiates. It would be another procession like many I had already witnessed. Surrounded by the juju men, the kanyeleng women, the ringing of irons, and hordes of onlookers, the ngangsingolu would dance to the time-honoured place from which, accompanied only by the kintangolu, they would shuffle slowly away into the bush, as the sun disappeared among the trees. It would be, for those not actually going to the bush, a moment of anti-climax.

But for many of the visitors, the interest of attending the conveying of the initiates lay less in its ostensible purpose than in the events that would take place in the village afterwards. Negotiations had been underway in unobserved moments for several days, and that night, as Daouda's disco sounded from one side of the village and the rhythms of the drums from the other, men and women united only by desire would slip away into the darkness together. On that night, everyone would have a person. On that night even Sirrah Bajie, Ndey-Touti and Jori Sanyang would be taking lovers, because in that place, and on that night, all women were free. A woman could make love with a stranger in front of her husband, and he would not be able to do anything. This was known in Jola as *busangkab*, and it was the traditional way of celebrating the departure of the young men for the bush. If I stayed I would have to take part. There could be no avoiding it.

It was all becoming too much, I couldn't face the thought of making love on the floor of the jujuo with someone I'd never seen before, with the rest of the village grunting and heaving all around me. I was exhausted, and I was desperately thirsty. But there was no water in the village. The wells were by now completely dry. And the next day there would be the wrestling and the army, and still there would be no water.

The Mandingkos were gathering together into their own group to 'push' the initiates towards the bush with the rhythm of the barawulo. Sullu, who was standing on the edge of the group, spotted me. 'You can't go now. Everything is just about to happen. Tonight everyone will have a person. You can have anyone you want. You can have as many as you like. You can have Fanta Toure . . .' I could see her somewhere in the distance. Perspective seemed to have disappeared as I looked into the vast gathering of people that moved over the plain of the village. They were spread out as though on some limitless tapestry, their size allocated not according to their nearness but to their symbolic import-ance. Despite the distance I could see Fanta Toure very clearly as she stood with her three friends, waiting. 'Do not disappoint your person,' said Sullu.

I was tempted.

'No,' I said. 'I'm going to go.'

'You are afraid of the kangkurang. This is why you want to go. The kangkurang will not come into the village again.'

'No, it's not that.'

'You should not go,' said Sullu taking my hand. 'One friend should not leave before another.'

'I know, but . . .'

It was just after seven. There was still time to leave before night fell.

The kangkurang did come into the village again. On the Sunday night it came looking for the kintangolu, many of whom had preferred to stay in the village, dancing and chasing women. This time it went into the houses. Any young man even remotely related to the ngangsingolu, even if he were not a citizen of the village, even if he were only of the same surname, would be dragged outside, beaten and taken to the bush. Inevitably some escaped and the following afternoon the kangkurang would come back to find them. When they were caught they were flogged all the way to the jujuo.

By the Monday, all strangers were expected to have left the village. It was not reasonable that the village should have to support them after that time. And in case anyone had not taken the hint, the kangkurang would come into the village on the Monday night to hasten them on their way.

During the period of initiation the ngangsingolu were completely in the hands of the elders. They were kept in a state of constant uncertainty and fear. At any moment the kangkurang might enter the jujuo and flog them without warning. They would see many things they did not understand. But they did not dare to ask what they were. Asking questions was bad. If you wanted to survive in that place you would say nothing. Any boy who was particularly rude or stubborn would be made to drink his own urine. He would have to kneel down and swill it from a tin like a dog or a pig while the kintangolu rained blows on him with their canes.

The ngangsingolu slept little. The drums beat day and night, and they were made to stay up singing till the early hours of the morning. They were not allowed to wash, so they were dirty, exhausted and run down, with only the sting of their guardians' canes to keep them awake.

The boys were constantly asked the meanings of the songs and the *pasingo* – the secret signs – they had been taught. If they did not know they would feel the cane across their backs – one stroke for each mistake.

> 'Where is the road?
> The road we are following,
> The great, ancient road.
>
> 'The road we are keeping to –
> The road our ancestors first took
> We also are following that great ancient road.'

That was the first song the initiates learned in the jujuo.

*

Many of the songs related to sexual taboos. A man should not allow a woman to lie on top of him when they were making love. He should not go to a place where a woman is giving birth. He should not have sexual contact with his wife after she is four months pregnant. Most important of all, he should not trust her. He could love his wife as much as he wanted, but he should never, ever trust her. More than that, he should watch her very carefully. And nearly all the threats that were used to pacify the initiates related to their sexual and generative power. They would be made to lie face downwards on the floor of the jujuo, while various 'devils' that had been summoned by the elders moved among them. They were told that if they looked up, they would never be able to have children.

One morning they would be woken early. 'What did you dream?' a guardian asked one of the boys. 'Nothing,' said the boy. *Thwack!* The guardian's cane came down on his back. 'Don't say nothing,' said one of the elders. 'You should tell them that you dreamt that your brother's wife killed four cocks and cooked them for you.' Immediately the kintango ran back to the village and told the boy's brother's wife of the dream. She was so honoured that the boy had dreamt of her while he was in the jujuo that she went to the boy's father and begged four cocks. Then she cooked them as well as she could with rice and oil and pepper and sent it to the jujuo for the boy to eat. When the food arrived it was placed before the ngangsingo. 'Here is your food,' said the kintango. 'Eat!' If the boy was stupid enough to move as much as a muscle towards that food, he would immediately feel the cane cutting into his back.

And when the food had arrived from each of the boys' relatives it would be massed together. Each of the ngangsingolu was given a handful or two, while the elders and the kintangolu gorged themselves on the rest.

Life in the jujuo was considered to be on a different plane from the rest of existence. To bear grudges for the shame and the cruelties one had suffered there was absolutely forbidden. The only way to get revenge was to wait until the children of one's tormentor were taken to the bush.

But the elders and guardians could not inflict punishment at random. A person could only be beaten if they did not know one of the secrets of initiation, or if they had infringed the etiquette of the jujuo.

Any initiated man could enter the jujuo. And in the evenings, the men of the village – the fathers of the initiates – would go and join with the singing. They and the kintangolu would test each other on the meanings of the songs and the pasingo, and they too could administer punishments on each other.

'Sympathy is something that you leave behind you when you enter the jujuo. You take it off like a shirt, and you leave it outside. This is why they call it *kei-wulo* – the bush of men. If you are not a *man*, you should not go there. For myself I have no friends when I am in the jujuo.

'To enter some of these jujuos, you may pass twenty-five pasingos – signs that are left on the ground, or gestures that they make to test if you are an initiate. I know all of them and I know all of the songs. I can enter any jujuo and sing them in Jola or Mandinka or Wolof. I have only ever been beaten once, and that was by the Serers. I did not greet them when I entered the jujuo. They said, "You should greet when you enter." And then they beat me.'

No woman would go near the men's jujuo. It was believed that if she entered, she would die 'automatically'. When the boys had been there for three weeks, they would be taken to the edge of the bush, so that their mothers would be able to see that they were still alive. But they would see them only briefly, and over a distance of some yards, before they were once again led away by their guardians into the bush.

By the time they left the jujuo, the boys would have become definitively distanced from the society of women. When they returned to the village they would live in their own house, or in the house of their elder brothers. From now on they would be under the men, and their mothers would have no further influence on their lives. It was perhaps because of this distance that their mothers became for them almost iconic figures of respect. There was no easier way to anger an African man than to insult his mother.

For anyone whose child or brother or relative had gone to the bush, the last day of the initiation was a great day. The boys would be taken to the river to wash, and then a big dance would be held in the bush. Many of the things that they had seen in the jujuo would be explained to them. They would see many strange, many inexplicable things on that day.

They would come leaping from the bush, waving branches of green leaves above their heads. The young women of the village, their sisters, would be waiting for them, and when they saw them coming they would make secret signs to them, to see what they had learnt in the bush. And as the boys came dancing towards them they would make certain signs they had been taught, with which to taunt women. And the girls would go 'Whooo!' and laugh, and hide their faces in shame. Then they would run ahead of the boys towards the village, singing and laughing and waving flags and branches of leaves.

Everyone would gather in the village, in the open area beside the bantaba. The initiates would sit at one end, with the kintangolu, who had guarded them in the bush, standing behind them. Then, from the other end of the square, the girls would come dancing towards their brothers. They would be doing a dance called the king dance. It was a very difficult dance. If you asked someone to do that dance for you, they would say they could not do it. But on that day everyone would do it.

Each girl would take a faneau – a very beautiful one – and place it around her brother's shoulders. Then the brothers would stand up, and they too would do that dance. And as they danced, their sisters would throw money at them.

15

NIGHT ARROWS

'Tubabo Marky la be ke
Tubabo ko mbitta mofing nyolia
Mbitta luwase la
Jang ning Kemeseng nyolia'

'Tubabo Mark is the cause of it all,
He says he wants to live with the blacks,
"I'm going to rent a house,
At Kemeseng Sanyang's place."'

My new house stood on the corner of the compound of Cho Kunda – one of the oldest compounds in the village – on the avenue that led from the bantaba to the mosque. Nearby, under a mango tree, stood a small bantaba at which the alkalo held meetings, and beyond it a gap between the houses led into the smoky, crowded yard around which the alkalo and his family lived.

'How many months have you been living in this compound with us?' bellowed Mariyama Sibo Djankeh, who was married to one of the alkalo's brothers. 'And not once have you come to greet us. All you do is go off attending Jola circumcision ceremonies.'

The house belonged to Kemeseng Sanyang, husband of Arabiatou of the Saniyoro Kafo, the man who had loaned the kafo the land for their groundnut farm the previous year. He was an amiable, scruffy man in his forties, whose clothes never seemed to fit him. He breathed heavily, giving the impression that if he once sat down he would immediately fall asleep. And though he was no fool, his career as a shopkeeper had been dogged by a series of disasters he was happy to recount to the accompaniment of great roars of laughter. In fact the house in which I was living had once been his shop. He had cemented the floor and dug in a long drop latrine in the yard at the back. So it was, by the standards of the village, extremely luxurious.

Two good-sized rooms led off a central corridor, the back door leading to a small, enclosed washing area fenced with millet stalks, the front directly onto a crumbling mud verandah banked with the droppings of the animals that slept there. Four wooden posts loosely supported the rusting eaves, which were bent down at one corner and up at the other, giving the house the appearance of a parcel perpetually in the process of coming undone.

Above my bed two corrugated-iron casements looked onto the covered alley that led into the yard where Kemeseng lived with Arabiatou and his elder wife Salinding, his mother Mba Juju and all the children.

It was the dry season, and there was no need of a mosquito net. I would lie on my back, positioning myself on the thin mattress of groundnut chaff so that the wooden slats didn't cut too sharply into me, the dry air like a blanket so soft and so thick it filled the whole room, and sleep would engulf me almost immediately. Often, however, I would wake in the small hours, the air bearing down on me with such force that I could hardly breathe. I would go and stand at the back door and look out at the grey night, feeling the relative coolness of the air.

The villagers always slept with their doors and windows closed, for they believed that at night demon archers fired invisible rays, 'night arrows', which if they hit one could cause all manner of disorders, from boils to septicaemia.

Sometimes one dog's bark would set every dog in the village howling wildly for what seemed like large portions of the night – the donkey who lived in the thatched shelter over the way braying in feverish union – until they suddenly stopped as abruptly as they had begun. It was said that on such nights devils were active in the village.

On moonless nights people were enjoined to point their torches always at the ground. If you raised it you would immediately hear harsh voices from the darkness telling you to extinguish it. As the Mandingkos said, *Suto mu sutiro le ti* – 'the night is a secret' – and it was better that that which it contained was not examined too closely. It was on such nights that the women walked abroad. When the moon was full they would rest.

Once or twice I was woken in the very dead of night by an abrupt knock on the door. I was immediately awake and on my feet, my blood racing. But it was only one of the sheep knocking against the door. Moments later I would hear them shuffling away along the side of the building, their bleats sounding oddly human, like some strange terminal moaning.

Each morning I was woken briefly at dawn by the shouting of children and the crashing of buckets and basins in the alley beside my bed, then the thudding of water against metal and the arguments of the women at the taps only twenty yards away. An hour or two later I would rouse myself and stumble up the street towards the camp, where I still kept my tape recorder and my notes.

The dust got everywhere. It blew on the light breeze through the cracks round the windows and doors. It covered the bed, the books, the seats, the walls. No matter how much the floor was swept it was still marbled with thin drifts of violet-grey dust. It was impossible to put anything down or touch anything without it or you accruing a residue of the stuff, and you had no sooner washed than you were covered again. The villagers, who washed standing on a small block of wood, pouring water over themselves from an old tin, would always wash their shoes before stepping back into them.

It explained why, though they had a voracious appetite for material possessions, they treated them with remarkable lightness. For in that environment it was impossible to keep anything in a pristine condition for long: scoured and stained by the dust, bruised by the handling of many children – within days it looked like an antique.

So the people reserved their lavial efforts for their persons and their clothes, and liked to change them once, twice or even three times a day, if they could. Visitors always commented on how superb they looked – stepping from the decrepitude of their houses – the men in their freshly-ironed robes, the women in their turbans and brilliantly patterned prints. This personal cleanliness was required by the religion; though it meant that the women and girls had to spend a large portion of their time washing clothes.

Although a woman could not go anywhere without first asking her husband's permission, a man would leave the village sometimes for weeks on end, without even informing his wife. I once passed a man of my acquaintance on his way to take the taxi to the coast. Later in the day I was talking to his wife, one of the members of the Saniyoro Kafo, when I realized she was not aware of his departure. She was very perplexed when she found out. She had not known that he had gone, and now she did not know when he would return. That, however, was masculine behaviour. It was how a man should behave, and a woman had simply to bear it.

My translator, Jojo Bajie, was someone who was acutely conscious of how he should behave. He told me that while a man might inform his wife of his actions, or even ask her permission, if he loved her very much, he himself would never ever ask his wife's permission about anything. He had once been engaged to be married. But although the girl was very beautiful, the affair had come to grief because of her unfortunate penchant for wearing trousers. She had even come to visit him wearing these trousers, while he was working at the clinic in Sibanor. He was very distressed, for he had heard that God had forbidden women to wear trousers. He had sent messengers asking her to please desist from this habit, but to no avail. Finally he was so mortified by his fiancée's attitude that he decided to break off the engagement. 'She was very stubborn, and I know that it would not have lasted. Whoever I marry must obey me immediately and without question.'

I have never come across anyone who was quite so conscious of being someone of a particular age. He played football, drank Chinese tea and chased women compulsively, not only because he enjoyed these activities, but because he was a young man, and playing football, drinking Chinese tea and chasing women compulsively were what young men did. When we were interviewing he was very loath to translate questions on any subject he felt to be outside the proper concerns of a young man of his age group – which seemed to be virtually everything. Jojo was a devout Muslim without really knowing anything about the religion. He prayed five times a day without understanding a word of any of the prayers. But he was not at all bothered by this ignorance. He would leave such knowledge to the *talibos*, those who had been educated in the Koran on behalf of the rest of their community, of whom there were at least one in every family – so that each member of the family would benefit from this person's knowledge in the next world. Jojo was an 'English scholar', and it was incumbent upon him to benefit his family in the here and now. He felt keenly the shame of 'only' working for me, while many of his age-mates had permanent contracts with 'foreign companies'. It was, however, employment of a sort, and he had, initially at least, been desperate for the position. I was thus very surprised when he came to me one evening and told me he would no longer be able to work for me. I asked him if he had found another job.

'No.'

So what was the problem?

'These questions that you want to ask the people; I don't think it's reasonable to ask such questions.'

But we'd been asking these questions for months. We'd passed through the stage of trying to find out about the circumcision, the most controversial area of enquiry. I couldn't understand why he was suddenly telling me this.

'You know, you are trying to delve very deeply into their culture. They may not like it. In fact I know for sure that they will not like it. These village boys, they may say that this man is trying to invade our culture, and they may become very annoyed.'

'Have any of them said anything to you?'

'No! But I am afraid of it . . .' He breathed deeply. 'You know you are going very deeply into these things, this . . . ku'lo. If anyone thinks I have been helping you it may be a big problem for me. They may try to do something against me.'

Like what?

'You know, a . . . juju, or a curse or something of that sort. They will do something to you and you will not know.'

I sighed.

'I have been worried about this for some time, and I don't think I can go on. So please, just release me.'

'Someone has been speaking to him,' said Pa Konte. 'They are just trying to frighten him, to keep him from helping you. There are some very wicked people in this place . . . They don't like to see someone succeed, so they are just trying to spoil your chance. I also will speak to him, and I know that he will continue working for you, because he respects me very much.'

Soon Jojo was back at work, but I could tell he was deeply, physically uncomfortable in the role of interrogator, particularly when we were among the women. Some of the questions – those relating to childbirth – made him wince with anguish. The Wolofs had a proverb that the person who translates the insult is the same as the person who has given it, and I could tell that he found it impossible to distance himself from the questions that he was asking. I was forcing him to go against the ways of his culture. He would do it, because that was what he needed to do to survive in the earth. But he did not like it.

Before the existence of the Arabic school, Islam was taught in the village as it had always been taught – at the *karanta*. In the afternoon the children would go to the bush to find firewood. Then in the evening they would light a fire, and the talibos, the elders who were educated in the religion, would teach them to read the Koran.

Ustas Toure, the well-laundered young man who ran the Arabic school, took a dim view of this form of education. 'The study of the Koran requires tidiness and cleanliness,' he said. 'To sit down on the earth and open the Holy Koran and read it is something which is distasteful to God. And they read it senselessly. A person can be in the karanta for thirty years and not know what they are reading.'

The Arabic school, like many others in the Gambia, had been set up by the Gambia Islamic Union – an organization partly funded by the Saudi Arabian government – to teach pure Islam through the study of the language sanctified by God. It had originally been called the 'Dulaba Islamic Arab Girls' School', the aim being to improve the standard of education among the women. But there were now far more boys than girls, particularly in the higher classes. There were only two girls in Class Five and none at all in Class Six. This was partly because parents kept their daughters at home to work, but it was also, according to Ustas Toure's observation, because the girls themselves were simply not interested in learning.

'In Mauritania, Morocco, Algeria, Libya, Tunisia, Sudan, Somalia – in these countries the religion is very powerful, because the women are following God's words. Many of them are very highly educated. But here in the countries of the blacks, women do not have the desire to learn about their religion – to find out about what they don't understand. Even my wife is not educated. I have tried to teach her myself, but she has resisted.'

In Dulaba, however, there were women who were keen to learn about their religion. The Imam's wives had gone to him and told him that women of the village were in danger of forgetting their religion, and would he please agree to teach them. So since the beginning of the dry season, a group of them had met every afternoon except Thursday and Friday in the Imam's house. They were fifteen in number, and all from his compound, the compound of Fili Kunda. The older women sat back, staring into space as they intoned the words of the suras. But the younger women, those who had been to the Arabic school, leant forward, craning eagerly over huge Korans.

Haminata Ndingo, Sajonding Minte's co-wife, was the best. She was a small, rather round woman of twenty-one. She had transferred to her husband's compound the year before, but had not yet had a child. She liked reading and studying, partly because she was good at it, but also because she believed that if she kept at it God might save a very good place for her in heaven.

When she was at the Arabic school they had taught her how to translate the suras into Mandinka. But she had forgotten most of what she had learnt there. Now she could not even translate her daily prayers into Mandinka. There was only one of the suras that she could say in her own language.

'I swear by the five o'clock prayer that we will all one day die. And those of us who agreed to obey the words of God, those who are doing very good things towards God, should advise each other of the truth. They should advise people to forgive each other.'

She was trying to understand, but it was very difficult since they were Mandingkos and not Arabs. She had the hope, however, that God would not punish them for it. And now she had heard that one day soon the Imam would be teaching them the meanings.

The last days of Sunkary Konong, the month before Ramadan, and the beginning of the fasting month itself, were traditionally the time of the *manyo bitto* – the ceremony in which people sent their daughters to live permanently in their husbands' compounds. Any act of virtue a woman performed towards her husband during Ramadan would be a great blessing for her in the next world, and the people wanted their children to have the benefit of these blessings. This year, however, the elders had decreed that, because of the very severe economic problems the village was facing, there would be no manyo bitto. The brides would be transferred without ceremony. Their hair would not be plaited. There would be no white faneau. And there would be no feasting.

The women protested. They said that the manyo bitto was their custom. They expected it, and they were prepared to make whatever sacrifice was necessary in order that it should happen. Some said that they would not allow their daughters to transfer until they could be sent in the proper way. But the elders were unrelenting. They said that the white faneau, the fani koyo, was not mentioned in the Koran, and if anyone said that anything bad would happen to these girls because they had not had it, they were fooling themselves. Finally the women gave in. Life was too short, they said, to keep these children at home.

The first of the manyos – Njonji Sise of Fili Kunda – was transferred four days before the beginning of Ramadan, on a night of thick, anonymous blackness. Soon after dinner the house of the women filled up with children and young women, the crashing of the basin resounding against the corrugated-iron roof. A pan of water stood in the middle of the floor. Soon the older women would be arriving to wash the bride.

'Please!' came a sudden male voice, quiet, but firm. 'We are almost in Sungkaro [Ramadan]. Have some respect.' A tall bulky figure could just be made out in the doorway, his pale gown glowing faintly in the dimness.

'Sungkaro!' called a woman's voice, incredulous from the darkness at the other end of the room. There was laughter.

'Yes,' said the man, bristling. 'So please leave it. There will be no washing of the bride tonight.'

'We will not leave it,' said one of the older women. 'The bride will be washed.'

'Yes.' I heard Sajonding's harsh voice. 'She is going to be washed.'

'Please', said the mother, a thin rather nervous woman. 'Be calm. This should not be a big problem.'

'She will not be washed,' said the father, his voice now rising. 'If you wash her, you will know.'

'Come on,' said the older woman. 'Get the water. We will wash her now.'

'I tell you, you will not wash her,' said the father. 'This is a Muslim place, and the Holy Month is almost upon us.'

'Please,' said the mother, almost beside herself. 'Everyone just leave. Don't insist upon it.'

There was a crash of metal and then a gurgling sound, as the father poured the bride's bathwater out into the yard.

'*Lai la ilahah!*' said the women, disbelieving. And then he was gone.

'But the washing . . .' said the mother in despair. 'People always wash their children before they send them to their husbands.'

When she had been blessed by the male elders of the compound, and advised on the modes of behaviour befitting her new status, the manyo was led off along the street towards her husband's compound by a great crowd of women and children.

Another manyo was at the moment leaving her parents' compound close to the bantaba, and as the two processions crossed each others' paths in the darkness, I somehow got detached from the first and found myself following the second up the main street towards Bajo Kunda. They were all singing, their voices filling the dusty darkness with the same refrain, over and over again:

> '*Hey Al Marky joobay jambaro!*
> *Hey Al Marky joobay jambaro!*'
>
> '*Hey look at Mark – the champion!*'

What had this to do with the transfer of the manyo? Nothing. It was just a song that they liked to sing and the fact that its meaning had nothing to do with the purpose of the celebration was neither here nor there.

I had long since ceased to feel flattered by such aggrandizement. I no longer even felt any embarrassment. I simply accepted it as the way things had come to be; the same as I accepted the fact that everyone, even the men, now referred to me as '*Jambaro*' – '*Marky Jambaro*' – 'Mark the Champion'. I would have been wrong to attribute any particular significance to this. It was all just for amusement. But there was no doubt that I had come to take their affection for granted.

When we reached the compound, the manyo sat down on a mat, draped in her faneau, and she and her husbands – her actual husband and his brothers and cousins – were lectured at some length by the elders of the compound on how they should behave towards each other. I sat down with my tape recorder in the midst of the elders. '*Yo! Ntolu la Marky*,' they chuckled. 'Our own Mark.'

'Ibraima,' said the head of the compound. 'Your parents have tried their best to give you this girl. So please, be in unity with her. She has come all the way from her parents' compound, expecting you to support her. So if you don't know how to behave towards her, it's of no use. Women are not powerful. All the power is with the men. So you should help her very much. This girl is here for you to show her the way – to advise her, to teach her what to do. May God save the place this manyo has come from. I'm praying for her both day and night.'

'*Amin,*' said the crowd. '*Amin.*'

When the prayers were over, the young women and the girls rushed from the compound, and the air was once again filled with laughter. They began to make their way along the north side of the village towards the compound to which Njonji, the first of the manyos, had been transferred. I became aware of the young men moving all around us in the darkness, like hyenas among a flock of sheep – for the manyo bitto was a night when everyone was at play.

Ahead of me I could make out Munya's tall, broad-shouldered form in the grey, foggy darkness, walking ahead of me in the centre of a group of young girls.

'There she is,' said Sullu, who had suddenly materialized at my side. 'You can have her. I will give her to you tonight.'

'I thought she was your person,' I said.

'She is tired of me.'

'But she's not tired of me?'

'No.'

As we entered the husband's compound, I was vaguely aware of a figure rising from among the group of young men sitting drinking Chinese tea in front of one of the houses. Suddenly he was calling me, and leading me among the milling figures towards the other side of the compound. It was Karanjaneh, the second son of the head of the compound.

He was pointing towards the far entrance of the compound, in the direction of my house. And he was telling me to leave the compound and not come back. Gasps of incredulity went up from the crowd. He said it in such a bland, deadpan voice that at first I thought he was joking. I told him to come back into the main body of the crowd where I would find someone to fully translate.

A stunned silence fell over the crowd, as his voice took on a fierce eagerness.

'This man has come here to steal the secrets of the women,' he shouted towards the elders, who sat grouped around the bentengo. 'He wants to take them away and write them in a book. This man is someone very wicked. If you see him talking to your wives, you should drive him away immediately.'

I suddenly didn't feel at all well. I could feel around me that sense of mounting chaos that in Africa seems to attend any kind of altercation – the sense that anything could happen, and that those around me, even those who wished me well, would be so caught up in the collective emotions they would be powerless to protect me. The fact that I could barely see what was going on added to my sense of panic. Did this person have a knife? I wondered.

The husband of the manyo and the young man's elder brother – the husband of Senabu of the Saniyoro Kafo – led me to one side, to where the father, the compound head, was sitting. He bade me sit down next to him.

'Don't pay any attention,' he said. 'He has been smoking tai nyamo. He doesn't know what he is saying.' He was a short, wiry man, his beard now almost white. He was not one of the scholars of the village. He was a farmer and a hunter, a tough, practical man with a ready and engaging laugh. He had built this compound from nothing. He had been the age of the second son when McGregor had first brought the MRC to Dulaba, shortly after the Second World War. McGregor had appointed him his representative among the people and he had fulfilled that function ever since. Now, however, his voice sounded sad and resigned.

'We no longer know him. He has spent so much time away from us, so much time at the coast, that we no longer consider him one of us. He has no respect for his mother, and no respect for his father. So how can we expect him to show respect to a stranger?'

He told me they thought I was the same as 'Kamble Fatty' – David Gamble, the anthropologist who had compiled the Dulaba census. He was always asking questions. But he had been familiar to them. They had called him 'the Curiosity Man'. And when the roofs of the village had been destroyed by storms, he had heard about it, even in Tubabidu, and he had sent money for the whole of the village to be reroofed in corrugate. This was why, he said, I did not surprise them, and they did not have two minds towards me.

At this point a figure burst through the crowd, his voice now almost hysterical. 'I swear that if he comes here again, I will wound him.' The husband of the manyo, a rather thin man, attempted to remonstrate with him. But he soon shrank back under the ferocity of Karanjaneh's onslaught.

'I swear it!'

'You'd better go,' said the elder.

The women, the ostensible subject of this incident, stood around us in the darkness, watching in silence.

'He is bad,' said Sullu, as we sat in his house some time later. 'He is my elder brother, but he is bad.'

'Why is he bad?' I asked.

'Because he disturbed you. It is bad to disturb people. We do not disturb tubabs in this village.'

The young man seemed an unlikely adversary. I had never been particularly friendly with him, but we had always been on perfectly cordial terms; though now I thought about it, had there not always been something not quite wholesome about that cordiality? Had there not always been beneath it an odd kind of bitterness – on both sides – that was only barely concealed? He was tall and slender, with red, satiated eyes, and a thin, rather nervous laugh. And although very black, he had a drooping moustache, which gave him an oddly oriental appearance. Like all the young men of the village, he always held himself very upright. I would see him often, standing on the forecourt of the MRC compound –

his form narrow but well-proportioned and elegant in its straightness, echoing that of the tree that stood outside my study window, smiling easily as he slapped hands with the MRC workers and all the others who moved endlessly, and with no apparent purpose, across that stage.

That African smile! How deceptive it could be. Interpreted by most outsiders as a sign of the innate simplicity and informality of the people, it was itself one of the formalities of their culture, as necessary as greeting, or shaking hands among the men. A person who did not smile was condemned in that society. And it seemed to me in retrospect that there had always been a particularly evident falseness, a strained quality in Karanjaneh's smile. I had always addressed him with rather abrupt familiarity as *morro* – mate. He had laughed, but he had perhaps not found it so very amusing.

And I, almost without realizing it, had been irritated by his presence there in the compound. For it seemed to me that his leisurely ways, his very physical elegance itself, were at the expense of the breaking, morally and physically, of the women. What was he doing, just standing there for hours on end? Why didn't he go out and do something to benefit his father and his mother and his sisters?

What right did he have to speak so proprietorially of the culture of the women? If I had offended them by my behaviour, they could have spoken for themselves. I would have been even more annoyed, if my instinctive reaction had not been one of guilt.

'He is confused,' said Sullu. 'He has no job. He was a long time in Kombo, working as a driver. But now he has no job. This is why his mind is not steady.'

I could see now the sense of inferiority that he, like many of the young men of the village, felt when measuring themselves against the Civil Servants. They were all blacks. They were all boys of the same age-group. But the chances those people had had – to get good jobs, to wear nice clothes, to help their parents – the village boys had not had. In refusing to allow a European school to be built in the village, the elders had been trying to save their community. But where had that left their children?

In the dry season, he had gone out into the world, like many others of his age-group. They had travelled to Kombo, looking for work. And it was there that they realized that they had nothing to offer. They had waited at the garages at Serekunda and Bakau – offering to clean the vehicles for the drivers, in the hope that they might be taught to drive. They had hung around by the hotels and on the beaches, along with hundreds of others, hoping to 'assist' the tourists. But mostly they had just sat. For even in these hopeless endeavours, the boys of Kombo, even those who had no schooling, were ahead of them.

Some, despite their lack of schooling, managed to succeed in business, found a trade or unskilled employment, and built their own compounds there. But most returned to the village just before the rains, to hack once more into the grey earth.

Now the school had been built, and the young people who were sent there would have as good a chance as any other young people in the country. But Karanjaneh and the others of his generation had missed their chance, and they would never have it again.

They had started evening classes for themselves in the Community Centre. The teachers had agreed to teach them Maths and English. Then the building of the new camp had begun, and they had all got jobs as labourers, and they were too tired to study in the evenings. Soon the new camp would be completed, and they would be back where they were before. Nowhere.

It was hardly surprising that, now he was back in the village, Karanjaneh should attempt to defend the women. For they were the ones who had made him the only thing that he was – a man. And no matter how poor he was, no matter how low he had sunk, a man was at least more than a woman.

But although I understood all of this, I no longer had the emotional energy to empathize. Whatever bitterness this person felt was his business. I would soon be leaving. The date of my departure was set. And from the moment I had booked my flight at the Gambia Airways office in Banjul, it was as though a spell had been broken. For the first time in many months I could envisage life beyond that place. I could imagine my life continuing outside Dulaba. More than that, I was looking forward to it.

Almost from the moment of my most intimate and most intense involvement with the people of the village, I had realized that what I wanted from them – what my background, my upbringing, my culture led me to expect from them – I would not have, I could not have.

'When you are young,' Father J had told me, 'everything will upset you. But then you toughen yourself. You must toughen yourself – so that nothing can hurt you.'

So during the long, lonely afternoons of the dry season, I steeled myself, as every African had done, against the idea that one could control one's destiny, against the idea that one could attain that which one's heart led one to feel one was entitled to. It was as though, buffeted by the dust and the hot winds, one's soul were drying out in the harmattan. And when the process was completed, I realized that the feelings that had bound me to that place were no longer there.

But I still didn't feel I was entitled to go quite yet. I still had time to live out in that place. Soon it would be Ramadan, and I felt I could not leave while the people were fasting, and I wanted to leave a further two weeks for the people to gather their strength. Besides which, there were still certain things I did not fully understand, certain questions I had yet to ask.

'Now you have a new person,' said Sullu, suddenly rousing himself from half-sleep. 'Munya.'

'She's interested?'

'Very.'

Her compound lay on the other side of the avenue from my house. Sometimes at night I would hear the strangers, young men working at the new camp, calling out to her to come and chat with them, or to bring food to them. Each of these exhortations was met with a stony and indifferent silence. 'Please, Munya! Have mercy on us!' they bellowed, to great guffaws from their fellows.

Sullu had told me that shortly after dinner, on the nights when there was no moon, she would come and visit me. She would knock on the side door that opened directly onto the street, and enter through the empty room that had once been Kemeseng's shop.

I was not sure of the wisdom of this idea. There would still be many people about at that hour and, moon or no moon, they seemed to be able to identify each other with great ease. In any case I was not sure that this was now the involvement I wanted with Munya. I wanted to understand her, to understand her inside herself.

She was, as I had suspected all along, not the daughter of Gunjur at all, but had been born in Karafa Kunda, the daughter of Gunjur's elder sister. But as Gunjur had no children, the girl had been sent to Dulaba as soon as she came from the breast, to be 'disciplined' by her aunt. So she had grown up knowing herself to be a citizen of Karafa Kunda, but never getting to know her real parents – indeed never having any desire to, since she called Gunjur her mother. And this had perhaps contributed to her slight sense of detachment. Not that she was alienated from the people of the village – indeed she was one of the most popular women of her age-group – but of all the women, she was the one I found it easiest to identify with, because she was the one who seemed least tied to her position, the least static in her responses to the world – as if she were somehow freer in her soul.

Many of the women appeared to have ceased to exist as free individuals from the moment they had transferred to their husbands' compounds at the age of twenty-one or twenty-two. But Munya, one felt, could still be anyone or anything. When I saw her in the street, on her way to and from Dr Sabari's house, darkly intent among her thoughts, it seemed that she, like me, was someone who only happened to be living in that place – that she was not yet completely physically and emotionally of it.

Her great friend Darbon Jammeh had never transferred. Before the time had come she had divorced her husband, and now she had left the village, probably forever.

And Munya, when she had first been given to her husband, would often refuse to go to him. She would tell Gunjur that she did not love him, that she would rather sleep in the bush. And she would run out of the compound and spend the night in the bush or in the shells of houses that were still being built. When her husband sent his clothes to be washed, or Gunjur told her that she should now serve some food for him, she would say, 'No, I don't love him. I'm not going to take anything to him.'

Nobody went to the marabouts. At least, neither Gunjur, nor her husband, nor the girl's real parents did. But after a time, Gunjur had observed that Munya went to his compound without complaining, and she took his food to him, and washed his clothes as a wife should.

Now she was twenty-two. And although she was happy living in her aunt's compound there were already several women younger than her who had transferred to their husbands. How many women before her, of singular, indeed belligerent independence of spirit, had gone without complaining – or if complaining, at least finally agreeing to remain there?

Darbon had resisted. She had done what most European women would like to think they would do under such circumstances. But all those others had not. And now, before the end of Ramadan, Munya also must go there. There was no question that she would not.

'Chah!' said Pa Konte, the morning after the incident in Minte Kunda. 'How can he know what you are doing? He does not know anything. They have been speaking to him. They are using him to try to disturb you . . . I wish I had been there. Anyone who insults you – I must fight them. There is no way out.'

Safi Mama, Gunjur and Awa Bajo arrived.

'I wanted to put you on my back and carry you like a baby,' said Safi Mama. 'I felt such sympathy for you.' But of course she had not said anything, for it was unthinkable that a women should intervene in such a dispute.

They told me to continue with my work, asking whatever questions I wanted. 'We will not mind,' they said. 'We will help you.'

In Dulaba, the worship of ancestors had not been practised – in a literal sense – within the memory of the people. For like most Muslim villages, they traced their history only from the moment of conversion. Ties of blood, and the names by which they were expressed, were none the less as important to them as they were to any pagan people. Each morning as they greeted each other, they would respond by using the time-honoured phrases used to 'praise' that person's name – 'Sise More', 'Seydi Minte', 'Jammeh Jilanko', 'Bajo Dibbah'. One would hear these phrases hundreds of times as the people continued to greet each other during the course of the day. 'Sise More' meant 'Sises are marabouts'. Everyone knew that. But otherwise the origin and significance of these phrases were unknown to most of the people. They knew only that these were the words that had always been used to maintain a sense of harmony and respect between the people of the village.

One often heard the young people educated in Western ideas complaining that while the soul and reggae singers were saying things that were relevant today, the griots, and the popular singers of West Africa, who were their spiritual and in many cases their physical heirs, were merely listing names. 'Youssou Ndour,' said one, referring to the most popular singer of the region. 'That man is howling in the air. He is just singing the songs the Wolof women sing at naming ceremonies. His music means nothing.'

In Dulaba too, the women's songs were crammed with names – of their friends, their age mates, their children, and the people of the male line into which they were married. They never seemed to tire of singing about themselves and each other. At times this constant, obsessive self-referral made them seem almost childishly parochial and self-absorbed. Yet it was one's name that linked one to one's ancestors – to the flesh that had given one life – and in preserving and calling forth these names, the griots were performing an essentially sacred function. So the women's singing was an assertion, a celebration of their physical closeness, their unity, their *badiya* – their 'relatedness' – as they called it: the very factors which gave the village such vigorous human life, and which they believed guaranteed their physical survival on the earth.

Now, however, for the first time, I felt this physical closeness as a negative phenomenon, as something that must inevitably exclude me. And although I continued to live and even sleep closely among them, I could feel the instinctive and automatic loyalty to one of their own blood, that went beyond any questions of moral or even of rational choice. It was as though the one flesh of the village were physically closing itself against me.

'They are like that,' Jere Jarjou had told me almost immediately after my arrival. 'If you go against one of them, they will all be against you.'

Many of the women who resented the amount of attention I had paid the Saniyoro Kafo, and even members of the Saniyoro Kafo who were not particular friends of my particular friends, did not now bother to hide their irritation at my presence. I would hear the young girls laughing at how that young man had threatened to beat me, and the children would say quite openly '*Marky, a mang betia*' – 'Mark is not good'. Among the men, now that they no longer felt obliged to maintain a mask of almost obsequious geniality, I observed a hardness I had never noticed before. I could now easily imagine the callousness with which they treated their women. Particularly among those close to the immediate family of the young man himself, there were feelings of genuine indignation. It did not matter that I had not done him any personal wrong; whether his feelings were even justified was beside the point. He was *ntolu la dingo* – our child – and I, a stranger, had upset him.

Those people to whom I had become particularly close, whom I had made my 'own' either by materially assisting them, or through assiduously cultivating the badiya – the relationship – between us, remained loyal. In fact during this period I became closer to them than ever before. But though there were several, such as Fatounding, who had been angry on my behalf, there was no possibility that these people could ultimately side with me against Karanjaneh. I was a tubab. I would soon be leaving. And when I left, I would go finally, and completely, as all tubabs did. But they would have to go on living with Karanjaneh. And no matter how much time he spent on the coast – even if he left the country altogether – he would be part of them. Through the laws of badiya that bound them all, he was their son, their brother, and their husband from this world unto the next. Friendship and love were for the earth. But marriage and badiya were for Alahira.

Everywhere I heard the words, '*Kumpa baliya a mang betia*' – 'Curiosity is not good'; '*Nyininkaro a mang betia*' – 'Asking questions is not good.' I now realized that it was this curiosity that was at the root of the problem. It hadn't occurred to me when I began my project that its aims would be fundamentally at variance with the values of the people it was supposed to be about. In Europe, questioning, criticism and analysis were tools, essential to understanding a world in which nothing was fixed, in which everything was in a state of continual flux. In Africa they were considered to be inherently negative and destructive phenomena.

I reflected with some bitterness that of all the Europeans who had come to that place, I was the only one who had come because of the people themselves. I was the one who had taken the most interest in them as individuals. And I was also the only one who had managed seriously to upset them.

I now realized how many of the people in the social groups in which I moved were not only highly ambivalent towards me, but had little love for each other. There were among them all kinds of invisible tensions – allegiances and hostilities – but because of the nature of that society, they remained unexpressed. Peace – the harmonious order of the group – was placed above the interests or even the rights of any individual, and to disrupt it by expressing resentment was to sin against the society that had given one life. So, apart from occasional outbursts of extreme violence, the placid surface of the world was seldom disturbed.

Just beneath it, however, was a paralysed and paralysing under-layer of resentment and mistrust. The people had a concern amounting to obsession with paying back any and every disservice they had been rendered. And as refusal was one of the few forms of resistance accorded them by their culture, they would have to wait, often for years, to do it. One day that person would have to come to them. One day that person would need something from them. And that was the time that they would look the other way. Meanwhile, they worked and played and sometimes even ate and slept side by side. Life had to go on.

If people were related, they were compelled to forgive each other almost anything. Indeed, proverbially, a relative could not 'refuse' another relative anything. Even relatives, however, were intensely suspicious and jealous of each other. And people generally were terrified of malice, not only of specific acts of magic and witchcraft, but of a general human malevolence they called 'wickedness'. Unlike in England, where the strongest emotion most people ever feel towards another human being is mild irritation, the Africans hated fiercely and completely. If they had been wronged, they did not speculate on the psychological or sociological causes of the other person's behaviour. They said simply that they were wicked. Nor did it occur to them to speculate that they themselves may have been in the wrong. Guilt was not, as far as I could ascertain, a characteristic African emotion. Indeed, even if someone were demonstrably in the wrong, they would blame the other person for the shame they had been made to feel.

Pa Konte was a charismatic, mercurial character who naturally charmed and offended many people with great ease. And as he was attractive to many women, he was naturally loathed by many men. He protected himself from this antagonism by bathing daily in liquid jujus he obtained from the marabouts.

'They just sit there,' he said, 'under the mango tree, smoking ganja and back-biting people. They have seen you going about your work. They say you have had the chance to come here and take something from here. But what have you given them? Nothing. So they have just looked for a way to try to spoil your chance. They have used this boy Karanjaneh to try to disturb you.'

I too knew who these people were. And it no longer surprised me that those who had spoken most patronizingly about the villagers' culture, who had referred to them as 'these illiterates', should declare themselves the most concerned when this culture was supposedly being invaded. I no longer really cared. I was leaving. I would leave them there to be consumed by their pathetic resentment.

But I was myself still far from completely eschewing African emotion. I had heard that Karanjaneh now regretted what he had said, that he did not know why he had done it. But still he had said nothing to me.

'Now you are a real African,' said Ramou Jagne, with some amusement. 'Involving yourself in all these petty arguments and disputes.'

She was right, of course. This man had caused me considerable inconvenience. And unless he came to me personally and apologized, I would never forgive him. And I would continue to hold the bitterness of it in my heart.

On the last day of the month, the Civil Servants held a small party at Ramou Jagne's house. We sat outside in armchairs, eating *chakhri*, a kind of millet porridge, from plastic mugs, under the utter blackness. It was, they said, the last bit of pleasure we would have for thirty days. For in Ramadan there should be no singing or dancing, no drumming, and not one single hand-clap. No one should commit adultery or even think lustful thoughts about anyone who was not their wife. 'Do you mean to say,' I asked Sullu, 'that no one in this village is going to commit adultery during Ramadan?'

'At night, it's not a problem,' he said. 'But people never do it in the afternoon. Firstly, God doesn't like it. And secondly, you won't be able to do it if you're fasting.'

The villagers waited one more day, until they had seen the moon, then everyone, even Sanyang, the Rastafarian, Kor, the Communist, and Pa Konte, who had said he would not, was fasting.

One of the purposes of the fast was to enable the Muslim to identify with the sufferings of the poor. But it had not occured to the people of Dulaba that self-denial might be somehow inherently good for them. They believed themselves to be the poorest people of the earth, and they had already had several opportunities for self-denial during the course of the year. They fasted because they were afraid of God, and because they wanted the blessings, for Alahira.

There was, they believed, one day in Ramadan that was more

auspicious than all the others. If you fasted on that day, you would receive more blessings than if you fasted on all the other days put together. If they had known which it was they would have fasted only on that day. Unfortunately, it was only the great marabouts, the chosen ones of God, who knew, and they didn't tell. So everyone else had to fast for the whole month. During the course of those days, however, they would buy for themselves any delicious thing they saw, for having suffered through the heat of the day, they felt they deserved something particularly nice with which to break their fast. Even the poorest people would try to find a little sugar to add to their porridge if they possibly could. So, far from helping people to economize, self-denial made Ramadan the most expensive month of the year.

Thus the previous week had been fraught with tension and anxiety: the Civil Servants all rushing around trying to find money to send sugar to their parents, everyone looking for places in fridges and freezers in which to store their water. For although the clay jars of the village kept the water at a perfectly adequate level of coolness, it was considered a matter of great prestige to be able to break one's fast with *fridgo kono gio* – water from a fridge. As there were only six fridges in the whole of Kiang, five of them in the MRC compound in Dulaba, and well over a thousand people in the village, this naturally created considerable antagonism.

But whatever the small absurdities of the fast, there was no doubt that the people really suffered.

The days would begin as normal – the early morning shouting at the taps as loud, if not louder than usual. But people returned early from the edge of the bush where they were fencing their gardens, and by the afternoon they had reached a state of speechless stupefaction – many looking close to collapse. And while the men liked to sleep through as much of the day as possible, the women had to continue their tasks – cooking, gathering firewood, carrying the great panfuls of water – into the early evening.

The Civil Servants ate two meals, one of delicacies – fried meat, chicken, fish, salads, eaten with bread – at the moment of sundown. And then our usual dinner of rice, at about ten, after the *nafilo*, the lengthy mid-evening prayer, which took place only during Ramadan. Even this second meal was more sumptuous than usual. Frequently there would be benakino with meat, and the durango would be laced with thick red palm oil.

The villagers liked to break their fast with 'local tea' – hot water infused with leaves from the bush, and a hunk of bread if they could get it. Most, however, ate their one meal straight away. And there was nothing very remarkable about this meal. Nor was there often very much of it.

On the third night of Ramadan, the 'great girls' of Salum Kunda, Munya and Jhibaila, were conveyed to their husbands. Jhibaila was to go immediately after sundown to Karafa Kunda in the ITC lorry. Munya would go later, for her husband's compound lay only twenty yards from the place where she had lived since she came from her mother's breast.

Shortly before sundown, I found her sitting on the bentengo in front of Gunjur's house – the woman she considered to be her mother, the one who had done everything for her.

Her head was lowered towards the ground, occasionally moving as she mulled things over in her mind. From time to time she would dab at her eyes with a rag.

'The whole village knows that she does not want to go there, that she does not love the husband,' Pa Konte had said. 'But they also know that she will go there.'

Did the husband know that she didn't love him?

'Obviously he must know.'

So why would he want to marry someone who didn't love him?

'Maybe he believes that she will submit. And if the marriage lasts, eventually she must, because when she has had four children, that is the time that a woman will know that she is lost and she will never leave that place. Even if she is prepared to leave herself, she will never leave the children there with the co-wife.'

A Jola woman, a stranger, who was staying in the compound, leaned over the mortar into which she was pounding. '*Manyo be kumbo,*' she sang with a laugh. 'The manyo is crying. *Ai Waali!*'

Others laughed too. I left, and I didn't return that night. Over the following days, however, I noticed that the clothes Munya had worn, the crimson head-tie and the dish-cloth vest, were now the property of Gunjur's co-wives. The manyo should leave these things behind, as she should leave behind the behaviour she had learned in her mother's compound.

'Woman, do not be fooled by the world. Everything you see in this earth will one day come to an end. We will all die. The trees will die, and these beautiful buildings that you see will tumble to the ground. Your husband is your way to heaven. So whatever difficulties your husband faces, you can face them with him. From these difficulties you're going to find your blessings for tomorrow. But don't think that if you cannot face them that there are people who are going to help you. We will never support you in anything now. You are not a child any more. You are a mature woman. What you did before by mistake, now you do it deliberately. The habits you had here you must leave behind when you go to your husband's compound. So don't look back. You have nothing behind you now.'

'You are going to face two people when you arrive in that place. So accept to be treated as a child there. Be forgiving. Forgiveness is something that is of great profit to a woman. May God make you a forgiving woman.'

'There are three kinds of women: a dog, a donkey and a human being. The woman who is a dog, no one can make her sit down. And when she comes and goes, she says what has happened to her, no matter what it is. A donkey, before it is happy, you have to beat it – so much that everyone in the village will come and look and say, "Hurh! You're going to kill her!" But the human being – she is the woman whose husband takes great care of her, because she has obeyed his words.'

Every few nights another of the manyos would be taken to her husband. Then the women would dance and sing as much as they liked. And though their husbands disapproved, they didn't say anything, for they knew how the women had been angered when the manyo's bath had been poured away. And while the older women washed the manyo and danced in the house of the woman, the young women and girls crowded around and onto the bentengo outside, leaping as one in the grey, muggy darkness, and chanting in time to the rhythms from inside the house: 'Hey! Hey! Hey!'

At one such event, a figure approached me, a child tied on its back. It was Munya. She was now confined to her husband's house for one week, leaving it only for the dances organized in her honour, or to attend the transfer of other brides. She asked me to come and chat with her at her husband's house the following day.

Sometimes at night there would be a few drops of rain, and the days were often overcast, the sky crowded with a bilious greyness. But they did not call this rain. It was known as *wammo* – the false rain – and the air remained thick and hot.

I couldn't see Munya as I passed through the compound, and not wishing to intrude on this time of seclusion, I went and sat with the women shelling groundnuts in the adjacent yard. As I was leaving, however, I was told that the manyo was calling me. I turned to see her standing smiling, her big frame filling the doorway of her husband's house.

In the newly plastered reception room, her new basins and enamelled bowls stood piled on a table with a cloth over it. A number of photographs were neatly framed on the wall above. The walls had not been whitewashed, but the mud retained its pristine pinkish-brown colour. A doorway led through into the bedroom. I sat cautiously in the wooden armchair closest to the outside door. Munya sat next to me. The ceiling of the room was open to the corrugated iron of the roof above, the roof it shared with the spare room next door, and the house of the women at the end of the block. It occurred to me that there would be little privacy in any of these rooms.

I started at the sudden deep voice from the bedroom, and looked through to see a well-built, handsome man – very dark in complexion – lying sprawled on the iron bedstead, the mosquito net folded neatly back around him. He looked back at me with an expression both furtive and slightly mocking – as though unsure whether to feel triumph at having caught me alone with his wife, or embarrassment at being found in this prone position. In the end he simply smiled back at me, a trifle helplessly. He was, I suppose, in mid to late thirties. It was difficult to see why anyone should take such great exception to him; except that he might ultimately have been rather wet – though, even if he wasn't, why should anyone love him?

I sat back down, and the conversation moved slowly along; a three-way conversation between the two of us in our armchairs and the disembodied voice on the other side of the wall. Munya leant forward in her chair, her elbows on her knees, her surprisingly short, stubby fingers fidgeting all the time with a shiny metal object. She would peer closely at it, pressing it against her nose, and then different parts of her face. On closer observation, it proved to be the wing mirror of a car. She seemed both abstracted – unselfconscious as a child – and at the same time deeply self-conscious. It was as though everything the husband said made her cringe with embarrassment.

The conversation moved on to the subject of politics. The husband supported the opposition party, the NCP. I asked Munya if she supported them too. 'The NCP are not good,' she said.

'Why's that?' I asked.

'I support Jawara,' she said. 'He is good.'

'Why?' I asked. 'Because your father supports him?'

'Yes,' she said, enjoying the frankness of her answer.

I looked at her. She was staring straight ahead, but in the mirror, pressed at an angle against her face, I could see one slanting diamond-shaped eye staring straight at me.

The American air raid on Tripoli had happened only a few days before. But while many of the Civil Servants had been horrified by this attack on African soil, the husband thought it had been a good thing. 'Those people have been disturbing Reagan,' he said. 'Now he has punished them very strongly.' He naturally thought that I, a European and an unbeliever, would take Reagan's part. I explained that not everyone in Britain supported Thatcher and Reagan. 'Your brain is very good,' he said.

All the time there was a hissing and a murmuring as he fiddled with his radio. After a time I began to notice something oddly familiar about the fragments of intelligible sound that impinged intermittently on my consciousness. Then, through the dense, heightened atmosphere of the husband's house, I became aware of another parallel atmosphere struggling through the buzzing and the static to break into ours. I thought I could hear English middle-class voices. They appeared to be engaged in some sort of argument. Then they became suddenly louder and clearer, and it was as if there were invisible presences around us in the room, shouting. It sounded like an afternoon play on Radio 4. He had tuned in to the BBC world service. It probably was an afternoon play from Radio 4.

'Why don't you just leave me alone?' said a voice.

'You've been saying that for years,' said another. 'You don't know what it means to be alone.'

'Get out!' said the first. 'Get out! Get out!'

Everyone was intrigued.

'This is in English,' I said. 'It's a husband and wife quarrelling.'

'Aha,' they said, almost together.

Now they knew.

Gradually the people were becoming used to fasting. I followed Binta Sise and Ramatoulai Jallo, the Fulani woman from Fili Kunda, to the salt flats in search of tiny fish. They caught them by damming the tidal streams that ran beside the laterite track across the flats. When they had walled off a section about six feet in length with handfuls of the soft mud, they began bailing out the water. Then, when the pool was almost empty, they sifted the remainder. Binta sprawled on the muddy bank, holding a battered, conical basket over the edge of the dam, while Rama poured basins of water through it. It was horrendously hot. All around us the rock-hard, salt-encrusted mud stretched into the distance – like a burnished steel plate throwing off white light in all directions. Even though they would not drink for many hours, the two women talked ceaselessly, paying the minimum amount of attention to what they were doing.

Binta had left the village at the beginning of harvest time, and gone to stay with her husband's older brother in Serekunda. It had been said that the whole family were going to live there permanently, but at the beginning of the circumcision she had returned. Now she said she could not begin to describe the sweetness of that place, and that she had been very annoyed when her husband had forced her to return. However, I recalled that when I went to visit the compound in Serekunda, during my Christmas break, she had seemed far from comfortable. Demba Tamba had said that in Kombo she would grow very fat and beautiful, because she would not have to do any farming there. She was indeed beautiful, but so much thinner I scarcely recognized her. She was tired, she said. Kombo was sweet, but Dulaba was also sweet. She would be returning to Dulaba in a week's time, and she seemed to be looking forward to it. 'Dulaba is very sweet!' she said again. There were a lot of women living in that compound. Maybe it hadn't been so easy to just move in with them – as they all knew each other, and the place, so well. Since she had returned to the village, however, she had seemed much quieter and more subdued, and genuinely appeared to regret the passing of that period of her life. But it had been her husband's decision, and that was all there was to it.

Rama was a good ten years older than Binta, but they lived in adjacent yards, and often worked and socialized together. She was very fair in complexion, and had a resigned and sadly used look about her.

She said that she would come to my room that evening, while Binta said she was keen to forge a relationship with Jojo, my translator. I said I thought he'd be more than interested.

'He is just a boy,' said Binta. 'I don't think he will know what to do.'

'If you try him, you will know,' I said.

'That's true,' she said.

I said I had heard that her husband had made a very good fence around her garden, and that she now loved him very much.

'That is not true at all,' she said. 'I wanted to divorce him, but this woman persuaded me not to.'

'Binta is always refusing to have sex with her husband,' said Rama. 'That is not good.'

Suddenly a silver speck appeared in the basket – flicking itself in great leaps backwards and forwards across the rough wicker. How it didn't just jump out of the basket, I had no idea. But the two women seemed not at all concerned. They just knew that it wouldn't. And even if it did, it would soon be replaced by another. Sure enough, as another bowlful of the grey-brown water hit the basket, there were another five or six of them. When they had five or six handfuls of the tiny fish, they scraped them into an enamel basin. Then, when the pool was completely drained, they went over to the other side of the track and began damming another section of the stream.

Further back along the track in the direction of the village, five young girls were engaged in the same activity. They stood in a line, stripped down to their be-chos, all bailing in time. They viewed my arrival with some circumspection in view of their nakedness. They hadn't yet been given to their husbands but they soon would be, and they were both defiantly aware of their bodies and puritanically defensive of them.

'Mark is looking at my body,' said one.

'Is that bad?' I asked.

'It's bad,' she said.

Another told me to come and help them.

'Hey,' chided the others. 'Do some work yourself. Don't spend all your time chatting with boys!'

'Mark,' said another. '*I ba dala to* – you're on the threshold.'

'And you,' I said, 'you're in the middle – *I ba tema.*'

They all crooned with hilarity and pleasure. This was what the young girls of today liked to say. One heard it at night, breathed seductively from the darkness as one passed along the village streets, or in the afternoons, called cheekily from under the mango trees where the women and girls sat shelling groundnuts. '*I ba dala to – I ba tema.*' It was a marvellous expression, and though I had been assured it meant 'absolutely nothing', they managed to wring every possible shade of lewdness from it.

When they had finished draining their pool, they lay on their stomachs in the water on the other side of the track, splashing themselves with the water they could not take into their bodies. 'Marky, come and bathe!' they shouted. Then they got up and went trotting away over the hard, sun-baked mud towards the mangroves in search of shellfish, covering their buttocks with their basins to shield them from my gaze.

Sona was now so massively pregnant that she resembled a great globe with legs. I found her sitting in the dust at the edge of the village, her limbs splayed out in front of her great girth as she jabbed into the dust with an iron bar flattened at one end. She was wearing a head-tie of canary yellow which flashed brilliantly in the sunshine, but she looked very drawn and exhausted. Into the holes she would place the fence-posts of her pepper garden. Every woman cultivated a pepper garden during the rainy season. Two years ago, Jarra Njai had been able to buy an iron bedstead with the money she had made from selling the fruit. But last year termites had eaten most of the peppers, and they ate the millet stalks and even the posts from the fences, making it easy for the sheep and goats to shoulder their way into the gardens and finish off the remainder. So this year, people were finding it very difficult to get seeds. Tumbulu, whose garden was nearby, had managed to get a few from a neighbour.

'You die in that garden,' she said. 'And then you harvest nothing.' She looked at the seeds in the palm of her hand. 'How small they are! How difficult it is to get them! And how quickly they are destroyed!'

It had become obvious that with periods, pregnancy and illness, few of the women fasted every day. Fasting, it was said, never killed anyone. But then it was also said that fasting was itself an illness. The previous year Sona had fasted for fourteen days before she had fallen ill. This year, in spite of her condition, she had fasted until this very day. She had decided that tomorrow she would stop. Jarra Njai, remembering the difficulties she had faced last time she was pregnant, had decided she would not break her fast at all. Nor did she intend to make up the days after she had delivered. It would count against her in the afterlife, but that was too bad. Natoma, however, who at thirty-five was pregnant with her eighth child, refused to stop fasting. She had gone on a journey to Brikama. And though Muslims were not supposed to fast when pregnant or while travelling, she had insisted on fasting through both conditions. The result was that when she turned up for work, she would virtually collapse through the doorway, and would soon be found sprawled on the sofa. She carried out her tasks as though in a stupor – as though it were an effort of will to drag her limbs, let alone her stomach, through the house.

When a woman was in labour, children would be driven from the house of the women. But this was to avoid confusion rather than to prevent them from seeing what was happening. And naturally they would manage to prise their way back onto the scene the moment the delivery had taken place. Indeed, if it happened at night, the children would remain in their beds, and usually slept through the whole drama. A young girl approaching puberty would be made to stay well away, however, and thus when the time came for her to deliver herself, she would have little idea of what would happen to her.

No matter what agonies she underwent there, she would be told to keep quiet. For crying was thought to prolong labour. A woman who cried out would be ridiculed, as would a woman who showed discomfort under any other form of pain.

Birth was in the hands of the musakebas – the old women – and the girl's husband, the father of the child, would be far away from all of this. It was believed to be inherently bad for a man to be in the place of delivery. Indeed, they were taught during initiation that if a man was present while a woman was giving birth – unless she had no one else to help her – he would have bad luck for the rest of his life. Even in the week of confinement following delivery, a man would avoid his wife, for fear that his jujus would become contaminated by her presence.

I saw Tumbulu standing motionless at the old mango tree where she and Mba Filije did their pounding, the pestle poised in mid-air. The blood appeared to have completely drained from her face, only her blue, tattooed lips having retained any colour. Her sunken eyes looked straight at me, but she didn't seem to see me.

'What's the matter?' I asked.

'What do you mean?'

'Is there a problem?'

'I'm fasting. That's the problem.' Then she greeted me at length and continued pounding.

It was now hotter than ever. In the morning, as I prepared to leave the house, I would wonder what it was, this pressure on the world, bearing down on one's brain through the iron roof and increasing moment by moment. Then I would realize that it was the day heating after the cool of the night.

The women returning from their gardens at midday would collapse under the mango trees that ringed the south side of the village. Soon there would be a great group of them lying fast asleep on the pathway. The remains of last year's crops, raked together and burnt, lay around them on the grey earth in thick, black bars. Nothing stirred except the eagles wheeling in the empty sky.

Sometimes in the early evening there would be clouds, spun by the wind into odd, disconcerting shapes, like strange automatic writing against the sky. Yet these symptoms of impending relief offered little comfort to the people, who slumped against the verandah posts waiting for darkness, their eyes glazed, their flesh dull and listless, as though the very blood in their veins were weighing them down. This, they said, was *sanjo*. It was rain. But the sight of clouds was no guarantee that it would come soon, or that it would even come at all.

People would still feel weak after the first breaking of the fast. The men would go to the mosque, so, in the compounds, the mid-evening Ramadan prayers were led by the young boys. Their shrill voices would be heard piping up over the roof tops – 'God is great! God is most great!' – while in the darkness behind them, their mothers and sisters rose and knelt with metronomic precision.

Then, after their second meal – if they had it – they would begin to revive. A great crowd would gather outside the Quarters, where Daouda's television had been set up. The quality of the image was not particularly good, but Daouda's family had stared agog through every moment of transmission since the thing had arrived – even though the programmes, from Senegal, were nearly all in French. Now, however, the television was being used for the purpose for which it had been bought: the World Cup. Tonight it was England v Morocco! Everyone, except Daouda and myself, was loudly rooting for Morocco – not for political, ethnic or religious reasons, but simply because they were winning. At half-time there was, as usual, an interlude of 'international music'. A young woman of Levantine appearance, swathed in diaphanous scarves, sang as though in the throes of an orgasm – 'I can't wait for you to touch me'; the words were oddly phrased, as though she did not fully understand their meaning. The crowd hooted and roared with laughter throughout, and kept looking at me to see if the song evoked any response. 'Tubab music,' they kept saying. 'Tubab music.'

And every day there was newsreel footage from South Africa of – largely white – policemen beating and shooting into crowds of unarmed black demonstrators. It is difficult to describe the effect of seeing images of such speed and ferocity in that slow-moving society in which television had been unknown until a few weeks before. The whirling blur of grey and white figures, the flailing whips and batons, the vehicles flashing past as they drove apparently at random into crowds of cowering people; everything was rushing, careering as though it was all about to come pouring from the screen. The fact that none of us could understand a word of the accompanying commentary added to the sense of distress.

Ndey-Touti would look from the television to me and then back again. There was no point trying to explain that the tubabs of South Africa were quite different from the tubabs of England. She had never heard of South Africa, and it wouldn't have meant anything to her if she had. She didn't know what a map was. For her it was all part of the global tension between the white and black. And if it didn't exist to the same extent in her country, that was due purely to God's mercy.

Fatounding and Isatou were now well over the first forty days of their mourning, and I felt that sufficient time might have elapsed for me to be able to interview them about their position. I was told by various people, particularly Jojo, who would have to translate, that this would be an unreasonable, even an inhuman thing to try to do. I agreed with him. But I felt that it was something I had to do. People on television programmes did such things. I also should try to do it.

I found Fatounding sitting on the floor of her late husband's house, shelling groundnuts with his mother, N'na. Virtually all of the ground-nuts had been partially eaten by maggots, and they crumbled to powder between their fingers. I asked Fatounding if it would be all right for me to come and talk to them with the tape recorder. She said it was not a problem. I could come now or whenever I wanted.

Isatou had at first seemed the more resilient, the more buoyant of the two in the matter of facing up to the husband's death. Recently, however, she had become increasingly moody and withdrawn. I would see her at the Infant Supplement Centre, her daughter Haminata slumped prost-rate on her knee, staring off into the middle distance as she poured the porridge heedlessly into the child's mouth. 'What's the matter?' I would ask. '*Mbe miro*,' she would say. 'I am thinking.'

Now she came out of the cooking hut. 'I don't want to talk,' she said. 'There will be a time when I will want to talk. But it is not now. It will not be for a long time. The way I talked to you after I'd had my child, I cannot do that now. I *cannot*! For us to talk, where we are now, it is not good. It is bad.' She said these words brightly, however, and with no element of reproach.

So, wanting to be sure that I had understood absolutely correctly, I returned a short time later with Jojo. By now they were all three sitting, shelling groundnuts. She restated her position, adding that, 'We are young women. We cannot talk about these things.' By now I could see that she was very upset. Fatounding looked down at the groundnuts as she cracked them against the concrete floor. 'I said it's not a problem,' she said, 'but please leave it.' She had a look about her, a mixture of sadness and annoyance and hurt that looked quite heart-rending on that big, tough face. I thought we'd better leave before she burst out crying. 'Maybe when we've taken off these tikos and these big jujus, we'll be able to talk to you. But while we're wearing them, we cannot talk to you about these things. Chatting is fine. But talking properly and answering questions – we cannot do that.'

I realized then that the emotions of grief and loss, which we feel to be 'spontaneous' and 'natural', feelings which have an existence, a validity in their own right, were for the people of the village contained and in a sense described by the rituals of death – the keening, the putting on and the taking off of the tikos and jujus. It was useless to ask people if they 'meant' their keening – if it was sincerely felt or a ritualized display. For them there was no distinction between the two. Thus the reason they could not talk to me was because they were wearing the tikos and safos. Of course they recognized that they felt sadness as well, but it was not distinct from these other elements. In this way they were saved from having to delve too deeply into the meanings of that sadness.

The women of Dulaba believed that there were certain people that they *should* marry – people who by virtue of their descent they were particularly eligible to marry. And even if they did not marry one of these people, they might still refer to them as their husbands.

Traditionally a woman would place a cord around her brother's daughter's wrist within hours of her birth, and claim her as the future wife of her son. Although this practice was becoming less and less common, many of the women still married people to whom they were very closely related. Jarra Njai's mother was her husband's first cousin. Sona's father and her husband's father were of the same grandfather. Munya's husband's mother was her aunt. Such a person was clearly much more to you than just a husband. Indeed, traditionally, a woman would never refer to her husband by his name. She would call him *nkoto*, my elder brother.

All this added to the sense of inevitability – that you were marrying this person not only because of a whim of your father's, not even solely because God had guided him to choose that person for you, but because this, according to the traditional law, was the person that you should be with. Thus the compulsion to accept him was very great – not only because of the force of your family's opinion, the moral and even the physical pressure that would be exerted upon you, but because of your own sense of yourself, your feeling of who you were. To question the 'rightness' of that man as the person for you would be to question your very existence.

At last I felt I had the answer to what I had regarded as the enigma of

Fatounding's personality. As long as I had known her I had wondered how I would describe a personality that seemed to exist only in physical terms. Standing there in front of her, it was obvious that she was one of the most notable personalities among the women. But objectively, there was little to distinguish her from hundreds of thousands of other women. She had not done anything that would not be expected of a woman of her people. Nor had she not wanted to do anything that had been expected of her. She didn't consider herself to be an individual – freely able to adopt or reject one way of life or another. It wasn't so much that they were physically imprisoned by their way of life. It was the way of their tribe, their people – the physical substance that had given them life. It was the first thing that they had seen, and having watched themselves and everyone around them being created by its processes, even as their grandmothers had been, they believed themselves to be made from it. Fatounding was a Mandinka woman. That was what she believed herself to be, and she had no conception of herself as anything other than that.

Now, when I saw Munya in her husband's compound, she seemed more clearly defined as a personality. As she sat with the other women, under the mango tree, she seemed more womanly, more considered in her movements and her manners. She was not, as she had been in her adoptive mother's compound, someone who just happened to be there as part of the place – part of its physical fabric – but a separate individual who was having to find her way among all the other women who had come to be married in that compound. It was as though on transferring she had become an adult – instantaneously.

On most days, however, her adoptive mother, Gunjur, still took the son Omar to the Supplement Centre. He was much healthier these days, and although small for his age, he was an endearing child – very fair in complexion, he was always making hard, monosyllabic cries of enthusiasm. There was still a roughness in the way Munya treated him; a lack of naturalness and affection in her movements towards him, as though she wasn't sure who he was, or he represented something she didn't like.

But eventually, Munya too would try to accept her husband and his children, because one day he would be the one who, with one foot in the earth, would pass her into her grave.

At about nine on the morning of the twenty-seventh day of Ramadan, a cow was slaughtered in the street, outside the entrance of Baba Kunda, so that the meat could be sold for the prayer-day feasting. A small crowd gathered as Jarjei's father, wielding a long, straight cutlass, severed its gleaming haunches. Then the gut was split and the slippery grey intestines came spilling out into the dust. The head had been more or less completely hacked off and lay on the ground, its eyes staring listlessly at the buildings opposite.

Everyone had been up until dawn for the Kitimo, the commemoration of the revelation of the Holy Koran. It was always a happy occasion, not only because of the gratitude the people felt for their holy book, but because it signified that Ramadan was almost at an end. This year, however, the people had had little opportunity to sing the su-kwo, the songs of the Almighty God, that they loved so much. For the sermons by the two young Koranic teachers had been extremely long. And surprisingly for these two mild-mannered and courteous young men, they were sternly, even harshly judgemental. For hour after hour they fulminated against pagans of every kind; Rastamen, Hindus – 'who worship their mother's private parts' – and particularly Britain as represented by Action Aid and the Catholic Relief Services.

As a Briton and the only representative of the forces of unbelief, I should no doubt have felt uneasy. But it was difficult to imagine that this rhetoric was going to make much difference to the people's attitude towards me – or indeed towards anything else. In fact, as it approached four o'clock it was difficult to tell if anybody else was even awake.

Now more and more people were arriving for the dividing of the meat. Daouda was there, Lamin and Buba Samate arrived in the MRC Land Rover. My person was also there. And as I had not seen her for some time, I took the opportunity to have a good look at her – to appraise her disinterestedly – really for the first time. There she stood, leaning against the millet-stalk fence of the compound, a big enamel bowl resting against her knees. Indeed, whenever I saw her she seemed always to be heaving some great basin or bucket or bowl around with her. Like all the women, she walked very slowly – though on two occasions, when she thought she was unobserved, I had seen her running, rather awkwardly, but with pleasure. She always looked very clean and neat, and she was so cool and demure – her round, black face pretty, but seemingly bland – it was hardly surprising that she often just seemed to melt into the crowd of women and that I had scarcely noticed her for so long. And yet her large eyes – the whites standing out with great clarity against her overall blackness – missed nothing. She saw the cutting of the meat. She saw those who were arriving, and who was talking to whom. Her compound was situated not far from where the old dispensary stood among a grove of mango trees. It was there that the ITC fieldworkers, who came with Dr Snow, stayed on their monthly visits to Dulaba. And on their last visit, I had seen her strolling along the path through the trees, apparently nonchalant, but her face wearing the same slightly set expression it had when she passed through the compound gates to my house. I could tell that she drew strength from these assignations, and the sense of independence they gave her. For while, like all the women, she took orders from the men in every moment of her everyday life; in the secret world, it was she who was in control. And with time, the secrecy, and even the danger, had come to have a value in themselves. It was difficult to imagine that she believed herself to be possessed by a spirit when she went to people. She looked like somebody who knew exactly what she was doing.

One of the men took an axe and began splitting the shins of the animal, which were then hacked into sections with knives. The joints of meat were hurled onto the nearby bentengo, shortly followed by those handfuls of slippery intestines that were considered worth eating.

Two days later, on a grey, overcast morning, Jarra Njai delivered. I ran to the compound to find her lying on the ground at the back of the house of women, beside the cooking hut. She lay on her side, facing me, her head resting on her hands, her knees drawn slightly upwards. Near her the afterbirth lay in a kind of sprawling mass, and in front of her the child on a pile of not very clean rags. Nafi Saho's mother-in-law sat on a block of wood, staring at nothing. These elements were laid out on the ochre dust like motifs on a heraldic shield. Nothing moved. Jarra Njai's eyes were slightly open, but only the whites showed. The back of her faneau was matted with dust and blood. And near her head was a further pool of blood, thick and dark, like crimson oil-paint. In it lay a piece of rope, mysteriously attached to a grinding board.

Jarra Njai's mother, Mba Filije, appeared with a panful of water, and suddenly the yard was full of people, all carrying panfuls of water. Mamanding Janno was laughing uproariously. 'When Mark heard the news that Jarra Njai had delivered, he went running off up the road to this compound so fast that his trousers started falling down.' Everyone laughed. Even Jarra Njai managed a titter.

Janno looked at the child. 'May God prolong this child's life. May God make her to be a Muslim, to have shame, and to be a very good girl.'

The child was covered in whitish slime, matted into a greenish mass in its hair. Filije, munching on a chewing stick, picked it up and began vigorously rubbing it with a soapy rag. The child did not protest as it was held up, sometimes by one hand only, and thoroughly doused till its pink skin began to appear. Then it was quickly wrapped in another cloth of less than pristine condition.

The afterbirth was buried in the sand in the washing area. The grinding board, which with the piece of rope had been used to draw it from the body, was placed over it, to prevent witches getting to the afterbirth, and through it harming the child.

An hour later Jarra Njai sat on the floor in the middle of the house of the women, looking very wan. The place was unusually neat and tidy. The beds were all made, the floor had been swept and there was a minimum of rubbish littered about. The baby lay on the nearest bed, wrapped in a cloth. Her husband's mother handed her the baby, and she took it and began to breastfeed it.

The children, who had been sent to Filije's compound to keep them out of the way, returned to look at the child. Jarra Njai's father also arrived with the husband, Kemoring. The moon, he said, had been seen in Mauritania, Mali and Guinea. The people in Banjul and on the coast had stopped fasting and were praying today. He too had stopped fasting, and he wasn't very pleased that the rest of the village had continued. 'They just do it to disturb people,' he said.

Jarra Njai was exhausted. But she did her best to contribute to the conversation. It was a happy day. It was the last day of Ramadan, and she had delivered safely.

That afternoon the women and girls washed the clothes in preparation for the prayer day. And as it grew dark, the people stood in the compounds clutching plastic mugs and old tins full of tea, waiting for the moon. Dark pink clouds gathered ominously in the lower part of the sky, while, high above, the first stars appeared. But of the moon there was no sign.

'There it is, there!'

'Where?'

'Over there.'

'Can you see it?'

'No.'

'I can see it.'

'You liar.'

'They've seen it in Li Kunda.'

'They can see it there, but we can't see it here.'

As I left the compound, I bumped into a man walking quickly from Li Kunda. 'We've seen the moon,' he said.

'Where?' I asked.

'We saw it before,' he said.

I rushed down the village street, tripping over the hem of a pale blue robe I had borrowed from Sanyang. I was late. It was nine-thirty in the morning and the sun was already hot. Further down the street, I could see a great crowd, their white robes gleaming in the hazy sunshine. The elders of the founding compounds led the people of the respective *kabylos* to the mosque, stopping off along the way to collect the people of their subject compounds. These were the people of the kabylo of Li Kunda, and as I joined them they moved off along the lane between the compounds of Mbara Kunda and Bakary Kunda, all hands raised in prayer. Each person was only murmuring, but *en masse* it sounded like the throbbing of a great train. The dust rose into the sunlit air.

The only thing beyond the burial ground was the light of the sun, which made it impossible to look ahead. We sat down on our mats ready to pray directly into it, as though facing some great and terrible power – which of course we were. Overhead the outstretched branches of the baobabs, shining like iron, reached up to receive the full glare: the light that made that place so different from where I came from.

16

NDEYSAN, THE MOON AND STARS!

I returned from the coast, the MRC Peugeot laden down with the food for my 'leaving party'. It was an event that had been eagerly awaited, almost from the moment of my arrival, and in accordance with MRC tradition I had to organize it myself, in honour of the people who had participated in my work. These parties, mixing the traditions of the Europeans and the Africans, were always fraught with mysterious tensions. Certain people would refuse to attend – often the very people for whom the event had ostensibly been organized. There were incomprehensible and often violent arguments during the cooking and serving of the food, rumours of jealousy and rancour among other sections of the community, and always the amount of food that actually ended up in people's bowls seemed rather less than what had been provided. To the outsider it was impossible to know exactly what was happening. But it was said darkly by those who knew about these things, that 'this thing had not been done correctly', that 'too many hands had gone into the food'.

In order to try and circumvent some of these conflicts, I had decided that I would invite every woman in the village to my party. It had become obvious, however, that to provide *benakino*, rice cooked in oil – which had become the accepted, and thus the expected party food – for all these people would be prohibitively expensive. I had decided instead to cook *nyankatango* – rice steamed with dried fish, pounded raw groundnuts, and the black seeds of the netto tree – a marvellously dry, earthy and satisfying dish. Demba Tamba and Yaya Bojang had been aghast at the impoverishment, the shameful parsimony of this suggestion. 'If you do that,' said Demba, 'the only people who will go will be Pa Seydu [Lamin Jarjou's two-year-old son, known as the most disreputable person in the compound] and Ramou Jagne's children.'

What was wrong with nyankatango? I liked it.

'These people want oil,' said Yaya. 'If they squeeze the food in their hand and the oil trickles down to their elbows, they will be happy. If it does not, they will condemn you.'

'You saw George. He did not give them rice, he gave them bread and *achora* – this sauce of oil. And they complained that he gave them only a *biskitiparti* – a biscuit party.'

'But there was no rice at that time,' I said.

'That does not matter.'

In the end I realized I would have to take their advice, even though it would mean bankrupting myself. As the Mandingkos said: *'Duniya beteng ne'* – 'This is the way the world is.'

The car was filled with sacks and carrier bags of 'Irish' potatoes (what they called *pomdeterro*), crimson-skinned sweet potatoes (which they called *patato*), aubergines, cassava – the immense tubers protruding from the back of the car like tree trunks – *kani ba* (big peppers), red chilli peppers and black pepper. There were bay leaves, garlic, three different kinds of Maggi stock cubes, and six kilos of tomato paste. There were five packets of attaya, and five long plastic bags packed tight with sugar like white bombs. My fridge at home was full of onions grown in the Kurung Kafo garden, and every time I opened the door they would come tumbling out all over the floor.

There remained the question of how I was going to get the oil. There was none in Dulaba or any of the neighbouring villages, and in the markets at the coast it was available only by the cupful, which was an extremely expensive way to buy it. Pa Konte, however, had a friend who worked in the government store in Sibanor. The Catholic Relief Services sent oil for the children's 'dietary supplement'. But they always sent too much, and his friend sold off the remainder by the barrel to whoever was prepared to pay. 'Isn't that corruption?' I had asked. Pa had laughed. 'Of course it's corruption. You think you can live in the Gambia and not be corrupt?' I had given him the money to buy two barrels.

It was dark by the time I reached Dulaba. I had no sooner dragged the party provisions into the house when Jarra Njai appeared at the french windows. I showed her everything I'd bought. She was very pleased. 'This is very good,' she said, and she told me to lock it all up safely.

Some time later she returned with Ami Marong. Ami also looked at the ingredients – the 'materials' as they were called. 'This is very, very good,' she said. Although it was by now quite late, they insisted on having a meeting, with Jojo being called over from the Quarters to translate. To put it simply, they wanted to have complete control over the running of the party. I told them that if I asked one kafo to organize it, I would be accused of favouritism. I wanted to get all the leaders from the women's kafos together to discuss how the party should be organized. Then, with everyone watching everyone else, I felt sure that nothing would go missing. Jarra Njai and Ami were most distressed by this idea. They had been discussing and planning this event since shortly after my arrival. There was no kafo in Dulaba that I had taken as much interest in as theirs. Nor was there any kafo that had helped me and done as much for me as they had. They had a moral right to organize this party. If the other kafos became involved, it would be taken completely out of their hands. They were children compared to Safi Mama and the rest, and they could not argue with them. They said if I left it with them, the party would be a great success. Everyone would eat and dance to their satisfaction. I said I wasn't so sure. I could imagine the blame that would be heaped on me by the rest of the population.

All right, they said. There would be three bags of rice. I should give one to them, one to the Saniyoro Kafo of Karafa Kunda, and one to the rest of the village women. I said there was absolutely no way I was going to do that. They left, with everyone feeling annoyed and suspicious of everyone else.

It took me a long time to go to sleep that night. I thought longingly of the moment when my plane would take off from Dakar. As I finally drifted into sleep, I could see the plane, with me aboard, ascending into the darkness, as the sugar I had bought for the party came cascading from the heavens.

I awoke in the early hours of the morning with the cold, desolate conscience of a murderer – the sudden realization that the oil that Pa was going to buy on my behalf in Sibanor was not part of any surplus, but would be taken from the mouths of the children for whom it was intended. In my heart of hearts, I had known it all along. What had I been thinking of? I wondered. What's happened to me here? How could I have let things go that far?

As soon as it was light I would go and beg a place in the car of Susan Lawrence, who was leaving that very day. I would go to Nioro Jattaba, near Sankandi, where Pa was working, and tell him not to go to Sibanor. Then I would go on to Serekunda, where I would buy the oil by the cupful as any decent person would have done in the first place.

At dawn, I met Jojo on the verandah of the Quarters. He had lived most of his life in Sibanor, and said it was quite true about the oil. 'What they sell is the children's oil. The women who have come to get it for their children will be standing watching. They will know what is happening, but they won't say anything.'

Whatever happened, Pa must be stopped from going there.

I managed to get myself a place in Susan's car, only to be told that Pa would be working miles out in the bush and I would never be able to find him. Jojo was supposed to be going to Tankular to buy the fish for the party – it having been impossible to procure sheep or goats at anything other than punitive prices. Now I learnt that there was a fish shortage – something to do with the wind disturbing the surface of the water. I decided that the party, which was to have been held on the Saturday, two days later, would have to be postponed until Monday. Meanwhile I was told that the elders of the Saniyoro Kafo were waiting to have a meeting with me in Jarra Njai's compound.

In the event, one of Pa's colleagues kindly agreed to go to Nioro Jattaba on his motorbike to retrieve the money for the oil, and Richard, who could see this party developing into a painful, long-running disaster, offered to let me have oil from the Supplement Stores, on the condition that I replaced it before I left. I had no idea how I was going to do that, but I agreed. The date of the party was moved back to Saturday. I went to Tankular and Joli with Alioune Sware, and we told the fishermen we would buy everything they could catch.

On my return, I found Natoma and Mabinta sitting waiting for me in the living-room of House One. They said that as the people who worked for me, they would feel very ashamed if they had no hand in the organization of my party. I said I didn't think that would be a problem, as many people would be going to Jarra Njai's compound to take part in the cooking. Mabinta said that since they were both of an older age-group than Jarra Njai, it would be quite out of the question for them to go to her compound. Wouldn't it be better if the Saniyoro Kafo brought the food to Mabinta's compound, and did the cooking there? I said I'd think about it.

At the end of the afternoon, I received messages telling me to come to Tankular immediately, where my fish was waiting for me, and to come to Jarra Njai's compound immediately, where the Saniyoro Kafo were meeting. I went first to the meeting with Alioune. There the kafo sat, grim-faced and businesslike. What exactly was going on? they wanted to know. Who was this party supposed to be for? For them? For the Saniyoro Kafo of Karafa Kunda? Or for every woman in the village?

'Mark used very harsh words with me last night,' Ami Marong was saying. 'I couldn't understand what they were, but I could tell they were very harsh.'

I said that the party was for all the women of the village. The Saniyoro Kafo of Karafa Kunda were guests, but the main point was to provide something that every woman in Dulaba could attend, because the people who had helped me and been kind to me were not confined to one kafo. There was no woman in Dulaba who would not feel hurt if she did not come to my party.

'All this is quite true,' they said. 'But who is going to be organizing it?'

'You are,' I said.

'And where is the cooking going to take place?'

'Here.'

A wave of relief passed through the crowd.

'Is that all right?' I asked Jarra Njai.

'Mark,' she said, 'you have disturbed me very much today. But now things are all right.'

I asked her if she could inform the heads of the other kafos.

'I've already done it,' she said. 'Any woman can come to the cooking. And we're going to ask the falifos of each of the kafos to come and help, so that they can observe and see that everything happens in the proper way. This is going to be a very successful party. Let no one go to the fields on Saturday!'

At Tankular we found an enormous fish, about five and a half feet in length, lying waiting for us on the beach. A huge Serer woman named Netty Ndoye Jopp had asked one of the fishermen to save it for us. I reckoned we would need at least another three like that. She said she would try for us again the following morning.

The next day was Friday, however, and many of the fishermen had gone to the mosque rather than to the river. One of the men at Joli had apparently caught several large fish during the night, but his wife had failed to give him our message and he had sold them by the time we arrived. Malamin Bajo from Dulaba had pulled two large and beautifully marbled fish from the Bintang Bolon, and Netty Ndoye, who made her living from drying fish, had saved a bucketful for us. But it was still nothing like enough. The party was now only a day away. Everything depended on the night catch at Tankular.

In the afternoon, Mabinta and Natoma paid another visit to my house. Why didn't I have two parties, they asked? One for the villagers and one for the Staff. They would organize the one for the Staff. By now I was too weary to really listen. Mabinta was the negotiator, but Natoma put the case more succinctly. 'Why don't you just give Mabinta and me a bag of rice?' she said. 'All that rice for a party is too much. Susan Lawrence gave her staff a bag of rice when she left. Mabinta and me. What will we do when you've gone?' It was a good question.

The great day arrived. We were slow to leave for Tankular. Sona had delivered during the night; there had been some complications, and Alioune had had to drive her to the Methodist clinic in Sibanor in the early hours of the morning. Now she and the baby were both fine. It was a boy and very big, and everyone was very happy about it. I took the fact that Sona had delivered safely on the morning of my party to be entirely appropriate. I wanted it to be a day of big events and big emotions.

We met the canoes arriving at the wooden pier, which was once again crowded with fishermen, housewives, dealers and the driers of fish. None of the canoes were massively full. One man had gone specially for us, and we bought everything he had. Near the neck of the landing stage we found a pile of small and rather thin fish.

'Why not have these?' suggested Pa. 'They're very nice in benakino.'

'You know, personally I don't favour them,' said Jojo. Pa and Alioune rounded on him and when Jojo had been thoroughly disabused regarding his culinary opinions and his position in the universe, we bought the fish.

It all made a good-looking pile on the floor in the back of the Land Rover. But bearing in mind that I was expecting three or four hundred guests, I was not convinced it would be enough. Perhaps I could try and get a small goat to add to it. No, no, no, no, no, said my advisers. Firstly, fish and meat never went well together, and secondly, this was enough. In fact it was too much.

Willing hands pulled the fish from the back of the Land Rover. Pa said he would stay there in the compound until all the food was cooked. 'Otherwise everything is just going to disappear,' he said.

Soon a great crowd of people were there helping with the cooking. Many of the kafo members were there. The kafo mothers – Penda and Kanikunda – were there. The falifos of all the other kafos were there. And of course, Mabinta and Natoma were there.

My person was also there, and it made me very happy to see her fully involved in the cooking at my party. She was the assistant leader of her kafo, and I thought how well the position suited her. She told me she had gone round and invited every single person in the kafo to the party, and I believed her. She had an air of thoroughness and capability about her, the look of someone on whom many people would rely. I sometimes saw her and the leader of the kafo standing together in the street, conferring about the affairs of their group. They always looked very intense and conspiratorial, speaking in low tones. They seemed somehow formidable, and one longed for the time when the gifts of such people would be put to the service of something greater and more profitable than this subsistence agriculture which was so grindingly, punishingly laborious, and from which they received so little.

She never danced, or at least I never saw her dancing. At the dances organized by her kafo, she would be one of those who held the circle together, holding back the children and over-eager onlookers who threatened to turn the event into a sprawling, chaotic mêlée. She would lead the clapping, and dart into the circle to bend and clap beside those whose dancing she admired. But she would never actually dance herself. Yet she often stayed long at dances; standing towards the back among the ranks of her own age-group – coolly watching, laughing at the antics of the *luburrdhe* – the clowns of the group – and very occasionally shaking her body wildly in unison. I loved her for her coolness and her imperturbability, but even more for the sense of delighted, childish exultation she evinced in the rare moments when one glimpsed this exterior melting.

As I approached the thorn tree at the back of Jarra Njai's compound, in the meagre shade of which the cooking was taking place, she came dancing towards me, swaying, smiling as she brandished the great spoon with which the benakino would be stirred.

'*Aiyo!* Mark is here!' she sang. '*Ndeysan*, the moon and stars!'

This is a great day, I thought.

In three enormous iron cauldrons, 125 kilos of rice were cooked in six gallons of oil. Twelve one-kilo tins of tomato puree were used (though one of them was the only thing to disappear – the cause of a considerable amount of rancour). There were onions left over, half a bag of rice, and of course there had been far too much fish. The cooking began at ten, and went on till five in the afternoon – each stage accompanied by a great deal of heated debate. Altogether six of the great potfuls of benakino were cooked. And as nothing could be eaten until the last grain of rice had been cooked, each was served up as soon as it was ready into big enamel basins which were locked in Kemoring's house for safety.

At about three, the guests began to arrive, and by four there were great crowds of people – women and children of all ages – milling about between the compound, the kankango, and the roadway outside. Hunger and the intense heat lent an edge to the sense of expectation. Finally, each of the kafos carried its basin of food to a secluded spot – in one of the nearby houses, gardens or fields – and squatted down to eat.

Afterwards, as I watched the women dancing under the mango trees beside the Supplement Centre, I felt nothing but relief that this event, the natural climax of my time in Dulaba, was over. And although the dance was the biggest I had witnessed, I sensed that for the women, too, this display of enthusiasm was something of a formality. For although they loved dancing and they loved eating – and they rarely ate food as sumptuous as had been provided that day – for them the most significant moment had come when the ingredients were unloaded from the Land

Rover, when they had seen the appropriateness of the gesture that had been made. I had done what they wanted. They had seen it, they had held it in their hand, and that was the most important thing.

Sarah had found Sona lying flat on her bed. The neck of her womb was fully dilated, but the baby's head was still very high in the pelvis. Sarah estimated that she had been in that position for about half an hour. She appeared to be in a great deal of distress and was not pushing properly. Sarah got her off the bed, sitting up on the floor and pushing. But after a further half hour nothing had happened. It was possible that the baby's head was too big for the pelvis. If that was the case it would have to be delivered by caesarean section. It was more likely, however, that the baby was big and his head would not go through until it was positioned correctly in the womb. It would probably happen eventually, after hours of labour, but Sarah didn't want to subject the baby to that kind of pressing and squeezing for more than a certain amount of time if she could help it. Anyway it was obvious that Sona was so exhausted that she was unable to push effectively any longer. She decided to take them to Sibanor, to the Methodist clinic, where there was a vacuum extractor. They could use mechanical force to change the position of the baby's head and if it was only a relative obstruction it could be delivered vaginally.

Sona was laid down in the back of the Peugeot, two of the old women from her compound sitting beside her. By the time they reached Sibanor the baby's head was visible at the opening of the vagina. But even so it had been a tight squeeze. The midwife had had to rend the skin between the vagina and the rectum, and still it had been a struggle to get the baby's shoulders out, and the rent had torn; though at that point the pain of contraction had been so drastic that Sona had hardly noticed.

It was sewn up without anaesthetic, which was in short supply. But it was conceivable that without this assistance, Sona or the baby, or both, would have died. In the Gambia, many women who had already given birth successfully several times died in obstructed labour. If she had delivered in, say, Tankular, without professional assistance, it was highly likely that the baby would have died at birth. It was possible that the obstruction had not been serious enough for the mother to have died in this instance, because the baby had come down on its own eventually.

On the Saturday evening, both Sona and the child were fine. The following evening, however, the child was referred to the MRC hospital in Fajara. It had been a traumatic birth, and he was now seriously ill.

Tumbulu Sise sat on the bentengo outside her house. She had a sore near her mouth, which had made her cheek swell up and was causing her considerable discomfort. She had just come from the taps. Her big plastic bowl had split open, so she had had to spend all that time queueing and going to and fro, just to fill a bucket. She had just sent Salimata off with it again. It was all going to take twice as long. What she wanted was one of the big iron 'pans' that most of the other women had. But they were very expensive. The plastic bowls were cheaper, but they broke very quickly.

She looked at the roof of the house. The grey, brittle thatch was very dilapidated. When the rains came the water would pass straight through onto them as they lay in their beds, and they would become ill.

Weren't they planning to fix the roof before the rains?

'This is what the owner of the house says he is planning to do,' she said. 'But whether he will do it or not I don't know.'

Who was the owner of the house?

'My husband.'

There was only one small bed in the half of the house where she and the children lived. The eldest son had been sent to stay in her mother's compound, but the rest of them, her eldest daughter, Salimata, the younger son, Ibraima, the baby, Binta, and herself all shared this one bed. Sleeping was sometimes difficult as Salimata would roll around and throw her arms about as she slept.

She was scarcely recognizable even as the person who had returned hungry from the Royal Victoria Hospital. She had lost that 'full, rich' look, the look that made it difficult for Sarah to imagine that she had gone without food for nearly two weeks.

It wasn't that she had starved outright over the intervening months. It was the petty difficulties of wondering what they would eat from day to day that had worn her down. This week they would have rice, but the next week they would not. So they would just have to sit and wait till she or the husband were able to get something – either that they were lucky enough to be given, or what they could get from working. The coming rain was the only hope she had that the year ahead would not be as difficult as this one had been. But if the rain failed and she again harvested nothing, or her crops were all eaten by insects, she would bear it. Since she had left her mother's house and come to live with her husband, things had been difficult. And she had borne it. So if it happened to continue like that – on and on and on – she would still bear it.

Natoma was now the only person who was bringing money into her compound. She alone was responsible for feeding her husband, their seven children, her niece Mariatou, her mother, and Fatou, the baby she looked after. The co-wife was almost as old as the husband. She had one child, a grown-up daughter, married in Serekunda, who sometimes sent her money, but otherwise she was also reliant on Natoma, even though they still did not cook together.

Natoma's eldest daughter, Fatou, had returned from Brikama, where she had been staying with her husband, so that she could deliver her first child in her mother's compound. She was seventeen, and had not yet fully transferred to her husband. She had, as they said, only been borrowed. And not having any form of paid employment, her husband had been unable to give her any money to contribute towards her keep.

When the child was born, it was named virtually without ceremony. What charities there were – munko, but no kola-nuts – had been paid for by Natoma, since the child's father had not deigned to turn up – a fact that had caused them all considerable consternation.

Now Mutar, the eldest son, who was in his first year at secondary school in Serekunda, was home for the holidays. During term-time, his uncle – his father's younger brother – took care of his board and lodging. But Natoma had to provide his uniform and school fees. This year it had cost her one hundred and fifty dalasis. What he did about books she had no idea. Maybe the uncle had helped him. She only knew that if the boy needed money, he would send a message, and she would send whatever she had.

Tijian, the second son, had taken his Common Entrance Exam, and if he got a place at secondary school, he too would be going; though who would pay for him, only God knew.

When her daughter finally transferred to her husband, she would have to be provided with her clothes and cooking utensils. Some of these things would be paid for from the bride-price. But nowadays the smallest cooking pot cost eighty dalasis. And if the father received three hundred dalasis from the husband, he would not give it all to her. He would give her no more than one hundred dalasis.

Natoma was pregnant with her eighth child. She had been earning fifteen dalasis a week from the two mornings she spent cleaning my house. That was her only income. When I left, she and her family would have no means of support. It had been her intention to go onto 'family planning', but she had heard from the talibos – the men who were educated in the Koran – that whoever took a pill to 'burn their stomach from delivering' had killed a living person. Now she was afraid to take that pill. For even if you were exhausted in this world, you would still have to be judged in the next.

Since she had transferred to her husband, Munya had been complaining to Sarah that Dr Sabari was not paying her enough. 'I tried to explain to her that he doesn't earn as much as the rest of us – he doesn't get the expatriate allowances – so he can't afford to pay so much, but it didn't seem to sink in. Now he's getting very fed up with her. She's always late and not turning up because she says she's ill. He asked me the other day if I could recommend anyone else, so I think she may have reached the end of this one.

'It's only since she was transferred that she's been complaining about the money. Maybe her husband's been getting on at her that she should be earning more. She says she's got new responsibilities now. Maybe it's her domestic chores that are making her so unreliable.'

On the sali lungo – the prayer day at the end of Ramadan – I had noticed the extraordinary shifts in her behaviour. In the early evening in her husband's compound, as she was doing the cooking, she was brusquely, almost rudely assured; the long torso bending forward to scrub the bowls, the voice incessantly raised in a high shout, berating the compound children and the neighbours over the fences. Later, at around ten, she came to my house for a salibo, with Mama Njai and Konyaji, the tall girl from Karafa Kunda who had just transferred to their compound. They were all decked out in their very best clothes – spectacularly tailored *dendikos* in the gaudiest materials, with matching faneaus tightly wrapped. Their head ties were thickly rolled so that they had an almost Elizabethan appearance. They had powdered their faces to make them fairer, and drawn in eyebrows arching sharply from the bridge of the nose. They were wearing all the jewellery they possessed. I dreaded to think what they'd have looked like if they'd had enough to be too much. I had no salibos to give them, but said I'd make them a cup of tea. 'That's fine,' said Mama. 'We'll have bread with it as well.' Munya followed me to the kitchen to help me make it.

She seemed so different from the cocky, almost belligerent person I'd encountered at Mintering Kunda; almost hysterically frisky and giggly, dancing up the corridor after me. She seemed a good ten years younger than she had a few hours earlier. Whereas before her movements had had a weighty but sinuous inevitability about them, now they were light, almost whimsical.

Back in the living-room, Mama Njai told me that their fellow kafo member, Luwanding, had been divorced by her husband that very afternoon for attacking her co-wife. Konyaji said that Mama Njai had herself been beaten by her husband earlier in the evening. It was a lively conversation, everyone sounding off to their heart's content. Munya let out numerous gurgling guffaws, twisting nervously in her seat, and seemed at times almost to be trembling as she munched on her hunk of dry bread.

'She's a hopeless mother,' Sarah had said. 'She hasn't got a clue when her child's ill. She brings him out of hours and she never brings him back when you ask her to. It's true, he has got this kidney problem, but she's not helping. Maybe she doesn't care. Maybe she's just gormless.'

The following day, at the tulungo held by her kafo for the naming ceremony of Buba Samate's child, Munya wore a different face again. She arrived late, looking rather drawn and strained. The second-best style singer in the kafo, she seemed abstracted from what was going on around her, mouthing the words only tentatively, as though unable to bring any conviction to them. She looked like someone who had just received some critical news. I wondered if perhaps she had just been given her notice by Dr Sabari.

It wasn't hard to see why her life was in such a mess. On the one hand she was living the life of a typical village woman – not knowing 'what is time', pacing her day by the movements of the sun and the time it took to perform her given tasks – a farmer, a rearer of children, a dutiful second wife. And on the other hand she was someone who was active in the secret world; someone with the beauty and personality to attract many men, and with the appetite to make something of it, to play her hand in that world. And now, in order to try to free herself from the drudgery of the traditional labours, she was trying to make her way in the world of the tubabs, where things had to be done with a quite different sort of precision. It was hardly surprising that she was confused, that she couldn't cram everything into her day. And now she was pregnant with a second child.

On the Sunday evening, Pa and I went to Jarra Njai's to discuss what would be done with the food left over from the party – particularly the half bag of rice, to which many people would no doubt lay claim. Jarra Njai said that this rice was now entirely in *her* hands, since in this village whenever there was an event which required a lot of cooking, whatever was left over always stayed in the compound where the cooking had been done. Now I knew why everyone had been so keen to have the cooking done in *their* compound. I felt Jarra Njai – and everyone else – had been a little less than direct with me about this. There were sharp words between her and Pa, who also felt he was entitled to some of the food for having stayed in the compound watching the cooking in the heat of the day. Didn't we know, she said, that when the Professor left, the people who organized his party had taken huge amounts of the food, and no one else had got any of it? Also, she said, one of these people had been given a bowl of the food to take to Pa, but she had been seen passing through the village with it late at night, taking it to one of her relatives. I doubted the veracity of this story, but the sense of grievance was real enough.

Earlier in the evening I had visited Fatounding's compound, where she and Isatou and N'na were now completely alone. Although they were supposed to be in the care of the late husband's family until the period of mourning was over, they had not been given any food or money for some time, and were now eating only one meal a day. If it hadn't been for the bowl of party food that had been taken to them, they would not have eaten the night before.

I suggested to Pa that since Fatounding and Isatou were our fellow kafo members, and they were in the same compound as Jarra Njai, it would seem appropriate that some of the rice should be given to them as a charity. Pa however said that Jarra Njai and her people would take this as a great insult, and they would simply tell us to take all the rice and do what we wanted with it.

In the end it was agreed that some of the rice should be given to Fatounding and Isatou, and the rest be disposed of by Jarra Njai in whatever way she felt was right.

I was due to leave Dulaba around the middle of the Thursday afternoon. Time rushed towards that moment with the force of a meteorite hurling itself through space. Meanwhile there were a hundred details to be seen to, and two hundred inconveniences, all too tedious to be mentioned here. The oil that I had taken from the Supplement Stores had to be replaced. On the Wednesday lunchtime, as I was about to go to Karafa Kunda, where I would buy it by the cupful, Sullu arrived at the house and told me that my person had come to see me twice the day before, and would come again. I told him to ask her to come at half-past two. It was now one-thirty. I wondered if I would make it back in time.

I had no sooner finished dragging the great drum of oil into the kitchen than I saw her walking across the compound forecourt towards the house. Then she was there.

I bade her sit down. 'You've come to see me,' I said. 'Yes,' she said. We sat nervously on the edges of our chairs for a few moments. Then I said 'Come on,' and led her into the darkened study. She looked around, at the room she hadn't entered for some months. Then she sat down on the bed beside me.

'It's a long time since you've been here,' I said.

'Yes,' she said. 'I had something to keep me from here.'

'What was that?'

'Cooking and fetching water.' She stretched out on the bed. 'I left the washing half-done.'

As we passed back out through the door, I laid my hand on her shoulder in an uncharacteristic gesture of affection. 'I love you very much,' I said.

'Do you?' she asked.

'Kende ke,' I said. 'Very strongly.'

She seemed pleased.

'What time will you leave tomorrow?'

'In the middle of the afternoon.'

'I'll come and see you off.'

Then I did feel happy.

I did not cry when I left Dulaba – not openly, in front of the people as I had been afraid I would. But then I had already cried many times over that event already. How many times when I left Dulaba, for weekends or for the Christmas break, had I been reduced to tears at the thought of the moment when I must leave that place for the last time? How many times as I had watched the tubabs – the Professor and Helene, Sharon and most recently Susan Lawrence – climbing into the Peugeot to leave Dulaba, probably never to return, had my eyes smarted on their behalf? But now, now that the moment had finally come, I felt that I knew too much – that I knew these people too well to feel sentimental about them. I was drained of emotion. And I felt then that, if I stayed, ultimately I would be destroyed – not by the people, though there would be some who would wish for that; nor even by the place itself, but by my own sense of unbelonging – my unbelonging to the climate and to the culture, or at least to those aspects of the culture that I knew I would never be able to accept. I felt that no matter how much I tried to fit in, I would continually be disgorged by the culture as an alien and inimical presence.

We dropped Jojo at the Serekunda road junction, from where he took the bus to Banjul. Jarra Njai and Tumbulu, both dressed in the kafo ashobi, had come along to escort me towards my destination. I would give them the taxi fare back, and after spending the night with relatives in Bakau, they would return the following morning. As we sped through the villages of Fonyi, Alioune, who was driving, explained that I really should give them something for this. In their culture, if someone escorted you such a great distance, you should give them something to make them happy and show your appreciation of their efforts. If I did not, others would ridicule them on their return.

Alioune dropped me at the MRC compound in Fajara, and, after having a last look at the sea, only one thing remained to be done.

Sona was with her child in the ward on the other side of the compound. I spotted her immediately, sitting with her mother by the last of the long row of beds. The child lay in the middle of the bed, swaddled in cloth, completely motionless, his eyes closed. Two tubes led from an appliance fitted over the head; one to the baby's nostril, the other under the covers beside its foot. 'He is a little better,' said Sona, 'but only a little better.'

The mother was about to leave. She was staying with relatives in Bakau village, and would not be back until the morning. She told me to stay and keep her daughter company.

When she had gone, Sona pulled back the clothes to show me the child's navel. She said the doctor had told her that the knife the nurse had used to cut the child's umbilical cord at Sibanor had not been good. I couldn't quite understand the significance of this, though it was obviously very important to her. But if the child was ill, she herself looked radiant – better than I'd seen her looking for months – her body glowing in the muggy, rather blue light of the ward. Her happiness, her evident relief at the birth of the child was offset by her concern for his survival, which still hung in the balance. But she showed none of the anxiety – fear mounting almost to hysteria – that a European might have felt in her position. For she knew that whatever God had placed upon her and the child, no human being could change or remove. All she could do was to stay with the child, and not flinch from doing whatever she was asked to do for its welfare, to do it as well as she could, and not a second later than it needed to be done.

On the window-sill above the bed, a narrow plastic funnel was floating in water. She asked me to pass this to her, and with the greatest care she fixed it to the pipe leading to the baby's nostril. Into this she poured some thick white liquid which she said was medicine, and then squeezed milk from each of her breasts into it. She carried out this process slowly, gravely and very precisely, clearly attributing great importance to it, and clearly proud of all this machinery that had been called into use solely for the benefit of her child. She had pinned her hopes upon it.

The woman in the next bed watched this operation through narrowed eyes, as she no doubt had done dozens of times before. Her child had no tubes and no equipment surrounding it, and she was clearly peeved by this lack. This younger woman in the next bed not only had all these things for her child, she had her mother to help her, and tubabs coming to visit her. As Sona began to carefully return the funnel to the basin of water, the woman snapped triumphantly, 'You forgot the water!' Grinning with embarrassment, Sona reconnected the funnel and poured in a measure of water. Throughout the whole of this procedure, the baby remained entirely unconscious.

'So you're leaving tomorrow,' she said. 'I'd like to follow you to Dakar. But at the moment, I'm not going anywhere. I cannot leave here.'

I said that her husband had told me to tell her that he would be coming to visit her the following day. She smiled broadly.

'That's very good,' she said.

'Your *jambaro*?'

'I swear to God.'

I saw her then for the first time as what she had always been – a dutiful wife. Then it was time for me to go.

'Are you going to take the cassettes of my songs with you?'

'Yes,' I said. 'Is that good or bad?'

'It's good,' she said.

The Saniyoro Kafo did not have a groundnut field that year. Their seed nuts had been destroyed by maggots along with those of more than half of the other villagers. It was their intention to plant sesame instead, but in the event the agricultural demonstrator was dismissed along with one tenth of the country's civil servants in austerity measures imposed by the IMF, and there was no one to provide them with the seeds.

The rains came late and finished early, and the harvest was poor compared with that of the previous year. During one of the first storms, Tumbulu's house collapsed while she and her children were asleep inside it. They survived. Fatounding and Isatou did marry Kalamatta's younger brother. But they remained living in the compound in Dulaba, and he rarely made the journey from Serekunda.

Sona's child lived, but was found to be partially sighted and suffering from cerebral palsy. He was believed by many of the people of the village to be a devil. Sona went into a rapid decline – unable to sleep or retain any food, her body going almost white. She was treated at the MRC for post-natal depression, but as she began to get weaker and weaker, she was sent twice to Fajara for tests. She was finally discovered to have an enzyme deficiency, and was put on permanent medication – a special fluid being flown out from England. Slowly she began to recover. Had she lived in any other village in the Gambia, other than Mankono or Karafa Kunda, she would almost certainly have died. Her husband took Tumbulu's daughter, Salimata, as his third wife. Sona went to live with her mother in Karafa Kunda. May God give you long life, success and happiness in whatever you do. May God bless us, guard us and lead us in the right way.

GLOSSARY

Alahira, the next world.

badiya, the condition of being related.

bantaba, the meeting place of the men; usually a low platform of logs in the centre of the village.

batut, unit of Gambian currency: one hundredth of a dalasi.

benakino, rice cooked in oil with fish or meat, and vegetables.

dalasi, unit of Gambian currency: in 1985 five dalasis to the pound, by late 1986 twelve.

dempetengo, pounded rice flakes.

denkilo, singing, song.

durango, groundnut sauce.

falifo, the 'administrator' of a kafo; the person who takes news to the people, extracts fines, distributes kola nuts at meetings, naming ceremonies and funerals.

faneau, a length of cloth tied at the waist to form a skirt.

Fulani, a pastoral people; typically of a fair, reddish complexion and aquiline features. Originating in the mountains of central Guinea, they have driven their flocks into every country of the savannah.

griot, a praise-singer or musician (f. Creole: *grius*).

jaliba, jalo, a griot (Mandinka).

jambaro, champion, hero.

juju, an amulet (f. French: jou-jou – toy).

jujuo, the house of the initiates.

kabylo, one of the wards of a village, centring on one of the founding compounds.

kafo, a social group of people of the same age; traditionally people who were circumcised at the same time.

kankango, the open area at the back of each compound, where the men cultivate maize and millet during the rainy season.

kijo, the women's percussion; specifically calabash drums, also basins, mortars, grinding boards.

kintango, one of the guardians of the initiates (pl: kintangolu).

ku'lo, secret, secrecy.

kunfanunte, possessing second sight, the power to see witches.

kutcha, red sorrel leaves; a sauce made from these.

manyo, a bride; a woman *transferring* to her husband's compound.

manyo bitto, the ceremony of the transfer of the bride.

marabout, a holy man, a maker of jujus (f. Arabic: *murabit*, Mandinka: *moro*.)

munko, raw rice pounded into a damp, gritty mass with sugar; distributed at naming ceremonies and funerals.

ndeysan!, an expression of sympathy or regret; sometimes also used to convey admiration (Wolof). Mandinka: *ai waali!*

ngangsimba, the mother of the initiates.

ngangsingo, an initiate, male or female (pl: ngangsingolu).

nimbara, all-purpose greeting or affirmation; literally, 'you are working'. The appropriate response is to say the person's surname.

nyakaboyo, women's initiation.

nyakaboyo dula, the place of initiation.

safo, an amulet made by writing from the Koran.

salibo, a tip or gift given on a prayer day.

Serer, a people living in western Gambia and Senegal; closely related both to the Jolas and the Wolofs. Many who now consider themselves to be Wolofs are in fact Serers.

seri, darling, lover (f. French: *chéri*).

seyuwrubaa, the three Mandinka drums.

Sirif, the family of Haidara, from which many of the greatest marabouts in West Africa are drawn, claim descent from the Prophet through his daughter Fatima. They are known as Sirif (Sharif), have certain privileges under Islamic law, and are believed to have great spiritual power. They have thus established an identity that goes beyond mere ethnicity.

talibo, a scholar of the Koran.

tiko, a head-tie; scarf tied by a woman to form a turban.

tubab, a European, a rich person, anyone not of African origin. (Wolof f. Mandinka: *tubabo* – person from across the great *baa,* the sea).

tulungo, a dance, literally 'playing'.

Venti Latir, Wolof dance in which the hips are suggestively rotated in a manner supposedly reminiscent of an electric fan ('ventilateur').